The Official Book of
THE
DALMATIAN

TS-254

Facing page: *Anticipation...waiting for the morning run. Photo submitted by Dr. James E. Seltzer.*

Distributed in the UNITED STATES to the Pet Trade by T.F.H. Publications, Inc., One T.F.H. Plaza, Neptune City, NJ 07753; distributed in the UNITED STATES to the Bookstore and Library Trade by National Book Network, Inc. 4720 Boston Way, Lanham MD 20706; in CANADA to the Pet Trade by H & L Pet Supplies Inc., 27 Kingston Crescent, Kitchener, Ontario N2B 2T6; Rolf C. Hagen Inc., 3225 Sartelon St. Laurent-Montreal Quebec H4R 1E8; in CANADA to the Book Trade by Vanwell Publishing Ltd., 1 Northrup Crescent, St. Catharines, Ontario L2M 6P5 ; in ENGLAND by T.F.H. Publications, PO Box 15, Waterlooville PO7 6BQ; in AUSTRALIA AND THE SOUTH PACIFIC by T.F.H. (Australia), Pty. Ltd., Box 149, Brookvale 2100 N.S.W., Australia; in NEW ZEALAND by Brooklands Aquarium Ltd. 5 McGiven Drive, New Plymouth, RD1 New Zealand; in Japan by T.F.H. Publications, Japan—Jiro Tsuda, 10-12-3 Ohjidai, Sakura, Chiba 285, Japan; in SOUTH AFRICA by Lopis (Pty) Ltd., P.O. Box 39127, Booysens, 2016, Johannesburg, South Africa. Published by T.F.H. Publications, Inc.
MANUFACTURED IN THE
UNITED STATES OF AMERICA
BY T.F.H. PUBLICATIONS, INC.

THE OFFICIAL BOOK OF
THE
DALMATIAN

THE DALMATIAN CLUB OF
AMERICA

Am-Can. Ch. Korcula King of Harts, owned by Sam and Flo Hart and Dr. Charles Garvin. Before his untimely death, "King" was a Group winner in the USA and Canada.

Contents

Preface 6

History of the Dalmatian 8
  Whence Thee Cometh? • The Dalmatian Becomes the Coach Dog • The Dalmatian Becomes a Firehouse Dog • The Dalmatian Comes to America • The Dalmatian as a Competitor • Major Inactive Kennels in the USA • Active Kennels in the USA Established Prior to 1965 • Dalmatian Trends in the 1990s • A Log of the DCA's Legacy • Mrs. Flora M. Bonney's Notes on the DCA's Leadership • History of the DCA's National Specialties • Dalmatians Around the World

The Dalmatian Standard 123
  The AKC Standard and How to Apply It • Illustrating the Standard • Dalmatian Type • Dalmatian Gait • Coat and Color

Characteristics of the Dalmatian 173
  Personality and Temperament • The Dalmatian's Abilities and Activities

Selecting a Dalmatian 206
  Responsibilities of Ownership • The Dalmatian as a Family Pet • What You Should Know About Canine Development • Choosing the Pet Dal Puppy • Putting the Pieces Together • Buying a Show Puppy

Raising and Training the Dalmatian 233
  General Care • Nutrition • Training • Socializing Your Puppy • Early Obedience Training • Proper Toys • Understanding Pack Structure • Corrections • Puppy Problems

Dalmatians in Conformation 256
  What is a Championship? • Training Classes • Training Methods • Conditioning • Matches • The AKC, Superintendents, and Shows • Show Procedure • Advertising • Junior Showmanship • A Lifetime of Friendships

Dalmatians in Obedience 298
  Obedience Training • Kindergarten Puppy Training • The Purpose of Obedience Trials • What Dogs May Enter Obedience Trials? • AKC Obedience Titles • The Dog World Award • The Dalmatian's Personality and Trainability for Obedience • Types of Obedience Training

Breeding Dalmatians 326
  General Information • Genetics • Selecting the Stud Dog • Stud Owner Responsibility • Breeding the Bitch • Pregnancy • Whelping • Raising the Litter • Puppy Placements • Breeder Responsibility

Deafness in Dalmatians 363
  The Hearing Ear • Historical Research • Home Testing • The Development of Clinical (BAER) Testing • The BAER Test Protocol • Genetic Inheritance

Your Dalmatian's Health 369
  Urinary Tract Problems and Control • Other Possible Health Problems • Flea and Tick Control • Skin and Coat Disorders

You and Your Veterinarian 401
  How to Choose a Veterinarian • Aiding the Veterinarian in Dalmatian Care

The Senior Dalmatian 404
  Saying Goodbye • Arrival of the Next Dalmatian

Living with Multiple Dalmatians or Dogs 407

Appendix 417

Index

Preface

The honor of being entrusted with the authorship of this book is in itself an awesome thing. The learning experiences we have encountered as we researched, questioned, and assembled information for you have been both exhausting and rewarding. During these three years we have been humbled more than once by the realization that there is a lot more to learn about our spotted friends. It has been our goal to provide you with accurate, current information as best as we can so that it can be useful to you in your life with Dalmatians.

We are indebted to the many Dalmatian fanciers who have contributed their knowledge in specific areas (listed in alphabetical order):

Charles and Linda Cyopik (Canadian History)
Marilyn Dromgoole
Raymond Fitzsimmons (Mexican History)
Elaine Gewirtz
Karen Goff (British History)
Ann Marie Hammarlund (Swedish History)
Meg Hennessey (Pictures)
Tom Hufford, DVM
Suzanne Hughes, DVM
Walter Johnson (Statistics)
Carolyn Krause (Fire Safety Education and Tracking)
Robert Lawson (Australian History)
Amy Lipschutz, DCA Historian
Susan MacDonald (South African History)
Jessica MacMillan (Artwork and Captions)
Cathy Murphy (Obedience)
Linda Myers (Road Trials)
Nicholas Neutzling, DVM
Andrea Paccagnella (South American History)
Lisa Paxon, DVM
Ron Rajala (Photography)
Sidney Remmele, DVM
Dr. James Seltzer
Vivian Sterne (Canadian History)
Dr. George Strain (Deafness)
Peggy Ann Strupp (Fire Safety Education)
Prudence Stuhr (Obedience)
Alfred Treen (DCA History)
Bernard Voelkelt (German History)
Carroll H. Weiss (Uroliths)

Susan Brooksbank

Sue MacMillan

Sheila A. Whymore

Firesprite Firebird O'Land, a puppy owned by Norma Baley and Bryna Comsky, has caught the attention of Ch. Firesprite Stingre O'Saratoga, owned by Ray and Norma Baley.

History of the Dalmatian

WHENCE THEE COMETH?

The exact origin of the Dalmatian is not known. Because there is a province on the Adriatic coastline named Dalmatia, many people assume that this is the birthplace of the breed. However, there is no concrete proof that this is true. Alfred and Esmeralda Treen, in their book *The New Dalmatian, Coach Dog—Firehouse Dog,* state, "Probably the first printed use in English of 'Dalmatian' to designate our breed was in 1780, when a translation of Count de Buffon's *Natural History* was published in Scotland."

The summer 1977 issue of *The Spotter,* published by the Dalmatian Club of America, has an article about the origin of the term "Dalmatian." Apparently, in a discovery made in Chousnick Castle in Bohemia, there was a letter from Jurij Dalmatin (1546-1589), a Slovenian poet, to Alena Meziricska Lomnice, a Bohemian duchess. Jurij writes to thank Alena for the "Turkish Dogs" she had given him and tells her that the breed had become so popular that the people were calling them "Dalmatins." Hence, the term Dalmatian is tied to the Dalmatia coast on the Adriatic Sea. This, however, does not prove that the breed originated from this area or even that the "Turkish Dogs" had spots.

During extensive research for their book about Dalmatians, John and Monica Brooks found two writings which confirm the use of "Turkish Dogs" in battle. The first writing was from Jan Findejs, a Czech Dalmatian fancier who authored a section on Dalmatians in the Czech book *Psi Spolencenskych* (Domestic Dogs). Apparently, four Turkish

Bromholm Dalmatian, by Flemish painter Pieter Boel, depicts a Dalmatian of the 17th century.

The Braque de Bengale is from a work by Claude Fessard in 1767. This dog closely resembles the Istrian Pointer, which is believed to be related to the Dalmatian.

Dogs were captured during the Battle of Mohaca (1526) by Micklos (a courtier of King Louis Jagello), who then bred them and gave some to his friends. The second writing was from Dr. George Hagen, a German historian who confirmed Findejs's story and added that the spring of 1573 is when Alena sent the dogs to Jurij. By 1579, Jurij had bred and given "several tens" of the dogs, called Dalmatins, as presents. The Brooks raised the question, "Why is spotting of the coat never mentioned?" Their research indicates that "Turkish art and literature yield no evidence of the presence of spotted dogs."

The Treens report in *The New Dalmatian, Coach Dog—Firehouse Dog* that the British authority Harry Glover "suggests that the Dal may have been confused with a spotted Mastiff, a larger, more powerful dog." The Treens further state that Glover's suggestion lends credence to the "possibility that the spotted dog of Dalmatia is not a Dal at all but an Epirote or Molossian Mastiff."

Molossian hounds of antiquity are mentioned in Greek and Latin classical works. Molossus was an eponymous hero. Achilles's son married into his family and settled in Epirus, an area south of the mountainous region between Greece and Dalmatia. According to the Treens, "...it is possible that these dogs were taken into Dalmatia by the ancients. They were used as shepherd dogs and as dogs of war, guarding the mountains for their masters."

The Dalmatian is a combination of many lines. It is definitely an old breed, 300 years old in England alone. Regardless of the early body types the Dalmatian possessed, the most striking feature of the Dalmatian has always been his small, round, distinctive spots. It is through this one feature that historians have been able to follow the Dalmatian's existence. There are several plausible theories as to the Dalmatian's lineage.

Clifford L.B. Hubbard, author of *The Dalmatian Handbook* (1957), believes that the

Dalmatian is "almost a direct descendant of the Istrian Pointer (Istrianer Braque) who may in turn have been created by cross-breeding small Harlequin Great Danes with certain Pointers native to the region which is now known as Jugoslavia," and that "the Istrian Pointer often carries small blotches or patches rather than pure spots." Hubbard writes that the breeders of that time were more concerned with pointing ability than with markings. He believes that "the Dalmatian inherits his almost excessive love of open-air pursuits and friendliness towards horses from the Istrian Pointer." The Brooks report that "the modern Istrian short-haired hound is white but smaller than a Dalmatian (18–23 inches at the withers), and coat markings do not predominate. However, speckling of the ears is regarded as evidence of pure blood, and the nose, lips, and eyeliner are deeply pigmented." Istria is in the northwesternmost part of the former Yugoslavia and lies next to Jurij Dalmatin's country of birth—Slovenia.

Franklin J. Willock, in his book *The Dalmatian,* states that the naturalist writer William Youatt (*The Dog,* 1847) "depicts a Dalmatian of racey and somewhat Fox-hound type, badly marked." Youatt also connects the Dalmatian with the Great Dane and says that in Denmark, the dog was used as a draught animal known as the "Danish Dog." Hubbard also writes that Youatt believes the Dalmatian "to be a small variety of the black-and-white Great Dane."

"Idstone" (Rev. Thomas Pearce), who Hubbard thought was a student purely of dogs, thought that the Dalmatian came from the Pointer. In Idstone's book *The Dog* (1872), he writes, "It is my opinion that, except in colour, he is a Pointer with Pointer instincts, which only require cultivation." Captain Thomas Brown, in *Biographical Sketches and Authentic Anecdotes of Dogs* (1829), describes the Dalmatian as "something betwixt the British fox-hound and English pointer...The pure breed has tanned cheeks and black ears. He is much smaller than the large Danish Dog."

Catherine Gore, in her book *Dalmatians,* writes of four lines that she believes the Dalmatian descended from. She believes that the Bengal line and the harlequin Great Dane contributed to spotting patterns, that the Istrian Pointer introduced pointer characteristics, and that the Talbot, a pre-eminently houndlike guard dog, gave the Dalmatian his guarding instincts.

Since there were no written records of the Dalmatian's origin that have been authenticated, art forms have served as the logical recorders of the Dalmatian's development. Alfred and Esmeralda Treen, in *The New Dalmatian, Coach Dog—Firehouse Dog,* write "the earliest known pictures portraying dogs which could be an original form of Dalmatians can be

This rendering of the Braque de Bengale was done by F. Chereau in 1790.

found in a fresco (circa 1360) in the Spanish Chapel of Santa Maria Novella in Florence."

The Flemish artist Jan Fyt's (1611-1661) painting entitled *Diana and Her Nymphs* has a Dalmatian sitting on the right side of Diana. He also painted *The Hunting Party* for Emperor Maximilian. *The World Encyclopedia of Dogs* describes this dog as "rather heavily built but most obviously Dalmatian, amoung other types of hunting dogs." This book also describes *A Musical Party* by the Dutch master Pieter de Hooch (c. 1650) which "shows a patched Dalmatian romping in the foreground."

The renowned Italian animal painter of the 17th century Francesco Castiglione painted "two dogs of unmistakable Dalmatian type, with the conventional spotting, and heads which would not be in disgrace even today." This painting is entitled *The Hawking Party* (1716) and it once hung in Dresden, Germany.

Federigo Zuccari's painting *The Emperor Frederick Barbarossa Before Pope Alexander III*, which hangs in the Doge's Palace in Venice, depicts a "spotted dog but one of heavy build and considerable size, a dog, moreover, lacking anything like the bal-

Reinagle's **Coach Dog of Reinagle** *depicts a spirited and active Dalmatian.*

Clifford Hubbard describes the following nine works of art in *The Dalmatian Handbook*:

The Flemish painter Pieter Boel (1622-1674) painted an oil entitled *Bromholm Dalmatian* in the mid-17th century. This was known to be in Mr. Martin S. Fisher's collection and a picture of it was published in *The Sporting and Dramatic News* in 1939. It was also reproduced in Clifford Hubbard's *The Dalmatian Handbook* as the frontispiece. It depicts a Dalmatian with dark ears and small spots.

anced beauty of the orthodox Dalmatian."

Henry Roberts, in 1749, published a print which "includes two powerful dogs of Harlequin Great Dane type with what is definitely spotting rather than blotching." Their ears are houndlike and dark.

In 1767, Claude Fessard's second engraving in a large work entitled *Braque de Bengale* depicts a dog that is "so much like the Istrian Pointer of 200 years ago that there can be little doubt that the Braque de Bengale, the small variety of Great Dane, the Istrian Pointer and the Dalmatian are blood relatives."

11

In 1790, Thomas Bewick showed a Dalmatian as "a robust and well balanced dog plentifully spotted." He also did a woodcut of himself in a carriage with a Dalmatian that had cropped ears.

It is believed in 1790 that F. Chereau also rendered a Braque de Bengale in his first engraving in a folio work called *Nouveau Livre d'Animaux*. "She is short in tail, and rather flecked than spotted, but lies somewhere between the Fessard (engraving) and the modern Dalmatian." She has a large patch covering her right eye, head, and part of her ear.

In the 19th century, actually in 1804, Reinagle's *Coach Dog of Reinagle,* engraved by Scott, shows cropped ears. The dog also appears in Volume Two of Taplin's *The Sportsman's Cabinet* (1803–04), depicted with a patch on his head, guarding his master's coachyard.

In 1827, Abraham Cooper R.A.'s painting of a dog named Victory shows "a rather heavily spotted dog with a Pointer-like head who was bred in Norfolk." It appears as an

An 1870-era Autotype print found in its original frame by Peter Capell, authenticated and dated by the Art Institute of Chicago.

A close-up of the Coach Dog of Reinagle's head, showing the cropped ears.

engraving in *The Sporting Magazine.* Hubbard states that from then on "most of the pictures of Dalmatians are portraits of named dogs, pets of various celebrities and early show dogs."

Because Dalmatians have been found in many areas of Europe, it is thought that they wandered with groups of traveling Romany gypsies. However, there is no known evidence to substantiate this. The Dalmatian also has been reported to have been a sporting dog in the capacity of pointer and tracker, a draft dog in Denmark, a shepherd, and a sentry on the borders of Dalmatia and Croatia. During World Wars I and II he was employed for war work. He also has been in the spotlight in circus acts.

THE DALMATIAN BECOMES THE COACH DOG

Although depictions of spotted dogs have been documented for centuries, it has only been approximately 200 years since the breed was specifically described as a coach dog in the English language. The term "coaching" in connection with dogs usually means a dog trotting under a carriage axle, close to the horses' heels. The Dalmatian's coaching position depends on his preference. The main positions are under the rear or front axles or under the pole between the wheeler and the leader horses. The Dalmatian's intelligence has been displayed in his ability to keep close to the horses' heels or underneath the front axle and to stay with the carriage even in the busiest of streets. When the carriage was standing, the Dalmatian would either go to the front and watch the horses or lie down under the carriage; either position was a guarding one.

In England, the Dalmatian was bred for coaching and for guarding his master's coach. His innate love of horses and his coaching ability earned him the title of "coach dog," and he lent style and dignity to the carriage. Coaching required a dog with well-padded feet, solid bone, and a capacious chest—a dog of endurance. In the early days of coaching, the Dalmatian's ears were cropped and he often wore a padlocked brass collar. This was done to protect the dog in the event he was attacked by stray dogs he encountered along the trail.

In 1878, Mr. J.H. Walsh, known as "Stonehenge," stated that "the Dalmatian will run close by a horse's heels," and he gave a detailed description of the breed

Ch. Hopi Kachina Indian Summer, UDTX ("Indi") chooses a position between the rear wheels.

which assigned values to the various aspects of the dog, much like the current breed standard. He assigned 10 out of the total 100 points to legs and feet, stating that "in legs and feet the Dalmatian ought to be perfect, as his sole employment is on the road. The feet must be strong and close...and the horny sole should specially be regarded as of necessity thick and tough."

Indi in coaching position behind the carriage.

Coaching the modern way! Ch. Bearded Oaks Astra's Lyra, CD looks like she's waiting for a ride.

Mrs. Fred Kemp writes in *Pedigree Dogs,* "It was no uncommon sight in Devonshire during the period when farmers' wives used to ride 'pannier' to market, to see a pack-horse accompanied by a Dalmatian...his duty being to guard his master's goods...Only one instance have I found where a Dalmatian actually followed a stage coach and this was on the London and Brighton road in 1851. This dog was known to make the trip of seventy-four miles for eight successive days. He had a strong objection to being carried upon the coach and it was his being placed on the top, from feeling of humanity on the part of the coachman, which cost him his life. He jumped off and fell between the wheels, one of which passed over his neck and killed him."

Edward Noble also described travel in England in the late 1800s, "At the time the roads leading in and out of London were nothing more or less than muddy country lanes, full of holes and cart ruts, but by degrees these were improved, and people who lived only a few miles out of London were enabled to drive in much more fre-

quently and with more comfort. The roads, however, were infested with highwaymen, so as a protection 'running footmen' were introduced. As time went on (these foot-men) were gradually replaced by dogs, and the most showy dog that could be found for the purpose was the Dalmatian." Mr. Noble continues, "Most other dogs soon tire of hard roadwork and refuse to accompany a carriage day after day for the fifteen or twenty miles which is probably the average distance travelled by private conveyances; but the Dalmatian is always pleased to be so

A Dal owned by Judy Bible coaches at the Kentucky Horse Park during National Specialty week.

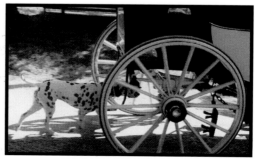

Hapi Dal Easy to Spot, owned by Julie Stubbings Sandoval, poses by the wheels of a carriage.

employed, and if he is allowed the run of the stables and enough food, has all that he cares for. Of his own accord he places himself close behind the heels of the horses...and rarely leaves his berth for any temptation, except when the carriage is stopped."

In *The Complete Dalmatian,* originally copyrighted in 1947 and updated in 1954, Milo Denlinger writes, "There seems to be some difference of opinion as to whether the Dalmatian's

Ch. Centurion's Cultured Pearl with leopard Appaloosa friend I'm a Pepper, both owned by Elise Moloney.

love for horses is inherent or the result of his environment. As with human beings, some are horsy and some are not...At the beginning of the last century the dog was kept as a good traveling servant, a sort of outrider. Besides his attendance on the carriage on the road, he also guarded it in the inn yard at night as well as his master's luggage while he slept."

Mr. Denlinger continues, "In the early days the dog usually preceded the horses; later, his proper position seems to have been changed to behind their heels or under the body of the carriage itself. If in his native home, wherever that may have been, he is used for sporting purposes, in England he has always been regarded as a suitable appendage to a carriage, and his love for horses is firmly implanted. For the first half of the last century (about 1850) or still later, one or more of these dogs was almost always found in a stable of any importance."

In the British Isles it was the custom to breed a large and heavy-type Dalmatian, but according to H. Fred Lauer in his 1907 book *The Dalmatian,* American Dal breeders as early as the 1900s were breeding moderate-sized Dalmatians for coaching because the American coaches were built closer to the ground. If the tradition of a Dalmatian

dictated that he be a coaching dog, then in America he would have to be smaller to coach under the axles.

As automobiles rose in popularity, they gradually replaced horse-drawn carriages, and with them, the opportunities for Dalmatians to engage in the one activity that set them apart from other breeds.

Rudi (Dal) and Blackie give a Christmas gift to their friend Trigger. Owned by Nancy Werhane.

Members of the Puget Sound Dalmatian Club pose with a horse-drawn carriage in Seattle's historic Pioneer Square at the 1992 Pioneer Square Fire Festival.

THE DALMATIAN BECOMES A FIREHOUSE DOG

The Dalmatian earned the title "firehouse dog" because of a series of events and his personality. It has been established that the Dalmatian had an innate love for horses and was at home in the stable. This, coupled with the fact that the early "fire trucks" were horse drawn, caused the Dalmatian to become associated with the firehouse. There are accounts of Dalmatians in various fire departments across the USA in which they have been visibly present riding on the trucks on the way to fires, inside burning buildings, and even rescuing people. Early accounts state that the Dalmatian was often seen running in front of the horse-drawn trucks, barking at the people as if to say "get out of the way."

Several Dals have been well-known fire dogs over the years. In 1917, Kate Sanborn wrote in her book *Educated Dogs of Today* about "Bessie" of Engine Company No. 39 in New York City. "For five and a half long years Bessie cleared the crossing at Third Avenue and Sixty-seventh Street for her company, barking a warning to surface-car motormen, truck drivers, and pedestrians, and during all that time she led the way in every one of the average of forty runs a month made by No. 39."

Bessie was owned by Lieutenant Wise and was also shown by him. She won second place in a special class for Dalmatians owned by fire fighters at the 1910 Westminster Kennel Club show held at Madison Square Garden. However, her notoriety was as a firehouse dog. She was given a street car pass which enabled her to ride to and from the station. She also wore a brass helmet on her collar signifying her status as a fire dog. Lieutenant Wise, in an interview with Kate Sanborn, reported that "Bessie would always follow me into a burning building in the old days and stay

Ch. Korcula Midnight Amanda ("Mandy") is the mascot for the Heartland Fire Historical Society and Museum, Inc. Owned by Dianna Teeter and photographed by Bob Lovell.

Above: Always fired up and ready to go! Crossroads Checkers, CDX is owned by Marilyn Gaffney.
Below: Am-Can. Ch. Tuckaway Bottoms Up Gusto, CD ("Gus") poses with a City of Orlando fire truck.
Owned by Janey Baughn.

one floor below the fighting line, as the rule required. We had to establish that rule for fear a dog might cause a man to stumble if retreat was ordered. Bessie, I think, knew as much about the risks we ran as we did, but she stuck to the rules and always waited a floor below the men handling the nozzles."

When the horse-drawn fire wagons were replaced by fire engines, the Dal began to be less prevalent around the stations. However, in the 1930s and 1940s mascots began to reappear in firehouses.

In the 1970s, "Shadow" in Rock Island, Illinois; "Sparky" trained by Lt. Larry Poage in Fayetteville, Arkansas; and another "Sparky" who joined the Los Angeles Engine 103 Company were all firehouse mascots. "Freckles," the Anderson, Indiana Fire Department mascot, lived at Firehouse #7 until her retirement in 1983. At her burial, she received the same tribute that firefighters receive and alongside her grave a pair of firefighter boots, an ax, and a disconnected hose nozzle were placed.

Cee Kay Becker Thatcher, UDTX is the official fire safety education mascot of the Springfield, MO Fire Department. Owned by Carolyn Krause, photographed by Jim Mayfield.

Dal pup Cally is right at home at the firehouse!

In 1980, the men of Chicago's Engine 22 won a case to keep their mascot "Caesar" when the city attempted to evict the dog from the firehouse. The men of Engine 44 in Manhattan had a Dalmatian mascot for 15 years, and when he died, they where given a six-month-old Dal pup named "Sparky."

Dals are also firehouse dogs in other countries. Firechaser Phoenix (Kitt) is the official mascot of the Melbourne Fire Museum in Australia. He has given demonstrations around Australia, starred in a video, and was featured on a segment of the TV program *Talk to Animals* as a children's fire safety educator.

A Dalmatian poses with Smokey the Bear at the 1991 Pioneer Square Fire Festival in Seattle.

THE DALMATIAN COMES TO AMERICA

The Treens, in their research for *The New Dalmatian, Coach Dog—Firehouse Dog*, located two items which indicate George Washington owned and bred coach dogs. In a letter from George to his nephew he describes purchasing a dog for his bitch "Madame Moose" in order to service her. The original letter is in the Library of Congress. The second item was in Washington's *Ledger B.* "In it on August 14, 1787 he notes the amount he paid for the coachdog—15 shillings."

One hundred years later, in October 1887, "Bessie" was whelped and was the first Dalmatian registered with the AKC. She was registered in 1888 as #10519, and she was owned by Mrs. N.L. Harvey of San Francisco. "Bessie" was white, black, and tan. Her breeder and pedigree are unknown.

In 1897, the AKC Stud Book (Vol. XIV) has recorded "Ruth H." (#444682), a black and white bitch whelped on July 26, 1896. She was owned by Mr. Fred Hull of Danbury, Connecticut and bred by Mr. William Cary of Winchester, Illinois. Two years later, the black and white bitch "Good Times" (#59453), owned by Mr. J.B. Thomas, Jr. of New York City, was registered (Vol. XVI). She was bred by Mr. Hull and "Ruth H." was the dam. Since that time, Dalmatian registrations increased and dogs were imported.

The following is a non-inclusive listing of Dalmatian imports. The first list is arranged in order by birth date for reference purposes. The second list is an alphabetical listing of the remaining known imports.

Eng-Am. Ch. Buffrey Jobee was imported to the US from England at seven years of age. He had a remarkable show career in both countries and was a top-producing stud dog as well. Owned by Benito Vila.

22

Imports with Known Birth Dates

1900s—Ch. Windy Valley Snowstorm 5/1/03
1910s—Eng-Am. Ch. Penwortham Bosco 8/28/11
1920s—Eng-Am. Ch. Queen of Trumps of LeMel 6/21/23
1930s—Ch. Coeland Black Magic 3/21/31
Ch. Highwood Don Juan of Tattoo 10/2/35
Eng-Am. Ch. Moonmagic of Chasfield 8/29/36
Ch. Astwood Qui Vive 9/8/36
Ch. Four-in-Hand Mischief 9/20/36
Ch. Colonsay Jookery of Four-in-Hand 4/4/38
Ch. Boojum of Wells of Four-in-Hand 4/8/38
Ch. Elmcroft Coacher 1/31/39
1940s—Ch. Nigel of Welfield and Stock Dal 6/4/42
Ch. Penny Parade of Williamsdale 4/10/44
Ch. Welfield Guardsman of Stock Dal 6/4/44
Ch. Igor of Kye of Williamsdale 3/16/45
Am. Ch. Jason Widdington of Stock Dal 4/9/45
Eng-Am. Ch. Beau of Hollyroyde 6/2/47
Eng. Ch. Twink of Towpath 9/19/47
Eng-Am. Ch. Colonsay Storm 9/10/48
Washakie Bolehills Barbara 7/23/49
Eng-Am. Ch. Cabaret Charivaris 8/21/49
Ch. Cabaret Cocky Chap of Four-in-Hand 11/8/51
Eng-Am. Ch. Tantivvey Godetia 6/9/48
1950s—Ch. Widdington Kandy 6/27/51
Ch. Cabaret Cheryl of Four-in-Hand 11/8/51
Ch. Cabaret Courtcard 6/16/52
Eng-Am. Ch. Jo-Bandit of St. Botoff 9/18/52
Eng-Am. Ch. Colonsay Blacksmith 4/19/54
Ch. Washakie Matesar 10/4/54
Ch. Colonsay Tantivvey Claudia 6/20/55
Ch. An English Rose of Colonsay 8/21/57
1960s—Am. Ch. Merithew Grand Slam 10/7/62
Ch. Colonsay Olaf the Red 4/16/63
Am. Ch. Broadmoor of Birch 9/3/63
Ch. Duxfordham Yessam Marquis 4/23/64
Ch. Calash Fife Major of Ascotheath 4/15/66
Am. Ch. Ascotheath Little Slam's Pip 5/18/66
1970s—Ch. Duxfordham Alladin 5/9/76
 Eng-Am. Ch. Buffrey Jobee 4/1/77
1980s—Ch. Washakie Bellamie 2/26/80
Ch. Knightstone Huntsman 9/16/85
Int-Arg. Grand Ch. Zagreb Enforcer 12/30/85
Int-Arg. Grand Ch. Zagreb the Challenger 12/31/88

Remaining Known Imports

Am. Ch. Bittersweet of the Wells of Sarum
Am. Ch. Margharita of Ascotheath, CD
Mesra Dilemma
Tantivvey Rose of Tattoo

An important line of descent started with Ch. Twingates Blue Bonnet ("Bonnie"), BOS at DCA in 1973. Owned by Alberta G. Holden.

Bonnie's daughter by Ch. Coachman's Caliber was Winners Bitch at DCA in 1976: Ch. Pill Peddler's Christmas Holly ("Holly"), owned by Teresa Vila and Alberta G. Holden.

Holly produced a son by Ch. Estripe de Montjuic: Ch. Iman de Montjuic was BOB at Westminster in 1977 and winner of the St. Louis Specialty in 1978 and 1984. Owned by Benito Vila.

Iman ex Ch. Tizona de Montjuic produced Ch. Volanta de Montjuic, the top-producing Dalmatian bitch in history with a record 17 champions. Owned by Benito Vila.

One of Volanta's top-winning offspring (by Eng-Am. Ch. Buffrey Jobee), Ch. Farga de Montjuic, is a multiple BIS, DCA, BOS, and specialty BOB winner. She was ranked in the Top Ten Dalmatians and produced five champions. Owned by Benito Vila.

Farga, bred to Ch. Judici de Montjuic, produced mulitple Group and Regional Specialty winner Ch. Sabre de Montjuic. Owned by Benito Vila.

Above: Ch. Four-In-Hand Mischief was a top winner on the West Coast in the late 1930s. He won 18 BIS, sired 18 champions, and was BOB at DCA in 1940. Below: Ch. Elmcroft Coacher was imported from England by Williamsdale Kennel and was an important stud dog in the 1940s, siring 27 champions.

Above: Ch. Washakie Belleamie ("Cheerio") produced five champions from her only litter. She was bred in England and owned by Penny Linke. Below: Ch. Knightstone Huntsman ("Oliver") is one of only seven Dals to go BIS from the classes and is the only English import to do it. Owned by Edith and Nelson Gladstone.

THE DALMATIAN AS A COMPETITOR

Conformation Competition

The Dalmatian's role as a show dog began in England, where in December 1860, Dalmatians were entered at the Birmingham Exhibition. The judge, thought to be "Stonehenge" (Mr. J.H. Walsh), withheld the ribbons because he thought that the quality of the Dals was lacking merit.

In the early 1860s in England, Mr. J. Harrison's "Carlo" was the chief winner until his son "Crib," owned by Mr. Lloyd Price, took over. Between 1866 and 1874 he was the most prominent English Dalmatian. In 1875, Mr. J. Fawdry's "Captain" became the breed winner for several years. "Captain" first was named "Traviser," then "Uhlan," and, finally, "Captain."

Patched and tri-colored Dalmatians were not disqualified from competition in the early years. Vero Shaw, in his work *The Book of the Dog* (1881), writes about the quality of Dalmatians in England at that time as well as about the tri-color Dals. "No where in England are they (Dals) to be seen in such numbers as in a radius of a few miles from the Crystal Palace, where they are not only numerous, but in many cases much above the average in good points. In a few instances we have noticed fair specimens of the tri-colored variety, so rarely found good." It is interesting to note that in the third edition of *Dogs of the British Isles* (1878) by J.H. Walsh, the description of the Dalmatian mentioned tri-color markings, stating that "sometimes there is a stain of tan about the head and legs but clear jet black is more highly valued than black and tan." By 1948, the British standard did not mention tri-color.

In America, the first conformation competition was held in 1874, in Memphis, Tennessee, but there were no Dalmatians entered. Records indicate that the first Dalmatians were shown in the USA in 1883, but there was not much support from the Dalmatian fancy until 1903. The first Dalmatian champion recorded by the AKC was in 1904. He was a black and white dog named Ch. Edgecomb D'Artagnan who was owned by Miss M.W. Martin and bred by J.S. Price, Jr. It seems that the Dalmatian became popular as a show dog within a short period of time after that, largely due to the formation of the Dalmatian Club of America (DCA), which supported the entries at the shows in the Northeast. The DCA also began its own specialty shows in 1926.

In the early show days, a dog was not required by the AKC to be registered in order to compete in conformation classes. If a dog was able to win one point within three shows, the owner could then apply to the AKC to have the dog registered. The number of required points for a championship was originally ten, and today it has increased to 15.

Mr. Fawdry's famous dog Captain, whose name was changed several times and who was a breed winner in the 1870s.

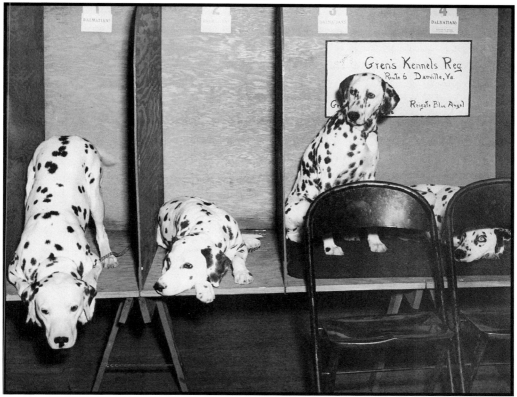

A bench show in the 1950s. Photo submitted by Margie Doane.

The early Dalmatian competition was centered in the East, mostly around southern New England, New York, New Jersey, and Virginia. In the South, the shows were often held in tobacco warehouses because the railroad tracks ran alongside of them and the train was the mode of travel at that time. The trains would pull alongside of the warehouses and the dog exhibitors would disembark. The handlers often rode in the baggage cars with the dogs to make sure that the dogs were safe.

Some shows were supported by wealthy patrons such as Mrs. Geraldine Dodge of New Jersey. She financed the Morris and Essex all-breed show, which was held on her estate. This show and the Westminster Kennel Club show were the two most prestigious dog shows in the country. Upon Mrs. Dodge's death, the Morris and Essex show was discontinued. However, her love for the canine world has been generously supported by the founding of the Morris Animal Foundation.

The early shows were benched and competitors were required to be in attendance from 8 a.m. until 5 p.m., as the shows were designed mostly for the public to enjoy the various breeds. Dogs were allowed off the bench one hour prior to being shown in order to be exercised and groomed. Females in season and young puppies could be crated if necessary. There was a healthy exchange of information among exhibitors, and they often helped each other hold their dogs for grooming. The dogs of the same breed were benched together, which allowed the fancier to get to know the dogs in a more intimate way than by just observing the dogs in the show ring.

June 1950—The Dalmatian Club of Southern New England's first sanctioned match. Left to right: D. Doane and Ch. Tailgate of the Walls, W. Sammet and Ch. China Doll of Dalmatia, J. Doane and Ch. Beloved Scotch of the Walls, J. Whiting Verre and Ch. Shadrach of Whitlee, and C. Theissen and an unidentified dog.

Obedience Competition

Obedience competition was sanctioned by the AKC in 1936 and several Dalmatian enthusiasts, such as Harland and Lois Meistrell, supported this part of the Dalmatian's competitive career. The Treens write, "The first Dalmatian entered in an obedience class was Captain Fiske, exhibited by Louise Geddes Fiske in the Novice A class of the Eastern Dog Club, Boston, MA, February 21–22, 1937." By 1939, a Dalmatian was awarded a Companion Dog title. This honor went to Meeker's Barbara Worth, owned by George S. Walker.

The early obedience point system had a different scale for each class. In 1948, it was changed to a 200-point system for every class with a qualifying score of 170 or better required for a "leg." Three legs at the same level are required to receive an obedience title for each of the following: Companion Dog (CD), Companion Dog Excellent (CDX),

Duchess of Dal Downs (left) earned her CDX in April 1953 and Pamela of Dal Downs earned her UD in October 1951. Owned by Mr. and Mrs. R.L. Sullivan.

Ch. Dal Downs Dicie of Shadodal, UDT was the first female Dal to hold the titles Ch., CD, CDX, UD, and TD. Owned by Mr. and Mrs. R.L. Sullivan.

and Utility Dog (UD). Obedience Trial Champion (OTCh) and Utility Dog Excellent (UDX) are obedience titles also offered by the AKC.

In the beginning years of obedience com-petition, a Utility Dog Tracking title was offered for a short period of time. It was different from the UDT of today, as the early title required a dog to pass a tracking test before competing in the Utility class. Today,

Ch. Dal Downs Nordic, UDT was the son of two UDT parents: Labyrinth Obviously, UDT and Ch. Dal Downs Dicie of Shadodal, UDT.

a dog can earn a Tracking Dog (TD) title at a tracking trial, which is a separate event. If a dog has a Utility Dog title and a Tracking Dog title, the owner can combine both and add a Utility Dog Tracker (UDT) to the dog's name.

Since 1972, the Dalmatian Club of America has offered obedience competition at its National Specialty on a regular basis.

Road Trial Competition

The first road trial held in America was in 1906 in Wissahickon, Pennsylvania with an entry of seven. The same horse and carriage was used for each dog. Judging was based 75% on the dog's working ability—the closer to the horses' heels and the longer he remained under the coach, the higher the score. All the dogs ran at the same time to see which was able to keep closest to the horses. Twenty-five percent of the score was based on the dog's conformation. "Ponto," owned by William Anson of Chestnut Hills, Pennsylvania, received the winning ribbon.

According to H. Fred Lauer's book *The Dalmatian* (1907), a second trial was held that year at the York, Pennsylvania show. "A handsome pair of Cobs to a break wagon" was the equipment used. There was an entry of six and each dog ran by himself with Mr. Lauer officiating. Dr. George Pottiger of Gamburg, Penn-

sylvania owned the winner, "Pottiger's Bell."

Mr. Lauer also wrote that an exhibition was given afterward with the first through third place dogs coaching together. "It was amazing to see how one dog would pass the other dog out in order to get close to the horses' heels."

Specific rules were not written down for these early trials; they simply were established at the beginning of each trial.

According to the DCA *Rules and Standards Handbook*, published in 1921, the DCA wanted road trials showing a Dalmatian running under a trap to be a feature at outdoor horse shows. "The rule governing these trials is as follows: a one-horse four-wheel trap of sufficient height to enable the dog to travel with shoulders under front axle must be used. The working qualities of the dog to count 75%, and the show qualities to count 25%."

Wendell Sammet and Roadcoach Frou Frou are presented with the winning Road Trial ribbon in 1949.

Shortly after World War II, DCA members Lloyd and Stella Reeves, Mrs. Alfred Barrett, and Harland and Lois Meistrell revised the road trial rules to accommodate exhibitors on horseback so that carriages were not required, and, therefore, there would be a greater number of suitable locations to conduct trials. Most of these rules listed in these 1948 regulations were in standard dog show language stating such predictable basics as, "The Road Trial Committee shall have power...to suspend or debar from handling or entering dogs in any Road Trial of the Club any person who uses abusive language to the judges or Officers of the Club, or who has been found to the satisfaction of the Road Trial Committee to have conducted himself improperly in any measure connected with the Road Trials...All dogs must be registered or eligible for registration in the AKC Stud Book...The entrance fee must accompany every nomination...Dogs affected with any contagious disease, shall not be permitted on the grounds or kennels where the Trials are to be run...Each heat shall be conducted in such a manner as to give each dog an opportunity to display the qualities under judgment...Dogs will not be penalized for leaving his handler but must remain within calling distance and must Hock on command."

Some other sections of the rules are unexpected, but are nonetheless fascinating to read. Section 4 of Chapter 1 states, for example, that "Castrated dogs or spayed bitches shall be debarred from competition in the events held by the Road Trial-giving Club, and any such dog proven to have been so run, with the knowledge of the owner or handler, or both, shall be debarred from competition in the events held by the Club." Rule 9, Section 1 states, "The judges shall call to order a handler for making any unnecessary noise, or for a disorderly conduct calculated to in any way interfere with the opponent's dog. It shall be the duty of the Judges to call the offending party to order and see that this rule is at all times strictly enforced." Section 2 states, "A handler may speak or whistle or use hound whip or hand or work dog in any way he may deem proper, if not contrary to these rules, but he shall not make any unnecessary noise, or interfere with the opponent's dog in any way." Rule 10, Section 1 reads, "A warning bark is desirable, but dogs may not be excessively noisy or babbling." Section 2 declares, "Any chasing of animals, wild or domestic, shall be considered undesirable." Rule 10, Section 3 states, "Judges shall consider the conformation of the dogs as it reflects on their ability to maintain such a pace as is necessary to keep up with horses at any pace up to approximately 18 miles per hour and for such length of time as a horse can travel." Section 4 states, "Handlers shall ride at a reasonable cross-country hacking pace. Walking where ground is rocky, boggy, etc.; trotting a good third of the time; cantering where trail permits. A good hunting pace should be shown across open field or stretch of trail to allow dogs to show range and speed. One such exhibition is sufficient."

These rules were used at a road trial held on November 14, 1948, for which the "conditions" were described as follows: "Trial will start on Dedham Country and Polo Club field and finish at Miss Amelia Peabody's Mill Farm on Dedham Street, Dover. Distance approximately 10 miles. Bridle Path will be marked." The entry fee was one dollar, there was one mounted judge and two foot judges, and trophies were awarded to the "first four places and for the best puppy in the trial."

Another road trial was held around this time at the Rice Farms in Huntington, Long Island, where Roadcoach Frou Frou, CD, owned and handled by Wendell Sammet, was the winner. After this time, although many Dal fanciers continued to personally enjoy Dalmatian escorts on their horseback rides, formal road trials vanished.

In 1989, due to the efforts of DCA member Linda Myers and others, the DCA Board appointed a Road Trial Committee that had fine-tuned the road trial rules and once again the Dalmatian is demonstrating his ability to coach. In 1994, the Dalmatian Club of America Board of Governors approved an updated version of the Road Trial Regulations which were suggested by the Road Trial Committee. As the rules currently stand, they attempt to give a Dalmatian the opportunity to display the skills that logically would be required for him to be considered a safe, effective escort to either a rider on horseback or a carriage driver. The exercises require a dog to do the following:

1. Come directly to his handler when called.

2. Hock on command for a distance of 200 yards.

3. Hock past a distraction.

4. Sit or down and wait for a period of two minutes.

5. Demonstrate his ability to keep up with a galloping horse for 100 yards.

In addition to the successful completion of these five exercises displaying his suitability as a coach dog, the Dalmatian also has to pass Pre-Course, Mid-Course, and After-Course Soundness Checks by two veterinarians and complete a distance of 12.5 miles within three hours for an RD (Road Dog) title or 25 miles within 6 hours for an RDX (Road Dog Excellent) title to demonstrate that they have the endurance called for in their breed standard. Since 1992, whenever the National Specialty location is conducive to this event, the DCA has sponsored a Road Trial.

At the 1993 DCA Road Trial, Bell Ringer's Redrock Puccini, CD, RD (left) won the 12.5-mile class, and Ch. Harmony of Cheshire T. Redrock, CD, RDX won the 25-mile class. Pictured with owner/handler Peggy Ann Strupp.

MAJOR INACTIVE KENNELS IN THE USA

Many of the original Dalmatian breeding kennels were large kennels with extensive breeding programs and hired kennel managers who lived on the property. As time marched on, these large kennels became less numerous and have been replaced by breeders whose kennels are on a much smaller scale. The following are summaries of some of the earlier breeding kennels that are now inactive.

Altamar

Altamar Dalmatians, located in Woodland Hills, California, and owned by Maria Johnson, began in 1960. The kennel name is derived from "All Tack" and "Maria" (Tack was Maria's first Dalmatian).

Coachman's Classic (Tack) was purchased in 1954. He became Altamar's stud dog and earned American, Mexican, and Canadian championship titles as well as a CD obedience title. He was Best of Breed at the 1958 DCA National Specialty. He won Groups and was the recipient of the Will Judy (*Dog World*) award. Tack also won fame as the model for "Pongo" in the *101 Dalmatians* animated feature film.

Above: Am-Can-Mex. Ch. Coachman's Classic, CD ("Tack") was the foundation sire for Altamar Dalmatians. He was also the model for Pongo in Disney's animated 101 Dalmatians. Right: Ch. Williamscrest Dainty Dancer ("DeeDee") was Altamar's foundation bitch. She was the model for Perdita in 101 Dalmatians.

Above: Ch. Altamar's Aristos ("King") was a homebred Altamar champion and Regional Specialty winner. He is shown here winning under Mrs. L.W. Bonney, owner of the influential Tally Ho Kennels. Below: Ch. Altamar's Acheson ("Grinch") was BOB at the Dalmatian Club of Southern California's 1972 specialty. He also sired several champions.

Am-Mex. Ch. Williamscrest Dainty Dancer, purchased in 1959, became Altamar's foundation bitch. She was a Group winner from the classes and was never defeated by her sex. She was the model for "Perdita" and three of her puppies sired by Tack were models for the pups in *101 Dalmatians*.

Ch. Blackpool Crinkle Forest was a big winner in the 1960s, earning six BIS, many Group wins, and BOB at the 1966 DCA show. Owned by Ed Jenner and Barbara Peters.

Blackpool

Nick and Barbara Peters's Blackpool Dalmatians is basically a cross between Willowmount and Crestview kennels. This combination produced one of the top winning bitches, Ch. Blackpool Crinkle Forest, who won the DCA National Specialty twice as well as six Bests in Show. Blackpool also imported a liver dog from England, Ch. Colonsay Olaf the Red.

Colonial Coach

William and Laura Knowles's kennel, founded in 1945 in Illinois, was taken over

Ch. Blackpool Red Nora, CDX (L) finished her championship with several BOB over Specials, but is best known as an obedience dog. Owned by Sue MacMillan.

Ch. Colonial Coach Cheshire was a well-known winner in the Midwest in the early 1960s as well as the sire of 19 champions.

by Ron and Natalie Fleger in 1964. The Knowles were able to purchase all of the Dalmatians from the O'Dal Kennel, which added to the Colonial Coach breeding program. The Colonial Coach prefix can be found in many of the pedigrees of top winning dogs.

Dals were Best in Show at DCA National Specialties: in 1960, Ch. Crestview Diamond Jim and in 1976, Ch. Crestview Dan Patch. This kennel has had many Dals win regional specialties as well.

Ch. Crown Jewels Oriental Pearl, CD is a top producer with seven champions, among them specialty winners and Group placers. Owned by R.P. Zemke.

Crestview

Violet McManus of California started her breeding program under the guidance of Mr. Leo Meeker of Four-in-Hand Kennels and all of the Crestview stock goes back to Ch. Four-in-Hand Mischief. A few years after the kennel began, Jim McManus participated actively with the dogs and handled many of them to their championships. Two Crestview

Crown Jewels

Vern and Norma Price began their kennel in the Midwest in the 1950s with a bitch trained for obedience competition. Colonial Coach Kennels played an important part in the Crown Jewels foundation stock. One of the more well-known Dals from the Crown Jewels Kennel is Ch. Crown Jewels Black Diamond, who sired 42 champions.

Ch. Windgap's Honey Bee was the foundation bitch for Dottidale Kennels.

Dottidale

Amy and Elli Lipschutz established the Dottidale Kennel in 1960 in Croton on Hudson, New York with the foundation bitch Ch. Windgap's Honey Bee. Her son Ch. Dottidale Jo Jo became their major stud dog. The kennel was moved to a "built to order" facility in Milbrook, New York in 1972 and then, in 1984, it was relocated to Liberty, Kentucky.

Ch. Dottidale Jo Jo, the top winning liver Dalmatian in 1967; his son, Ch. Dalhalla Thunderbolt; and his grandson, Ch. Bell Ringer's Sundance are in many pedigrees today. Amy and Elli are no longer breeding Dals but have a few Beagles and have rescued a retired Greyhound.

Four-in-Hand

Leo Meeker, a Californian, imported several English Dalmatians. The most well known was Ch. Four-in-Hand Mischief, who won 18 Bests in Show and was the sire of many Best in Show Dals. This kennel is in the pedigree of many of today's California Dals. Two Four-in-Hand Dalmatians won DCA National Specialties: Ch. Four-in-Hand Mischief in 1940 and Ch. Four-in-Hand Blackberry in 1946.

In the Valley

This is the prefix used by Mrs. George Ratner. Many of these Dals, such as Ch. Tin Lizzie In the Valley and Ch. Barney Oldfield In the Valley, can be found in extended pedigrees. Mrs. Ratner owned the well-known Ch. Roadcoach Roadster when he was one of the top winning Dals. He won the Group at the Morris and Essex show in 1955 and under new owners he won Best in Show at this show again the following year.

Ch. Roadcoach Roadster, handled by Charlie Meyers, winning the Group at Morris and Essex in 1955. Owned by Mr. and Mrs. Barrett.

Above: Ch. Dottidale JoJo pictured in 1966. One of the first big-winning livers, JoJo was breeder-owner-handled to all of his wins. Below: Ch. Dottidale Buster Brown (L) shown finishing in 1966. He was one of Dottidale's first homebred champions.

Above: Ch. Dottidale Marco Polo is another of Dottidale's liver-spotted champions. Below: Although Dottidale was known for its livers, they did have a few champion blacks. This is black-spotted Ch. Dottidale Captain Nemo.

Oseau

Lloyd and Reba Oseau of California were very active in obedience but they also purchased Ch. Crestview Dan Patch, who became a Best in Show winner in 1974. They imported a bitch in whelp, Widdington Kandy, from England. She became a champion and three of her pups earned obedience titles.

Above: Am-Can. Ch. Coachman's Chuck-A-Luck was the #1 Dalmatian for several years and an important sire. Originally owned by John and Mary Kay Blair, later owned by Mr. and Mrs. Al Treen. Below: Going BOB at DCA in 1959 is Ch. Green Starr's Undergraduate (L). She was also a multiple-Group winner and BOS at DCA in 1958. Owned by Pennydale Kennels.

Pennydale

Arthur and Muriel Higgins's Dals retired the DCA Challenge trophies at the National by winning Best of Breed, Best of Opposite Sex, Best of Winners, Winners Dog, and Winners Bitch. Their Dals also won three times at the Chicagoland Specialty and the Dalmatian Club of Southern New England Specialty.

Pryor Creek

Alfred and Esmeralda Treen began their kennel in Southern Illinois and later moved to Milwaukee. Their foundation bitch was Ch. Saint Rocco's Polka Dot, CD, and the foundation dog was Ch. Fobette's Fanfare, CDX. He became the grandsire of Ch. Coachman's Chuck-A-Luck, owned by John and Mary Kay Blair, who was a Best in Show winner and the sire of two Best in Show get: Ch. Lord Jim and Ch. Roadking's Rome.

Quaker's Acre

In 1948, Mary Munro Smith started breeding Dalmatians in Florida with a bitch from the Quaker's Oats Company. Mary was interested in obedience but had many championships on her dogs as well. This prefix can be found on pedigrees in 18 different countries.

Reigate

George and Mary Leigh Lane began breeding Dals in the late 1930s in Franklin, Virginia. Mary Leigh started with a bitch from England that was not registered and was undershot, but after finishing her championship was registered as Ch. Lady Culpepper of Reigate. (Many of the earlier dogs in the USA who were not registered were allowed to become so after proving they measured up to the standard.) She became the dam of the Lanes' most famous dog, Ch. Reigate Bold Venture, who won Best of Breed at the DCA National Specialty twice. Many kennels purchased their foundation stock from Reigate. Mrs. Virginia Wiseman, who co-

Ch. Reigate Bold Venture was a BIS winner, BOB at DCA in 1944 and 1945, and the sire of 24 champions. Owned by Reigate Kennels.

owned and handled many of the Reigate dogs, started Gren Dalmatians with Reigate dogs. Her first Reigate Dal, "Snitchal," often trotted along when Mrs. Wiseman would ride on horseback for 20 miles. Mrs. Wiseman said, "These old Dals had good substance, bone, and feet required for such a trip." Ch. Gren's Coal Tar, a Best in Show winner, was her top winning dog.

Roadcoach

Alfred and Mary Barrett established their kennel in Massachusetts in the 1930s. They used the Tally Ho, Tattoo, Hollow Hill, and Reigate kennels in their breeding program and acquired Strathglass stock when it no longer bred Dals. Four Roadcoach dogs have won the National Specialty and the Barretts were two of the owners of Ch. Roadcoach Roadster, winner of 17 Bests in Show.

Stablemate

Sylvia Howison's foundation bitch was Charlie's Pretty Penny sired by Ch. Dal Duchy's Georgeous George. Sylvia acquired Am-Can. Ch. Willowmount Baron Brown by accident as he had been abandoned. She trained and showed him to his championship and he became the top stud dog for this kennel.

Ch. Reigate Native Dancer was WD at DCA in 1954 and also became a Group winner. Owned by Mr. and Mrs. Myron W. Greene, II.

Tally Ho

This well-known kennel was owned by Mrs. Flora Bonney of Flushing, Long Island. She was the secretary for the Dalmatian Club spanning several decades. In 1912, when Mrs. Bonney's dog Windholme's Kip won Reserve Winners at the Belmont Park show, it encouraged her to start a kennel. The original kennel was wiped out by an eccentric neighbor who poisoned all the dogs. However, the kennel was started again in 1917 with two bitches from Mr. Weekes of York, Pennsylvania. One of these, Tally Ho Make Merry, was the dam of Ch. Tally Ho Last of Sunstar, the first DCA National Specialty Best of Breed winner. Five Tally Ho dogs won the National Specialty six times and a Tally Ho bitch was the first bitch to win Best of Breed at the Nationals. Mrs. Bonney's breeding program involved outcrosses every few generations and she imported many dogs from England.

Mary Barrett showing Ch. Roadcoach Roadster to BOB at Westminster in 1955 under judge Harry T. Peters, Jr.

Tomalyn Hill

The Nelsons started exhibiting in New Jersey in 1940 and they were helped in their breeding program by Mrs. Bonney of Tally Ho. The Nelsons' daughter, Evelyn Nelson White, was the most active participant with the kennel. She purchased Ch. Four-in-Hand Blackberry from Leo Meeker and used him extensively as a sire. He was Best of Breed at the 1945 DCA National Specialty. Ch. Tomalyn's Air Cadette was Best of Opposite Sex the same year and Tomalyn's Rascality came from the classes to win the same honors at the 1949 Nationals.

Williamsdale

Charles Williams's kennel in Cincinnati, operative from 1938 through 1976, was given to the kennel manager, Martin Milet, in 1955. The foundation bitch for Williamsdale was Her Majesty of Williamsdale. Mr. Williams imported two English stud dogs, Am-Can. Ch. Elmcroft Coacher, who sired 27 champions, and Ch. Igor of Kye of Williamsdale, who sired 16 champions. In 1953, one of Igor's sons, Ch. Williamsdale Rocky, won Best of Breed at the DCA National Specialty. Other imports included Eng-Am. Ch. Penny Parade of Williamsdale, Ch. Colonsay Tantivvey Claudia and Eng-Am. Ch. Beau of Hollyroyde.

Mary Barrett showing Ch. Roadcoach Spice (L) to BOB at the 1962 DCA Specialty under judge Mrs. Flora Bonney.

Above: Am-Can. Ch. Willowmount Baron Brown going BOB at the 1973 Western Reserve Dalmatian Club Specialty. Owned by Sylvia Howison. Below: Ch. Tally Ho Sirius was BOB at DCA in 1939 and 1941.

Above: Ch. Spotlight's Spectacular (L), "Penny," is the top-winning Dalmatian in breed history. Bred by Stephen and Connie Wagner, owned by Isabel Robson.

ACTIVE KENNELS IN THE USA ESTABLISHED PRIOR TO 1965

Albelarm

Since the 1940s, Isabel Robson has been involved with Dalmatians. When she was a teenager, she received a Dalmatian from a friend who, like Isabel, was involved in hunter horse competition. Later, Mrs. Robson purchased her foundation bitch from a litter sired by an import, Ch. Nigel of Welfield, and a Stock-Dal dam. Albelarm's foundation male was Ch. Lorbyrndale We Hail. Today, Albelarm is located in Glenmore, Pennsylvania.

Above: Ch. Albelarm Starr of Summerhill was a BIS winner and Top Ten Dal for four consecutive years. He is one of the Top 25 Dals of all time. Owned by Edith and Nelson Gladstone. Left: Eight-year-old Ch. Green Starr's Colonel Joe going BOB at DCA in 1982 from the Veterans class. Owned by Mrs. Alan Robson and Mrs. David G. Doane.

Mrs. Robson imported Eng. Ch. Cabaret Charivaris, who was the Winners Bitch at the 1952 DCA National Specialty, Tantivvey Georgina, and Pateshull Pucelle (liver).

Albelarm has owned several Best in Show winners: Ch. Coachkeeper Blizzard of Quaker's Acre (liver dog); Ch. Green Starr's Shamrock (bitch), who won three Bests in Show; Ch. Green Starr's Colonel Joe, who won 35 Bests in Show and the DCA National Specialty four times; and Ch. Spotlight's Spectacular (liver bitch) bred by Stephen and Connie Wagner, who was acquired after winning Best of Breed at the 1993 DCA National Specialty and who has won 66 Best in Show awards. She was also Best of Breed at the 1995 Westminster show, Group winner at the 1996 and 1997 Westminster shows, and the number one Non-Sporting dog for 1995 and 1996. These accomplishments earn her the "spotlight" as the number one all-time winning Dalmatian in America.

Bespeckled

Ken and Nan Nagler of Bespeckled Dalmatians, Upper Marlboro, Maryland, have concentrated their efforts along obedience training and competition routes. Their first Dalmatian, Lightning Sparks, UD, was purchased in 1956. His daughter, Ch. Princess Lillian, CD, and her daughter, Ch. Princess Lois of Loki, UD, were bred to dogs from the Never Complain Kennels. In 1973, Bespeckled Becky was purchased from the Never Complain Kennels and eventually

became a champion UD. Since that time, the Bespeckled prefix has been used.

Coachman

Bill and Jean Fetner's Coachman Kennels in Missouri pointed their first Dalmatian, Kingcrest Jack Tar, in 1942. Their kennel was registered with the AKC in 1950. The foundation bitch, Ch. Fobette's Frishka, CD, and the foundation dog, Ch. Fobette's Fanfare, CDX, were a result of linebreeding on Ch. Four-in-Hand Mischief. Coachman has concentrated on a linebred program since that time.

Three of the Coachman Dalmatians have won Best of Breed at the DCA National Specialty: Ch. Coachman's Classic, CD, Ch. Coachman's Callisto, and Ch. Lord Jim, owned by Bill and Carol Victor, who won twice.

Top to bottom: Ch. Bespeckled Becky, UD; Bespeckled Jean, UD; Ch. Bespeckled Kelly, CDX; Ch. Old Coach Trilj, CD; Ch. Bespeckled Freckles, CDX; Ch. Bespeckled Charlemagne, CD. Owned by Ken and Nan Nagler.

Ch. Fobette's Frishka, CD was the foundation bitch for Coachman Kennels.

Coachman's first homebred champion, Ch. Coachman's Cup O' Tea (L). Owned by Phyllis Fetner.

Ch. Coachman's Hot Coffee (L) was BOB at Westminster twice.

Ch. Coachman's Red Carpet (L) was owned and shown by Kevin Fetner.

Ch. Coachman's Carbon Copy is from a litter of seven champions. Breeder-owner-handled by P. Jay Fetner.

Ch. Coachman's Lucky Cuss was owned and handled by Dr. Christopher Fetner.

$1.00

Saddle and Bridle

MARCH 1971

Carte Blanche   *Coachman Champions*   Hot Fudge

Two famous Coachman "cover girls"—Ch. Coachman's Carte Blanche and Hot Fudge—in an oil portrait by Walter L. Brown. This beautiful painting appeared on the cover of Saddle and Bridle magazine.

Dalmatia

Wendell Sammet's Dalmatia Kennels in Bryantville, Massachusetts, came into existence in 1945 with the purchase of a three-year-old bitch, Roadcoach Frou Frou, for obedience and possibly conformation competition. She completed her CDX and was the winner of one of the two road trials held in 1949.

"Frou" was bred to Ch. Roadcoach Racing Colors, an outcross which produced Dalmatia's first homebred champion, Ch. China Doll from Dalmatia. "Chinky" was the 1949 DCA National Specialty Best of Breed.

This kennel produced Ch. Boot Black from Dalmatia. "Boot" won Best American Bred in Show, an award given at that time because so many of the imported dogs were winning Best in Show. His offspring, Ch. Colonel Boots from Dalmatia was Best of Breed at the 1954 DCA National Specialty.

Dalmatia went on a sabbatical for 25 years as Wendell was busy handling and being an agent for several breeding kennels. Since 1990, the kennel has become active again.

Wendell Sammet with the famous Am-Can. Ch. Boot Black from Dalmatia, the sire of many champions.

Dalwood

Dalwood Dalmatians is a small, selective breeding kennel in Palos Verdes Estates, California, that was established by Georgiann (Peggy) Rudder. The foundation dog for the line was Paul's Mischievous Bandit, CDX, whelped in 1953. The foundation bitch was Ch. Dalwood's Princess Candy Tuft, CDX, whelped in 1955. There were a number of Four-in-Hand dogs on both pedigrees including Int-Am. Ch. Four-in-Hand Mischief. Some other well-known kennels on the pedigrees were Reigate, Stock-Dal, and Williamsdale.

The first Dalwood Dalmatian litter was whelped in 1957, and the dogs were bred exclusively by Peggy until 1963 when Carol Haywood joined as a partner. In 1986, Int-Am-Mex. Ch. Dalwood's Knight Edition, 1978 World Show Champion and multi-Group winner, was the top sire with five champion get.

The multi-Group winner Int-Am-Mex. Ch. Dalwood's Knight Traveler and Ch. Dalwood's Dream Girl were in the top ten in 1986. Ch. Dalwood's Knight E Nite was a DCA Award of Merit winner in 1991.

One of Dalwood's claims to fame is the nationally recognized group of Junior Handlers that has handled Dalwood Dalmatians. Diane Haywood (Bartholomew), Jean Marie Lloyd, Ron Lloyd, and Heather Haywood Johnston have done the honors.

Ch. China Doll of Dalmatia and Roadcoach Frou Frou in a "woody"—a wooden-sided station wagon. Owned by Wendell Sammet.

Above: Paul's Mischievous Bandit, CDX was the foundation dog for Dalwood Dalmatians. Owner-handled by Peggy Rudder. Below: Ch. Dalwood's Princess Candy Tuft, CDX was the foundation bitch for Dalwood. She is pictured here at age 12.

Wendell Sammet and his first homebred champion, China Doll of Dalmatia, who was Best of Breed at both Westminster and DCA.

Ch. Colonel Boots from Dalmatia, owned by Wendell Sammet.

Ch. Tioga Georgio of Dalmatia being shown as a puppy.

Int-Am-Mex. Ch. Dalwood's Knight Edition was the first big star for Dalwood.

Int-Am-Mex. Ch. Dalwood's Knight Traveler was a Group winner and Top Ten Dal.

Ch. Dalwood's Mr. Clown, shown by then 13-year-old handler Jean Marie Lloyd.

Ch. Dalwood's Dream Girl was a multiple-Group winner and a Top Ten Dal in 1986.

Green Starr

After selecting the maiden names of their mothers for their kennel's name, Dr. and Mrs. David G. Doane began the Green Starr Kennel in New England in 1947. Since that time the kennel has been located in upstate New York, Virginia, and presently, in Jonesborough, Tennessee. A note of interest—in Ireland, "Green Star" is the title of a champion certificate.

The foundation of today's kennel was established with Ch. Beloved Scotch of the Walls and Shad's Dotter of Whitlee. Both were grandchildren of Ch. Reigate Bold Venture. The Doanes consider Ch. Green Starr's Darling Dotter to be the best Dalmatian the kennel has produced.

Three Green Starr Dals have won Best of Breed at DCA National Specialties and several Green Starr Dals have won Best in Show honors. The best-known Green Starr Dal in recent times is Ch. Green Starr's Colonel Joe, a multiple Best in Show and DCA Best of Breed winner.

Hopi Kachina

Ray and Cathy Nogar became enchanted with Dalmatians when the riding stable they bought on their honeymoon came with a male Dalmatian named "King." The Nogars, who now live in Espanola, New Mexico, established the Hopi Kachina line when Hopi Noki Kachina was bred to Ch. Melody Dynamatic (owned by C.E. Flock, Jr.). From this litter Ch. Hopi Kachina Melody Mocha went Best of Opposite Sex at the 1977 DCA Specialty and won the Veteran Bitch Class in 1983. Ch. Hopi Kachina Indian Summer, who was the DCA Best in Futurity winner in 1980, was the first champion UDTX in the breed. Four other bitches have won top honors in DCA

This little boy grew up to be Lt. Stephen Doane, who shared his family's interest in Dals and dog shows. He is with Ch. Green Starrs Dynamite and Green Starrs Bit of the Walls.

Ch. Green Starr's Colonel Joe, "Cass," at the age of nine, taking it easy in the Doanes' front hall. Owned by Margie Doane and Mrs. Alan Robson.

Futurity and Sweepstakes competitions and three Hopi Kachina Dals have won Award of Merit honors at DCA Specialties.

Jaybar

In 1963 in California, Barbara Niemeyer purchased her first Dal, Bobby's Bobbie of Tarzana. She later was bred to Ch. Broadmoor of Birch, an English import, and produced Jaybar's first champion, Am-Can. Ch. Dandy Dan of Coachmaster, who became one of the leading liver sires. One of Jaybar's owner-handled Group winners that Barbara enjoyed showing was Am-Can-Mex. Ch. Jaybar's Black Label.

Above: Ch. Beloved Scotch of the Walls was the foundation sire of Green Starr Kennels. Below: Ch. Green Starr's Follow Me Mark (left) and Ch. Green Starr's Jenny's Mark (right) pictured with Mr. and Mrs. David G. Doane. "Mark" is "Jenny's" sire.

Ch. Green Starr's Masterpiece (L) was one of the first champions for Green Starr Kennels.

Ch. Green Starr's King Pin was one of the first homebred Green Starr champions.

Ch. Green Starr's Dazzler was BOB at Westminster. Owned by Mr. and Mrs. Milton Smith.

Ch. Hopi Kachina Melody Mocha (L) went BOS at DCA in 1977, handled by Ed Flock.

Ch. Hopi Kachina Kawaika (L), Best in Futurity at DCA in 1993.

Am-Can-Mex. Ch. Jaybar's Black Label, owned by Barbara Niemeyer.

59

Korcula

Dr. John and Betty Garvin's Korcula Kennels began in 1965 near Columbus, Ohio, with their foundation bitch, Ch. Korcula Salona, CD ("Corky"), and foundation male, Ch. Dogtowne's Firechief Rocky, CD. The prefix Korcula was chosen because it was a city-state of the old Dalmatia province. Salona was chosen as the name of their first Dal because it was the capital city of Korcula.

The Garvins' son, Charles Garvin, MD, was well known as a Junior Handler and he trained and handled "Corky" and "Rocky" to their championship and obedience titles. Currently, Charlie and his wife Lynn are breeding and handling the Korcula Dalmatians from Marion, Ohio.

Korcula has been known for a strong bitch line as there have been important breeding bitches in each generation from "Corky" to "Lace" to "Hannah" to "Serenade" to "Sissy," and the list goes on. Ch. Korcula Salona, CD, was the top Dal bitch for five years and was Best of Opposite Sex at the 1968 DCA National Specialty. Her great-granddaughter, Ch. Korcula Midnight Serenade, was Best of Breed at the 1981 DCA

National Specialty. She was the first bitch to win this title since Ch. Blackpool Crinkle Forest in 1965 and 1966. Serenade's daughter, Ch. Korcula Midnight Mistress, "Sissy," is the dam of 16 champions including three Best in Show winners.

In the late 1980s Korcula gave the males a chance to do their thing and Ch. Korcula Midnight Star Bret D, co-owned with Debbie Zink, was the number one Dalmatian in 1989 and 1990 as well as the 1991 Best of Breed at the DCA National Specialty. He is the sire of Best in Show, Best in Futurity, and Best in Sweepstakes winners.

Labyrinth

Christine Dyker's involvement with Dals began in 1947 in Silver Spring, Maryland. Labyrinth's foundation male was War Eagle Taps and the foundation bitch was Polka Dot Salute to Reveille. One of "Dot's" daughters, Ch. Labyrinth Sleighbelle, became one of the top-producing dams of the breed as well as the granddam of two well-known Dal sires, Ch. Tuckaway Traveler Indalane and Ch. Count Miguel of Tuckaway.

Ch. Korcula Salona, CD was the Garvins' first Dalmatian and the foundation bitch for Korcula Kennels.

Ch. Korcula Midnight Serenade ("Sarah") finished at 14 months of age. She was BOB at DCA in 1981 and the dam of nine champions.

Am-Can. Ch. Korcula Midnight Star Bret D and breeder/owner/handler Dr. Charles Garvin, relaxing after "Charley's" eighth BIS. Charley is one of Sarah's top-winning offspring.

Ch. Korcula Salona, CD, going BOB from the Veterans class at the 1972 Pittsburgh Specialty. Corky was the top owner-handled Dal bitch from 1967–1971.

Ch. Korcula Midnight Margie finished under breeder-judge William Fetner. "Margie" was a Regional Specialty winner and the dam of eight champions.

Ch. Labyrinth Sleighbelle at 12 weeks. She was a top producer with nine champions that included Group winners, specialty winners, and top-ranked dogs and producers.

Labyrinth Dals have been contributors to Brazilian and South African breeding programs. Am-SA-Zimbabwe Ch. Labyrinth Big Spender was the 1993 Dalmatian of the Year in South Africa.

Long Last

Lorraine Donahue's 1947 registered kennel, founded with Reigate stock, is located in Owing Mills, Maryland. She imported several English dogs from the Washakie Kennels in the 1950s and Eng-Am. Ch. Colonsay Blacksmith, the Best in Show Dal at the British Dal Club Specialty in 1957. Lorraine's top obedience dog was the first Dal bitch to receive a UDT title. Spur of Victory, UDT won perfect scores in Open and Utility four times as well as numerous High in Trial awards. In the 1970s and 1980s an important sire

Above: Poca Dot Salute to Reveille was the foundation bitch for Labyrinth Dalmatians and the dam of the top-producing "Sleighbelle." Below: Am-RSA-Zim. Ch. Labyrinth Big Spender was a specialty winner in the US as well as a Group winner, BIS winner, and sire of champions in South Africa. He returned to the US to become a top producer. Owned by Christine Dyker.

63

Ch. Long Last Living Legend sired 26 champions including Group winners and placers, Regional Specialty winners, a DCA Futurity winner, and a DCA WB. Owned by Kitty Brown.

was Ch. Long Last Living Legend. He is ranked among the important sires of the breed and has many top winning offspring to his credit. Lorraine commented that she had saved the name "living legend" for a special dog and that he was it.

When Lorraine died in 1980, the kennel was turned over to Christina Jackson who, with the help of Elaine Thomas in recent years, has carried on the breeding program. Several Dals from this kennel have won at the regional and national Sweepstakes and Futurity levels. Ch. Long Last Black Chrome was Best Senior in the Futurity and Winners Dog at the 1984 DCA Nationals. Ch. Long Last No Frills, a liver bitch, was Best of Opposite Sex at the 1980 DCA Nationals and Ch. Long Last Solar Flare, a liver bitch, was given an Award of Merit at the Colorado Nationals.

Majestic K'ls

Majestic Cleopatra, purchased in 1963, marked the beginning of Tom and Barbara Harrison's Majestic K'ls in California. "Cleo" was principally Four-in-Hand bred. Although she was bought as a family pet, her one breeding to Ch. Crestview Mr. Bently of Beaux produced Ch. Majestic K'ls Ebon of Pearl.

Majestic K'ls Ebon Mischief, a bitch, was the next addition to the kennels. Bred to a male from the Cleo/Bently litter, she produced the first Majestic K'ls champion, the multiple-Specialty winner Ch. Majestic K'ls Bold Fella. He was Winners Dog at the 1968 National Specialty.

All Majestic K'ls Dals are tightly linebred on "Fella" and through him to the Crestview and Four-in-Hand pedigrees. In the late 1960s and early 1970s Coachman and Watseka pedigrees were added to the breeding program.

Ch. Labyrinth Tuckaway Julep came from a combination that produced many champions.

Ch. Labyrinth Oscar Madison produced many champion offspring despite his untimely death.

Ch. Long Last Link to Paisley was 1979 DCA Best in Futurity and sire of 14 champions.

Ch. Long Last No Frills (L) went BOS at DCA in 1980.

Ch. Long Last Black Chrome went BOW at DCA in 1984. He was BOS at DCA in 1985.

Am-Can. Ch. Long Last Perfect for Paisley, CD was 1989 DCA WD and the sire of over 40 champions.

Melody

Jack White, DVM, bought his first Dalmatian, a Green Starr-bred bitch named Calculator's Miss Sincerity ("Sindy"), while he was stationed in Texas training horses for the Army. In 1963, Sindy was bred to Ch. Long Last Ripcord. This first litter produced Ch. Melody Sweet, CD ("Sweet"), who until 1993 was the breed's top producer with 16 champions. Two Melody dogs have won Bests in Show: Int-Am-Mex. Ch. Melody Ring of Fire, CD and Ch. Melody Dynamatic, owned by C.E. Flock, Jr.

Ft. Collins, Colorado, has been the home of Melody Kennels since 1968. Beth White joined the team in 1971 and has become the major exhibitor of the family. The Whites also raise cattle and Appaloosa horses.

Dalmatians from this kennel are usually liver-spotted. All resident dogs earn the Companion Dog (CD) obedience title and all owners of Melody puppies are encouraged to train for a CD.

Ch. Melody Sweet, CD was the foundation bitch for Melody Kennels and the dam of 16 champions, becoming one of the breed's all-time top producers.

Int-Am-Mex. Ch. Melody Ring of Fire, CD, winning the Group on his way to BIS. He was also BOB at DCA in 1975.

Pill Peddler's

Pill Peddler's Kennel was established in 1961 in Amherst, Massachusetts, with Skipper of Rabbit Run. The kennel name was derived from the fact that the owners, Dr. and Mrs. Eugene Holden, were a doctor and a nurse. The kennel is currently located in Dunn, North Carolina.

The first foundation bitch was Ch. Dalquest Belle Charm from In the Valley Kennels in Pennsylvania and the second foundation bitch was Altamar's Annette from the Altamar Kennel in California. When Mrs. Reeves, owner of Rabbit Run Dals, decided to give up breeding Dals, she sent all of her breeding dogs to Pill Peddler's.

Ch. Tuckaway the Pill Peddler won three Bests in Show prior to being killed by a hit and run in his own yard.

Above: Ch. Melody Rocky Top Cheerio, CD was a multiple-specialty winner. Below: Ch. Fire Brand (L) was Best in Futurity at DCA in 1989 and became a multiple Group winner.

Above: Ch. Skipper of Rabbit Run was the foundation for Pill Peddler's Kennel. Below: Ch. Rabbit Run Thunder Storm was handled by Alberta Holden at the Providence County Kennel Club in 1967.

Above: Am-Can-Ber. Ch. Twingates Blue Bonnet was BOS at the 1973 DCA under judge Mrs. Alfred Treen. Handled by Barbara Partridge, owned by Alberta Holden. Below: One of the more recent Pill Peddler dogs is Ch. Pill Peddler's the Nurses Aide, shown here winning in 1993.

Royal Oaks

Eric and Ardith Dahlstrom's kennel is located in northern California. Ardith has been active with the breed since 1963, starting with an outcross bitch under the mentorship of the Hares of Tallara Kennels. Royal Oaks has concentrated on bloodlines from Leo Meeker's imported Colonsay Dals at his Four-in-Hand Kennels. The foundation bitch for Royal Oaks was Ch. Royal Oaks Liberty Belle, who became one of the top producing dams in the breed. Ch. Royal Oaks Ragtime Rambler sired the Best of Winners recipient at the 1990 DCA National Specialty in Anaheim, California.

Above: As a Junior Handler, Ardith Moyer (Dahlstrom) handled Gemini of Tallara, owned by Lloyd and Briziade Hare. Below: Ardith Dahlstrom handled future champion Royal Oaks Ragtime Rambler to Best in Sweeps at a Dalmatian Club of Northern California show.

Ch. Royal Oaks Liberty Belle was the main foundation for both Royal Oaks and Rambler Dalmatians and the dam of nine champions.

Tioga-Coach

Hope Smith acquired her first Dal, Roadcoach Tioga, as a pet in 1941. By 1945, the Tioga-Coach Kennel was established in Marblehead, Massachusetts, with basic breeding stock from the Roadcoach Kennels (Ch. Roadcoach Tioga Too). During the late 1940s the kennel moved to Lake Forest, Illinois, where outcross breedings occurred to improve temperament. Since moving to Hamilton, Massachusetts in 1957, the breeding program has been basically linebreeding on Ch. Lord Jim as closely as possible. The outcross breedings have been sired by Ch. Green Starr's Colonel Joe and have produced quality, but smaller stationed, Dalmatians.

In 1993, Mrs. Smith acquired a black and white bitch, Ch. Deltalyn N Penwiper KisnCuzn, who was bred by Robert and Judith Rivard and who won a total of 23 Best in Show honors. This was a new record for a bitch as the previous record of eight Bests in Show was held by Ch. Swabbie of Oz-Dal and Ch. Godin's To Be Or Not To Be.

Hope Noyes (now Mrs. Walter Smith) showing Ch. Roadcoach Tioga Too, CD to BOW at the Chicago International in 1949 under Mrs. Flora Bonney.

Williamsview Shane was the original foundation sire for Tuckaway Kennels. Owned by Dr. Sid Remmele.

KisnCuzn was also the number one Dalmatian in 1993 and won Best of Breed at the Westminster Kennel Club show in 1994, after which she was retired to her original owner, Barbara DiMino of Penwiper.

Tuckaway

In 1963, amid the blue grass of central Kentucky, Sidney Remmele, DVM, established Tuckaway Kennels. The foundation bitch was Ch. Garland Pride, "Tuck." Her call name was the basis for the kennel being named Tuckaway. The foundation dog was Williamsview Shane, who was purchased from the Williamsview Kennels in New Jersey.

The breeding program has consisted of intensive linebreeding with very few outcrosses. The most famous litter was sired by Ch. Coachman's Canicula bred to Ch. Labyrinth Sleighbelle. This litter produced seven champions who were each important sires and producers in their own right. In 1969, Tuckaway purchased Ch. Coachman's Canicula, who was Best of Breed at the 1973 DCA National Specialty. Other dogs with Tuckaway in their pedigrees, Am-Can. Ch. Tuckaway Bottom's Up Gusto, CD, Ch. Tuckaway Augusta, and Ch. Tuckaway Winged Foot, are Best in Show winners, and three Tuckaway dogs have won the DCA Sweepstakes.

Above: Westminster 1953: Ch. Boot Black from Dalmatia was BOB, owner/handled by Wendell Sammet; Ch. Roadcoach Tioga Too, CD was BOS, owner-handled by Hope Noyes. Below: Ch. Deltalyn N Penwiper KisnCuzn, winning one of her many Bests in Show. In 1993, she was ranked #1 Dalmatian, #3 Non-Sporting, and #16 All-Breeds.

Above: Ch. Labyrinth Sleighbelle ("99") was the foundation bitch for both Tuckaway and Labyrinth. Owned by Christine Dyker and Dr. Sid Remmele. Below: What an impact this litter had on the breed! Left to right: Ch. Coachman's Canicula (sire), Ch. Tuckaway Bold and Brave, Ch. Tuckaway Gallant Man, Ch. Tuckaway Jason James, Ch. Labyrinth Tuckaway Julep, Ch. Tuckaway Dinah, Ch. Labyrinth Sleighbelle (dam).

Above: Ch. Coachman's Canicula ("Nicky") was BOB at DCA in 1973, a multiple Group and Regional Specialty winner, and the sire of 21 champions. Owned by Dr. Sid Remmele. Below: Ch. Tuckaway Augusta, pictured going BIS. He was also Best in Sweeps and BOW at DCA in 1991. Among his champion get is the Top Dalmatian in the US for 1994, 1995 and 1996 Ch. Spotlight's Spectacular.

Although she did not finish, Lola of Watseka produced three champions including the top-producing Ch. Tamara of Watseka.

Ch. Tamara of Watseka was a top-producing dam with 13 champions. Owned by Sherry and Carol Schubert.

Watseka

Watseka Dalmatians came into existence in 1960 in Illinois when Don and Carol Schubert acquired Lola of Watseka. After deciding to breed to the strongest part of her pedigree, they bred to Ch. Colonial Coach Cheshire. One of the champions from that breeding was Ch. Tamara of Wateska, who became one of the top producing dams in the breed.

The Schuberts' mentor, Nelson Radcliff, encouraged them to acquire Ch. Colonial Coach Carriage Way. Thirteen champions resulted from linebreeding to Tamara. One of these champions was Ch. Panore of Wateska, who won 10 Bests in Show and three DCA National Specialties. He was also the leading sire of his time. With "Carriage Way" as the foundation, a stud line has been established by Champions Panore, Jack Daniels, Dylan, and Tennyson.

Williamsview

William Hibbler began the Williamsview Kennels, located in Lebanon, New Jersey, in 1940 with a bitch whelped in 1939 from the Tattoo Kennels in Pennsylvania. She was bred to an English import, Ch. Elmcroft Coacher. From that litter, the bitch Williamsview Patrician was bred to Ch. Reigate Bold Venture, which produced the first Williamsview champions in 1946. In the 1950s, Williamsview Riptide was Best of Breed from the classes at a DCA National Specialty.

Several of the present-day kennels have the Williamsview prefix in their pedigrees.

Ch. Colonial Coach Carriage Way was a multiple Group winner and the sire of 38 champions. Owned by Donald and Carol Schubert.

Ch. Panore of Watseka with his breeder/owner/handler Carol Schubert. Panore was a multiple-BIS winner, National and Regional Specialty winner, and top-producing sire with over 40 champions.

Above: Ch. Williamsview Carbon Copy was the first homebred champion for Williamsview Kennels. Owned by William Hibbler. Below: Ch. Williamsview Gaiety, owned by William Hibbler.

Above: Williamsview Jody, owned by William Hibbler. Below: Ch. Williamsview Gambler's Luck, owned by William Hibbler.

DALMATIAN TRENDS IN THE 1990s

Dalmatian breeders in the USA have become better educated through the Dalmatian Club of America's educational programs and research committees that continually inform the membership on topics ranging from hearing research and statistics, immune deficiencies, and urolitic stone research to better breeding practices. This assimilation of information has resulted in breeders' becoming more aware of the benefits of breeding healthier Dals and testing with BAER hearing equipment.

Dalmatians, on the average, are taller than those of the 1930s and 1940s. Today's Dals also appear more elegant, with perhaps less bone than the dogs of the 1930s and 1940s.

A topic of discussion among many breeders is how it has become increasingly harder to breed a Dalmatian with a shoulder layback that will allow the dog to attain the reach so many breeders are seeking. Some pedigrees also contain Dalmatians with less and less bend of stifle. Perhaps with the renewed interest in coaching and road trials, breeders will take these structural problems more to heart and continue to breed a Dal that is able to trot for 20 miles with the flowing easy cadence it should have.

Spotting patterns for the majority have become increasingly more pleasing to the eye. Spotting patterns in the liver dogs have improved and are larger and more open.

Temperament is much improved and breeders are more aware of socializing their puppies and informing the buyers about what to do for the puppies in the various training periods. Buyers are being encouraged to attend good obedience training programs just for general behavior at home. As a result, many owners are competing in obedience for the first time with their Dals and really enjoying it. Agility training is also becoming more popular as owners discover that their dogs really love to go over, under, and through the obstacles.

Breeders are doing less linebreeding as stud dogs are being used all over the country. Frozen and extended semen has increased the availability of a wider variety of stud dogs. Semen is being shipped all over the world, especially to places like England and Australia that are hard to reach due to quarantines or distance.

The breed has jumped in popularity largely due to the second release of Walt Disney's *101 Dalmatians* film and video, the Hollywood 1996 remake with Glenn Close and over 200 live Dalmatians, and the use of many striking Dals in advertisements. All have contributed to the rise in demand for the breed and many average pet owners have responded by breeding their first litters. The American Kennel Club ranked the Dalmatian as ninth in popularity in 1993. By 1995, the breed was ranked out of the top ten, to the relief of many a fancier.

A LOG OF THE DCA'S LEGACY

Only eight Dalmatians had been registered with the American Kennel Club when an elite group of twenty gentlemen and six ladies established the Dalmatian Club of America. Discussed during 1904, the DCA was formally organized in 1905.

The need for support of the breed was great. While the first Dalmatian was registered with the American Kennel Club in 1888, only seven more had been registered by 1905. In 10 of those 17 years, no Dalmatian had been recorded in the AKC's Stud Book.

The club began action at once. By February 2, 1905 it had published a booklet listing the club rules, the officers, and the members of the club. The booklet also included the Dalmatian standard as recommended by the Dalmatian Club of America. The standard presented by the newly formed club was basically the 1890 British standard slightly modified. Some wording had been tightened and the general appearance paragraph was moved to the end of the text to appear just before the scale of points. The DCA also applied for membership in the American Kennel Club.

The DCA immediately began a program offering trophies and prizes at selected all-breed shows. It was specified in the DCA's rules that the club would reserve from its funds only sufficient money to meet its expenses. The balance would be offered annually in prizes. A silver medallion was designed to be used on trophies and to be presented separately.

This was all done during the DCA's first year! During the same year, 15 Dalmatians were entered in the AKC's Stud Book.

By 1913, without any fanfare, the Dal's height was specified as between 19 and 23 inches and the weight difference between dogs and bitches was eliminated. The standard then remained unchanged until 1950.

Within the next two years the original club membership of 26 grew to 43. In 1913 there were only 39 members, and by 1921 membership had shrunk to 22. Then, membership began to grow again. The original rules limited the number of members to 50, but gave the Board of Governors power to increase this number. The Board did so in 1937.

In 1941, a committee was appointed to rewrite the DCA's rules. The committee presented a constitution and by-laws to the DCA membership at the 1942 annual meeting. They were adopted and the old set of rules was repealed.

On July 11, 1950, the American Kennel Club approved an addition to the standard on gait, and changes in the scale of points were made to accommodate it. Ten points were given to gait: five points were taken from legs and feet and five points were taken from color and markings. The new paragraph read: "Gait—Length of stride should be in proportion to the size of the dog, steady in rhythm of 1, 2, 3, 4, as in the cadence count in military drill. Front legs should not paddle, nor should there be a straddling appearance. Hind legs should neither cross nor weave. Judges should be able to see each leg move with no interference of another leg; drive and reach are most desirable."

However, in 1950, the AKC did not approve an attempt to disqualify dogs taller than 23 inches at the withers. At the time, the AKC looked with great disfavor on adding a disqualification in any breed which might lead to unpleasant incidents during its administration in the show ring. The AKC was not convinced that the height would endanger the future of the breed. At the annual meeting on February 12, 1962, the members voted to approve some additions and modifications to the standard to overcome problems encountered in the ring and in the whelping box. The paragraph on general appearance was moved to the beginning and the phrase "poised and alert; free of shyness; intelligent in expression" was added. Other additions were made to highlight faults and to settle disputes. There was also some tightening of language to make the standard more useful to newcomers to the breed. The AKC's position had changed and for the first time, the faults and disqualifications of the Dalmatian were spelled out. Disqualifications specified were any color other than black or liver, any size over 24 inches at the withers, patches, tricolors, and undershot or overshot bite. The proposal was submitted to the AKC, published in the *Gazette,* and on December 11, 1962, was approved by the Board of Directors of the American Kennel Club.

The 1962 standard remained in effect for 27 years. A recommendation by the Standard Committee to change the standard was returned to the committee by the membership on February 9, 1975. The committee was restructured the next year and was instructed by the membership to clarify the descriptions of the patch and the gait. In 1981, the proposed changes received less than the two-thirds majority required by the AKC. Later, another committee was formed. This committee produced the present standard which was approved by the American Kennel Club on July 11, 1989, and became effective on September 6, 1989.

SPRING 1971

Dalmatian Club of America

The Spotter evolved into a magazine with pictures and advertising in 1971.

Membership continued to grow and by the time the club was 50 years old it had 172 members. This was, of course, in 1955. A mimeographed bulletin was printed from time to time when enough material had accumulated to make it worthwhile. It was called *The Spotter* and its first issue was a membership list. In 1967, *The Spotter* began regular publication on a quarterly basis. It became a magazine with pictures and advertising in 1971. Membership growth accelerated, and by 1976 the club had over 500 members. The DCA began its 75th year (1980) with 647 members.

The Dalmatian Club of America was incorporated under the not-for-profit law of the State of New York in 1962. The club's by-laws were brought into compliance with the state laws and the policies of the American Kennel Club. Provisions were made for "new blood" as well as for continuity of knowledge and experience on the Board of Governors. The goals stated were: "to promote and advance the breeding, care, train-

ing and exhibition of, and collection and dissemination of information concerning Dalmatian dogs, and to that end to define and publish a Standard for Dalmatians, encourage and hold dog shows, exhibitions and matches, promote and engage in research in breeding, care, exhibition and standards of Dalmatians."

The Dalmatian Club of America held its first specialty show in 1926 as part of the Nassau County Kennel Club's all-breed event in Mineola, New York. The policy of holding an annual show was adopted and there has been one each year since with the exception of 1929, 1934, and 1942. The first 12 specialties were held in the New York/Philadelphia area. In 1940, the DCA's 13th specialty was held with the International Kennel Club in Chicago. 1940 was also the only year until 1984 that the DCA held two specialties; the other one was held in Far Hills, New Jersey. 1940 was the first and only time that the DCA's specialty was held away from the East Coast until 1958 when the 31st show was held at the Thistledown Race Track in North Randall, Ohio.

Although many of the eastern members complained about going "way out West" to the Ohio specialty, the DCA Board of Governors recognized that the Club had members across the nation. Some regional clubs had been organized and were starting to hold their own specialty shows. DCA's show was now being referred to as the National Specialty. In 1960, the show moved out of the East again to be a part of the Santa Barbara Kennel Club show in California.

From then on, the policy of moving the "national" around the country has been followed. This provides members and other Dal fanciers in various parts of the country with the opportunity to see many of the top Dalmatians in competition. It also enables members from coast to coast to get better acquainted and to exchange information and ideas.

The number of Dalmatians entered in the specialties grew. While 33 Dals had been the average for the first ten specialty shows, by 1975, the entry was passing the AKC's limit of 175 dogs for a single day's judging. The DCA found it necessary to add a second judge. This was not the first time that the DCA used multiple judges at its specialties. In the four shows from 1947 through 1950, three judges were used—one each for dogs, bitches, and intersex competition. There was a significant increase in entries for these shows. They averaged 97 dogs in competition compared with the average of 57 for the previous five years. There is no explanation as to why the practice of using multiple judges was stopped. During the following five years the average number of entries dropped to 67. The election of specialty judges was traditionally very closely held until early in the 1970s when it was thrown open to nomination and balloting by the entire membership.

The program of cash prizes at all-breed shows continued into the 1960s. Senior DCA members may recall seeing a note in all-breed premium lists and catalogs stating: "The Dalmatian Club of America will offer the following prizes, open to members only: There must be 10 or more Dalmatians present and competing in the breed." The cash prize program in its last several years included a prize for "Highest Scoring Dalmatian in Obedience Trial, qualifying score required."

An obedience trial was not always a feature of the National Specialty. It was sometimes omitted when an independent specialty was held and it was always omitted when the Dalmatian classes of an all-breed show were used for the specialty. No trial was held in 1967

because entries at previous eastern shows were so low that qualifying scores were not possible under the AKC regulations. Obedience was passed over again in 1971 for the same reason. Following that show, however, the Board of Governors decided that in the future, the Dalmatian Club of America would always hold an obedience trial with its National Specialty. Obedience classes gave Dalmatian breeders an opportunity to demonstrate the intelligence and temperament of the breed. The Board believed that this decision might motivate future chairmen and obedience buffs to train or recruit enough entries for legal legs at all levels. The 1971 decision was strengthened in 1980 when the Board voted to offer a bronze medallion at all regional specialty shows as well as at the National Specialty for the Dalmatian winning the Highest Score in Trial in the regular classes, provided there was a sufficient number of dogs in competition at each level to form a legal leg.

DCA medallions are given for a variety of accomplishments. This bronze medallion is awarded to specialty Best of Breed and High in Trial winners.

A sweepstakes designed to increase the number of entries at the National Specialty was started in 1967. Ten years later, another program designed to encourage specialty entries as well as better planning for breeding quality Dalmatians was the Futurity, inaugurated in 1977. Another ten years later, in 1987, the first DCA tracking test was offered at the National Specialty in Colorado.

The DCA's 53rd National Specialty, in 1980, was celebrated as its Diamond Jubilee. A part of the celebration was the publication of a paperback entitled *DCA Commemorative Keepsake 1980*, dedicated to the Dalmatian fancier in the hope that its contents would inspire an ongoing commitment to the physical and emotional betterment of the breed.

While road trials had been held in the New England area during the early years of the DCA, they were sponsored by local groups and barely survived the two big wars. There was a 40-year gap without road trials until a group in the Pacific Northwest took over. The Puget Sound Dalmatian Club held a trial in 1989, and interest in other parts of the country grew. In 1989, the DCA appointed a Road Trial Committee and since 1992 has sponsored road trials during the National Specialty week if the specialty location was conducive to these events.

The silver medallion designed in 1905 is still used today. It is given for Best of Breed at the National Specialty and as a presentation piece. Each DCA president receives one when going out of office. In 1980, the DCA sent a pair of medallions to England for the British Dalmatian Club to award to the Challenge Certificate (CC) Dog and Bitch at the specialty held in London in connection with the first World Congress of Dalmatians.

Meanwhile, during the 1940s, a few regional clubs began forming to support the breed. The first to be recognized by the American Kennel Club was the Northern California Dalmatian Club, which held its first show at Golden Gate on January 29 and 30, 1949. The following year, the Southern California Dalmatian Club held its first show, followed in 1952 by the Southern New England Dalmatian Club, and in 1956 by Chicagoland Dalmatian Club. By June of 1994 there were 28 regional Dalmatian clubs licensed by the AKC. There are another dozen local Dal clubs in various stages of development.

The Board of Governors recognized a need to improve its relations with the growing number of regional clubs and a trial meeting of representatives of the various local clubs was held on October 11, 1973. As a result, the Regional Club Council was created on February 10, 1974 to provide a liaison with the parent club and to share information, ideas, and procedures useful to the regional clubs. The Council was formed to assist the regional clubs in finding better ways to serve their members and the breed and for improving communication with the DCA.

The AKC delegates in attendance at the December 1980 quarterly meeting were introduced to what was a new concept in judges' education. A 15-minute audio-visual presentation on the Dalmatian breed standard had been developed with the full cooperation of the DCA by a committee comprised of breeder-judges who had presided over a National Specialty. The concept was well received and extended to other breeds. As VCRs became more popular, these presentations were converted onto videotapes for most of the breeds recognized by the American Kennel Club.

During the 1970s and 1980s, the Dalmatian Club of America presented its members with a number of considerations that enlarged their frame of reference and stimulated constructive thinking about the health, welfare, and future quality of the breed.

A Judges' Education Committee was created to assist aspiring judges, particularly those coming from other breeds, to understand Dalmatian type and to correct misconceptions that were perpetuated by some established judges, particularly color confusion. Initially, this was done largely through mailings, workshops, and seminars. In 1988, the committee completed *A Review of Color in the Dalmatian*, a videotape which has become a very effective educational tool for breeders and exhibitors as well as for judges. It corrects mistaken ideas many judges have had regarding patches, tri-colors, dark ears, and confluence of spots, and it explains the genetics of color and markings.

Two widespread problems, deafness and bladder stones, were reviewed in depth at the second World Congress of Dalmatians in Philadelphia during the week of the AKC's Centennial Show in 1984. The concept of using frozen semen for breeding was also discussed. A new scientific tool to test hearing, the Brainstem Auditory Evoked Response (BAER), was introduced to the fancy. It tells whether a dog can hear with both ears, only one ear, or not at all. The DCA added a Research Sub-Committee on Deafness to gather information on BAER-tested Dalmatians and to recruit a group of associates with scientific backgrounds to help analyze the data collected. Developments have been published in *The Spotter*. One major advance in the scientific hearing studies for Dalmatians occurred at Louisiana State University where the research

has been recently expanded to cover deafness in all breeds of dog. This was made possible with the help of a substantial grant from the AKC. So far, 45 breeds have been identified as having a serious problem with deafness. It is hoped that the broader base of study will provide breeders with a solution to the problem. Meanwhile, many Dalmatian breeders are avoiding breeding unilaterally deaf dogs.

Another problem that is prevalent in Dalmatians is high levels of uric acid and

The DCA Commemorative Keepsake was produced in 1980 and was available at the National Specialty.

85

the frequency of resultant bladder stones. The search for a method of eliminating bladder stones has been going on since at least 1940, when a large-scale survey in the United States and Great Britain failed to find any Dalmatians with low acid levels in their urine. A high level of uric acid leads to bladder stones. Without any Dalmatians that produce low levels of uric acid, breeders are unable to breed out this genetic defect.

In 1973, a crossbreeding experiment was started with the approval of the DCA's Board of Governors. An appropriately sized white champion Pointer bitch with a low uric acid level was bred to a purebred Dalmatian. Selected progeny were backcrossed to purebred Dalmatians for five generations. With the support of the DCA Board, two fifth-generation backcross puppies (31/32 purebred) were registered with the AKC on February 7, 1981. Considerable controversy among the members of DCA culminated in a negative vote of the membership. On August 11, 1981, the AKC Board of Directors put a hold on the registration of any offspring of the backcross Dalmatians.

There are two studies presently in progress which may have the potential for solving these genetic problems. Funded by the American Kennel Club, the Morris Animal Foundation, and the Orthopedic Foundation for Animals, geneticists at the University of Michigan and veterinary specialists at Michigan State University are conducting a five-year study of all breeds which may produce techniques with the potential to identify and classify defective genes. Meanwhile, an independent group has been carrying on the Dalmatian Backcross Project with descendants of the registered backcross bitch.

Since the 1960s, educational programs have been occasionally presented in connection with an annual meeting or a National Specialty. In 1982, the Board created a Membership Educational Committee to ensure an ongoing program for DCA members.

There was considerable discussion in the late 1960s about the need for a uniform ethical approach for breeders and exhibitors of Dalmatians. A committee was established and several drafts of a code were presented until finally, in 1979, the *Ethical Guidelines* were published. This was revised and the revision was approved by the membership in 1994.

In the 1980s, the by-laws were revised to enable the annual meeting to be held with the National Specialty. The fiscal year was changed to eliminate confusion about administrative matters, such as which members had paid their dues and which were eligible to vote.

The DCA appointed an Endowment Committee in the 1980s to act as a vehicle for establishing a separate tax-exempt Research and Education Foundation. After considerable groundwork was done, in 1994 the Endowment Committee made a concerted effort to develop the structure for a Foundation, its by-laws, and a timetable to reach its goals. Toward the end of 1995, the incorporation documents for the Dalmatian Club of America Foundation, Inc. (DCAF) were legally transacted. History was in the making as this was the first body in the world solely dedicated to research and education concerning the Dalmatian. The Foundation was structured under the U.S. tax code so that all contributions, donations, or gifts were fully tax deductible to the donors. By the end of 1996, its first year, the DCAF had raised considerable funds from a broad section of DCA members and regional Dal clubs, which were used to establish a base to commence to fulfill its mission.

The popularity of the breed, as measured by the number of registrations, grew. In 1987, 11,291 Dalmatians were registered with the AKC, ranking them in 27th place, and in 1988, 14,109 Dalmatians were registered. The number of Dalmatian registrations continued to soar and in 1991 had one of the biggest increases of the 134 breeds recorded. 30,225 Dalmatians were registered that year, putting the breed into 15th place.

In 1992, the Dalmatian cemented its claim to the title of America's "fad breed" according to the AKC *Gazette.* Dals were the 15th most popular breed again in 1992, with 38,927 registrations. This was 8,702 more than the 30,225 Dalmatians recorded in 1991, a whopping 28.8 percent gain. In 1993, Dalmatians reached a "top ten" placing of ninth among the 137 breeds registered. There were 42,816 Dals registered, an increase of 3,889, which was 10 percent more than in 1992. However, total AKC registrations dropped 1.4 percent.

In 1994 there was a slight decline—there were 195 fewer Dalmatians registered than in 1993. By 1995, the number of Dalmatians registered with the AKC dropped to 36,714, which was 5,907 less than in 1994. This dropped the breed's rank to 11th.

Dals can claim to be the first breed to zoom into popularity because of the home video explosion. The media attention given to the Walt Disney movie *101 Dalmatians* and its ready availability for home video must have been a contributing factor to the Dalmatian's rapid rise in popularity. This has been supplemented by the frequent use of Dals in print media ads and television commercials. In September 1991, a Breeder Referral Coordinator was appointed by the DCA Board. In August of 1992, the DCA appointed a National Rescue Coordinator. Rescue work had been and continues to be carried on by many of the regional clubs. The DCA operates with 22 special committees

including Endowment, Historical, Junior Showmanship, Public Education, and Standing Rules, in addition to those previously mentioned. The Dalmatian Club of America's membership passed 1,000 in 1991.

MRS. FLORA M. BONNEY'S NOTES ON THE DCA'S LEADERSHIP

Mrs. Flora McDonald Bonney served as the Dalmatian Club of America's secretary from 1915 until her death in January 1967, a total of 52 years. Although she never served as the president of this club, she was widely respected as an authority figure. She was very generous in her financial support of Dalmatians, often contributing large silver trophies and catering sit-down dinners for all of the club members and exhibitors after the DCA National Specialties.

In 1954, Mrs. Bonney wrote a few pages for a pamphlet published by the DCA entitled *Dalmatian Club of America.* The following about the leadership of the DCA is an excerpt from those pages.

Mrs. Flora Bonney was a widely respected Dalmatian authority and contributor to the breed.

"The Dalmatian Club of America was organized in 1905 and the original officers were: president—Alfred Maclay; vice president—Harry T. Peters; secretary-treasurer—J. Sergeant Price, Jr. The club started with twenty-six members, among them such pillars of the breed as Howard Willets; Joseph B. Thomas, Jr.; Mrs. C.F. Denee; Percy Drury; H. Fred Lauer; Dr. Henry Jarrett and Miss Rachael Holmes.

"When I joined the club, in 1913, Harry T. Peters was the president, Arthur Whitney, of the Rocksiticus Kennels, vice president and Theodore Crane, secretary-treasurer. Alfred B. Maclay was the delegate to the American Kennel Club. In 1915 pressure of business forced Mr. Crane to retire as secretary-treasurer and as no-one else seemed to want the job it was given to me. Mr. Peters was succeeded as president by Mr.

J. Sergeant Price, Jr. was one of the founders of DCA and a long-time club member.

IN MEMORIAM

J. SERGEANT PRICE, JR.

A Founder of the Dalmatian Club of America

and

Honorary Vice President

Whitney, who was followed by John C. Weekes; Mrs. Hastings Arnold became president after Mr. Weekes and after a few years turned over the office to Franklin J. Willock. The next president was Mrs. Alfred W. Barrett and now we have Miss Evelyn S. Nelson. May I inject a personal note right here and say I consider that I have been very, very fortunate to have had the privilege of serving under these different presidents, all of them sincerely interested in the breed, kind and helpful at all times and dignified presiding officers.

"To the best of my knowledge, the Club has only had three delegates to the American Kennel Club. Mr. Maclay who served until 1937; then Dr. John P. Homiller and now Mr. Alfred Barrett.

"Of the founders of the Club only one continued as a member until he died, this was J. Sergeant Price, Jr., known affectionately as "Uncle John" to some of us. He was one of the first members to pay annual dues each January and always sent his contribution to the Specialty Shows with speed. Mr. Price died in the summer of 1948. His great interest was in the Dalmatian as a working dog and his dogs were trained to run under his coach-and-four, which was one of the sights to be seen in Fairmont Park, on the outskirts of Philadelphia.

"At the instigation of Mr. Willock, and due in large to his work and support, the first Specialty Show of the Dalmatian Club of America was held in May, 1926...Had it not been for the unfailing support and interest of Mr. Willock, and the hard work of Mrs. Homiller during the late 1920s and early 1930s, Dalmatians would have suffered greatly and the Club shrunk down to midget size."

HISTORY OF THE DCA'S NATIONAL SPECIALTIES

Franklin J. Willock was instrumental in organizing the first DCA specialty show in 1926. This show was held in Mineola, New York, with an entry of 25. From the 19 dogs in conformation, judge Mrs. C.G. West chose

Ch. Tally Ho Last of Sunstar (dog) as the Breed winner and Gladmore Gaylass as Best of Opposite Sex.

1928, with a total entry of 27, was the first time a bitch, Ch. Tally Ho Fore Thought, won Best of Breed at a DCA specialty, and 1932, with a total entry of 38, was the first time a class winner, Tally Ho Kathleen (bitch), won BOB. There were no shows held in 1929, 1934, and 1942 due to world events and the 1943, 1944, and 1945 National Specialties were held in conjunction with the Westminster Kennel Club shows.

Dalmatian Specialty at Oyster Bay, Long Island (Mrs. Bonney's estate). Pictured are: Cyrill Malone, Evelyn Nelson White, Marjorie van der Veer, Helen Powers, and Elviria Firuski.

In 1947 at Far Hills, New Jersey, the entries reached over 100 for the first time. This was also the first year that a three-judge panel was used: one for dogs, one for bitches, and one for intersex. A three-judge panel was used for the next three years. Beginning in 1970, the number of entries consistently exceeded 100.

The Dalmatian Club of America traditionally offers armetale as trophies at the National Specialty. Everyone wants to win a "DCA pitcher."

All of the early specialty shows were held in the New York, Pennsylvania, or New Jersey areas until 1940, when Chicago hosted an entry of 52. 1960 was the first year that a specialty was hosted on the West Coast. Santa Barbara did the honors with an entry of 92.

Shortly after the American Kennel Club sanctioned obedience competition in 1937, Dalmatians were in the midst of the competition. However, on the national level, obedience competition was sporadic. There

Futurity classes were added in 1977 to encourage breeders to strive for better quality in their breeding programs. Unlike the Sweepstakes classes, where prior nomination is not required, the Futurity rules state that a bitch must be nominated prior to whelping and each puppy that the breeder decides is worthy of nomination must be nominated prior to four months of age. Cash prizes are awarded for first through fourth place in each class and Best Junior, Best Senior, and Best in Futurity.

Erin's Nutmeg Candy, CD, TD is the dam of eight champions including specialty winners and top producers. Owned by Ann Thornhill and Sharon Lyons.

were no obedience classes offered between 1939 and 1947. In 1972, the DCA Board decided to offer obedience annually at the Nationals and the number of entries has grown each year. Early obedience pioneers were Harland and Lois Meistrell, Mary Munro Smith, and Bob and Marge Sullivan.

In 1967, Sweepstakes classes were added to the National Specialty. These classes are open to Dalmatians up to 18 months of age. A Best Junior, Best Senior, and Best in Sweeps are chosen from the first place winners in the age categories. Cash prizes are awarded based on the number of entries and a sliding percentage scale.

The first time a tracking test was offered at the National Specialty occurred at the 1987 Nationals held in Fort Collins, Colorado. Of the six teams competing, the dogs that qualified were Phil Gallagher's Disney's Conscience Guides, CDX (who was also the first Dal to show at a DCA tracking test and to earn the first TD title awarded from such an event), and Erin's Nutmeg Candy, CD, TD, owned by Ann Thornhill. A total of four other tracking tests have been offered at the Nationals since the original one in 1987.

The first DCA-sponsored road trial in connection with a National Specialty occurred in 1992 in Reading, Pennsylvania.

Ch. Hushabye Hannah of Hoo Doo, CDX, RDX, owned by Linda Myers, was the High in Road Trial winner. Since that year, a road trial has been held in conjunction with the National Specialty and has been a popular event, as it allows the Dal to fulfill his role as a coaching dog.

In 1996, the first agility competition was held at the National Specialty in Olympia, Washington. It drew a good entry and the High in Agility Trial winner was Ch. Country Kate's Mandolin of MGR, CD, TD, owned by Karen

judges needed for the regular classes: usually one for bitches and one for dogs with one of the judges also judging intersex or Best of Breed. The number of obedience entries has also reached new heights, requiring two judges. Road trial and tracking competitions occur when the location of the Nationals permits.

With activities such as the annual DCA meeting, educational programs, ID tattooing and hearing tests for the dogs, judges' seminars, and a variety of social events, the DCA National Specialty week offers something for everyone.

Ch. Tuckaway Winged Foot, winning the first DCA Top 20 event. A multiple-BIS and specialty BOB winner, "Jack" is owned by Carrie Jordan, Tom Harris, and Frances Remmele.

and Stan Larson of Bellingham, Washington. That same year the first Top 20 competition, a black tie presentation of the top qualifying conformation dogs, also drew a lot of interest from spectators and competitors alike. Three judges polled their selection and chose Ch. Tuckaway Winged Foot, owned by Carrie Jordan, Frances Remmele, and Tom Harris, as the winner.

Today the National Specialty spans a five- to six-day period with Futurity and Sweepstakes competitions each having well over 150 entries. The total number of Dalmatians entered in the Specialty averages over 600. There are two

DALMATIANS AROUND THE WORLD

Australia

Dalmatians in Australia are just like those from any other country—fun-loving, energetic, and pleasant family dogs. Australia is well suited for the Dalmatian; it is a large, diverse, young country that was dependent on horses for travel in its early years. Hunting found a place for the Dalmatian, as rural owners discovered the dogs to be excellent at retrieving game from the rivers and lakes, as well as flushing out game from the vast fields. The Dalmatian's stamina, soft mouth, desire to please by retrieving, and enjoyment of swimming and having fun are major contributors to his hunting ability.

It was in the early 1800s that the first details about the breed became available from paintings of a gathering on the shores of Sydney depicting a Dalmatian. Little else was discovered about the breed in Australia until 1886, when four Dalmatians were exhibited in Melbourne, Victoria, at the Victorian Poultry and Kennel Club show. There was also a record of another Dalmatian in Brisbane around 1887. It was not until the 1930s that the Dalmatian became a presence in the show ring. Dals were first shown in Sydney, the home of the original breed club, and then they appeared in Melbourne, Brisbane, and Adelaide during the 1940s. The Dalmatian can now be found country-wide, and he enjoys his deserved popularity.

In 1930, Mr. and Mrs. Hurst imported two Dalmatians from Kent, England. They were Ch. Quintus of Caefel and Florenza, who became the foundation stock of the Hursts' kennels. This commenced the surge in the breed's popularity.

Ch. Jancsi of Korchula was an outstanding dog of the 1940s. His sire was part of a litter of six lovely males, which was whelped under quarantine in 1936, out of an English import. Jancsi is in the pedigree of many Dals that have been successful in the show ring. Other imported Dals that have contributed to the breed's improvement and are deserving of notice are Ch. Colonsay Roll of the Dice, Eng-Aust-NZ. Ch. Clydevale Mastermind, Ch. Chasecourt Cheers, Northpleck Crackerjack, and Eng-Aust. Ch. Psychic Power at Pampard.

Many Dalmatians "down under" were imported from England from the mid-1980s to the 1990s. However, imports from the United States from time to time brought new bloodlines into the country. History was made when frozen semen from one of the most famous American Dalmatians, Ch.

"Dalmatian puppies getting to know some unique Australian baby animals." Commissioned by Robert Lawson and painted by Australian artist Deidre Hunt.

Dalmatians "Down Under" love to swim and retrieve.

Fireman's Freckled Friend, was taken to Australia during the early 1990s. Consequently, many wonderful and top-winning Dals were bred from this semen, thus expanding the bloodlines from the two top Dalmatian-producing countries (England and America) and further establishing genetic quality "down under."

Those Dals and others produced many fine progeny and are responsible for the strength of the breed in Australia today. One fine example occurred in 1980 at the largest all-breed show held in Australia, the famous Melbourne Royal, when Ch. Cherrymount Lucette was awarded Best in Show over nearly 7,000 dogs. No other Dalmatian has ever won such a major award. That day was her day and everyone, including Lucette herself, knew it. She was the double grand-daughter of Ch. Chasecourt Cheers, who was imported from the United Kingdom.

A dog must be six months of age or older to be eligible to begin accumulating the 100 points he needs to become a champion. The points must be received under four or more different judges. Dogs compete with the champions to win the Challenge Certificate (CC) for his sex, and only that winner receives points. The Challenge Certificate winner receives five points, plus one point for each dog of the same sex exhibited, up to a maximum of 25 points. The two Challenge Certificate winners compete for Best of Breed. If a dog wins Best Exhibit in Group, he receives up to 25 points unless he already received 25 points in the Challenge Certificate competition. There are no points awarded for Best of Breed or for the runner-up in the Group competition.

The six regular conformation classes for each sex are: Minor Puppy (6 months old), Puppy (6–12 months old), Junior (9–18 months old), Intermediate (18 months–3 years old), Open (6 months and older), and Australian-Bred (6 months and older). Dog breeds are divided into seven Groups, and Dalmatians are in the Non-Sporting Group.

The first breed club, the Dalmatian Club of Australia, was formed in Sydney on Australia Day, January 26, 1943. The club was renamed the Dalmatian Club in 1972 and then the Dalmatian Club of NSW, Inc. in 1996 to reflect the emergence of other state breed organizations. The next Dalmatian club, the Dalmatian Club of South Australia, was formed in 1947, dissolved after awhile, and reformed in 1972. The Dalmatian Club of Victoria started in 1952.

The Dalmatian Club of Queensland was formed in 1972, then dissolved, followed by the Dalmatian Association of Queensland in 1973, the Dalmatian Club of ACT (Australian Capitol Territory) in 1977, and the Dalmatian Association of Western Australia in 1996.

By the beginning of the 1980s, Dalmatian clubs around Australia were very active in improving the breed, publishing newsletters, and promoting activities for Dalmatians and their owners. The Dalmatian Club of New South Wales hosted the very first Australian Dalmatian convention. The theme for this historic event was deservedly "Dalmatian Destiny Down Under." All of Australia and New Zealand were well represented at the convention. It received acclaim from all factions of the dog world for its innovative approach.

Such a gathering resulted in what can only be described as one of the most major advances in the future of activities, knowledge, and cooperation between clubs and their members. The positive impact of the convention resulted in the first Dalmatian National Specialty championship show in 1982, which was held in Melbourne in

conjunction with the second Australian Dalmatian convention and hosted by the Dalmatian Club of Victoria. At this convention it was decided by all to form the National Dalmatian Council (of Australia). In doing so in 1983, it became the first national breed body in Australia, setting the stage for many other breed clubs to follow. This bold and historic move changed the course of history not only for Dalmatians but also for all other breeds in Australia.

Besides his popularity as a companion, show dog, and obedience dog, the Dalmatian also made his mark in many other areas. A circus dog, "Dagwood" the Dalmatian, was the lead dog in an act at the Taronga Zoo in Sydney during 1959, entertaining adults and children alike. Ch. Dumbledeer Jake, UD (the first Dal to obtain a CDX), thrilled crowds as he jumped through rings of fire during the 1960s. Many Dals became mascots for fire departments around the country and were instrumental in a number of dangerous rescues. Ch. Dumbledeer Glenn, AOC, was possibly one of the best known Dals bred in Australia. He was the first Dal to obtain his TDX title and he also received acclaim for his starring role in the film *Led Astray*. This wonderful film was supported by the government and shown in schools around much of the country to teach children about responsible ownership and control of dogs. *Led Astray* won the "Creative Excellence" award at the USA's Chicago Film Festival for its quality production and important message. At the famous "Moomba" (Aboriginal for "let's

Aus. Ch. Cherrymount Lucette (L) after winning BIS at the famous Melbourne Royal.

get together and have fun") festival in Melbourne, Dalmatians were a main feature of the parades during the 1970s and 1980s. The Dalmatian Club of Victoria had special floats to display the wonderful breed to the thousands of people who lined the streets to watch this annual event.

In 1987, Firechaser Phoenix (Kitt) was appointed the official mascot of the Melbourne Fire Museum. Kitt has given numerous demonstrations for fire aware-

perament under pressure, ability to get along with children, and amazing versatility.

The Dal developed in Australia as a result of international interaction as the country itself was developing. The most famous media production in the world depicting the breed was Walt Disney's animated *101 Dalmatians*, which was produced in the USA, written by Dodie Smith from England, and featured Australia's famous actor Rod Taylor as the voice of Pongo.

Firechaser Phoenix, also known as Fire Dog Kitt, with one of his firefigher friends.

ness and has often performed rescue work in smoke-filled areas. He also spends time at the Royal Children's Hospital as part of a juvenile awareness program, stars in a video entitled *Machines Aren't Toys*, and is featured in a segment on the TV program *Talk to Animals* as a children's fire safety educator. He has traveled thousands of miles to attend functions and to educate people. An excellent example of this Dalmatian's ability was a 65-mile trip to Darling Harbour to perform two major demonstrations in front of over 40,000 excited people. Kitt really exhibits the Dalmatian's wonderful tem-

The Dalmatian "down under" has earned international recognition and Australian Dal breeders share a common belief:

The Dalmatian is what he is,
and should stay as he is today.
It is our duty to ensure that we continue
to breed him that way.

Canada

The Canadian Dalmatian standard is very similar to that of the USA, however, the Canadian standard does not have a height disqualification and does regard blue eyes as a fault. Many Canadian Dals have American and English bloodlines in their pedigrees and a few have been imported from other countries.

There has been a valuable exchange of information as well as friendship between the Canadian and American Dalmatian breeders. The resultant exchange of scientific research and resources will benefit all Dalmatians.

Canadian Dals earn their championships after successfully obtaining ten points under three different judges. No "majors" are required, as they are in the USA. Points can be earned for each Group placement with five points being the maximum for Group One if there are enough dogs in that Group to warrant that many points.

Puppy classes are divided into 6- to 9-month-olds and 9- to 12-month-olds. A Best Puppy is chosen for each breed and then competes for the Best Puppy in its Group. The seven Group winners compete for Best Puppy in Show. There are no points awarded for winning the Puppy Group or Best Puppy in Show.

The Dalmatian Club of Canada started as a newsletter, entitled *Transcanadals*, the first issue of which was mailed in November 1966. The number of subscribers was modest; the mailing list in February of 1967 contained 34 names, but it was mailed from coast to coast. There were regional "reporters" and Dalmatian news was exchanged across the country. The number of interested subscribers grew and the Dalmatian Club of Canada was formed and recognized by the Canadian Kennel Club as a national club in July of 1969. Three of the original board members, Nilda Dorini and John Powell from British Columbia and Vivian Sterne from Ontario, are still members of the club, as are founding members Catherine Blinko and Jacques Carpay. *Transcanadals* is published bi-monthly by the club and mailed to all members. Currently the club membership is approximately 200, including several members from the USA and a few from Europe.

It is very difficult to run a national club in a very big country with a relatively small population. The Canadian Kennel Club requires that a national club be divided into five areas: British Columbia, the Prairie Provinces, Ontario, Quebec, and the Atlantic Provinces, with

At age 11 months and 3 days, Can. Ch. Beachcomber's Mint Mark was the youngest Dal to go BIS in Canada and the #1 Dal in Canada for 1983. Owned by Bertha Little.

Am-Can. Ch. Countryroad Cool Million is a Canadian-bred and owned BIS Dal who has produced a number of American champions, winners, and top producers. Owned by Charles and Linda Cyopik.

directors in each area to handle local affairs. The national officers are president, vice president, secretary, treasurer, and editor of *Transcanadals*. Most business has to be conducted by mail, including the annual meeting, which sometimes makes communication a little difficult. The lifeline is the newsletter, *Transcanadals*, the editor of which is perhaps the most important officer of the club!

The area directors generally organize an annual "booster" for Dalmatians at a local all-breed show. The booster tries to attract an increased entry of Dalmatians at the show by offering extra prizes and rosettes. Only clubs recognized by the Canadian Kennel Club are allowed to organize boosters, but no special classes or judges are allowed. Often the directors organize a get-together of people and dogs at the booster to encourage exhibitors to travel some distance to attend. The first such club booster was held in Toronto in 1969 with 21 Dals entered.

The first National Specialty was held in 1978 in Calgary, Alberta, and since then a specialty has been held every year in a different part of the country. The specialties are usually held in conjunction with all-breed shows and attract about 50 Dals, except in 1986 when an independent specialty and obedience trial in Windsor, Ontario, attracted approximately 100 Dals thanks to great support from American friends and neighbors. A second independent specialty was held in Vancouver in 1994.

England

Even though the first Dalmatian Club in England was formed in 1890, by the early 1920s there were very few Dalmatian champions recorded. In fact, at the Kennel Club show at the Crystal Palace in 1920, there was only one Dalmatian exhibited.

In 1925, at a meeting at Crufts, the Southern Dalmatian Club was conceived by seven exhibitors in order to encourage interest in the Dalmatian in the southern part of England. Mr. Kemp was elected

president, a post he served for 22 years. Mrs. Kemp was elected honorary secretary-treasurer and Mrs. Mackie was elected chairman. According to Eleanor Frankling in *The Dalmatian*, the club had 34 members a year later and 60 members in 1927.

In 1930, the Southern Dalmatian Club held its first specialty show at Tattersalls in Knightsbridge. It was a success, with a record entry of 458. Mr. W.J. Nichols and Mr. James Saunders were the judges. That same year the North of England Dalmatian Club, formed in 1903, held its first show in Bolton. It was judged by Mr. Geoffrey Gush and Mr. Fred Wardell.

The Southern Dalmatian Club changed its name to the British Dalmatian Club in 1930. Because of its rapid growth in membership and its widely expanding boundaries, it became a national club. In 1933, championship status was obtained for a show held in April. Today, the club holds this show in March one week prior to the Crufts show.

Eleanor Frankling cites the names of some of the well-known breeders and kennels of the 1920s and 1930s in *The Dalmatian*: "Mr. and Mrs. Kemp (Coldharbour), Mrs. Bedwell (Rugby), Miss Parson, Mr. Proctor, Mr. Fish (Penwortham), Mrs. Wigglesworth (Goworth), Dr. and Mrs. Hackney, Major Pirie, Miss Evelyn Barnes (of the Wells), Miss Veasey (Hyders), Mr. J.B. Newman (of the Highway), Miss Shirley Mallion (Silverden), Mrs. Gatheral (Phaeland), Miss Clay (Tantivvey), Miss Monkhouse (Cabaret), Mr. Willie Greenwood (Tandem), Mr. Gush (Roadcoach), Mr. Frank and Mr. Fred Makin, Mrs. Bloomfield (Welfield), Miss Millie Stephens (Coeland), Miss B. Stevens (Gambia), Captain, now Sir Ambrose, Keevil (Caefel), Mrs. Bland (Four-in-Hand), Mrs. and Miss Beal (Stubbington), Mrs. Leighton Yeomans (Astwood), Mrs. Eggo (Mesra), Mrs. Gore (then Duxford, now Duxfordham), Mr. Emerson (Orchid), Mrs. Nixey (of Birch), Miss Smither (Aldham), Lieut.-Commander Hamilton (Dibden), Miss Grant-Ives (Standsure), Mrs. Ratcliffe (Littleknowle), Miss Paterson (of Brow), Miss

Am-Can. Ch. Alfredrich Handsome Tall N' Dark is Canadian bred, owned, and handled. In the US, he is a BIS and National Specialty winner as well as a top producer. Owned by Richard Millaire and Al Kay.

"CH. GOLDEN DAWN OF COELAN."

Eng. Ch. Golden Dawn of Coeland, a liver bitch from 1934 owned by Coeland Kennels.

Eng. Ch. Coeland Leader, a liver dog from 1934 owned by Coeland Kennels.

A head study of Eng. Ch. Coeland Leader (L).

Miss Stephens of Coeland Kennels with (left to right): Coeland Black Magic, Am. Ch. Golden Dusk at Coeland (L), Eng. Ch. Golden Dawn of Coeland (L), Coeland Kado.

Macfie (Colonsay), Mrs. J. Williams (Modsley), Mr. and Mrs. Byrd (Spurstow), Mrs. Walford (Midstone), Mrs. Moseley (Highwood), Mrs. Curphey (Muggins), Mrs. Walker-Smith (Bookham)."

The war years of the 1940s virtually brought the championship shows to a halt. The British Kennel Club did allow radius shows to be held. Radius shows were restricted to exhibitors within a 25-mile radius. Unfortunately, a dog could win often without defeating any of his own breed. This gave a false sense of the dog's merit. Even though breeding activities were curtailed during this time, a nucleus of a few good dogs survived to help continue the breed.

1945 saw the return of the activities of the British Dalmatian Club and the North of England Dalmatian Club. However, the old Dalmatian Club had lost most of its members and officially disbanded in 1947. The first post-war Dalmatian show was held in October 1945. This was an open unbenched show with an entry of 263. Mrs. Wigglesworth judged the dogs and Miss Barnes judged the bitches. Nine-year-old Ch. Mahlib Jifft was Best in Show.

The post-war years saw the Dalmatian continue to advance, although there was a slight slump in 1953 and 1954. Today, both clubs hold a championship show as well as an annual joint show. In 1968, Mrs.

Eng. Ch. Brythennek Basil Fawlty, winner of 10 CCs and BOB at Crufts in 1985 and 1987. Bred by Paul and Chris Stannard, owned by John and Val Watson.

Eng. Ch. Spring Classic By Apaloosa, JW (L), winner of 29 CCs and 24 BOBs, including Crufts in 1988. He was also a multiple-Group winner.

Woodyatt's bitch Ch. Fanhill Faune, winner of 20 Challenge Certificates, was Best in Show all breeds at Crufts.

The number of registered Dalmatians has declined during the past 25 years— there were 2,916 in 1969 compared to 2,235 in 1993. Their status, however, is improving because the two breed clubs are determined to safeguard the Dalmatian's future.

Two publications of the British Dalmatian Club are its monthly newsletter, entitled *Spots of News*, and its *Handbook*. The *Handbook* began in 1934 and was printed until 1939. It was revived again in 1949 and is now printed every three years. Each volume begins where the last volume left off and contains statistics and records of breed history. There are also illustrations of the leading dogs of that time.

In English shows, there are several classes in which dogs can be entered. These classes are divided by sex and a dog can be entered in more than one class at a show. Minor Puppy is a class for 6- to 9- month olds, Puppy is for 6- to 12-month olds, and Junior is for 12- to 18-month olds. The Post Graduate class is for dogs 18 months and older until the dog has five wins at this level or earns a Challenge Certificate. A dog is eligible for the Limit class until he has seven wins in that class or has earned three

Eng-Am. Ch. Washakie Dancing Brave has won 19 CCs and was the #1 Dal in 1994. During his stay in the US, he finished his American title. Bred by Mrs. McClelland, owned by Karen Goff.

Challenge Certificates. The Open class is for any dog and this is the class that the champions usually enter. The winners of each class compete for Best Dog and Best Bitch, and a Challenge Certificate is awarded for each.

There are two types of shows recognized by the Kennel Club. An open show is the smaller of the two with an average of 1,500 dogs entered. It is usually not benched and no Challenge Certificates are awarded. The 30 championship shows per year award Challenge Certificates, are benched, have an average entry of 10,000–15,000 dogs, and span a three- to four-day period. Dogs are benched only on the day they are being shown. There are two Group awards, first and reserve, and the seven Group winners' expenses for returning on the last day for the Best in Show competition are paid for by the Kennel Club.

The most prestigious championship show is Crufts, which is held in March of each year. To be eligible to enter Crufts, a dog must meet one of the following requirements: win first or second place in a Minor Puppy or Puppy class; win in a Junior, Post Graduate, or Limit class; or be a champion.

Dalmatians are in the Utility Group and

Eng. Ch. Pickled Walnut from Pampard is the top-winning bitch of all time in the UK with 27 CCs under 27 different judges. Bred by Mrs. Booking, owned by Pamela Marshall.

there are usually 100–150 Dalmatians entered at a championship show. Since there are large entries in the classes, with only two Challenge Certificates awarded per breed and only two Group placements, there is a lot of emphasis placed on winning Best of Breed.

Dogs shown in England can earn two awards from the British Kennel Club: a Junior Warrant and a Challenge Certificate. A win in a class at an open show earns one point and a win in a class at a championship show earns three points towards the 25

three Challenge Certificates under three different judges to become a champion. Since the non-champions must compete with champions for the Challenge Certificates, it can be a long process in obtaining the required number of Challenge Certificates for the championship. Most of the dogs in England finish their championships at a later age than dogs in the USA.

Germany

Dalmatians have been living in Germany for many hundreds of years. This was docu-

Eng. Ch. Washakie Indian Summer, JW has 12 CCs and 6 BOBs, including Crufts in 1994. She was #1 Dal bitch in 1993. Bred by Karen Goff and Mrs. McClelland, owned by Karen Goff.

points required for a Junior Warrant (JW) award. A dog who wins in several classes at a show can accumulate points for each win. These points must be earned between the ages of 12 and 18 months in order to be eligible for the award. A JW may be attached after the dog's name if a Junior Warrant is awarded to the dog.

A Challenge Certificate is earned by winning Best Dog or Best Bitch in the breed at a championship show. A dog has to win

mented by the artist Gerald Terboch in 1650 when he depicted a Dalmatian in his painting *Allegory of the Munster Peace Treaty*. Today, this painting can be seen at the Munster County Museum.

The chapter about Dalmatians in Ludwig Beekman's *Geschichte und Beschreibung der Rassen des Hundes* (History and Description of Breeds of Dogs), published in 1895, was written by Dalmatian breeder Mr. C. Willy Brandis of Braunschweig

(Brunswick). He stated that many Dalmatians had been living at the Braunschweig Court as companion dogs but, unfortunately, had degenerated due to inbreeding and were finally eliminated from the Court. Mr. Brandis started breeding in 1885 and within ten years had bred approximately 40 Dalmatians.

In 1879, two Dalmatians were entered in a special class at the Hannover Dog Show. At the second International Dog Show in Hannover in May 1882, four Dalmatians were entered and two were awarded prizes. First prize went to "Harmony," owned by Mr. Royal of London. "Circa," owned by Mr. Brandis, was awarded second prize. Circa's conformation was considered better than Harmony's, but Circa had cropped ears.

After World War I in 1918, approximately 150 Dalmatians were living in Germany but most of them were old dogs. Some even appeared to be the progeny of crosses with other breeds. These facts made breeding quality Dalmatians very difficult.

To improve breeding conditions and the quality of dogs bred, a number of Dalmatian enthusiasts got together in 1920 and formed a breed club they called Club for Dalmatian Friends, later to be renamed *Deutscher Dalmatiner Club von 1920 e.V.* It was the second Dalmatian club to be founded in Europe, the first being the British Dalmatian Club of 1890. In 1924, the club staged its first specialty show for Dalmatians with an entry of 15 dogs.

The advent of the Nazi regime changed

(Left to right): Eng. Ch. Konavlje Miss Gorgeous, Eng. Ch. Illyricum Pandora, Eng. Ch. Pompadally Persephone, Eng. Ch. Phaeland Phorgetmenot, Eng. Ch. Phaeland Patron, Eng. Ch. Colonsay April Jest.

Thereafter, entries at shows grew steadily. There were 14 Dalmatians in Frankfurt am Main in 1887, 17 in Kassel in 1889, and 19 in Frankfurt in 1891, including two English champions, "Acrobat" and "Berolina" owned by Mr. H. Droesse of England. The main German breeders of those days were Mr. Brandis of Braunschweig and Mr. Hugo Damm of Berlin, who started breeding in 1886. Mr. Damm's best dog was Ch. Nero, an excellent hunting dog, who together with "Mars-Dalmatia" and "Putty-Dalmatia" were the most prominent breeding Dalmatians at the time.

many aspects of breeding dogs in Germany. Until then, breed clubs had enjoyed a certain independence, keeping their own stud books and records, while still being affiliated with the all-breed association *Deutsches Kartell für Hundewesen* (German Cartel for Dog Affairs). In Nazi Germany, the Cartel was eliminated and breed clubs became a part of the *Reichsgruppe Deutsches Hundewesen* (Reichsgroup German Dog Affairs), which was part of the *Reichsverband Deutscher Kleintierzuchter* (Reichs Association of Small Animal Breeders). Registration rules became more stringent and, of course, non-Aryans were not allowed to be members in any of the clubs or organizations.

During World War II, breeding activities became virtually impossible. Breeders were sent to fight in the war and orderly meetings of club members ceased to exist. Breeders and dogs were displaced or killed as part of the war's senseless destruction.

When peace was finally restored, it took some time until dog clubs could become active again. Allied rules did not permit gatherings of any kind for a few years following the war. Despite very difficult economic conditions, breeders started breeding again on a small scale, hoping for better times.

Breed clubs resumed their activities in early 1948, only to be disrupted again by the division of Germany into East and West. In the Federal Republic of Germany, the *Deutscher Dalmatiner Club von 1920 e.V.* (DDC) assumed the role of providing support for Dalmatian breeders. In the German Democratic Republic, East Germany, the Breeders Association for Great Danes and Dalmatians assumed that responsibility.

For over 40 years German Dalmatian breeders were forced to pursue their interest under very different conditions. While quality Dalmatians were bred in East and West Germany alike, the principal difference was in the disposition desired in the breed. West German breeders concentrated

Cobbin-End Choirboy ("Simon") was an English import and the winner of 3 CACIBs and 1 Reserve CACIB.

on breeding good family dogs with gentle dispositions. Their counterparts in East Germany were required to breed dogs that also showed an aptitude for guarding and protecting. Thus, aggression was introduced into the breed.

Since the reunification of Germany in 1989, the East German breeders merged with the DDC. Membership in the club grew to about 1200 members and about 600 Dalmatians are bred every year. The club is governed by the fundamental guidelines of the Fédération Cynologique Internationale (FCI) and integrated into the *Verband fur das Deutsche Hundewesen* (VDH), the Association for German Dog Affairs, an organization comparable to the American Kennel Club.

In addition to the DDC, two smaller Dalmatian clubs were founded in recent years. Both of these clubs are dissenter clubs, formed by individuals who were not happy with some of the policies of the old clubs. These clubs are the *Dalmatiner Verein Deutschland* (Dalmatian Club Germany) and *Club fur Dalmatiner Freunde* (Club for Dalmatian Friends). Both clubs are fully recognized by the German VDH and they maintain stud books and organize regional and club shows.

Since the beginning of 1994, a serious effort has been under way to form a European Dalmatian Union. The concepts of cooperation and equalizing individual breed standards are not new in Europe. In 1978 an attempt was made to integrate, but the time was not right. Today, the chances for a successful European Dalmatian Union are much better. In Germany and other European countries there is a strong need to enlarge the existing gene pool. Since the fall of the "Iron Curtain" in 1989, many dogs have crossed the border into Germany. However, many eastern European countries have little or no breeding requirements and do not issue certified pedigrees. Thus, international cooperation today is more important than ever in order to ensure quality Dalmatians for future generations of Dalmatian fanciers.

Above: Int-Deutscher Ch. ES 82 Arko von Muhlenbache. Below: Int-Deutscher-VDH Ch. Bundessieger, Europasieger, Clubsieger Erle v Nordenstadt.

In order for a Dalmatian to be certified for breeding by the DDC, the Dalmatian must participate in at least two VDH-sanctioned dog shows and receive a minimum evaluation of "very good" in the Open class. In addition, all Dalmatians to be used for breeding must be evaluated by a three-judge panel as to their conformation to the standard and they must undergo a personality and temperament evaluation. These evaluations are held once a year in each of the German states and the German Dalmatian Club chooses the three Dalmatian specialist judges who will conduct the evaluations. Dogs are not eligible for evaluation until they are 15 months old.

Int. Ch. Arro von Germannswald, three-time Clubsieger winner.

Males can not be used for breeding until they are 18 months old and females cannot be used until their third heat cycle. Hip dysplasia and deafness are also issues of concern. Dalmatians to be used for breeding must be certified as free of hip dysplasia. Since 1994, Dalmatians must be BAER tested and unilaterally deaf dogs are not given breeding certificates.

In 1995, the DDC celebrated its 75th anniversary. In commemoration of this event, the club hosted the very first All-European Specialty in May of that year.

The DDC also publishes a quarterly magazine entitled *Dalmatinerpost*. It features articles concerning health issues and showing, as well as photos of recent winners and breeder advertisements. Since breeding stock is required to be x-rayed for dysplastic hips, the magazine also publishes the names of the dogs who are free of dysplasia and certified for breeding.

Dalmatians who are shown in conformation competition in Germany must be at least six months of age. However, a dog can not receive a point towards a championship unless he is over 15 months of age, in the Open class, and wins first place. A total of four points are needed for a championship and a period of 366 days must lapse between the first point and the last point awarded. Three of these points must be under different judges.

Conformation classes include the Puppy class, for dogs six to nine months of age. The puppies are rated with written evaluations but no placements are awarded. The Youth class is for dogs 9–15 months of age. The dogs are placed first through fourth and rated, and the winner may compete for Best of Breed. The Open class is for dogs 15 months of age and older. As in the Youth class, the dogs are placed first through fourth and rated, and the winner may compete for Best of Breed.

The Champion class is open to all champions and winners of the Youth and Open classes. The Veterans class, offered at international all-breed shows, is for dogs eight years and older. The winners do not compete for Best of Breed or Best in Show, but a Best Veteran in Show award is given.

Challenge Certificates are awards that can be won during competitions and are requirements for the champion title. A CACIB is the Challenge Certificate for International Champions. It can be awarded to the best dogs and bitches out of the Open, Working (no classes for Dals), and Champion classes. A Reserve CACIB can be awarded if the judge finds the dog's quality to be close to that of the first CACIB. If a CACIB is awarded to a dog that is already an international champion, the FCI awards the CACIB to the dog awarded the Reserve. Four CACIBs under three different judges with 366 days lapsing between the first and the fourth

CACIB are required for a dog to become an international champion.

There are two national Challenge Certificates. The CAC is the title for a German champion. It can be awarded to each dog winning first place in the Open, Working (no classes for Dals), and Champion classes. If a dog receives a CAC and is already a German champion, the certificate is transferred to the Reserve CAC winner. A VDH Certificate must be awarded to every dog that has been rated Excellent first in the Open, Working (no classes for Dals), and Champion classes. Four VDH Certificates are required for a VDH championship, with 366 days lapsing between the first and fourth certificates.

Mexico

Dalmatians have long been popular in Mexico, although formal records of their first arrival are nonexistent. A number of prominent Mexican personalities owned and bred Dals in the 1930s and 1940s. General Manuel Avila Camacho, President of Mexico from 1940 to 1946, is perhaps the best known, and he is said to have imported his stock. A few years later, Don Ramon Beteta, a highly regarded Minister of Finance in the 1950s and the father of Mario Ramon Beteta, a Minister of Finance in the 1980s, began keeping and breeding Dalmatians. Don Ramon's widow, Mrs. Elizabeth Beteta, continued actively breeding and showing at least into the 1980s and

Int-Mex. Ch. Elvy, owned and bred by Dr. Jose Maria Crucet. She won the 1983 Mexican National Specialty in 1983.

maintained a Dalmatian Club membership. Other earlier breeders were members of the Rivera Torres family, Mr. Manuel Buch, Mr. J.A. Jaurequi, and Mr. Luis G. Maurino, who was active from the late 1960s through the 1980s (kennel prefix Culich) and a founding member of the Dalmatian Club of Mexico in 1975.

Since those earlier times there have been two major spurts of activity in the breed: the first in the late 1950s and early 1960s, and the second from 1970 through the late 1980s. The first of these was a

abandoned the breed and dissolved his kennel. The quality of the line gradually deteriorated and eventually disappeared.

The second spurt of activity occurred through the efforts of numerous people. It began in 1970 with the formation of La Mancha Dalmatians by Raymond F. Fitzsimmons and Alejandro Gonzalez, and it lasted through the late 1980s. La Mancha, which had been started with Culich stock, imported a Green Starr foundation bitch from the USA and bred with the American kennels Melody, Blackpool, and Green Starr. Puppies were placed in show homes, show activity increased markedly, and the breed became prominent in the Mexican Kennel Club's annual winning statistics. Dals placed either first or second in the Non-Sporting Group from 1971 through 1975.

The biggest impact on the breed, however, was the formation of the *Club Dalmata de Mexico*, AC (Mexican Dalmatian Club) by a group of 22 fanciers in 1975. It became the official club for the breed in Mexico and had as many as 75 members. Founding

World-Americas-Int-Am-Mex. Ch. Don Juan Tenorio de La Mancha, three-time winner of the Mexican National Specialty and a BIS winner. Owned by Raymond Fitzsimmons.

tremendous effort by one individual, Dr. Philip Chancellor, who bred and exhibited under the Dalmex prefix in the late 1950s and the early 1960s. He maintained about 80 dogs and 50 runs at peak activity, imported stock from England and the USA, bred up to 15 litters annually, and showed in Mexico and the USA, winning Bests in Show in both countries. After a serious disagreement with the American Kennel Club when one of his dogs that had won an all-breed show in the USA was declared ineligible for the award and all previous awards were requested returned, he

officers were Raymond F. Fitzsimmons, president; Emilio Barajas, vice president; Rodolfo Saldana, secretary; John Hogan, treasurer; and Enrique Castillo, vocal. The club participated actively as a member of the Mexican Kennel Club and, from 1980—1982, Mr. Fitzsimmons represented all member breed clubs on the board of the Mexican Kennel Club.

From 1976 through 1985, the Dalmatian Club sponsored 11 National Specialty shows. The largest entry was 78 dogs in 1979. The 1975 USA National Specialty winner, Int-Am-Mex. Ch. Melody Ring of

Fire, won the Mexican title in 1980. There were two multiple winners: Int-Mex. Ch. Don Benjamin de La Mancha won in 1978 and 1979, and World-Americas-Int-Mex-Am. Ch. Don Juan Tenorio de La Mancha won in 1982, 1984, and 1985.

Two brood bitches also made outstanding contributions. Int-Am-Mex. Ch. Pennydale Deacon's Daughter finished nine champions, including three international champions, one world champion, and three National Specialty winners. She won the Mexican Kennel Club's award for "Brood Bitch of the Year, All Breeds" in 1976.

The second bitch was her granddaughter, Int-Mex. Ch. La Mancha's Impossible Dream. She produced eight Mexican champions, seven of which were also international champions and one which was a world champion. At the 1984 USA National Specialty, she was named Best Brood Bitch and her son won the Puppy Sweepstakes. Two of her offspring won the Mexican National Specialty a total of four times, and she was Dalmatian Brood Bitch four times.

El Archiduque de La Mancha winning the DCA National Specialty Sweepstakes in 1984. Owner-handled by Ray Fitzsimmons.

There are four Dalmatian all-breed Best in Show winners in Mexico, including two Mexican-bred and two American-bred dogs. The Mexican dogs were Ch. Dalmex Chicharrin in 1961 and World-Americas-Int-Am-Mex. Ch. Don Juan Tenorio de La Mancha in 1983. The American dogs were Am-Mex. Ch. Little Slam's Jack of Hearts in 1976 and Am-Mex. Ch. Briarfield Princess Sonrisa in 1992.

World-Int-Mex. Ch. Floria Tosca de La Mancha (left), owned by Ernesto Macip; and Int-Mex. Ch. Don Benjamin de La Mancha (L) (right), owned by Alejandro Gonzales and Ray Fitzsimmons, going BOS and BOB at a Group IX (Toy and Non-Sporting) Specialty.

Unfortunately, formal Dalmatian Club activity has virtually ceased since the late 1980s. The last specialty show was in 1983. Mr. Fitzsimmons's departure late that year and Alejandro Gonzalez's untimely death in 1988 undoubtedly had serious effects on the club's status. The coordinated breeding, showing, and educational programs of the club no longer exist although individuals still work within the existing gene pool. There have been some recent quality imports from the USA and Canada. It is hoped that some dedicated Dalmatian people will emerge to restart what was, until recently, a vibrant breed club.

SA Ch. Mossgiel Candlelight (L) was the #1 Dalmatian in South Africa in 1990 and 1991. Owned by Sue McDonald.

South Africa

In September 1895, Caesar and Minka, sire and dam unknown, owned by A. Kunne, were the first Dals registered with the South African Kennel Union (now the Kennel Union of Southern Africa, KUSA). Two of their progeny, males named Tiger and Hans, were registered along with the pair. None of these older-type registrations seem to exist in the pedigrees of the present-day South African Dals.

Very little else is known about the development of the breed during those early years. The next recorded highlight came almost 50 years later, in 1941, when the first champion was crowned in the breed. He was Dalma Phantom, a dog bred by P.D. Pappas and owned by Mrs. E.W. Ruger of Port Elizabeth.

Although details are sketchy, it is evident that after World War II, a number of quality Dalmatians were brought into South Africa by British immigrants, and these dogs provided the foundation stock upon which the leading kennels of the day were based.

Among the known imports were three bitches: Ch. Clausentrum Red Dimples of Collaton (UK), Ch. Mariscat Marigold of Dallmalli (UK), and Ch. Labyrinth Star Dot Star (USA). The five dogs among the imports were: Ch. Fanhill Festivity of Traveare (UK) and Ch. Harpsichord Adagio of Kilshane (UK), who featured strongly in pedigrees of top winners in the late 1960s and 1970s, Ch. Mesabi of Watseka (USA), Ch. Labyrinth Liveryman of Dallmalli (USA), and Countryroad Polar Star (Canada). Recently, Ch. Labyrinth Big Spender of Dallmalli (USA) was on loan for a year exclusively to the Dallmalli Kennel.

By the early 1960s interest in the breed around the Johannesburg area had grown to the extent that the creation of a club was considered viable. The Dalmatian Club was formed on December 11, 1961, by the leading Dalmatian breeders on the Witwaterstrand at that time. At the first general meeting, Mr. Peacock was appointed chairman, Mrs. Roseveare undertook the duties of secretary, Mr. Bell became treasurer, and Mrs. Bell and Mrs. Roseveare undertook joint editorship of the club's newsletter.

The club grew rapidly, and by July it had 45 members. In August 1963 the club held its first trophy show in conjunction with the Goldfields Kennel Club championship show. Five floating trophies were offered for competition and over 20 Dalmatians attended. In 1975, the introduction of a new KUSA ruling enabled the club to qualify to hold a specialist championship show. Membership grew and the number of dogs present at the shows was sufficient enough to obtain a license. The first championship show was held in Johannesburg on October 10, 1976, and attracted an entry of 48 Dalmatians. Best of Breed was won by Ch. Doriben's Mojave of Dallmalli.

The club went through a period of inactivity and declined in membership, but a major membership drive in the early 1990s increased the membership to over 100. Today the club is active in the areas

Am-SA-Zim. Ch. Labyrinth Big Spender is an American Dal who became a Group and BIS winner in Zimbabwe, and a Group winner and the #1 Dal for 1993 in South Africa. Owned by Christine Dyker.

breed championship shows are held in various parts of the country during the year, and Dals are judged according to the British standard. South Africa is divided into centers by the Kennel Union. Dogs must earn a total of five points (Challenge Certificates) under different judges in a minimum of two centers to achieve champion status. One of the Challenge Certificates must be earned after the dog is 18 months of age, and points won before the age of nine months do not count. Challenge Certificates carry a value of one point unless there are ten or more dogs in competition. The value then increases to a maximum of two points.

Dals are the same happy clowns no matter where they reside! SA-Zim. Ch. Dallmalli Inthenews runs on the dunes in Umgazi, Transkei, South Africa. Owned by Carol Immelman.

SA Ch. Dallmalli Starsandstripes is a Group winner and the #1 Dalmatian in South Africa in 1989. Owned by Carol Immelman.

of education, rescue, judges' seminars, and both open and trophy shows.

The Dalmatian Club is one of over 200 canine associations that are affiliated with the Kennel Union of Southern Africa. KUSA recognizes over 100 breeds which are classified in seven Groups, and Dalmatians fall within the Utility Group. Over 30

SA Ch. Dalmalli Hawk is the only multiple BIS-winning Dalmatian in South Africa and the breed's all-time top winner in that country.

The breed has enjoyed a fair share of success in the Group ring over the years. Five Dalmatians have won Best in Show awards. They are Ch. Johnstown's High Life (1950s), Ch. Yumani Ceasar (1963), Ch. Meerlus Argus (1974), Ch. Doriben's Mojave of Dallmalli (1976), and Ch. Dallmalli Hawk (1983–1988). Ch. Dallmalli Hawk is the only Dalmatian to have won more than one such award and is also the breed record holder in South Africa with a total of 136 Bests of Breed, 84 Group placements including 21 firsts, and 5 Bests in Show.

The South African breeders have a small, relatively sound gene pool from which to draw and are making sensible decisions about its use. Provided that the breeders continue in this direction, the breed can look forward to a positive future.

South America

All South American countries follow FCI rules for obtaining championships and there are several types that can be earned. The international championship is obtained by winning four CACIBs, and at least two of these must be awarded by different judges from different continents. The Latin American championship is awarded at special championship shows organized by Sicalam, which are held once a year in a different South American country, or by the few judges that can award the CACLAB certificates. A dog has to win four CACLABs to earn this title. Each South American country has its own championship and grand championship title.

Currently there are several South American countries that have either organized clubs or Dalmatian enthusiasts:

Int-Arg-Sud. Ch. Zagreb Enforcer was a specialty BIS winner and the #1 Dalmatian in Argentina for 1987. Owned by Andrea Paccagnella.

Int-Arg-Sud. Ch. Caravan Zagreb the Challenger was a BIS winner in Brazil, specialty winner in Argentina, and the #1 Dal in Argentina for 1990–1992.

Arg-Sud. Ch. Zagreb Hollywood is an Argentine Group winner and the #1 Dalmatian for 1989.

Argentina—During President Peron's first presidency (1955) he imported a Dal from the USA to match his Pinto horses. Today, the rural people and gauchos recognize Dalmatians as "Peron's dogs" even though there is no record of Peron's Dal being a sire.

The first Dals imported and registered were in the 1960s from German and English bloodlines. The first registered litter born in the country was in 1965 from the Domino Kennel. This kennel bred over 80 litters in a 15-year period and is responsible for increasing the popularity of the breed in Argentina.

In the late 1970s new bloodlines were introduced, mostly from Brazilian-bred dogs that came from American and English stock. Many Dalmatians were imported in the period from 1980—1985. Dogs came from the Gypsy Rose Kennel in Brazil, which bred or owned dogs from the Paisley, Watseka, and Melody Kennels in the USA. Other dogs came directly from the Green Starr, Croatia, and Indalane Kennels in the USA. All of these kennels had a great influence in changing the type of Dalmatian in Argentina.

The first Dalmatian specialty show was held in 1979 and currently there are four specialty shows being held per year. The first Argentine Dal to become an international champion was Ch. Domino Uxmal. Other Dals that have had an important influence are: BIS winners Int. Ch. Von Achen Ali of Almeida and Ch. Final Act de Nutwoot; number one Dal sire of all time Raindrop of Gypsy Rose VII; number two sire of all time Int. Ch. Zagreb Enforcer; number one dams (tied) Ch. Zagreb Private Blend and Ch. Pan's Crystal de Albo Atrum; and Int. Ch. Zagreb the Challenger.

In June of 1993, the World Championship Show (FCI) was held in Argentina for the first time and the Best of Breed and world champion titles were won by an Argentine-bred Dal, Ch. Zagreb Hallmark.

Brazil—In 1961, the Dalmatian Club of São Paulo was founded and in 1975 was officially proclaimed the Dalmatian Club of Brazil. The first specialty was held in 1961 and was won by Ch. Flying Boots from Dalmatia, a USA import. To receive a championship in Brazil, a dog has to win five CACs and a bitch has to win four CACs as well as one Best of Breed.

The American kennels which have had influence in Brazil are Dalmatia, Limestone, Watseka, Paisley, and Long Last. The English kennel Oudenarde also has been influential.

Dalmatians that have influenced the breed as winners and producers are: number one dog all breeds and number one Dal sire Ch. Paisley Torch of Kirkland, Ch. Oak Tree of Gypsy Rose VII, Ch. Limestone Zara Padraic, Ch. Dollar Tree of Warlike Eden, Ch. Vicor of the Ebony Spots, and Ch. Gypsy Rose VII.

Chile—In Chile, the first Dals were indirectly imported from the Washakie Kennel in England and various American kennels via Mexican breeders. Since 1967, breeders have been sending their females to be bred to Argentine stud dogs and have also imported stock from Argentina to improve the quality of the Chilean Dals.

There is no Dalmatian club in Chile, but currently there are a few breeders and exhibitors who are working to form a club. To earn a Chilean championship, a dog has to win four CACs.

Uruguay—There is no Dalmatian club in Uruguay, but the breed is as popular there as it is in Argentina. A championship title is awarded by winning three CACs.

Sweden

To earn a championship in Sweden, a dog must earn three Challenge Certificates from two different judges after reaching one year of age. Challenge Certificates are awarded for Best Dog and Best Bitch in each breed at championship shows. An international championship requires four Challenge Certificates from three countries.

The Dalmatian has never been one of the more common breeds in Sweden, a fact which has worked in the breed's

Above: Int-Am-Can-Gr. Ch. Annle N Belrins Dylan Flyer finished his American title, and then went to Brazil and became a BIS winner and the Top Non-Sporting Dog for several years. Owned by Dr. Salem Antonio Salamao. Below: Int-Am-Br-Gr-NAC Ch. Paisley Torch of Kirkland (L) went to Brazil after finishing his American championship. Owner-handled by Alberto Salim Saber Filho, he was the #1 Dog All-Breeds in Brazil for 1980.

favor. Ever since the very first dog show was held in this country in July 1886, the Dalmatian breed has been represented at shows; however, from the end of the 19th century to the 1950s, only a few Dals were shown on each occasion.

During the first part of the 20th century, breeding of Dalmatians was very limited in Sweden and close inbreeding was very common. In the beginning of the 1950s hardly any Dalmatian breeding existed at all and the breed was nearly extinct.

In the beginning of 1954, Ann-Marie Hammarlund happened to find a really nice Dalmatian puppy that was inbred on the last remnants of the breed. He was named Kief and he grew into a very good specimen and soon became an international and Scandinavian champion.

From this dog along with Wendell Sammet's American dog Ch. Fleetwood Nu-Boot of Dalmatia and a number of imported bitches from Colonsay and Jellmont in England, a Swedish line was established. In the mid-1960s Swedish Dalmatians had reached such a high level of quality that they became competitive abroad. In 1960, Int-Swedish-Danish Ch. Dallas Inkspot won Best of Breed at the Utrecht show in Holland, and soon after that, Dallas Joyful Christmas finished her championship in Canada. A few years later another dog was imported from the USA, Garrett's Ice Cream Check Mate, who became an international and Scandinavian champion. New blood is frequently added to the breed with dogs and bitches imported from England.

Int-Nord. U Ch. Dallas Super Star, a winner of the 1970s. Bred by Ann-Marie Hammarlund, owned by Peter Soderquist.

Dallas Facsimilia (lying) and her daughter Dallas Valonia Gardens (standing). Bred and owned by Ann-Marie Hammarlund.

S U Ch. T-Cart Rasima (L). Bred and owned by Solveig Jensen.

In 1962, the Swedish Dalmatian Society (S*venska Dalmatiner-Sallskapet*) was founded by a handful of enthusiasts. At this time, the interest and activity in the breed was constantly increasing. Although the overall Dal population in Sweden was rather small, it was not unusual in those days that the breed was one of the more numerous at dog shows. The club also started to arrange special club shows, inviting authorities from other countries to judge. At some of these shows more than 100 Dalmatians were entered. At that time, even though breeders were few, one could definitely say that the Dalmatian had finally obtained a firm foothold in Sweden. Dogs were exported to Denmark, Norway, Finland, Canada, and later, even to England.

Int-Nord. U Ch. SV-92 & 93 Skartoftas Clothilde, the top-winning Dal in Sweden for 1992 and 1993. Bred by Viktor Kaller, owned by Annika Lellep.

Albicans Dappled Peg is winning in Denmark and Sweden. She is from a litter sired by Am. Ch. Proctors Dappled Hi-Flyer through the use of frozen semen. Bred by Ake Cronander, owned by Annika Lellep.

121

It was encouraging that several very interested and serious people started breeding, and currently there are at least 40 breeders who really care about the breed. Now the breed is in good hands.

About 400 Dalmatians are registered each year and in spite of decreasing numbers in many breeds today, the demand for Dalmatians seems to be constant.

In 1992, the club sponsored the purchase of an EMG machine so that BAER testing could start. By the end of September 1994, 82 adults and 163 puppies had been tested. Dogs and bitches used for breeding are tested at the expense of the club. There are hopes that in the near future the club will be able to present valuable documentation about the hearing status of the breed in Sweden. However, the long distances in a sparsely populated country make it difficult for many Dalmatian owners to get their dogs tested. In order to provide testing, the club has started to move the machine to different locations within the country.

In 1993, semen was imported from the American dog Ch. Proctor's Dappled Hi-Flyer and, by artificial insemination, Swedish Ch. Skartoftas Clothilde had eight puppies in March of that year. Some of the puppies from that litter are already winners at Swedish and Danish shows.

Int-Nord. U Ch. Dallas Leading Lady, bred by Ann-Marie Hammarlund and owned by Solveig Jensen.

Swedish Dalmatians are sometimes successful in obedience trials. Occasionally, they are also used as sled dogs and for tracking.

The Swedish Dalmatian Society, with 1,262 members in 1993, produces four or five issues annually of its newsletter, *Dalmatiner Kuriren.* Each issue contains numerous Dalmatian photographs and articles of interest. The editor is Ms. Asa Bohom. The society is under the able leadership of the Chairman, Ann-Marie Hammarlund, Hjalstavik, S-746 93 Balsta, Sweden; and the Honorary Secretary, Ms. Decilia Thonssen, Sjogard 6497, S-462 93 Vanersborg, Sweden.

The Dalmatian Standard

A breed standard is written by an official group, usually a national breed club. It is the instrument which breeders, fanciers, and judges use to evaluate dogs of that particular breed. For breeders, the standard is especially important in that they use it as a blueprint to ensure the continued quality and consistency of the breed.

THE AKC STANDARD AND HOW TO APPLY IT

Following is the current breed standard for the Dalmatian as set forth by the American Kennel Club. Comments about and explanations of each section of the standard are in italics.

General Appearance—The Dalmatian is a distinctively spotted dog; poised and alert; strong, muscular and active; free of shyness; intelligent in expression; symmetrical in outline; and without exaggeration or coarseness. The Dalmatian is capable of great endurance, combined with fair amount of speed.

Since the Dalmatian's purpose was that of a carriage dog, the emphasis here is on balance and fitness, which are essential for a trotting dog that was expected to cover many miles in a day's work. The Dalmatian should be an athlete, neither lumpy and over-muscled nor soft and flabby. His spotting sets him apart from all other breeds and he appears confident and interested in his surroundings.

Deviations from the described ideal should be penalized in direct proportion to the degree of the deviation.

We are differentiating between not quite correct and very incorrect. A dog who is only slightly faulty in a specific area is not to be penalized as severely as one who is extremely faulty in the same area.

Size, Proportion, Substance—Desirable height at the withers is between 19 and 23 inches. Undersize or oversize is a fault. Any dog or bitch over 24 inches at the withers is disqualified.

This is a rather large allowable size range with no distinction made for size differences between dogs and bitches, although dogs are normally larger than bitches. A 19–20-inch bitch is rarely seen in the show ring. Most females fit in middle of the standard averaging about 22 inches, while most males are closer to 23 inches than to 22 inches. A smaller male should not be faulted if he has sufficient bone and substance, nor should a larger female be faulted, provided she is feminine.

The overall length of the body from the forechest to the buttocks is approximately equal to the height at the withers.

"Approximately" is the key word here, and the standard does not specifically ask

Winning show dogs must closely adhere to the breed standard. Ch. Dalwood's Pat E. Kakes, going BOB from the Veterans class at the 1990 Dal Club of Las Vegas Specialty.

Looking at top-winning dogs will give you a picture of what the ideal Dalmatian should look like. Ch. Green Starr's Colonel Joe is one of the all-time top-winning Dals.

for a dog that is square. A dog should not be penalized for being slightly longer than tall any more than another should be faulted for being too square. As the standard calls for a short loin, any extra body length must be in the length of the ribcage.

The Dalmatian has good substance and is strong and sturdy in bone, but never coarse.

The Dalmatian is required to have sufficient strength and substance to perform the tasks he was bred for. Dalmatians were originally used for many purposes including running with the carriage, guarding the horses from stray dogs, and protecting the carriage and its contents from highway-

One blue eye and one brown eye are quite common in the Dalmatian.

The **eyes** are set moderately well apart, are medium sized and somewhat rounded in appearance, and are set well into the skull. Eye color is brown or blue, or any combination thereof; the darker the better and usually darker in black-spotted than in liver-spotted dogs.

Although perfectly acceptable according to the Dalmatian standard, this dog's eye color could be darker.

According to the standard, blue eyes are acceptable.

men. A coarse dog would not have the stamina necessary to run with the horses for hours on end.

Head—The head is in balance with the overall dog. It is of fair length and free of loose skin. The Dalmatian's **expression** is alert and intelligent, indicating a stable and outgoing temperament.

Although the Dalmatian is not considered a "head breed," his characteristic sparkling expression mirrors his enthusiasm. A sharp, fearful, or bored look is neither typical nor correct.

It is not unusual for Dalmatians to have one or two blue eyes. Some dogs have eyes that are partially blue, either a sizable amount of blue or just a small splash of it; all are equally acceptable. Light eyes detract from the proper expression, and dark eyes are preferred. The eyes on liver Dals are not normally quite as dark as those on blacks, but they should still be as dark as possible, and should not be pale yellow or glassy looking.

Abnormal position of the eyelids or eyelashes (ectropion, entropion, trichiasis) is a major fault.

These are characterized by eyelids that roll either out (ectropion) or in (entropion) or by lashes that rub against the surface of the eye. Excessive tearing might signify a possible eyelid problem.

Incomplete pigmentation of the eyerims is a major fault.

As the color pattern of the Dalmatian is its most unique characteristic, the goal is to have complete pigmentation of the eyerims, which contributes to the proper expression.

The **ears** are of moderate size, proportionately wide at the base and gradually tapering to a rounded tip. They are set rather high, and are carried close to the head, and are thin and fine in texture. When the Dalmatian is alert, the top of the ear is level with the top of the skull and the tip of the ear reaches to the bottom line of the cheek.

A lovely head study of Am-Can. Ch. Korcula King of Harts. "King" was owned by the Harts and Dr. Charles Garvin.

The Dalmatian should not have thick, excessively long, lowset, or houndy ears, nor should they be set so high that they break over well above the level of the skull. The dog should be able to bring them forward and close to the cheek when alert.

The top of the skull is flat with a slight vertical furrow and is approximately as wide as it is long. The **stop** is moderately well defined. The cheeks blend smoothly into a powerful **muzzle**, the top of which is level and parallel with the top of the skull. The muzzle and the top of the skull are about equal in length.

and brown in liver-spotted dogs. Incomplete nose pigment is a major fault.

As it is true of the eyerims, the goal is to have a solid-colored nose, but the severity of the deviation must also be considered. Only the nose leather itself must be pigmented.

The **lips** are clean and close fitting. The teeth meet in a **scissors bite**. Overshot or undershot bites are disqualifications.

No mention is made of level bites or missing pre-molars. Youngsters whose heads are not completely developed sometimes appear to be very slightly overshot.

Neck, Topline, Body—The **neck** is nicely arched, fairly long, free from throati-

A profile shot of the famous obedience dog Touchstone's Hello Holly, UD. "Holly" was owned by Gilda Aquilera.

There is considerable variation in head type in the breed. Heads should not be too coarse or cheeky, nor should they be weak and snipey. Neither a domey skull nor a downfaced look is correct. Heads should be balanced and always in proportion to the size of the dog. The top of the muzzle and the top of the skull should be on parallel planes. The term "pear-shaped" is often applied to the head.

The **nose** is completely pigmented on the leather, black in black-spotted dogs

ness, and blends smoothly into the shoulders.

The dog should not be ewe-necked or have a thick neck or one that is totally straight. There is a correlation between neck length and shoulder layback, with straight shouldered dogs often having short necks.

The **topline** is smooth.

The term topline is correctly applied to an area including neck, withers, back, loin, and croup, but more commonly used for the

127

area from withers to croup. Wrinkles over the withers usually imply straight shoulders and poor neckset.

The **chest** is deep, capacious, and of moderate width, having good spring of rib without being barrel shaped. The brisket reaches the elbow. The underline of the rib cage curves gradually into a moderate tuck-up.

The standard calls for a deep chest and good spring of ribs to provide maximum room for lung expansion. A short or shallow rib cage or excessive tuck-up also reduce lung capacity. Barrel-shaped ribs do not allow the shoulder and upper arm to move smoothly, nor do they permit the dog to get his feet under his center of gravity and single track.

The **back** is level and strong. The **loin** is short, muscular and slightly arched. The flanks narrow through the loin. The **croup** is nearly level with the back.

The back is the area between the withers and the loin. The loin is arched because of the muscle structure. The flanks are the area below the loin and behind the rib cage. Too much dropoff in croup reflects a steep pelvic angle which does not allow the dog to fully extend his rear legs when trotting.

The **tail** is a natural extension of the topline. It is not inserted too low down. It is strong at the insertion and tapers to the tip, which reaches to the hock. It is never docked. The tail is carried with a slight upward curve, but should never curl over the back. Ring tails and low-set tails are faults.

This is how a Dalmatian's tail should not look.

The tailset is determined by the angle of the croup. A steep croup means a low tailset. The tail should not be coarse, nor should it be too short or too long. Some tails are straight and carried almost level, while others have some degree of upward curve. The tail should not be carried at too high an angle or with so much curve that it looks curled. Tails do reflect attitude to some degree, and a dog who is excited may carry its tail higher than a dog who is relaxed.

Forequarters—The **shoulders** are smoothly muscled and well laid back. The **upper arm** is approximately equal in length to the shoulder blade and joins it at an angle sufficient to insure that the foot falls under the shoulder. The **elbows** are close to the body. The **legs** are straight, strong and sturdy in bone. There is a slight angle at the **pastern** denoting flexibility.

Well laid-back-shoulders set properly on a deep chest are required for a breed which is designed to trot long distances with little effort. They allow him to take long strides and cover a maximum amount of ground in a minimum number of strides. Straight shoulders cause the dog to take short choppy steps or use extra effort to lift his front higher in an effort to lengthen his stride. If the shoulder assembly is set too far forward on the rib cage, the elbows stand out from the body and when the dog moves he swings his elbows out and turns his feet in. Straight leg boning allows the leg to swing forward in a straight line, with no twisting or wasted motion. A slight pastern angle allows the pastern to function as a shock-absorber when the dog trots on hard ground. Dalmatian pasterns are short for endurance and strength.

Hindquarters—The **hindquarters** are powerful, having smooth, yet well-defined muscles. The **stifle** is well bent. The **hocks** are well let down. When the Dalmatian is standing, the hind legs, viewed from the rear, are parallel to each other from the point of the hock to the heel of the pad. Cowhocks are a major fault.

When a dog trots, he is propelled by his rear. The well-bent stifle allows him to bring his rear foot far forward beneath his body and follow through with a long stride which ends well behind the pelvis and thrusts his body forward with minimal effort. Short hocks (rear pasterns) are required for endurance. Cowhocks prevent the leg from moving forward in a straight line. The twisting motion wastes energy and reduces drive.

Feet—*Feet* are very important. Both front and rear feet are round and compact with thick, elastic pads and well arched toes. Flat feet are a major fault. Toenails are black and/or white in black-spotted dogs and brown and/or white in liver-spotted dogs. Dewclaws may be removed.

The Dalmatian is supposed to be able to run with horses, for hours at a time, over rough ground. The thick pads act as shock-absorbers and protect the foot from sharp rocks and excessive wear. Compact feet prevent rocks from getting between the toes and bruising them.

Coat—The *coat* is short, dense, fine and close fitting. It is neither wooly nor silky. It is sleek, glossy and healthy in appearance.

Dalmatians' coats vary in length, thickness, and texture, but should ideally be short, thick, and fine. Dogs should be penalized for coat problems according to severity.

Color and Markings— *Color and markings* and their overall appearance are very important points to be evaluated.

It is the spotting that sets the Dalmatian apart from other breeds, and correct markings are very important when a dog is being judged.

The ground color is pure white. In black-spotted dogs the spots are dense black. In liver-spotted dogs the spots are liver brown. Any color markings other than black or liver are disqualified.

Dals occasionally appear in colors other than black or liver. Lemon-spotted dogs have distinctly yellow or orange spots all over their bodies, and an occasional dog is seen with one or two spots of a different color. This is not to be confused with a dog who shows several shades of liver, such as lighter ears.

Spots are round and well-defined, the more distinct the better. They vary from the size of a dime to the size of a half-dollar. They are pleasingly and evenly distributed. The less the spots intermingle the better. Spots are usually smaller on the head, legs and tail than on the body. Ears are preferably spotted.

Dogs should be neither too lightly nor too heavily spotted and the spots should be pleasingly distributed. Large areas where the spots have run together or large areas with no spots at all are not correct. Spots should be as separate and distinct as possible and they should not be intermixed with very small spots or "ticking." Dogs should not have solid black or liver ears. Even if they show a few white hairs and are obviously

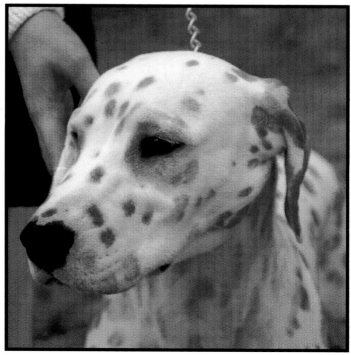

Close-up of an adult lemon-spotted Dalmatian. The color can also be much more pale.

129

not patched, they are not preferred, nor are solid white ears correct. Spots should be clear black or liver and not have white hairs mixed into them.

Tri-color (which occurs rarely in this breed) is a disqualification. It consists of tan markings found on the head, neck, chest, leg or tail of a black- or liver-spotted dog. Bronzing of black spots, and fading and/or darkening of liver spots due to environmental conditions or normal processes of coat change are not tri-coloration.

Tri-colors are not at all common and should not be confused with dogs who show normal variations in color. Dead hair, just before it is ready to shed, may not be

Above: Though not patched, this liver puppy is probably too dark for the show ring. Right: An example of light spotting. Although acceptable for the show ring, this pup could use more color (spots).

Dazzle is an example of a heavily marked puppy.

An example of a blank area on the dog's side.

An example of ticking or secondary spotting. Notice the small spots mixed in with the larger spots.

A black tri-colored Dalmatian.

A liver tri-colored Dalmatian.

Tail patch on a six-week-old puppy.

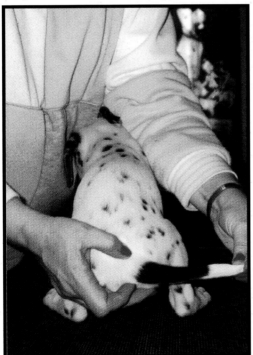

uniform in color. Liver-spotted Dals, like many brown breeds, are prone to sun fading and may show several shades of liver at the same time.

Patches are a disqualification. A patch is a solid mass of black or liver hair containing no white hair. It is appreciably larger than a normal sized spot. Patches are a dense, brilliant color with sharply defined, smooth edges. Patches are present at birth. Large color masses formed by intermingled or overlapping spots are not patches. Such masses should indicate individual spots by uneven edges and/or white hairs scattered throughout the mass.

Patches are normally found on the head or ears, occasionally at the base of the tail, and very rarely on the body.

Gait—In keeping with the Dalmatian's historical use as a coach dog, gait and endurance are of great importance. Movement is steady and effortless. Balanced angulation fore and aft combined with

132

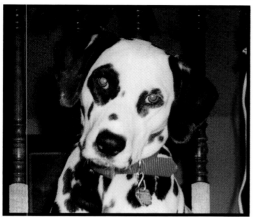

A very subtle eye patch.

Double ear patch—the edges are clearly defined; there are no white hairs within the patched area.

Leg patches on seven-week-old puppies.

Leg patch—although normally found around the head and base of the tail, patches can appear anywhere.

An example of blotching or "run-together" spotting on the neck and down the shoulder. This is not a patch!

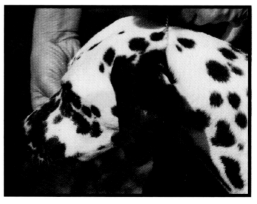

This dog has dark ears, not a patch. White hair can be seen dividing the spots.

powerful muscles and good condition produce smooth, efficient action. There is a powerful drive from the rear coordinated with extended reach in the front. The topline remains level. Elbows, hocks, and feet turn neither in nor out. As the speed of the trot increases, there is a tendency to single track.

Correct movement is very important. Proper construction, balance, and condition all contribute to a dog who can move easily and effortlessly for an extended period of time. All dog breeds with normal construction tend to single

The Dalmatian's temperament should be "stable and outgoing, yet dignifed." Banker's regal expression is dignity personified.

track. As a moving dog increases his speed, his legs tend to converge along a center line. As he trots he has no need to keep his legs spread apart for balance, and if he did not single track he would rock back and forth from side to side, which is inefficient in a trotting dog.

Temperament—Temperament is stable and outgoing, yet dignified. Shyness is a major fault.

Temperament is a most important feature. The dog should be self-assured and not intimidated by his surroundings; he should willingly submit to being handled by strangers. It must be assumed that the dog has been properly socialized so it is not correct to make allowances for shyness, as shyness is often associated with other temperament faults such as fear biting.

Scale of Points

General appearance 5
Size, proportion, substance 10
Head 10
Neck, topline, body 10
Forequarters 5
Hindquarters 5
Feet 5
Coat 5
Color and markings 25
Gait 10
Temperament 10
Total 100

The scale of points is included as a guide to the relative importance of each component of the standard.

Disqualifications

Any dog or bitch over 24 inches at the withers.

Overshot or undershot bites.

Any color markings other than black or liver.

Tri-color.

Patches.

Approved by the American Kennel Club July 11, 1989.

Effective Speptember 6, 1989.

Am-Can. Ch. Godin's To Be Or Not To Be doing a down-and-back pattern in the breed ring. Owned by Pauline and Helene Masaschi.

Illustrations of the Dalmatian Standard

1. A pleasingly spotted Dalmatian, very slightly longer than tall, with heavy bone and a proper body type with moderate tuck-up. He has a pleasing head, a moderately long well-arched neck set smoothly into his shoulders, a level back with correct tail set, and well-laid-back shoulders with his front correctly set under his shoulders. He displays moderate bend of stifle, short hocks, a slight angle to his pasterns, and good legs and feet.

2. This dog shows entirely too much throat skin.

3. This dog is ewe-necked. Compare it to the neck called for by the standard. Ewe necks often go along with straight shoulders and restricted gaits.

136

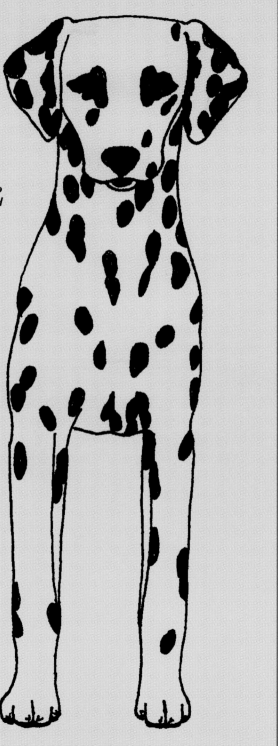

4. This dog shows legs that are straight, strong, and sturdy in bone. He has proper forechest (no hollow between his front legs) and his elbows are close to the body.

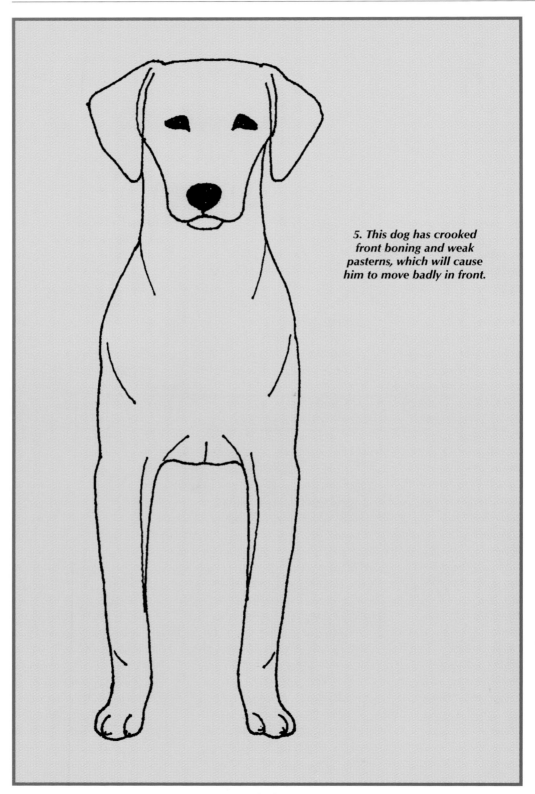

5. This dog has crooked front boning and weak pasterns, which will cause him to move badly in front.

6. *This dog is standing out at the elbows and is toeing in, which will also cause incorrect front movement.*

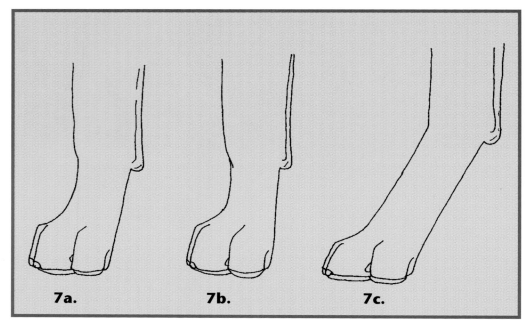

7a. *This correct pastern is slightly angled to act as a shock-absorber when the dog trots. 7b. This pastern is too straight and is usually found in conjunction with an excessively straight shoulder, causing the dog to move with short choppy strides. 7c. This pastern is too long as well as excessively angled. The dog will probably stand with his feet turning out and display sloppy front movement.*

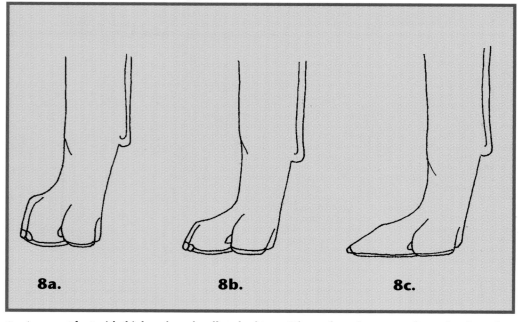

8a. *A correct foot with thick pads and well-arched toes. Often referred to as a cat foot. 8b. A hare foot, which is not round and compact and has less arch to the toes. The two center toes are appreciably longer than the outside toes. 8c. This is a flat foot, sometimes referred to as a paper foot. There is little arch and the toes are long and splayed. These feet would not hold up and are totally incorrect for a dog who has to trot for long distances.*

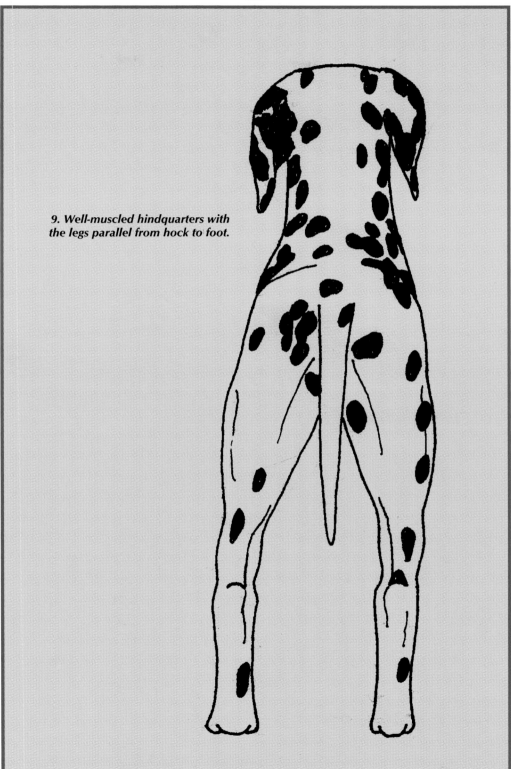

9. Well-muscled hindquarters with the legs parallel from hock to foot.

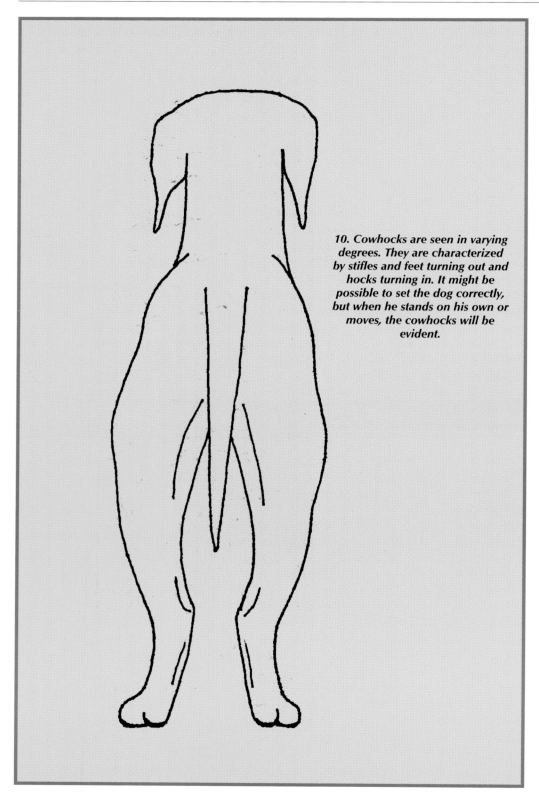

10. Cowhocks are seen in varying degrees. They are characterized by stifles and feet turning out and hocks turning in. It might be possible to set the dog correctly, but when he stands on his own or moves, the cowhocks will be evident.

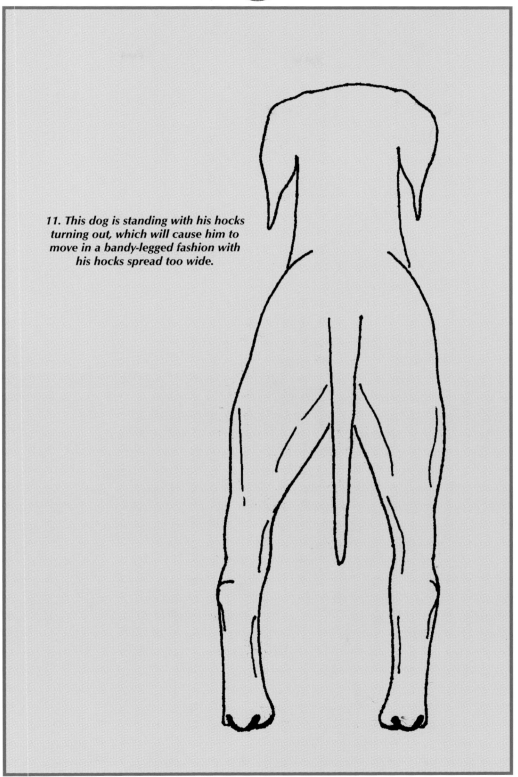

11. This dog is standing with his hocks turning out, which will cause him to move in a bandy-legged fashion with his hocks spread too wide.

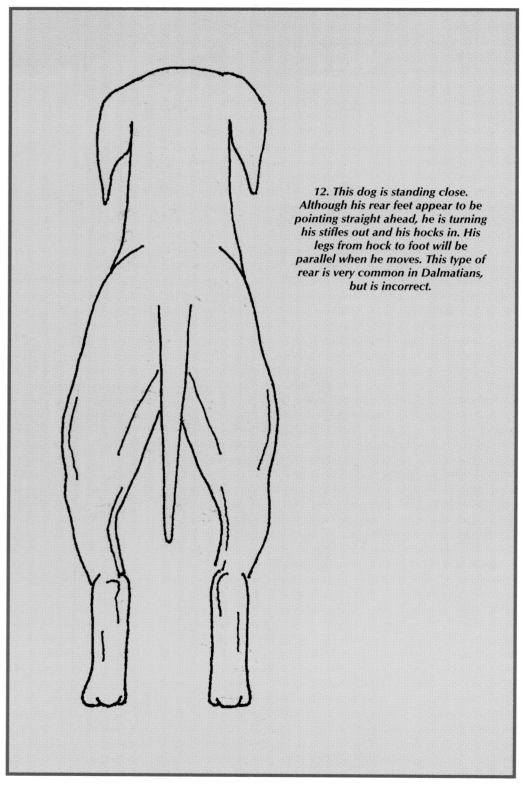

12. This dog is standing close. Although his rear feet appear to be pointing straight ahead, he is turning his stifles out and his hocks in. His legs from hock to foot will be parallel when he moves. This type of rear is very common in Dalmatians, but is incorrect.

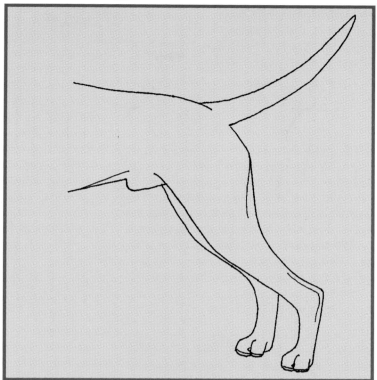

13. This rear is excessively angulated and would be considered "sickle hocked" as his angle at the hock is greater than 90 degrees and he will be unable to flex and straighten it when he moves. Excessively angulated dogs tend to stand cowhocked. They have more angle in the rear than in the shoulder, and this lack of balanced angulation can cause a variety of movement faults.

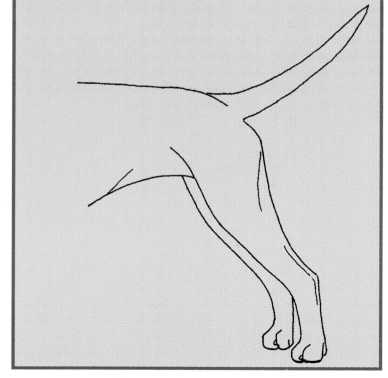

14. This dog is too straight stifled. His rear movement will be restricted and he will move with short choppy steps.

DALMATIAN TYPE

Type is the essence of a breed, the combination of characteristics detailed in each individual breed's standard that describes the picture of the ideal representative of the breed. Type enables the observer to instantly recognize and identify a dog as a member of a specific breed. The standard is considered a blueprint and defines the correct "look," personality, and construction for the breed, while providing breeders and judges with a basis for evaluating individual dogs. The Dalmatian standard attempts to describe a dog that should be able to perform a certain function; a dog that is agile, sound, and has great stamina, a dog that can follow a carriage or a horse for many miles a day.

A perfectly spotted dog who moves poorly is no more correct than a wonderfully sound dog who is very badly spotted. Both markings and soundness are essential parts of correct Dalmatian type and one must not be over-emphasized at the expense of the other. Correct temperament is also an important part of type, and a beautifully spotted dog who moves well but is extremely aggressive or shy does not display the personality and attitude called for in the standard.

No two people will interpret the standard in exactly the same way, and just reading the standard will not give the reader a feel for what an ideal specimen of the breed should look like. A feeling for type is best developed by observing superior specimens of the breed. Although the top-quality dogs will show a good deal of variation, they tend to embody the features that are important in the breed.

The Dalmatian standard assigns a total of 100 points to various aspects of the dog. Twenty-five percent of the points, or 25 points, are allotted for color and markings, making this one of the most important features of the breed and one that identifies the Dalmatian and sets it apart from other breeds. Yet if you subtract 25 from 100, that leaves 75 points that refer to features other than spotting. Remove another 10 points for temperament and 5 points for the coat, and the remaining 60 points deal directly with construction. Those physical features are related to size, proportion, and locomotion, so the standard actually emphasizes performance over spots. However, without his spots, the Dalmatian loses that part of his type that makes him distinctly a Dalmatian.

The following silhouettes are of recent top-winning Dalmatians. All are champions and Top 10 winners, and most are Specialty Best of Breed and Best in Show winners as well. There are dogs of both sexes and both colors, and all of them have satisfactory markings. Some are no taller than 21 inches, while others are closer to 24 inches.

Note the variations in outline among the silhouettes. Some of the dogs look just a bit like pointers, while others more closely resemble retrievers in outline. Without the characteristic spots to identify them, some are not easily recognizable as Dalmatians. Note the difference in neck length, leg length, and overall proportions. Some of the dogs are only moderately angulated, while others have a great deal more. Note that some of the front assemblies are set well under the dogs, while others are not at all. Toplines vary as well, with some being level with relatively flat croups, while others have more arch over the loin and steeper croups. Tailsets vary accordingly and if we were to see the dogs in action, tail carriage would vary as well.

While none of these dogs would be considered *perfect*, they are all quality dogs and satisfactory representatives of the breed. They vary a great deal in outline, and spotting would make some of them more easily recognizable as Dalmatians.

Illustrations of Dalmatian Type

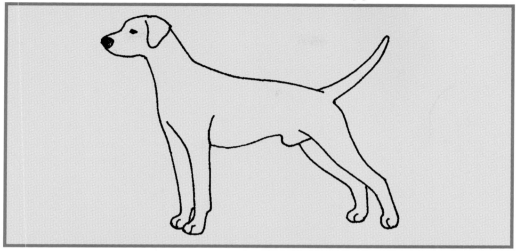

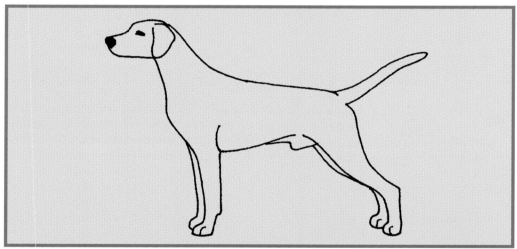

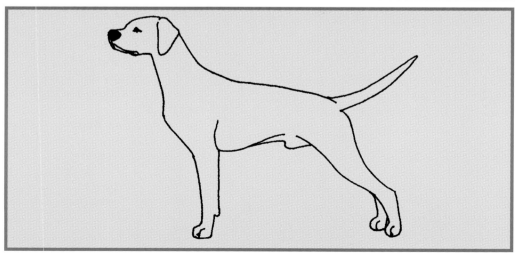

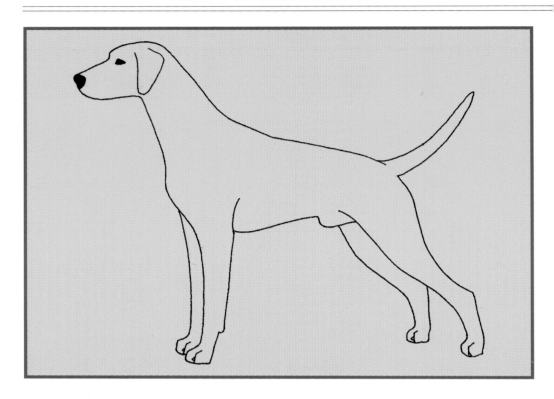

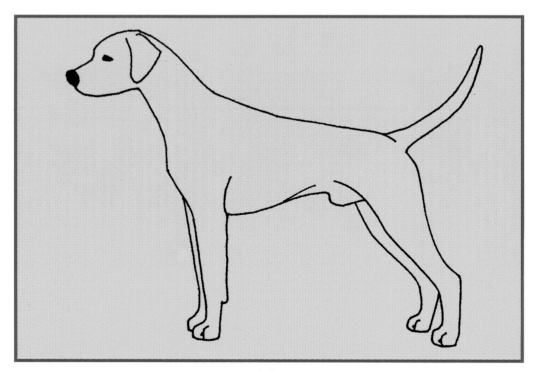

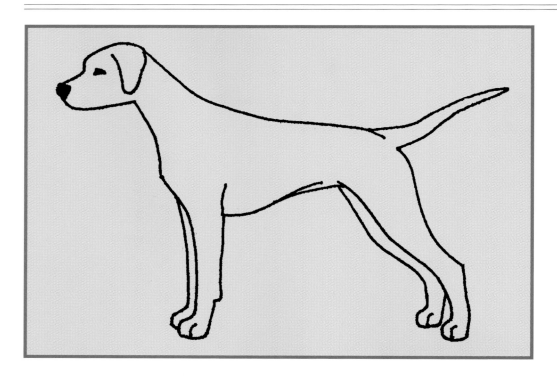

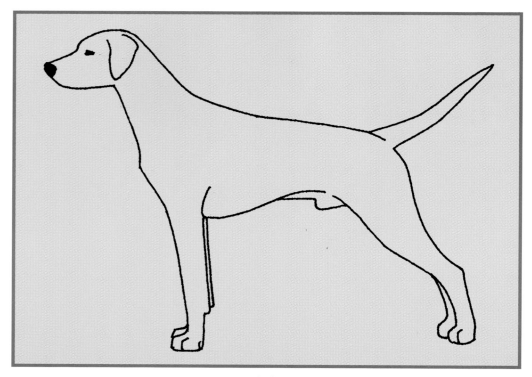

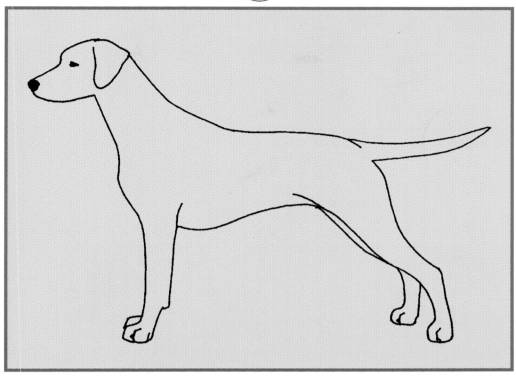

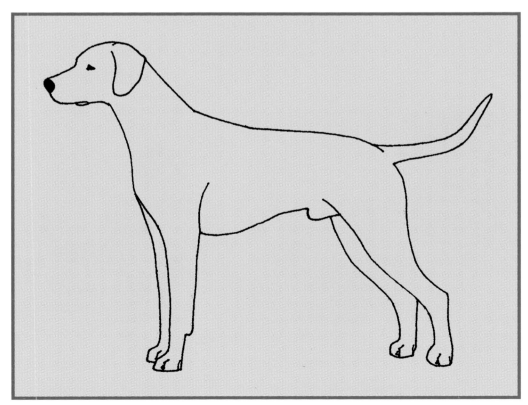

151

DALMATIAN GAIT

The standard reads, "In keeping with the Dalmatian's historical use as a coach dog, gait and endurance are of great importance. Movement is steady and effortless. Balanced angulation fore and aft combined with powerful muscles and good condition produce smooth, efficient action. There is a powerful drive from the rear coordinated with extended reach in the front. The topline remains level. Elbows, hocks and feet turn neither in nor out. As the speed of the trot increases, there is a tendency to single track."

Above: Bill and Cricket on the go! This photo was shot by Meg Callea in the Best in Show ring—and Cricket ended up going BIS. Owned by Kathryn Blink. Below: Ch. St. Florian Pisces Jordache doing what a Dalmatian was bred to do. Owned by Linda Fish and Dawn Mauel.

Illustrations of Dalmatian Gait

15. This shows a Dalmatian trotting with extended reach, powerful drive, and a level topline. Note that the front and rear movement is balanced with full extension of both the left front and rear legs, which are a similar distance above the ground. The right front foot and pastern move up and out of the way a fraction of a second before the right rear foot reaches its fullest forward extension. The Dalmatian should move with a level topline; the downhill sloping topline popular in some sporting breeds is not correct for the Dalmatian nor is the "running downhill" look of a too high rear. Note the head carriage. Trotting dogs do not move with a higher head carriage as that causes them to bring their fronts up, therefore shortening their strides.

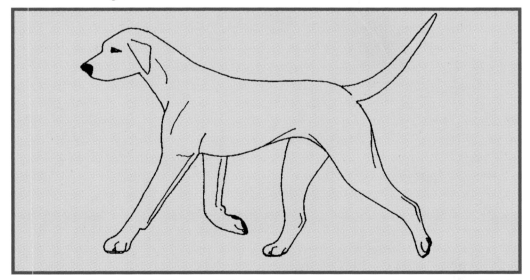

16. Compare this gait to #15. Note the limited forward reach and minimal rear extension. This dog may be lacking angulation on both ends, or if he is only straight stifled (lacking rear angulation) he may be shortening his reach so that front and rear are in balance. It is very important that the angulation in both the front and the rear be balanced. Dogs with straight shoulders and well-angulated rears may use their rearing muscles (which run from the point of the pelvis to the lower thigh) to lift their fronts and suspend the forward-most front foot a fraction of a second longer in an effort to increase reach to match rear drive.

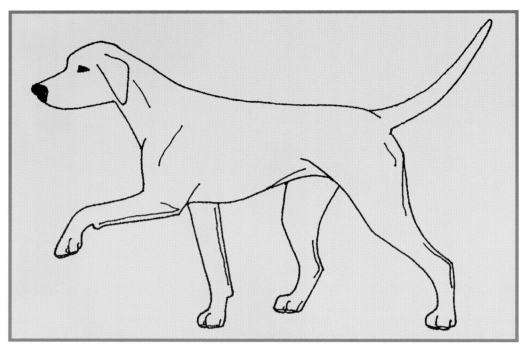

17. This dog is moving with a hackney action. Although it can be very flashy, the extra lift of the foreleg wastes energy and limits reach. Note that the front and rear action do not match.

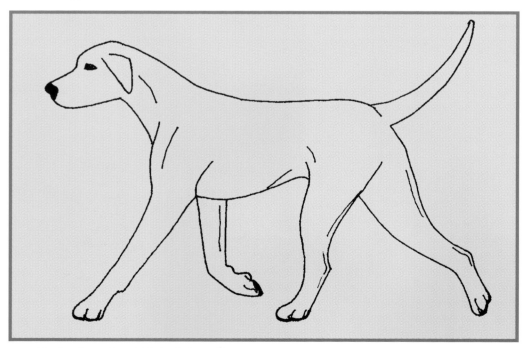

18. This dog is pacing, with both legs on the same side moving forward at the same time. This is commonly seen on young dogs or those with excessively long legs. It's an easy gait for the dog because proper foot timing is not required and the front and rear legs do not interfere. It's not correct, and the pacing dog usually rocks from side to side (like a camel) when he moves.

19. *This dog is showing correct front movement and is "single tracking." His front legs are converging along a center line. How much he will converge will depend on his speed, and a dog at a slow trot or in a small ring may only show a tendency to single track with his legs beginning to converge along a center line. The leg is in a straight line from elbow to foot, and his front feet are not crossing. The dog in picture #4 will presumably move this way.*

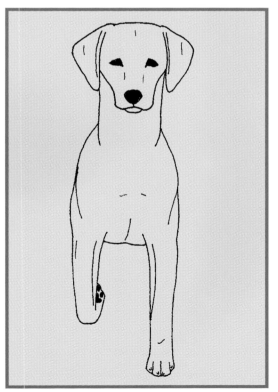

20. *This dog is making no attempt to single track and is tracking parallel instead. He will be rocking from side to side as he moves, wasting energy and reducing efficiency. His shoulders are probably set on incorrectly, or his rib cage may be too round in the area where the shoulders are attached.*

155

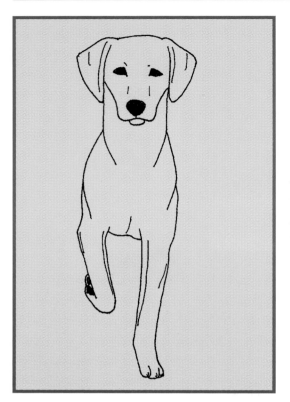

21. This is the dog with the crooked boning and weak pasterns pictured in #5. Note that his legs do not show the straight column of support necessary for correct movement.

22. This is the dog pictured in #6. As he moves, he swings his elbows out and his feet in. Notice that he is toeing in as he moves. This is not correct single tracking either, as the leg should be in one straight line from shoulder to foot.

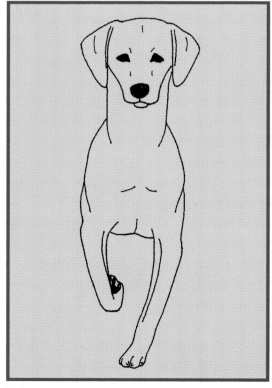

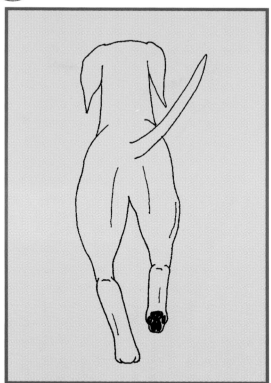

23. This is the dog pictured in #9. This movement is correct and he is single tracking. The leg is in a straight line from hip to foot, and the feet are converging along the center line and are not crossing. Again, the degree of single tracking will depend on a variety of factors, but the dog must show a tendency to single track as he moves away.

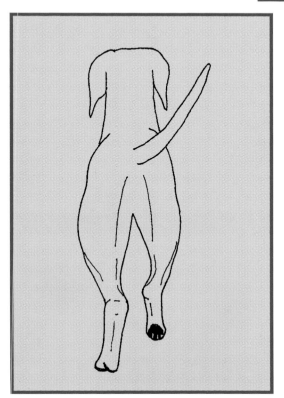

24. This is dog #10 moving cowhocked. He is swinging his stifles and feet out and turning his hocks in. This is a common and easily recognized movement fault.

157

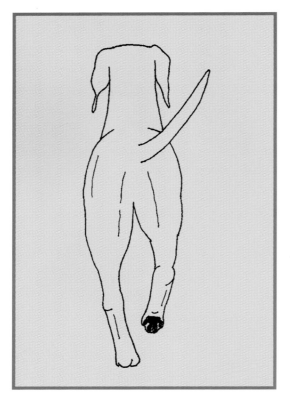

25. This is dog #11 moving wide in the rear, with his hocks turning out and his feet turning in. This is often not recognized as a movement fault and the casual observer may think this is exceptional movement. It is not correct, but is certainly preferable to dog #24.

26. This dog is moving close and is the dog pictured as #12. It should not be confused with cowhocks because the dog is not actually turning his hocks in as he moves. Rather than correct movement with the straight line of support from hip to foot, this dog shows one line from hip to hock, and a second (parallel) line from hock to foot. This type of rear movement, though incorrect, is extremely common in Dalmatians.

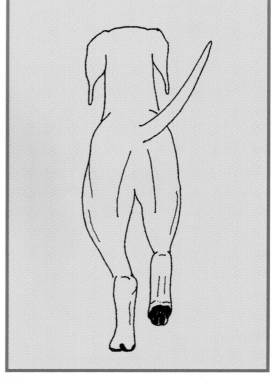

COAT AND COLOR

Although the Dalmatian is traditionally thought of as a black and white dog, liver-spotted dogs are neither rare nor unique and even the earliest texts refer to liver Dals. Also regularly mentioned in old books were black dogs with liver or tan on their faces and/or legs. An occasional reference was made to "blue" Dalmatians, but surprisingly little was said about lemon or yellow dogs. Eleanor Frankling suggests that crosses to English Pointers near the end of the last

Lemon-spotted puppy at seven weeks. Note the black nose, the black eyerims, and the faint color on the ears.

century may explain the appearance of lemons, while correspondence from the 1930s indicates that lemon may have been considered "faded liver."

While black and liver are by far the most common colors and the only ones allowed by the Dalmatian breed standard, a number of other colors and variations occur in the breed. Lemon-spotted dogs with either black or liver noses are by no means rare and appear regularly in some lines. Tri-colored dogs (they are actually bi-colored) can show up as either black or liver dogs with tan markings in the areas that are tan in breeds such as the Doberman. An interesting color

variation is the tri-colored dog with brindled markings in the tan areas. An occasional Dal is seen with brindling in all of its spots, and several Dals have been reported as being yellow or tan spotted with black hairs in some of the spots—possibly sables.

Several other color variations can show up unexpectedly and cause great concern. Black dogs are occasionally seen with one or more brownish spots, while liver dogs may show similar orange spotting. These odd spots are not in a uniform pattern such as that displayed by a tri-color, but may appear anywhere on the dog, either individually or in groups. Additionally, black-spotted dogs are seen with very faint shadowy brownish markings, usually on the insides of the forelegs, but occasionally down the front of the neck or on the head. Some of these color variations may be seen only in bright sunlight, at certain times of the year, or just before the dog sheds out an old coat. Liver dogs may show a slightly lighter shade of color in those same areas, or may be a darker shade of liver down the center of the back, especially when carrying an old coat. The ears on liver dogs are often a lighter shade than the body coat, and the dog may appear to have both black and brown spots. Like other liver breeds, some Dals sun-fade and show an uneven coloration.

Since any color other than black or liver is unacceptable according to the Dalmatian standard, there is a definite stigma attached to unusual coloration. Therefore, little re-

159

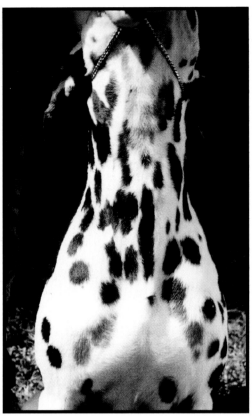

Close-up view of a black tri-colored Dalmatian. Tri-colors have tan spots in all the same areas as Dobermans (above each eye; on the muzzle, throat, and forechest; on all legs and feet; and below tail).

search has been done to explain the less commonly seen colors. While, in many breeds, variations in color are quite acceptable and new colors are greeted with enthusiasm, this is certainly not the case with Dalmatians. This chapter will attempt to explain the inheritance of the basic colors, as well as suggest possible explanations for some of the less common color variations.

The Basics of Color Inheritance

All cells in a living organism have a nucleus, and each nucleus contains chromosomes arranged in pairs. Dogs have 78 chromosomes arranged in 39 pairs, and each pair consists of one chromosome inherited from the sire and one chromosome inherited from the dam. The chromosomes

are made up of tightly coiled strands of DNA, and genes are segments of that DNA. It is easier to think in terms of the chromosomes as being strings of beads, with the genes being the individual beads on the string. Each chromosome pair (except for the sex chromosomes) also has paired genes, but although the gene pairs may occupy similar positions on the chromosomes, they may not be identical. Some genes have alternative forms of expression called *alleles*. A dog that is *homozygous* has two identical genes for a specific trait, while one that is *heterozygous* will have two different alleles of that gene. One of the alleles will be dominant and will have visible effects, while the other is recessive and will have no visible effects. The alleles are normally listed in descending order, with the most dominant allele in a series being capitalized. A dog's *phenotype* is what he appears to be, while his *genotype* is his actual genetic makeup.

Close-up view of a liver tri-color. Notice the tan spotting on the front legs and face.

Above and below: Close-ups of a tri-colored brindle Dalmatian. Note the black hair among the tan spotting.

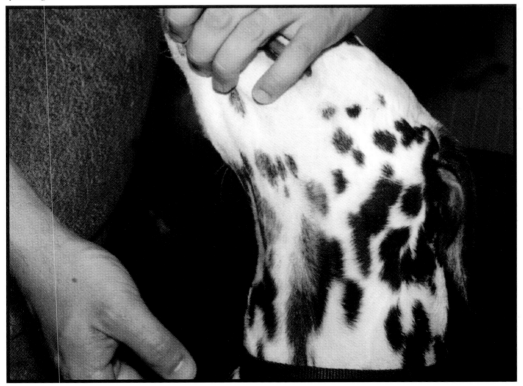

Brindle Dizzy cuddles up with her traditional black-and-white friend Sutphen.

Some genes at one locus have the ability to mask or cover up the influence of genes at another locus and are said to be *epistatic*. While dominance applies to gene pairs, epistasis applies to the reaction between different gene pairs. Other genes have very little individual influence, but in sufficient numbers can affect a main gene pair. These are known as modifying polygenes or *modifiers*. The amount of modification depends on the numbers of polygenes involved. Modifiers probably explain the obvious variations in some colors, such as liver.

There are a large number of gene pairs involved in the inheritance of coat color, but we will only discuss the ones that actually affect Dalmatians and are present in two or more allelic forms. The other genes will be present but only in one form, so the effect is always the same. Since color genetics is based on theory, the accumulated results from experimental breedings and survey results from breeders and geneticists do not always agree, nor do they all use the same lettering system to identify the genes involved. However, it is generally accepted that the basic theories apply to all breeds of dog.

B Series—This is the series that most affects Dalmatian breeders. There are only two alleles here, B which is dominant black, and b which is recessive liver. Black dogs always have black noses and black skin pigment, while liver dogs always have brown noses and brown skin pigment. The recessive b gene also affects eye color, so liver Dals normally have lighter colored eyes.

A dog that is BB is said to be "pure for black" and will never produce liver offspring no matter how he is bred. A dog that is Bb carries one black gene and one liver gene, and since black is dominant, this dog will always be black spotted. However, he will pass the liver gene on to half of his offspring, and is said to be "liver factored." A dog that is bb carries no genes for black, two genes for liver, and will never be black. He can only pass on liver genes to his offspring.

Remember that each of the dog's gene pairs (except for genes on the sex chromosomes) is made up of one gene from the sire and one gene from the dam. When a BB (pure for black) dog is bred to a Bb dog (liver-factored black), the BB dog can only contribute a B gene while the Bb dog can contribute either gene. Since none of the pups will get two b genes, none of them will be liver.

When a Bb dog is bred to another Bb dog, one-fourth of the offspring will get two B genes and be dominant black (BB), one-half of the offspring will get one of each gene and be liver-factored blacks (Bb), and one-fourth of the offspring will receive two b genes and be recessive liver (bb).

	B	b
B	**BB** (Black-pure)	**Bb** (Liver-factored)
b	**Bb** (Liver-factored)	**bb** (Liver)

When a Bb dog is bred to a bb dog, one-half of the offspring will get a B gene from one parent and a b gene from the other parent and be liver-factored blacks (Bb), while the other half will receive a b gene from each parent and will be liver (bb).

	B	b
b	**Bb** (Liver-factored)	**bb** (Liver)
b	**Bb** (Liver-factored)	**bb** (Liver)

163

There is no such thing as a dog who is "strong for liver," although that phrase is often heard. A dog is either pure for black, liver factored, or liver. A dominant homozygous black dog will *never* produce liver, while a liver or liver-factored dog will only produce liver when bred to another dog carrying the liver gene.

Color is not sex linked so it does not matter which of the parents have which color genes. Also remember that these numbers only work out over a large number of litters. Breeding a liver to a black and getting only black pups does not necessarily mean that the black dog is not liver factored. A repeat breeding might very well produce a liver pup. If a dog has a liver parent, it is *always* liver factored; but if both parents are blacks, you will not know whether the dog is liver factored until it produces a liver puppy.

There have been reports of two liver dogs producing all black litters, but color geneticists tend to discard those stories and assume that a mis-mating took place. There appears to be only one gene which produces liver (as opposed to several combinations which can produce yellow) and in hundreds of test breedings in a variety of breeds, liver has always functioned as a simple recessive.

E Series—This series also affects the Dalmatian because it is responsible for lemon Dalmatians. This gene determines where (or if) dark color (black or liver) will appear in the coat. The members of the series are E^{br} (dominant brindle), E (normal extension of dark hair), and e (absence of dark hair). This series is epistatic to the B series, which means it can affect the normal black or liver coloration. Dogs that carry EE and Ee allow for normal distribution of black (or liver), since E is dominant to e. However, if the Dalmatian carries ee it will be lemon spotted since recessive ee means that the dog can not have black (or liver) hair. Therefore a dog whose makeup is BBee or Bbee will be lemon with black nose and skin pigment, while a dog that is bbee will be lemon with a liver nose and skin pigment. The presence

A black-and-white dog introduces himself to a lemon.

Full view of an adult lemon-spotted Dalmatian.

of ee does not affect the skin pigment, only the hair color.

In the Pointer, dogs are divided into "lemons" and "oranges" based on the shade of yellow and the color of the nose, but it is much easier to refer to them as "black-nosed lemons" and "liver-nosed lemons." Lemon coloring may vary from a pale tan color to a rich bright orange. The brightly colored lemons can be rather attractive, but the pale dogs have a faded, washed-out appearance.

The E^{br} allele also affects Dalmatians and will be discussed further on in this text.

A Series—Also called the Agouti series, it contains some interesting color variations, though not all authorities are in agreement as to the hierarchy or even the existence of some of the alleles. The probable members of this series include A^s (which allows dark pigment over the entire body),

A^y (sable or tan, but not the same as ee yellow), A (agouti, and not present in the Dalmatian), and a^t (tan point pattern). Some authorities also recognize a^s, a saddle pattern where the black area is reduced and the tan area is extended, while others feel that brindle is actually part of the A series rather than the E series. We are basically concerned with A^s and a^t as this is the source of what we refer to as tri-colors.

Most Dalmatians are A^sA^s, which allows for the presence of black or liver hair in appropriate areas. A Dalmatian which was A^sa^t would probably appear normal as well, while a Dal that was a^ta^t would always have tan points, i.e., be a tri-color. If the dog was a^ta^tBB or a^ta^tBb, he would be a black-spotted dog except that any spots over the eyes, on the cheeks, inside the front legs, and down the chest would be tan. If the dog was a^ta^tbb, it would be a liver-spotted dog with

165

tan spotting in the appropriate places. It would also be less obviously a tri-color because of the variations of shading in both the liver and the tan coloration. Since a^t is recessive to the normal A^s, two tri-colored dogs bred together would only produce more tri-colors. Whether they were black tri-colors or liver tri-colors would depend on whether they were BB, Bb, or bb dogs. Also, if the dogs carried ee they would just be lemon dogs because the E series is epistatic to the A series and will mask the a^t. There is

sions of Dal standards referred to these "blue" spotted Dals as an acceptable, but not preferred, color.

S Series—The white spotting series contains S (any solid color other than white), s^i (Irish spotting such as the dogs with white chest and feet), s^p (piebald, which refers to basically white dogs with large areas of color), and s^w "extreme white piebald" (which is pure white except for possible areas of color on the head and ears or at the base of the tail). Dalmatians are all $s^w s^w$, which is not

Eight-week-old pups showing a variety of patches. These five patched pups came from a litter of eight.

some question as to whether A^s is completely dominant to a^t, which could explain some of the shadowy markings seen in the tan-point areas on otherwise normal-colored Dalmatians.

D Series—While Dal spotting is usually intense black or liver, there have been rare occasions where Dals have been observed that give the appearance of being dusty, dull, or faded. These Dals probably are homozygous for the recessive dilution gene d. Most Dals will carry the dominant intense pigmentation gene D, but some early ver-

always expressed as a completely white base color and therefore explains the presence of patches. Such areas of color are typical of s^w dogs. Since s^w is lowest in hierarchy in this series, most Dal crosses are solid-colored dogs or colored dogs with white feet and chest.

T Series—Dal spotting is considered to be a specialized form of ticking, and all Dals are TT, with the possible addition of ff (absence of flecking), which makes the spots uniform in size with an absence of white hairs within the spot itself. Considering the variations seen in spotting, perhaps not all Dalmatians are ff.

By way of review, some of the possible genetic color combinations include:

A^{s}A^{s}BBEEs^{w}s^{w}TTff—dominant black with normal spotting

A^{s}A^{s}bbEEs^{w}s^{w}TTff—recessive liver with normal spotting

A^{s}A^{s}Bbees^{w}s^{w}TTff—black nose, liver-factored, lemon-spotted

A^{s}a^{t}BbEes^{w}s^{w}TTff—tri-factored, liver-factored, lemon-factored dog who appears to be a normal black-spotted Dalmatian

a^{t}a^{t}BbEEs^{w}s^{w}TTff—tri-colored, liver-factored, black dog

a^{t}a^{t}bbEEs^{w}s^{w}TTff—tri-colored, liver-spotted dog

a^{t}a^{t}bbees^{w}s^{w}TTff—lemon dog with brown nose (Remember that the ee will cover the fact that the dog is tri-colored.)

If an a^{t}a^{t}bbee dog is bred to a A^{s}A^{s}BBEE dog, the offspring would all appear to be normal black-spotted Dalmatians, but they would be capable of producing tri-colors, livers, and lemons.

The E series apparently contains the dominant allele E^{br}, which allows brindling (stripe-like markings as seen in brindled Boxers and Great Danes) to appear on light-colored hair. It does not show through the normal black or liver spots, but does show through in the tan areas of a tri-colored dog, and tri-colors with brindled markings may actually be more common than tri-colors with clear tan markings. A brindled tri-color might be a^{t}a^{t}BBE^{br}E^{br}.

There are occasional Dals with completely brindled spotting, but this can not be explained as a lemon with brindling since E^{br} and e are both part of the E series and E^{br} is thought to be dominant to e. It may be that A^y also exists in Dalmatians. An A^{y}A^y dog could look similar to an ee lemon, although it might show an overlay of black hairs (explaining the sable which has been observed). An A^{y}A^y dog that was also carrying E^{br} might appear to be a distinctly brindled dog since E^{br} is epistatic to A^y and the brindling will show through, even though it can not show through the dark coat of an A^s

dog. A possible makeup would be A^{y}A^{y}BBE^{br}E^{br}, but no research has yet been done on this.

The presence of A^y might also explain some of the black-spotted dogs who show brownish shading on the insides of their legs. It has been suggested that such dogs might be A^{s}A^y. Another explanation of the

Dizzy the brindle and her owner.

167

shaded dogs is that A^{s}A^s by itself is not really a pure shiny black, but rather black with a reddish tinge to it. Selective breeding has introduced modifying polygenes that may not always be present. Some of the British Dalmatian correspondence from the 1930s mentions "rusty blacks." There has also been some reference to "bronzing" (not to be confused with the bronzing syndrome) where the black hairs take on a rusty look. However, the latter may just be color changes in an old coat before it sheds.

There are also dogs referred to as "mosaics" who are black or liver dogs with one or more off-colored spots, either brownish spots on a black dog or yellowish spots on a liver dog. They seem to appear randomly within the breed, and no one has come up with an adequate explanation although such spots could result from a somatic mutation affecting only a localized area. Such dogs do not seem to reproduce these problems, but one must always use great caution when using a Dalmatian with anything other than "typical" coloration in a breeding program.

Variations in Coat Color and Spotting

The modifiers mentioned previously are probably responsible for some of the variations seen in Dalmatian spotting. On black dogs the spotting ranges from huge brilliant jet black spots with crisp edges and no ticking all the way to small ragged markings that are little more than ticking. Coat type varies too, with the brilliantly colored dogs normally having softer shinier coats, and the raggedly marked dogs tending to have harsher coats. Although it is typical to see a large variation in the amount of color within a litter, it is possible to select for both spotting style and coat type, and spotting must always be considered when planning a breeding.

Ticking—The terms "ticking" and "second spotting" are used interchangeably and refer to the small spots that are often mixed in with the normal Dalmatian spotting. Most Dalmatian puppies have all of their normal size spots by four to six weeks of age, and spots that show up after that time do not become full-sized spots. Rolling a coat on an eight-week-old pup will show small skin spots that may come through as ticking. Ticking is not desirable, but when it shows up in an blank area it helps to even out the spotting pattern. Excessive ticking often goes along with ragged spotting or uneven spot size, and these can be difficult to eliminate in a breeding program.

A Dalmatian's skin pigment continues to spread for the dog's lifetime, which is why young dogs with missing eye or nose trim may eventually have complete trim. The colored hair of the spots grows from pigmented areas of the skin and a Dalmatian that is shaved down will still be a spotted dog. As the dog ages, the areas of skin spotting grow and small spots of skin color may begin to appear. When the dog is bathed, the additional skin color is quite readily visible. On some dogs, colored hair will grow from the newly pigmented areas, and the dog will get fuzzy edges to his spots and small flecks of color throughout his coat. Pigment seems to spread less on liver dogs and although they do not normally get the old age ticking, they do show a tendency to become increasingly gray on their faces and limbs.

Frosting—Frosting refers to white hairs mixed into the colored spots, and there are several types of frosting. Young pups sometimes have a fuzzy look to their spots because of an overlay of longer white hair. This often sheds out at about six weeks of age, leaving shiny clear spots. Other pups will have clear crisp spotting at the beginning, but develop fuzzy spot edges at seven to eight weeks when their spots start to grow quickly or "bloom." This often clears out in a few weeks but may last until the puppy coat is shed. Other pups have white hairs mixed in with their spots right from the beginning. These will normally shed out by the time the dog is an adult, but some dogs will always be frosty. In general, the dogs with crisp spots and deep color contrast will clear, while the dogs with more ragged spotting and less color contrast will remain frosty. These characteristics vary from line to line, but are all inherited features. Older dogs who were once clearly spotted may begin to look frosty as they develop fuzzy spot edges or turn gray as they age.

Liver Dalmatians—Liver color and markings have improved a great deal in recent years, and liver Dals are now often spotted as well as the best black-spotted dogs. With the increased interest in showing livers and the fact that a number of popular and widely used stud dogs are liver factored, this trend seems destined to continue.

Liver appears to come in three distinct shades and most dogs fit into one of these three categories. The modifiers appear to affect the size, shape, color, contrast, clarity, and pattern of the spotting, and perhaps even have some effect on the texture as well as the white background. Little actual research has been done, but accumulated observations have indicated some distinct and readily discernible tendencies.

Chocolate livers are dark chocolate brown. They tend to have all-over spotting patterns with dark chocolate noses, considerable face color, heavily spotted ears, and

Bleeding or spreading of the skin color is often seen in middle-aged and older Dals. It is first noticeable on the face at about six years of age, then it starts to show on the body. While liver Dals may gray as they age, blacks often show more pigment.

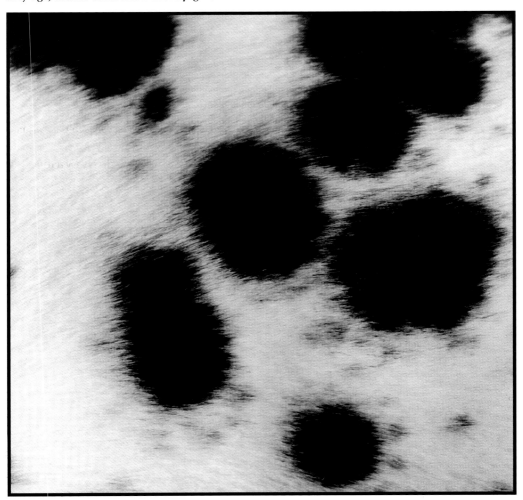

spotting all the way down to their toes. They usually have smaller spotting size and are born with complete eye and nose trim. Most have "liver patterns," which are recognizable even in black and white photos. Chocolate livers have brilliant white coats and do not normally fade in the sun, but they are sometimes questioned by show judges because their coats look almost black, particularly in bad lighting.

Red livers vary from an orangey color all the way to deep red and are characterized by their distinctly red-brown noses. They tend to have large, round, clear spots, little ticking, open-marked faces and ears, and minimal spotting on their legs. They tend to fade in the sun, often have a pale cream tinge to the coat color, and are more likely to be born with missing eye and nose trim. Red livers often show areas of orangey red on their muzzles, down the fronts of their necks, and on the insides of their legs, and their ears may be quite a bit lighter in color than their body spots. Well-marked red livers

rival the best black-spotted dogs for perfect spotting patterns and do not look "livery" in photos.

Brown livers are distinctly brown. They are not as intensely colored as chocolate dogs and lack the red highlights seen in reds. They are more likely to have somewhat ragged spotting, often have ticking, normally have complete trim, and usually do not have the crisp color contrast seen in chocolates or reds. They fade less than reds, but when they are out of coat they may show many different shades of brown. Brown livers can be well marked, but many tend to have an "antique" look to their spotting.

All three types of liver may appear in the same litters, just as there can be a variation in black spotting within a litter. However, the same modifiers seem to act on both blacks and livers, and jet black liver-factored dogs with large spots are the most likely to produce red livers, while black liver-factored dogs with less depth of color and contrast are far more likely to produce brown livers.

Am-Can. Ch. Paisley N Tucks Eureka is a chocolate liver. "Eloise" has two specialty majors, multiple Group placings, and a 1992 DCA Award of Merit. She is also a top producer.

Above: Am-Can. Ch. Paisleys Pointblank is a red liver. "Morris" is the only liver male to have won three BIS. He also has 6 specialty BOB and over 60 Group placings. Breeder-owner-handled by Sue MacMillan. Below: Paisleys Peachy Keen, CD is a brown liver. Pointed in the breed ring but a bit small to finish, "Peaches" was a ranked obedience dog as well as a top producer with seven champions.

Variations in Coat Length

Another inherited trait which affects the Dalmatian is coat length. While we think of the Dalmatian as a short-haired breed, that is not always the case. There are long-coated Dalmatians in several American bloodlines, and pictures from the Leakey archaeological expeditions in Africa show at least one long-coated Dalmatian, presumably of English breeding.

The gene L/l is for coat length with short-haired L being dominant. Long hair is a simple recessive and can show up whenever two dogs carrying the recessive l are bred together; it appears in many normally short-haired breeds. Although long coats are not common, the breed does show a wide range of coat length. Some Dals have hair no more than a $^{1}/_{2}$ inch long, while others have hair as long as two inches in length, complete with feathering on the ears, fringe on the legs, and a plume on the tail. Some of the longer coats are soft and fine, while others are coarser in texture. These variations are probably due to modifiers acting on short hair rather than the presence of the gene for long hair. Many young dogs shed out their long hair when they lose their puppy coats, while others gradually grow shorter coats each time they go through a seasonal shed. It seems that the longer-coated dogs also tend to have wavy hair, especially down the back of the neck and over the rump.

Coat Texture

There are many variations in coat texture, ranging from fine soft hairs to thick bristly ones. The standard describes a coat that is "short, dense, fine and close fitting...neither wooly nor silky...sleek, glossy and healthy in appearance." This is a single coated breed—there is no undercoat as is found in terriers and many sporting breeds. The desired Dalmatian coat consists of thickly growing short hairs that lay flat to the skin. They will be nearly impervious to rain, and dirt will remain on the surface of the hairs rather than penetrating to accumulate on the skin. If the coat is too long and soft, the hairs will "fluff" away from the skin and allow dirt and water to penetrate. If too stiff, the hairs will stand up away from the skin with the same results. It has been noted that dogs with thick soft coats seem to have fewer skin and coat problems than those with thinner harder coats. The sleek glossy appearance is the result of good breeding and proper nutrition.

An example of a long-haired Dalmatian.

Characteristics of the Dalmatian

PERSONALITY AND TEMPERAMENT

Before dog breeding evolved into a hobby and sport, it was practiced as a form of animal husbandry, with breeds being developed to serve specific purposes. Breeding pairs were chosen based on their ability to perform the desired breed function, hence certain characteristics became deeply entrenched in certain breeds. Obvious examples would be the herding breeds with their innate ability to round up animals and drive them in a group, or the sporting breeds with their instinctive attraction to birds.

For several centuries, the Dalmatian was selectively bred for and used as a coaching dog. He was medium-sized but sturdy in bone, and his well-developed muscles were covered by a closely fitting dense coat that shed road dirt very well. The work required him to trot at a steady pace mile after mile, thus developing a large capacity for and need to exercise. The coaching Dalmatian was an independent working dog; the coachman had his hands full controlling the team of horses and could not continually call out directions and orders to the Dalmatians accompanying the carriage. The Dal's job occasionally necessitated running ahead of the horses to clear the road of stray dogs threatening the team. It also required him to lie under the carriage and guard the master's possessions should the entourage stop at a roadside inn for a meal or a night's lodging. Once back at the stable, the Dal was expected to provide company for the horses and rid the barn of rodents.

The Dalmatian evolved with an almost boundless amount of energy. He was protective of his territory, excellent at hunting vermin, slightly dog-aggressive, self-reliant, and intelligent, and he had a strong desire to accompany his family wherever they went.

Those attributes suit a coaching dog just fine, but they can wreak havoc in the modern household. Yesteryear's need for a fine working dog has been replaced by today's desire for a suitable companion animal. Therefore, responsible breeders have been re-fashioning the Dal—toning down the extremes and blunting the sharper edges without losing the desirable characteristics that make the Dalmatian so appealing.

Once you understand how its history has shaped this breed, you will realize that those

Ch. All Around's Playin the Banjo checks out a Clydesdale horse. Owned by Jana Rodes.

very attributes so desired in a coaching dog eliminate the Dalmatian as suitable for some situations. Only the most dedicated owner can keep a Dalmatian happy in an apartment or in the small yard so common to a condominium. Structured daily exercise is a must, even for the Dal with a large fenced yard. The breed has a reputation for being hyperactive. While it is true that some Dals exhibit this tendency, it is usually seen as a result of an unstructured, undisciplined lifestyle. Give the Dalmatian a firm set of behavioral guidelines and a regular schedule and you will see the emergence of a happy family pet.

Remember the self-reliant, independent, intelligent coaching dog? His attitude must be shaped from the time he leaves his littermates; constant training is required to turn him into an obedient companion whose

Bret D's Midnight Breeze makes a new friend. Owned by Teresa and Pauline McIntyre and Marie (Debbie) Zink.

Chance of a Lifetime, UDT takes a break. Owned by Pat Mullin.

fine manners allow you to take him with you wherever you go. Slightly dog-aggressive? Obedience classes and outside socializing are the only way to reinforce your desire to turn him into an acceptable member of canine society.

The inherent intelligence of the average Dalmatian can get him into immense amounts of trouble. Most Dal puppy buyers take their new baby home thinking that they have plenty of time before obedience classes become a necessity. Unfortunately, by the time the owners realize their mistake, the puppy has *them* completely trained and at his mercy. If allowed to erupt, the Dal's need to dominate and control his environment will surface. The Dalmatian requires an owner with a take-charge personality who is willing to make rules and then gently but firmly enforce them.

When you first take your Dal puppy to the veterinarian and/or attempt to sign up for

Am-Can. Ch. Country Kate's Mandolin of MGR, CD, TD. Owned by Stan and Karen Larson.

obedience classes, you may hear a groan of dismay and disparaging comments about how unintelligent, unruly, and untrainable this breed is. However, the Dals that vets and trainers see as "unruly" are the ones that haven't received proper training right from the start. Don't despair—your pup can become a remarkably fun member of the family with a little time and effort on your part. Keeping the breed's history in mind, you can shape your Dal's attributes in a positive way that will result in a delightful companion.

The breed's intelligence surfaces in many ways. Dals love interaction with humans, frequently displaying their affection for one and all. Generally not a one-man dog, they are sensitive to the moods of all family members and respond accordingly. Dals are fun-loving and will demonstrate their sense of humor in a variety of ingenious ways, all of which will either amuse you or drive you to distraction.

The guarding instinct that developed in the coaching dog of yesteryear is still a part of the Dal's characteristics today. The breed's natural dominance and possessiveness com-

bine to provide you with a dog that will issue warning barks when his territory is invaded and he feels his family's safety is being threatened. The obedience training you give him enables you to help him understand that you are in charge of the situation and he can relax his vigilance.

THE DALMATIAN'S ABILITIES AND ACTIVITIES

In approximately the last two decades, the American Kennel Club has been putting more emphasis on the performance dog by encouraging clubs to develop and perfect both breed-specific and all-breed performance events. There is now a wide variety of activities within the sport where dogs can compete to win titles bestowed either by the AKC or by the parent clubs of the specific breeds.

Coaching

Most true Dalmatian fanciers can tell you exactly how each of the breed's physical features are described in the AKC standard. The same is no doubt true for fanciers of

Peggy Ann Strupp on Redrock's Moonlight, accompanied by Ch. Harmony of Cheshire T. Redrock, CD, RDX, CGC (foreground) and Bell Ringer's Redrock Puccini, CD, RDX, CGC during the speed exercise at the 1994 DCA Road Trial.

other purebreds. But is you took all of the AKC-recognized purebreds, stripped away their distinctive physical features, and lined them all up, you could still sort out many of the breeds by allowing them to demonstrate their instinctive qualities. Take them all to water and you would quickly find the retrievers. A few sheep would bring the herding breeds out of the pack. Display a rat

fair amount of speed." The specific sections of the breed standard describing size, proportion, and substance; neck, topline, and body; forequarters; hindquarters; feet; gait; and temperament all contain language that contributes to describing an ideal coach dog.

While Dalmatian fanciers can gauge to some extent how closely their dogs com-

Jana Rodes with IC Spots (Appaloosa) and Ch. All Around's Playin the Banjo, demonstrating the one-minute sit.

and you would soon sort out the terriers. Release a few birds and the pointers would be obvious. Introduce a horse and you would soon discover the Dalmatians. Even after nearly 100 years of travel by motor vehicles, the one quality that still sets our breed apart is his inborn affinity for horses. He is still, after all, a coach dog.

The Dalmatian standard describes a dog "capable of great endurance, combined with

pare to the breed standard by exhibiting them in dog shows, the judges' determinations are necessarily limited by the constraints of the size of the show ring. Based on observing dogs gait a few laps around a small ring, judges have to do their best to rate each Dalmatian's relative speed, endurance, and coaching capabilities. Dalmatian road trials, by requiring a Dalmatian to accompany a horse and complete either

12.5 or 25 miles within certain time constraints, allows a fancier to see without question if his dog's conformation holds up to the duty he was intended to serve. As Lois Meistrell, a participant in road trials during the 1940s, wisely pointed out in a letter dated August 20, 1988, "In our trials it was coincidence that some of the dogs entered were champions or of championship quality. It was not, however, coincidental that they placed among the winners. They had the conformation to sustain them."

inheritance of position preference in coach dogs. They presented their findings in an article in the February 1940 issue of the *Journal of Heredity*. They described several accounts of Dalmatians who would run under carriages on their own, and even an account of a two-and-a-half-month-old Dal puppy who would leave his playmates every day to paddle under the wheelbarrow of a lawn worker who passed by the group of puppies. Keeler and Trimble concluded in their study that "the tendency to run under

Jana, IC Spots, and "Banjo" in the Hocking position.

Accounts of Dalmatians performing in their historical role as a coach dog not only are fascinating, they also provide a greater appreciation of the recent revival of the road trial, an exciting opportunity for today's Dal to demonstrate his willingness and natural talent to perform in the same coaching tradition as his ancestors.

Clyde E. Keeler and Harry C. Trimble conducted a study at Harvard about the

a vehicle or to follow a horse is not the only characteristic of this mental trait which is inherited."

They presented data which shows that "Dalmatians differ individually with respect to the precise position which they take in running under a carriage when a choice is permitted." They also concluded that "something connected with these preferences appears to be inherited." Finally, they stated,

"It is possible that 'bad' (furthest away from the horse) coach following may be an expression of general timidity."

H. Fred Lauer, in his 1907 book *The Dalmatian*, explained that a traditional way of training a Dalmatian to coach is to first use a cart so that the dog can get close to the horse and the trainer can talk to and encourage the dog. The dog may not get too close to the horse at first, but will gradually move closer after several weeks. Eventually, when the four-wheeled coach is used, the trainer should not tie the dog to the axle as the dog may pull back and, as a result, get dragged. Such an experience may make him not want to coach again. If the dog does not come close to the horse on his own, the trainer can attach a 20-foot lightweight rope to the dog's collar and run the rope under the cart and up over the dasher. With the trainer holding the rope, the dog should be given slack and the horse should be started walking. As the dog comes closer,

the slack should be taken up. If the dog pulls back, he should be coaxed, not pulled, forward. If a trained dog is available, the trainee can be taken out with him—the trainee will soon go along with the trained dog on his own.

The Dalmatian's coaching ability is a pleasure to behold and has proven to be fun for both handler and dog. Those enthusiasts who so desire can earn coaching titles on their dogs. Currently there are two titles available; the RD (Road Dog) is the first level and the RDX (Road Dog Excellent) is the second level.

Tracking

A tracking dog must follow the scent trail of any person he is commanded to find. Dalmatians are usually superb trackers. They have excellent scenting ability and respond well to the positive methods used in tracking training. You can make a dog do many things, but you cannot force him to use his

All ready to road trial! Jana and IC Spots with eager Dals Brutus, Banjo, Bingo, BJ, and Bullet.

nose. Nearly all Dalmatians are capable of earning the Tracking Dog title, signified by the letters TD after the dog's name. Some Dalmatians have earned that most cherished and difficult title, Tracking Dog Excellent. To earn the TDX title the dog must have good scenting ability, brains, stamina, and most importantly, the willingness to work with his human partner. The new challange of Variable Surface Tracking (VST) is sure to demonstrate the practical value of tracking dog training, and Dalmatians are certain to excel at this test as well as the TD and TDX tests. A dog that earns all three tracking titles—TD, TDX, and VST—will also become an AKC Tracking Champion.

There is no such thing as a bad day tracking. In the tracking field there are no telephones, no sales quotas, no household chores, no cranky children, no unreasonable bosses. The trainer is spending time outdoors with one of his spotted friends. If the tracking training does not go as well as expected, then the handler has the interesting task of figuring out what went wrong and how to remedy the problem.

Tracking is one of the most non-competitive performance events sponsored by the American Kennel Club. Tracking tests at all levels are pass/fail events. There are no scores or placements awarded, and any suggestions to change this are vigorously opposed by the tracking community. In this sport, more than any other, each dog and handler team works in its own style and at its own pace. Every person watching, including the judges, fellow participants, and spectators, knows how many hours and how many miles each team has walked together in preparation for the test, and everyone is pulling for their success.

Dogs and handlers of any age can succeed at tracking. The youngest tracking certified dog of any breed is Ch. Paisley Poppycock, CDX, TD, who was certified to track at the age of 12 weeks. It is also common for elderly dogs and senior handlers to gain tracking dog titles.

The dog works in a harness to which a long tracking line is attached, and the handler holds the tracking line no closer to the dog than 20 feet. There are two judges who

Ch. Paisley Poppycock, CDX, TD as a puppy learning to track. At three months of age, "Poppy" was the youngest dog ever certified to track. Owned and trained by Carolyn Krause.

CHARACTERISTICS

The multi-talented Ch. Forrest Jilia O'Brogan, UDTX, CGC, TT, playing with a tracking article. Owned and trained by P. Karen McDonnell.

follow the dog and handler team. The dog must, in the agreement of both judges, work the track and indicate the article(s) left by the track layer. There is no time limit as long as the dog is judged to be working.

Many know the Dalmatian as a coach dog or firehouse dog but are unaware of the Dal's noble history as a war dog and guide dog for the blind. His bold, flashy appearance and often clownish personality may cause some to dismiss him as a dog without serious working ability. Dalmatians are proving this untrue as they are demonstrating their worth as tracking dogs all over the country.

TD Requirements:

A dog and handler must be certified as ready before being allowed to enter a test.

A TD track is at least 440 yards long and no more than 500 yards long.

A TD track must make at least three but no more than five turns.

A TD track is at least 30 minutes old but not more than 2 hours old.

There will be a flag at the start and a flag 30 yards down the first leg to indicate the direction of the first leg.

There will be one article at the end of the track; it should be a glove or a wallet of inconspicuous color.

TDX Requirements:

A TDX track is at least 800 yards and not more than 1000 yards long and makes at least 5 but not more than 7 turns.

A TDX track must be at least three hours old but not more than five hours old.

A TDX track has a flag at the start but no second flag to indicate direction of the first leg.

A set of two side-by-side cross-tracks will be laid across the TDX track about an hour after the TDX track was walked. These sets of cross tracks will intersect the TDX track in two different places.

There will be at least two obstacles on each TDX track.

There may be gullies, streams, roads, plowed fields, or anything else that challenges the dog's scenting ability.

TDX articles will be four dissimilar personal articles dropped at various places along the track.

VST Requirements:

A VST track is at least 600 but not more than 800 yards long and contains at least 4 but not more than 8 turns including both left and right turns.

A VST track must have a minimum of three different tracking surfaces—tracking on a variety of surfaces such as gravel, asphalt, or concrete is what sets VST tracking apart.

A VST track will have no physical barriers and will not enter buildings.

A VST track must be at least three hours old but not more than six hours old.

The track may be laid along fences and buildings and may be crossed by people, animals, and vehicles.

Four articles are dropped along the track and must be found by the dog.

180

Agility

Very much like a decathlon or steeple-chase, agility is as exciting to watch as it is to participate in. Roughly modeled after equestrian stadium jumping competition, agility competition was developed in England and made its official debut at the Crufts Dog Show in 1979. The exact rules and obstacles vary depending on the sponsoring organization, but in all cases the dogs race through an obstacle course and the dog with the best time wins. For beginners, the challenge is to have their dogs complete the course, but, for enthusiasts, speed and finesse are important considerations. The handler directs the dog through the course and may run or walk beside him but must not touch the dog or the obstacles.

Although the obstacles may vary somewhat depending on the sponsoring organization and the level of competition, certain obstacles are common to all agility trials, including the open tunnel, closed tunnel, A-frame, weave poles, dog walk, pause table, seesaw, circle/tire/window jump, and various other jumps. The obstacles are placed in

Ch. Centurion Cierra, CDX, TDX is also the dam of multi-titled obedience and tracking dogs. Owned and trained by Elaine Dodson.

Through the tire jump! Cottondale Woodland Lark, CGC, CDX, OAD was the first Dal to earn the Open Agility title in AKC agility. Owned and trained by Jim Bryson.

different sequences from trial to trial, but in all cases the handler will direct the dog through the course in the order specified by the judge. Dogs are faulted for mistakes and penalized for taking longer than the standard course time.

Jump heights vary from organization to organization, but dogs normally compete against dogs of similar size and level of experience, and the dogs with the fewest faults and best times win their classes or height divisions.

The United States Dog Agility Association (USDAA) was organized in 1986 and has been the leading agility organization since that time, offering agility trials in many parts of the country and awarding agility titles. They offered the Grand Prix of Dog Agility, held with the Astrohall dog show each August, and dogs had to win regional events to qualify for the Grand Prix. Such events gave agility the additional push it needed to become firmly established in this country.

Am-Can. Ch. Country Kate's Mandolin of MGR, CD, TD, ("Mandy") negotiating the agility weave

Mandy maneuvers over the teeter-totter.

Agility trials became an official AKC event in August 1995. Open only to AKC-registered dogs 12 months or older, titles are awarded for three qualifying scores earned under at least two different judges. Titles include NA (Novice Agility), OA (Open Agility), and AX (Agility Excellent). Dogs receiving ten qualifying scores in Agility Excellent competition are awarded the MAX (Master Agility Excellent) title.

Many Dalmatians and their owners are involved in agility at all levels of training and competition. Even puppy training classes often incorporate a few of the agility obstacles. Some Dal owners enjoy teaching their dogs to run the course with no thought

Mandy going over the agility A-frame.

Doing the crawl. Dal owned by Lindsey Jones.

of ever competing in agility trials. They simply do it because it is great fun and good exercise for both dog and owner. Learning to run an agility course is a tremendous confidence builder for the dog who is unsure of himself, and it provides a great change of pace for the dog (and owner) who might be feeling a bit "burned out" in regular obedience competition. It's also a fine "second career" for retired show dogs. Most Dals catch on to the exercises very quickly and run the courses with speed and enthusiasm.

Fire Safety Dogs

The Dalmatians that continue to fill the role of fire dog do so now in a unique and perhaps more important fashion than just as mascots. They function as educators, helping their firefighter friends carry the message of fire safety and prevention to children and adults. The fire dogs carry their smoke detectors and "911" signs proudly into schools, malls, and other public gathering places. They demonstrate "Stop, Drop, and Roll" and "Get Low and Go" as well as other

Through the tunnel. Dal owned by Peggy Brawner.

Agility training—going across the dog walk. Dal owned by Lindsey Jones.

safety maneuvers. These working fire dogs help educators gain what is called the "teachable moment." Lessons enhanced by the fire dogs are retained even by very young or handicapped children. Make no mistake, these are working dogs just as surely as any drug-detection dog, tracking dog, or other dog that gives service to mankind.

Some fire dogs fulfill additional roles working as therapy dogs. The recovery from injuries such as serious burns takes many months. Patients are often reluctant to interact with those outside their immediate circles of family and health-care professionals who have become familiar with the scars left by the flames. The fire dogs never notice scars and they greet all with a gentle wag and some snappy tricks or obedience routines.

Cee Kay Becky Thatcher, UDTX ("Becky"), owned and trained by Carolyn Krause, was the official mascot of the International Association of Fire Fighters Local No. 152 in Springfield, Missouri, until she passed away in 1996. Becky became the mascot on October 6, 1988 and had her own badge. Becky began working in 1986 as an educator with the firefighters who visited schools

Daisy demonstrates the "Stop, Drop, and Roll" to an attentive student. Children are more apt to remember safety techniques when practiced with a "fire dog."

Daisy teaches the students to crawl to safety when the house is full of smoke.

with a child-size fire engine they built called "Charlie's Angel." Becky would hold the "911" number while the firemen explained how to use the emergency number, and she loved demonstrating the "Stop, Drop, and Roll" method for what to do if your clothes catch on fire. The Springfield Fire Department's Fire Safety Award for Chil-

dren is now called the Becky Thatcher Award. It is a plaque, photo-engraved with Becky's picture.

Becky also worked with outpatients in the burn unit. The young burn victims seemed to benefit most from working with Becky. It was easy for Becky the fire dog; she didn't notice scars at all. Two other Dals owned by

Tos and Pucci demonstrate fire safety to a Girl Scout troop. Here, they show how to dial a telephone for help in case of an emergency. Owned and trained by Peggy Ann Strupp.

Cee Kay Becky Thatcher, a.k.a. "Becky the Fire Dog," received numerous awards for her fire safety work with children. She also held the TDX and multiple obedience titles. Owned and trained by Carolyn Krause.

Carolyn Krause are also working in the unit. They are Ch. Paisley Poppycock, CDX, TD and Ch. Daisy Dot Purrfect for Paisley, CD, TD.

Ch. Harmony of Cheshire T. Redrock, CD, CGC, RDX ("Tos"), owned and trained by Peggy Ann Strupp of Redrock Dalmatians in Soda Springs, Idaho, is an "Honorary Fire Fighter" with the Caribou County Fire Department. He travels with the fire-safety program to schools and malls in and out of the county, traveling up to 100 miles upon request. The children are delighted when Tos runs to the phone, picks up the receiver to call 911, and barks when asked his name and address.

Ch. Tramac Cinder Bandit, CDX ("Bandit") was the mascot for the City of Davis Fire Department in California from 1987 until his retirement in 1989. He then passed on his duties to his grandson, Can. Ch. Tramac's Sail Away With Me ("Nicky"). Bandit loved to accompany his owner Captain Jim Callea (Ret.) to schools during Fire

Prevention Week. He was always on hand when the mayor signed proclamations at the firehouse. Afterward, he could be found at the cookie and punch table, where handouts were easy to come by! His favorite events were the parades. In true Dalmatian style, he would trot alongside the fire truck for the length of the parade.

There are many Dals around the USA that serve as or have served as fire dog educators, including "Chief," who is trained by Judy Frolish of Saratoga County, New York and "Fred," (which stands for fire rescue emergency dog) of Anna Maria Island, Florida. The Westside Fire Department in Bradenton, Florida had "Heidi" for seven years and "Ember" for two years. Firefighter Kurt Lathrop was responsible for Ember's training, and they were the winning team at the St. Petersburg Festival of States Fire Department competition. Both Heidi and Ember remained as mascots until they died of illnesses.

Chief John McCarthy of the Ft. Myers

Ch. Tramac Cinder Bandit, CDX was owned by the Calleas of Tramac Dalmatians. Bandit was a real "fire dog"—owner Jim Callea was a fireman.

Beach Fire Department Station #2 reports that "Patches" will jump into his car if the window is open as if to say, "Let's go, there's a fire!" For 13 years this station has had three Dals, "Dolly," "Patches," and "Chelsea," as fire safety educators. Ch. Bearded Oaks Jigsaw Puzzle ("Jigs"), owned by Chief Jim Steffens of the Tallavast Fire Department in Florida, was also known to jump into the Chief's car if the window was down and then turn around and give a big Dalmatian-style smile.

The role of the Dalmatian as a fire safety educator was given prominence by the National Fire Prevention Association in 1951 when "Sparky," a stylized but easily recognized Dalmatian, became the official mascot. This artwork has been extensively used in public education and has been specifically effective in bringing fire safety to the home through school children around the world.

Scent Hurdle and Flyball

In these exciting relay events the dogs compete in teams, usually four to a team, and race over four jumps that are scaled to the shoulder height of the smallest canine participant. Minimum jump height is 10 inches, with a maximum height of 16 inches. The continual jumping demanded by this event puts additional stress on the dogs, thus requiring the jumps to be at a lower

Flyball—Mandy hits the pedal on the box to release the ball, which she will catch and bring back over a series of hurdles.

height than those in obedience competition. Hurdles are placed 10 feet apart and the course is 51 feet long from the starting line to the box.

The handlers stand behind the starting line, shouting encouragement to the dogs (who rarely seem to need any encouragement at all!). In fact, handlers of other dogs waiting their turn often have to restrain their overly enthusiastic animals, who are leaping and barking in anticipation of their turn to run.

In scent hurdle racing, a platform holding four dumbbells (one with his owner's scent) is placed at the end of the course. The dog must find the right one, pick it up and race back over the jumps. If he's wrong or if he misses a jump, he has to return to the end of the line and run again.

Flyball, which was developed in California in the 1970s, adds another twist. After jumping the hurdles, the dog hits a pedal on the front of a box. The pedal activates a lever on which a cup holding a ball is attached. The ball flies into the air, and the dog catches it and races back over the hurdles.

The most successful teams are usually composed of breeds who excel in obedience, but many different breeds may be seen, either in mixed teams or in teams consisting of only one breed. The fastest

Scent hurdle racing—Kaylor's Hurricane Indy, CD, TT, CGC, FDCh ("Indy") selects the dumbbell with his owner's scent and will return with it over the hurdles.

Indy, who is a Flyball Champion, returns over the hurdles with the tennis ball. Owned and trained by Katy Kaylor.

teams are often made up of breeds like the Border Collie, but the Dalmatian also does very well in these events. Active Dals who love to chase tennis balls usually enjoy the excitement of flyball, and they have the speed and enthusiasm to be valuable additions to flyball teams. The dogs love these games, as do the owners and spectators, as evidenced by the noise levels as soon as the starting whistle blows. Handlers shout, dogs

Scooter goes over the hurdles. Flyball titles are not AKC titles, but they are highly coveted. The fast and agile Dalmatian is a natural!

bark, and the crowd cheers on their favorites.

Exceptional teams can run the course in less than 20 seconds, and any time of less than 32 seconds earns a point toward flyball titles for each member of the team. A time of less than 28 seconds earns 5 points for each team member, and teams that complete the course in less than 24 seconds receive the maximum 25 points. A total of 100 points is required for the first flyball title. Titles that can be earned in flyball competition include FD (Flyball Dog), FDX (Flyball Dog Excellent), FDCh (Flyball Dog Champion), FM (Flyball Master), FMX (Flyball Master Excellent), FMCh (Flyball Master Champion), and FDGCh (Flyball Grand Champion). Although flyball is not an AKC-sanctioned event, the titles are eagerly sought by flyball competitors worldwide. Flyball is particularly popular in Canada, and in North America the sport is governed by the North American Flyball Association.

Therapy Dogs

The value of pet therapy is demonstrated by the many hospitals and institutions who once banned all animals but have now opened their doors and their arms to four-legged visitors and, in some cases, live-in companions. Various organizations are now testing and licensing therapy dogs on both a local and national level. Therapy dogs must be clean and well groomed, for both aesthetic and aseptic reasons, and these canine candy-stripers are taught not to jump on patients. Nails are clipped short so that unintentional scratches don't cause infection. Many therapy groups dress their dogs for the occasion—a Sunday bonnet, Easter bunny ears, or a Santa hat. The usual uniform, however, often is a colorful bandana around the neck or a T-shirt with a clever saying.

Two smiling faces! Therapy Dog "Zeke" visits with a youngster at the Children's Hospital in Detroit. Dazdell Kingfisher Zeke, CDX is owned by Bob and Pam Fisher.

A Dalmatian of suitable temperament and training can be a superb therapy dog. One of the most respected organizations sponsoring therapy work is The Delta Society in Renton, Washington. Two Dalmatian-handler teams were included in the first ten dog-handler teams to pass the stringent tests required for the Delta Dogs Pet Partners Program. Many Dalmatians work as therapy dogs, and many owners have found great satisfaction in volunteering their time and their dogs to perform a most useful and rewarding service. Although obedience training may prove useful in some situations, all that is normally required is a stable, reliable disposition and basic good manners. A gentle dog laying his head on someone's knee or climbing up beside a crying child requires no formal training, and a dog who can perform a few tricks will quickly bring smiles and laughter.

Animal-assisted-therapy dogs work with all age groups. Hearing impaired children have been inspired to learn their signs when they see a Dalmatian working on hand signals. A burned adult or child makes a

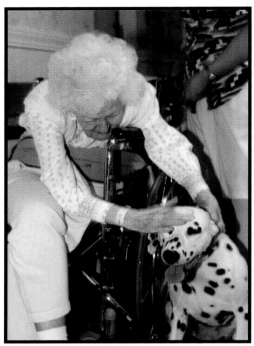

Gallopades Special Selection, owned by Donna Russo, enjoys the attention he is getting from a nursing home resident.

Zuma is a Pediatric Therapy Dog owned by Linda and Mason Kaufman. Here he's dressed up with his friends in the toddler classroom.

social contact he previously avoided, drawn to the clownish fire dog. Emotionally volatile, troubled adolescents and suicidal and otherwise seriously emotionally distressed individuals often respond to these spotted charmers. The dogs allow these patients to focus on a pleasant "now." The dogs don't care about the patient's yesterday or tomorrow; they just offer to share a small island of peace and pleasure.

Heartwarming stories abound. An autistic child speaks only to the dog that visits her every other week. A quadriplegic man is lowered to the floor on a gurney with rails so he can see, and a dog steps over the rails to lie quietly beside him. Severely withdrawn people who have not spoken for years speak first to the dogs, then to the dogs' owners, and eventually to their caregivers to ask when the dogs will be coming back. People who never leave their rooms on other occasions eagerly await the days when the dogs come. These are not isolated situations; they occur over and over around the world.

Every Dalmatian owner who participates in therapy dog work has a dozen stories to tell, many times with tears running down their cheeks.

Dogs have a calming effect and are often utilized, under supervision, with the mentally disturbed. Care is taken so that the animal is not threatened through jealousy or misdirected anger, but even the most disturbed patients seem protective of and appreciative of a dog's loyalty and devotion. Several Dalmatian owners who are also licensed psychologists report that just the presence of a dog in the room is reassuring, especially to children, and they regularly take their dogs to work with them. Other Dalmatians are approved to work in locked wards and perform a most valuable service under the most trying conditions. At least one prison holds training classes where abandoned dogs are brought to live with the prisoners, trained, groomed, socialized, and then adopted by new, loving homes. Both the dogs and the prisoners benefit from such programs.

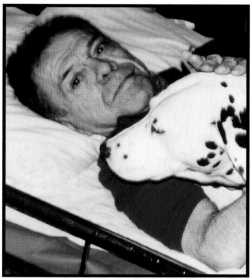

Ch. Coachman's Cluster Bee, CD, TDI is hard at work snuggling with a nursing home patient—not a very hard job for a Dal! "Honey" is owned by Susan Schweitzer.

If you have a Dalmatian with a steady, stable temperament, basic training in good manners, and a few tricks to show off,

A Therapy Dog group visits the Shriners Hospital in San Francisco. The Dal is Rambler Rose Tattoo, CDX, CGC, TDI. "Bailey" is owned and trained by Cathy Bones.

consider becoming involved in animal-assisted therapy.

The positive effect of dogs in a therapeutic setting has been documented in publications world-wide. New goals and programs are being established almost daily and therapy dogs and their handlers are being accorded the professional respect that they so richly deserve.

are some Dals, however, who work for their owners and allow their owners to be more mobile, independent, and self sufficient than they would otherwise be. Although not as widely used for these purposes as Golden Retrievers, Labradors, German Shepherd Dogs, and other such breeds who were bred specifically to work for their masters, Dalmatians are able to perform a variety of services.

Ch. Matchless Image of Folklore ("Jay"), accompanied by his owner-breeder Jan Warren, visits a nursing home and brings joy to some new friends.

Canine Helpers

Although most breeds of dog were developed for a specific purpose, few dogs actually see employment doing the tasks for which they were originally bred. While some Dalmatians are fortunate enough to share their lives with horses, and perhaps even participate in road trials or trail rides, Dalmatians are more likely to serve as family pets, jogging companions, or watchdogs. There

Seeing Eye Dogs—The most widely used service dog is the Seeing Eye dog or guide dog. There are at least 15 different guide-dog training organizations in the USA, and the breeds most commonly used are Labrador Retrievers, German Shepherd Dogs, and Golden Retrievers. At least 60% of the working guide dogs in the USA are black or yellow Labradors. Dogs trained as Seeing Eye dogs must be intelligent and willing workers, readily trainable, and large enough to guide their handlers but small enough to fit under restaurant tables and to board public transportation. They must be free of physical disorders and they are screened for eye problems and hip abnormalities. Some training schools have their own breeding programs while others purchase dogs locally, so popular breeds which are readily available are more likely to see widespread use.

Other breeds that are used in addition to the more common ones include Boxers, other retrievers, Border Collies, Huskies, Dobermans, Rhodesian Ridgebacks, Australian Shepherds, German Shorthaired Pointers, Standard Poodles, and Dalmatians. With the rise in Dalmatian popularity and the associated increase in availability, perhaps we will also see an increase in the number of Dalmatians trained as guide dogs. Their size, soundness, intelligence, and stamina seem to be characteristics which could make them quite suitable for this important opportunity to serve mankind.

Canine Assistance Dogs or Service Dogs—Following in the pawsteps of the other service organizations, training schools now offer the opportunity for increased independence to people who are confined to wheelchairs or who need assistance because of other physical limitations. Dalmatians are very suitable for such jobs as they learn quickly, respond readily to the positive methods used to train assistance dogs, are strong and agile, and require minimal coat care. The dogs are acclimated to wheelchairs and crutches and taught to open doors, activate light switches, push elevator buttons, retrieve various items by name, pick up things that are dropped, pull wheelchairs up ramps, and act as support for a person climbing stairs. Saddlebags are often part of the assistance dog's uniform and are used to carry purses, shopping purchases, or school books.

Most assistance dogs are trained by nonprofit organizations or by training schools, while others are trained by private individuals,

Assistance Dog—Culurien's No Jacket Required, CD, known as "Baron," and his owner Bill Kent.

Hard-working Touchstone's Topaz, CD with owner Melissa Eriksen, who feels that Dals can be trained for assistance work. "Topaz" has certainly lived up to her expectations.

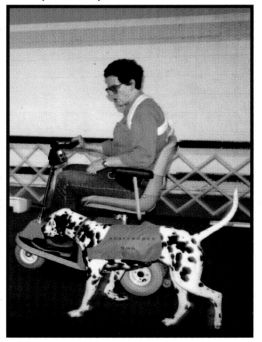

Bearded Oaks Astra's Ursa Major, CD ("Smokey") is a hard-working Assistance Dog owned by Dwight and Marianne Gill. Here, he brings Dwight the telephone.

sometimes even as a service to a friend. These dogs often receive more individualized training than any of the other service dogs because each person has very different needs and limitations. A busy working person who lives alone and is confined to a wheelchair may demand a dog who is trained to perform a large variety of tasks, while a child living at home may require only a "best friend" who can pull a wheelchair and retrieve items that are dropped.

Three well-known Dalmatians that are service/assistance dogs in the 1990s are

Smokey walks in the mall with Marianne and Dwight Gill.

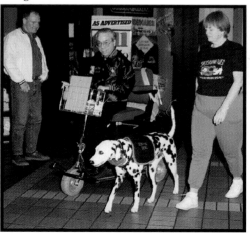

Bearded Oaks Astra's Ursa Major, CD, owned by Dwight and Marianne Gill; Culurien No Jacket Required, CD, owned by Bill Kent; and Touchstone's Topaz, owned by Melissa Eriksen. All of these dogs were present at the 1992 DCA National Specialty in Reading, Pennsylvania.

Hearing Dog—A specialized form of assistance dog is the hearing dog, a dog who is trained to work with deaf or hearing-impaired individuals. These dogs respond to sounds such as a babies crying,

Smokey collects a package from the cashier in the bookstore.

telephones ringing, doorbells, alarm clocks, and smoke alarms. They get their owners' attention and lead them to the source of the sound. Some of these dogs are trained by service-dog organizations, while others are taught by private trainers who will come to the house and train the owner's personal

PR Ch. Irishman's Lady Trixie with the Seal Team Platoon. "Trixie" joined owner Tom Keith as a member of the Navy Seals and accompanied him on jungle expeditions.

dog. Some organizations stress the use of homeless dogs for this task, thus providing a valuable service to the recipient as well as the dog! There are many reports of Dalmatians who are "self-taught" and alert their owners to a variety of sounds and situations.

K-9 Corps—Dogs were used extensively during World War II, perhaps as many as 25,000 in all, with at least 10,000 used for sentry and beach patrol by the Coast Guard. Combat dogs were trained to deliver messages, find the wounded, carry supplies, detect mines, alert to ambushes, accompany the point men, and patrol the borders. Only a limited number functioned as aggressive sentry dogs. The exploits of those dogs are well documented and many veterans owe their lives to four-legged soldiers. Dalmatians were included among the breeds used during the war, finding employment primarily as messengers and sentries. Among the Dalmatians who served were two donated by Ezio Pinza, who included some of

his own recordings in case the dogs got homesick!

Backpacking

The Dalmatian is an ideal breed for hiking and backpacking as long as the weather is suitable for a smooth-coated dog. Their tremendous stamina, love of the outdoors, and endless enthusiasm make Dals ideal companions for a walk around the block or a week's trip into the wilderness. Although dogs are not allowed on national park trails, most parts of the country have numerous hiking trails that are available to dogs and their owners.

A dog on the trail should always be leashed and wear a sturdy buckle collar with identification tags. If he has been microchipped or tattooed so much the better, but be sure he wears a tag as well. Although a retractable leash gives the dog more freedom, this type of leash can also get tangled in brush. A sturdy six-foot-leash gives the owner more control, particularly when meeting dogs or other animals on the trail. The dog should be current on his rabies vaccination, and you might want to consider a Lyme disease shot as well. Pack a good flea and tick repellent and don't forget the heartworm preventatives.

It is important that the backpack is carefully fitted, that the dog is gradually accustomed to carrying a load, and that the load itself is properly balanced. A dog should be able to carry a pack weighing as much as 35% of his own body weight, but it's better

Dals make great hiking companions—some even wear backpacks and carry their own supplies. This Dal accompanies his owner on a hike in Monte Cristo Peaks.

to start off with no more than 20% of the dog's weight until he is an experienced backpacker. The dog can carry his own food and water, an extra collar and leash, a towel, his brush, a Frisbee™, a Nylabone®, and clean-up bags. Clean-up bags should always be used. They can be placed in a zip-lock pouch and packed out with the rest of your trash.

If your dog is normally a couch potato, be sure to take the time to get him in proper condition before attempting a long hike or backpacking trip. Long walks, running beside a bike, and swimming are all good exercise for a Dalmatian. Let him get used to wearing his pack and carrying a light load of crumpled newspapers, then gradually accustom him to longer hikes and heavier loads. Remember that wearing a pack will affect the dog's balance until he is used to compensating for it.

If you will be hiking in an area where the water is polluted or might contain giardia, you will need to bring enough water for the dog to drink. Be sure to offer water often and know the warning signs of heat exhaustion and how to handle heat stroke. When hiking in cool weather, be sure to pack a pad for the dog to sleep on at night, and perhaps a blanket as well. Or, the dog can always share your sleeping bag!

Always keep your dog on lead when on a hiking trail and never let him interfere with other hikers or wild animals. When meeting hikers and other dogs, he should be under control—never lunging and barking. If you are hiking in an area where dogs are allowed off leash, remember that some irresponsible dog owner might have an aggressive dog running loose.

Canine Good Citizen

Due primarily to the growing amount of anti-dog sentiment, the American Kennel Club developed the Canine Good Citizen program as a way to promote responsible dog ownership. This is a non-competitive test in which the dog is required to display appropriate behavior while performing a series of ten simple exercises. The test focuses on the training and behavior that ensures the dog can function as a companion in the home, and it requires the dog to display appropriate behavior in public and in the presence of other dogs. Precision is not required, only good manners. Tests are open to both purebred and mixed-breed dogs since the anti-dog public does not differentiate between AKC-registered and mixed-breed dogs.

Tests may be sponsored by any AKC-recognized dog club or qualified dog-training organization. Some training schools offer Canine Good Citizen tests for the dogs who are graduating from their obedience classes and some Dalmatian clubs offer the CGC test in conjunction with their specialty shows. Dog owners are required to show proof of rabies vaccination as well as any locally-required licenses, as both of these requirements relate to responsible dog ownership.

The test is pass/fail and any dog that eliminates during the test will automatically fail. Dogs that growl, snap, or show aggressive behavior toward people or other dogs will be dismissed, as will any handlers who display unsportsmanlike conduct or abuse their dogs.

All tests are performed on leash and the handler may give the dog commands or encouragement but may not use physical force.

Hiking Dals on a footlog, crossing the White Chuck in Glacier Peak Wilderness.

Although the Canine Good Citizen is not an official AKC title, dog owners often use a CGC after their dogs' names. Many champion show dogs and top obedience dogs add the CGC to their list of titles and many pet owners proudly display the certificate. To receive a CGC certificate, the dog and handler are tested on the following items:

Accepting a stranger—A friendly stranger walks up and shakes hands with the handler while exchanging a few words. The dog must stay with his owner and show no shyness or resentment.

Sitting politely for petting—The dog must sit while the tester pats him on the head and body and circles the dog and handler. The dog must not show shyness or resentment.

Appearance and grooming—The tester brushes the dog lightly, checks his ears, and touches his feet. The exercise demonstrates that the dog can be examined by a veterinarian or handled by a groomer.

Walking on a loose lead—The dog and handler walk through the testing area with the dog under control. A few turns and at least one stop are included, but the dog does not have to maintain a formal heel position or sit when the handler stops.

Walking through a crowd—The dog and handler walk through a group of people, passing close to several of them. The dog may show interest in the people around him but must not interfere with them. The exercise demonstrates that the dog can behave properly in a group of pedestrians.

Sit and down on command/stay in place—The dog responds to the handler's commands and will stay where he is left while the handler goes to the end of a 20-foot line. The exercise demonstrates that the dog has received some type of training.

Coming when called—The dog is on a 20-foot line. The owner walks 10 feet away and then calls the dog. The evaluator can occupy the dog if he tries to follow owner as he walks away. This exercise demonstrates that the dog will come when called.

Reaction to another dog—Two handlers and their dogs approach one another, shake hands, and exchange a few words. The dogs may display interest in one another but must remain under control.

Reaction to distractions—This exercise tests the dog's reaction to something like a loud noise or a jogger. The dog may startle or show interest but should not

A Canine Good Citizen test was held in conjunction with the 1995 National Specialty.

panic, bark, show aggression, or try to run away.

Supervised separation—The dog is left with the tester or another individual while the handler goes out of sight for several minutes. The dog need not remain in position but should not bark, howl, or whine excessively and should not appear excessively agitated.

Hunting

Questions commonly asked of Dal owners often include, "Do they hunt?" and "Are they related to Pointers?" Most Dal owners are quite aware of the fact that their Dals probably could hunt, and it is generally accepted that the Dalmatian's closest relative is probably the Pointer. Certainly most Dalmatians appear to be very "varminty" if not "birdy."

As stable dogs, it is believed that the Dalmatian's tasks included being ratters, and indeed many Dalmatians today perform that job quite nicely. It is a rare Dalmatian that does not fancy it his job to protect his owner's property from all manner of small furry creatures, including rats and mice, squirrels, chipmunks, woodchucks, and even occasionally (and unfortunately) skunks and porcupines. Many owners can relate stories of carcasses deposited on the carpet by proud spotted hunters! While some Dals will chase squirrels and rabbits with little success, others are quite wily and soon become skilled hunters. The hunter learns to creep slowly and silently toward the intended victim, and with a tremendous leap, he scores a victory. Some Dals seem surprised to actually catch something and even let their victims escape, while others dispatch their victims with alacrity. Other Dals learn to watch for prey from the window, and when the door is opened they race out and use the elements of speed and surprise. Although a bit large to be an outstanding mouser, many Dals work very hard at their chosen profession, sometimes resulting in chairs pushed back from walls and overturned coffee tables!

Jim and Linda Fulks are professional sporting dog trainers who also train and compete with their Dalmatians. The Dal in this sequence is RFBCN Lidgate's Triever Watson, CD.

It is not unusual to hear of Dals who are used for bird hunting, and some are actually purchased with hunting in mind. While some Dals will point, most of them are more inclined to be flushers and work much like Springer Spaniels, scenting the birds and flushing them for their hunting companions to shoot. Since Dals are not normally bred for hunting instinct, most of them require a fair amount of training, but many hunters who use them insist that a good Dalmatian can work just as well as many sporting dogs.

Who says Dals can't hunt? Cassie hunts grouse and pheasant each fall—here she is with pheasants that she found, flushed, and retrieved. Owned and trained by Dan Jacobsen.

Dalmatians can also be taught to mark where the birds drop and retrieve them to hand, but most owners observe that the breed is certainly not inclined to be as soft-mouthed as sporting breeds. Birds are often delivered rather damp and rumpled, and a few Dals have been known to sample the birds on the way back! Dals seem to be used primarily on such birds as pheasants and grouse, and there are fewer reports of them hunting ducks. Although Dals are often good swimmers, they lack thick oily coats to protect them from the cold water, and several Dal owners have observed that their Dals don't seem to like the "taste" of ducks either!

Training problems also include some degree of difficulty in teaching a pointing Dal to hold the point for any length of time, and the fact that Dals tend to run so far and so hard that they flush the birds before the hunter is close enough to shoot them.

Yes, they can hunt, and more than one Dalmatian-owning hunter has won a bet with a hunting buddy who did not believe that some Dals can indeed hold their own in the field with the likes of springers, Brittanys, and pointers.

Jim and Linda Fulks are professional dog trainers who live in Oregon. They train and show retrievers in field trials and they also train their Dals in field work. Linda suggests, "In selecting a Dal to train in the field as a hunting retriever, the most important quality is trainability. All Dal owners know of the Dalmatian's burning desire to chase squirrels, rabbits, cats, etc. To work for a hunter instead of himself, Spot must be able to be trained to be called off such a hunt at any time. Another trait required for the retrieving Dal is that he must have good predatory instincts regarding game birds. I learned the hard way that the Dal must have bilateral hearing, as a dog with no directional hearing is more of a hindrance than a help in the field. It is also important that the Dal is not sound-sensitive so that he can be conditioned to the sound of a gun. A successful hunting retriever Dal should have mental stability and courage. In our limited experience with Dals we have found about 25% to have enough of these qualities to work successfully as retrieving gun dogs."

More Dalmatian Activities

The versatile Dalmatian has competed successfully in a variety of other activities.

Lure coursing—Many Dals have very highly developed "chase" instincts and that, combined with their speed and agility, make them very good at lure coursing. Although Dals can not enter the official competitions, many local associations will let breeds other

Lure coursing isn't just for sighthounds— Indi (owned by Pat Sayles) and Boomer (owned by Jane Beauchamp) love it! Many Dals have the required speed, agility, and chase instinct.

Sled dogs—These versatile Dals owned by Peggy Ann Strupp don their sled harnesses and festive coats to pull along a young friend, some holiday goodies, and the Christmas tree!

Crossroads Mountain Daisy, CDX, CGC enjoys a romp in the snow. Owned by Marilyn Gaffney.

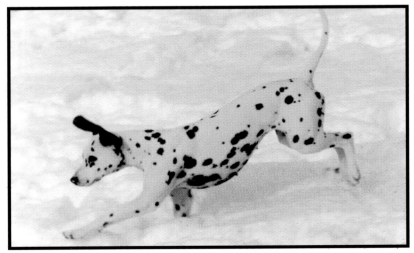

"Hey, what is this white stuff?" Mandy looks like she's been investigating! Owned by Stan and Karen Larson.

than sighthounds join them for practice sessions. Dal owners frequently relate how amazed the sighthound owners are at the Dalmatian's ability in this sport.

Herding—Many farm Dals learn to help with the chores and are able to herd cattle, sheep, birds such as turkey and ducks, and even pigs. Some are sent out to retrieve

Coachman's Chocolate E. Clair (L) leaps for a stick.

animals from a remote pasture, bring them into the farm yard or barn, and herd them into a specific pen. Although herding tests are not normally open to non-herding breeds, several Dals have earned Herding Instinct Certificates from herding breed clubs.

Weight pulling—Some years ago an unofficial weight pulling contest was held with a large all-breed dog show, and several Dalmatian owners decided to enter their dogs, since everyone knows how hard Dalmatians can pull! One of the Dals (a cham-

Picadilly's Alexis at Dynasty and Picadilly's Sir Nigel enjoy cross-country skiing. Owned by Stephanie and Cliff Seigneur.

pion at that) won his weight division against a number of breeds who were bred for the sport, and ended up in fourth place overall. Because of complaints from the chagrined draft dog owners, Dalmatians were not allowed to compete in subsequent years!

Sled dogs—More than a few Dals have learned to pull a sled and take the neighborhood kids for rides in the winter. There was apparently even a team of Dalmatians that competed in dog-sled races in California in the 1960s, and a few dog owners have used Dals in mixed teams in local competitions. Although many Dalmatians enjoy cold and

Dals enjoy all types of outdoor recreation—this Dal owned by Barrie Essner goes for a "sail" in the family pool.

Dals will play catch with anything! Ch. Markmaker Never Say Never, CDX, CGC ("Pica") leaps for a snowball. Owned by Carol Wells.

Ch. Odyssey's Star-Lite Dazzler, CD, CGC with his frisbee and ball. The Dalmatian's agility often makes for some spectacular catches.

control a dog who is wearing a prong training collar. Be sure to check the dog's pads from time to time, avoid running him on excessively hot asphalt or in extremely cold weather, and take along a supply of water, especially in warm weather.

Several Dal owners have entered their dogs in Schutzhund Endurance tests. To earn the AD title, the dogs are required to run 12.5 miles beside a bicycle in two hours or less, then complete a series of obedience exercises to prove that they are not exhausted.

Dals are also excellent Frisbee™ dogs and can make rather spectacular over-the-shoulder catches just for the fun of it. Be sure that the dog is fully mature, as a young, loose-jointed dog can injure himself with excessive jumping. A few Dalmatians have even found employment as golfers' companions, retrieving the golf balls while their owners practice their driving skills!

Step 2: The grab. Kindle leaps and makes the catch!

Step 1: The chase. Touchstone's Firestarter, CDX ("Kindle") goes for the frisbee. Owned by Leslie Stanley.

snow if they can keep moving, they are susceptible to frost-bitten ears if exposed to extremely cold temperatures for long periods of time.

Outdoor recreation—The Dalmatian's stamina and heritage as a coach dog make him an excellent companion for trail rides, biking, jogging, and in-line skating, as well as cross-country skiing. If properly conditioned, a Dal can easily go many miles and still be ready to play ball at the end of the day. The dog should have basic obedience training and good leash manners before attempting any of these activities, and it is advisable that skaters be proficient before attempting to skate with a dog. There are several bicycle attachments that make it easier and safer to bike with a dog, and joggers and skaters often find it easier to

A dog that truly exemplifies the Dal's versatility is Am-Bah. Ch. Ravenwood Yankee Clipper, Am. CDX, Bah. CD, CGC, VCCX, TDI. "Newley" is believed to be the first Dal to acquire a Versatile Canine Companion Excellent working title. Owned, trained, and handled by Kathy McCoubrey.

Selecting a Dalmatian

RESPONSIBILITIES OF OWNERSHIP

The purpose of any book on a specific breed of dog is to encourage responsible ownership of dogs in general and that breed in particular. By explaining the characteristics of the breed and outlining its basic needs, this book will help you determine if the Dalmatian is the right breed for you. Once you decide to purchase a Dalmatian, our goal is to help you become a happy Dal owner. If you have already purchased your Dalmatian without the benefit of advice beforehand, you can manage the situation successfully if you are willing to make the few adjustments this breed requires.

We have discussed the standard for Dalmatians as accepted by the American Kennel Club, we have talked about patches and off-color markings, and we have examined good and bad structure. These give you a good mental picture as reference for the general look of a Dalmatian. However, unless you are buying with the express purpose of breeding, all of these criteria are cosmetic and none affects the Dalmatian's ability to be an exceptional family pet provided he is owned by the right family. Determining whether your family is the right family is the beginning of your responsibility. Read about the characteristics of the Dalmatian and think about whether

Chewing is one of a puppy's favorite pastimes. Crossroad's Checkers, CDX, at four months of age, helps herself to a hunk of the wood pile.

Dals are always full of energy! Can you provide adequate exercise and a safe play area? Ch. Paradox Prodigal Dotter ("Zoe") is owned by Sandra Turner.

your family's characteristics are a good complement to the Dal. Do you have a safely fenced yard that the Dal can use to run off extra energy? Do you expect your new Dal to be a part of your family's life outside *and* inside the home to appease his need for companionship? Are you willing to start obedience training to guide his independent nature into more compliant behavior?

We live in a "throwaway society" today; too many people are participants in consumerism—buying without thought to consequences, making purchases for unsound reasons. Buying a living animal should not be comparable to buying a new outfit or new patio furniture that can be returned if not suitable. Millions of animals are taken to shelters by owners every year because no thought was given to the needs of these new pets and to whether the families would be able to cope with those needs. These innocent victims of our "need to buy" are then dumped in local pounds just for doing normal canine and/or feline activities: barking, digging, chewing, scratching, and urinating or defecating in unwanted places.

Don't be an unwitting victim of "soft sell" psychology—take responsibility for your decision-making. Be aware that subtle advertising techniques can subconsciously influence you into a purchase that you will regret, at the cost of an innocent animal's life. If that adorably pudgy Dal puppy just grabs your heart, go home and think about all the consequences of purchasing him before you pull out your wallet. The initial cost of a Dalmatian is nothing compared to the ongoing investment you will be making in this new family member. There will be medical costs such as initial vaccinations and yearly boosters, spay/neuter fees, training classes, toys, grooming tools, and the daily costs of good nutritious food, plus countless other expenses.

After you have thought it over and you feel that the family is ready to add a new member, take the next step in responsible puppy buying—do some research. Learn what constitutes a good source from which to purchase a puppy, what constitutes a good breeder, what a properly raised litter should look and behave like, and which puppy temperament will make the most suitable Dal pet. While the environment you are going to provide the new puppy will have a big influence on him as he matures, do not dismiss the importance of starting with a genetically sound specimen. Unfortunately, you cannot use *Consumer Reports* to research buyers and bloodlines. But be assured that there are conscientious breeders out there. It is your responsibility as a buyer to locate them and make your purchase wisely.

Once that Dal puppy is in your home it becomes your duty to care for him. He innocently trusts that you will provide for his needs in return for his limitless love. Food and medical needs are simple compared to the need for training. When you purchase a Dalmatian, you assume the responsibility for its welfare. Ownership is more of a partnership with the Dal, since he will be taking an active role in the family. The canine is a pack animal with a need to belong. Your family becomes his new pack, and you his new leader. You cannot frustrate his instincts without stunting his potential and limiting his contribution to the fullness of your life. Responsible dog ownership requires a

Am-Ber. Ch. Korcula John L. Lewis sits patiently while John Garvin, Jr. checks out some new attire.

Nothing makes a better pillow than a pile of snoozing Dals! Owned by Janice Brennan.

different outlook than in the past. Working dogs on the farm and in the hunt contributed to the "pack" or family every day by performing the jobs they knew to be theirs, but the main role of a dog in today's society is that of companion and family pet. To do this job successfully, dogs need to be guided into the role and allowed to fully participate in family life.

THE DALMATIAN AS A FAMILY PET

Children and Dogs

Children and dogs are a natural, and children and Dalmatians can be an exceptional combination. Dalmatians thrive on the activity associated with children in a normal, busy household. As in most good working relationships, the key is respect—the Dal must be taught to respect all humans, including children, and the children must be taught to respect the dog's rights as a living creature. A dog in the family is a marvelous learning experience for every child. There is, of course, the usual benefit of teaching the child responsibility for another's well-being. Added rewards come from observing and interacting with another species, accepting a non-human friend into your heart, and sharing the ups and downs of maturing in this world with a four-legged pal.

Some breeders feel that ownership of a family Dal should be restricted to that period when all of the "little people" in the house are at least 48 inches tall. Others feel that a Dalmatian can be integrated into a family at any stage, at any age. There are success stories to illustrate both sides of the argument. Either way, the dedication of every family member to making the relationship work will determine the end result. Dal puppies require a great deal of time and attention for the first two years of their lives. If there is a new baby on the way or children under two years of age in the household, you may not be able to devote the necessary time to the puppy and it might be wiser to hold off purchasing a puppy for several years. Then again, perhaps thought could be given to adopting a rescued adult Dalmatian. Careful investigation could turn up the ideal Dal candidate for integration into your family. If you do have younger children, carefully supervise their play with the dog until you are sure that

both children and dog have developed a good working relationship.

The first step is to teach the new Dal and the children to accept each other's presence in the household and to respect each other's status in the family. Children are taught how to act around dogs just as dogs learn how to act around children. When a puppy comes into your home, he brings only his experiences from within the litter

"This kid must have something good...why won't he let me have it?" Emma wonders as she runs along with young Chad Palmer. Emma is owned by Millie Palmer and Beth White.

Five-year-old Geoffrey Shimer poses with Rescue Me, CDX ("Mickey"). Mickey is owned by Leesa Huddleston.

Coachlane's Fireman's Blaze and his friends are "cool dudes" in their shades.

and the breeder's household. Perhaps he has never played with, or even seen, a child. His reaction to small children will be to treat them as playmates—littermates, if you will. You must supervise that play, teaching him *never* to put his mouth on humans of any size, and teaching him that playing with humans is quite different from playing with his littermates. An adult dog who bites children is generally the result of the owner's ineffectiveness as a trainer in allowing a problem to develop in the first place. The children must be taught *never* to abuse the puppy; abuse will bring out the natural instinct of self-preservation. Your job will be to establish an atmosphere in which the pup and the children can develop a secure relationship with each other.

The second step is to begin training the puppy by including everyone in the project. Training should begin immediately and *every* family member must learn to control the dog. There are plenty of good training books, tapes, and classes available, therefore, there is no excuse for failing to teach good manners to the family Dal. A good dog can be ruined by unintentionally

teaching it bad habits. For instance, never isolate the dog and its food as this fosters protectiveness. The puppy must be taught to tolerate the proximity of people, little and big, at feeding time. Setting the food bowl down in the middle of a busy kitchen may be an inconvenience to you, but it is excellent conditioning for the pup.

Sit with the pup while he eats his first few meals in your home. Dish the kibble out of the pan by hand and encourage the children to do the same. The puppy will relate the pleasure of food with the presence of humans. Another good method is installment feeding, where various members of the family give out portions of each meal to the pup at divided intervals, teaching him that when people come to his food bowl it is to give more, not to take away what is there. Bones, toys, and other doggy possessions should be handled the same way so that the pup is taught to share, not to protect. A box full of "doggy" toys kept on the floor in the puppy's play area is a deterrent to having him destroy the children's toys. When you buy a new dog toy, take an old one out of the box and put

Chad Garvin and Charley (both age nine) spend some quiet time together. Charley is co-owned by Lynn and Charles Garvin and Marie (Debbie) Zink.

Six-week-old Dal babies get super-socialized by this smiling bunch. Litter by Ch. Tuckaway Augusta out of Ch. Centurion Cultured Pearl, bred by Elise Moloney and Elaine Lindhorst.

it away for a while, exchanging it for another toy later on a rotating basis. Puppies can get bored with the same old things and look for a little diversity among the children's toys—forbidden territory!

Socialize your pup to children with plenty of dog treats on hand. Have the children offer the pup a small tidbit when they are first introduced, then hold regular sessions several times a day during the first week or

pup. The "come" command can be taught as soon as the pup has mastered the "sit." Using the treat reward for positive reinforcement easily teaches the pup to come, and then to sit when told. These two basic commands bring your Dal puppy under immediate control and will be the basis for the remainder of your training program.

What about the childless or teen/adult household? Is child socialization necessary

Where's Riker? This three-month-old Dal pup (if you can spot him) prefers toys of his own kind! Owned by Donna McCluer.

two, repeating this activity. Combined with teaching the command to "sit," this is a very useful tool. The pup learns to sit when approached by a child, and associates children with treats. All of the regular training commands can be reinforced with treats— the child gives a command, the pup obeys, a treat reward is given. The pup makes a positive association with the children, and the children learn that they can control the

in this case? Absolutely! The world is not childless and the puppy will need to understand proper behavior around miniature humans. Perhaps you could "borrow" children from the neighbors to help with your training program. There are added benefits to this: neighborhood children are less likely to tease a dog they know well and who will come, sit, etc., for them on command, and a dog is less likely to bark at familiar neighborhood children because they are not strangers to the dog and there is no need for him to protect his territory from children he interacts with regularly.

Where Will He Sleep?

If the Dal puppy learns to eat and play in the midst of family activity, should he be expected to sleep there also? Yes and no. The very young puppy needs a great deal of rest and will flop down for a snooze whenever the mood strikes. The only problem with this is that he will need to urinate as soon as he awakens. If you are not there to immediately take him outside, a mistake will be made on both your parts. His mistake is forgivable—he is only answering nature's call; your mistake in leaving him unsupervised will encourage him to use the house rather than the backyard for elimination. The solution is to train the Dal pup to sleep comfortably in a crate that is placed in a quiet corner of the main living area (*not* in the far corner of the garage or behind the closed laundry room door).

This sleeping beauty is Tattersall Tasmanian Devil (L). It's not uncommon to see young Dal pups sleeping with all fours in the air.

Puppies owned by Donna McCluer have their own "pad."

213

A true "den" animal, a dog can make a bed out of just about anything! Lizzy makes herself right at home.

The canine is a "den" animal and is quite comfortable sleeping in a confined area, in fact, usually prefers it! When he awakens he will call to be let out, preferring not to soil his sleeping quarters. You take him outside, praise him for being such a good pup in asking to "go out," and give him a treat reward. Housebreaking will progress rapidly using the crate as a teaching tool. He will consider his crate a safe haven, retreating to it when life gets to be too much. Putting him in the crate when you leave the house for a while will keep him safe and you sane. An extra rug or blanket in the kitchen or near your favorite chair is also a good idea. It will give him a place to take his chew toys and can be used for mild discipline and control. "Go to your rug" should be part of his vocabulary and is very useful during the family's dinner or when you need him clear of the immediate area.

Where Will He Play?

Outside accommodations for the family Dal should include a safely fenced yard, outside toy box full of playthings, a very large container of water, and plenty of shade. In the working household, a shaded dog run with a dog house is the ideal way to safely confine your Dal and yet allow him

a minimum of exercise. Upon your arrival home, you can turn him loose for a session of fetch in the back yard to burn off that initial display of enthusiasm and then take him inside for family interaction. As he matures you may want to consider installing a "doggy door" for his daytime use. If you began his training on day one, he will understand his place in the family structure. By the time maturity sets in and he loses that puppy energy (usually not until age two with the Dalmatian), he will have learned a healthy respect for your possessions, understand proper behavior, and be trustworthy when left alone.

How large does this "safely fenced yard" need to be? If you will take time to play "throw the ball" or "catch me if you can" games, then a small yard can be adequate. The key is in how you use the space, not how much space you have. A Dalmatian left alone for days on end in a yard the size of a football field will be more unhappy and get into much more trouble than a Dal in a very small yard whose caring owners play action games with him daily and then bring him inside to be an important part of their lives. A retractable lead (leash on a retractable spring) for walking your dog allows him to go out away from you and then back, covering extra ground during your walks yet remaining under your control. After *thorough* obedience training, perhaps off-lead runs in a nearby park can become part of your routine or kept for a weekend treat. Be a good neighbor and always clean up after your animal. A zip-lock baggie in your pocket will do the job and can be dropped neatly into the nearest trash container or even brought home for disposal. Many people train their Dals to respond to the "hurry up, out" command, which translates to "go outside, do your duty quickly, and we'll go for a walk." This cuts down on the possibility that you will have to clean up a deposit on the neighbor's lawn.

An obedient Dalmatian is a pleasure to take on family outings. He will be a source of pride as well, for you are sure to receive compliments on the behavior of this beautiful animal. Being included in family activities keeps the average Dalmatian out of trouble. If left to his own devices, the Dalmatian will be very inventive in passing idle time! The Dalmatian's need for activity is higher than the average dog's, but the activity level in a normal family household will be enough to keep his mind and body occupied. If excluded from this rewarding activity, he will undoubtedly get into trouble and become a problem pet.

WHAT YOU SHOULD KNOW ABOUT CANINE DEVELOPMENT

A short discussion with any veterinarian will tell you what you need to know in order to determine if a litter of puppies is physically healthy. Look for bright sparkling eyes, no discharge from eyes or noses, happily wagging tails, and little bodies that are plump without having extended bellies. Any excrement you see should be formed, solid to semi-solid, and should not have an excessively strong odor. Coats should be shiny and bodies should be clean and sweet-smelling. The pups should be happy, active,

A Dal needs a safely fenced area in which to play outside, and Mandy looks like she has a place to call her own!

Keeping watch over their domain are Ch. Volunteer Fireman's Discovery and Ch. Volunteer's of Touch of Soot, owned by Jacqueline Delaney.

and alert to events in their surroundings. You can determine a puppy's general physical health by observation, but how do you determine his mental health and his suitability as a pet?

Beginning in the early to mid-1990s, a number of studies were undertaken to explore the dynamics of puppy-raising in

215

an effort to determine the important relationship of genetics to the environment. The "nature vs. nurture" argument is ongoing, but studies have led to the discovery of some very important facts concerning the whelping and rearing of a litter of puppies. Knowledge of these facts will help you pick the best prospect for a successful pet.

Stages of Development

Early in this century, the advent of the Seeing Eye dog program and the use of dogs in the military required the development of methods for determining which pups in a litter would make the most successful trainees. It was too costly to keep, raise, and train an entire litter only to have two or three pups actually grow up able to cope with the stress of a working environment. By building upon some of the studies already completed and keeping accurate records of their own breeding successes, the Seeing Eye in Morristown, New Jersey was able to improve their success rate immensely. By recognizing important developmental periods universal to all puppies and by applying proper stimulation and training during those periods, they brought out the best that each puppy was capable of. You can do the same with your own puppy once you get him home, but there are some important developmental periods that occur prior to your purchase that the breeder must have handled properly in order for you to achieve maximum development in your pup. Various studies of canine and wolf populations have identified three distinct stages of development which have been termed the neonatal, the socialization/stimulation, and the enrichment stages. Their names somewhat describe the "state of mind" the puppy is in during each period. Because so much happens to a puppy during his first few months of life, the three major stages are broken down even further to: the neonatal period, the transitional period, the socialization period, the juvenile period, and adulthood. The first three months of a puppy's life encompass the first three sub-stages of development. His foundation is built based on the genetic codes programmed into him from his parents. This basic developmental period is divided into: neonatal from birth to two weeks, transitional from two to three weeks, and socialization from three to twelve weeks.

The Neonatal Period

The neonatal period is characterized by strictly physical development and needs. The nursing mother is the puppy's main influence, so her health and attitude are of prime importance. If she has been bred at every heat or at too young an age and has diminished physical resources to nurture the pups, their start in life will be poor. If her attitude is not calm and reassuring, the pups may become fearful or aggressive through negative imprinting.

The pups cannot hear or see and they locate their food source by smell or touch; therefore, they must be capable of righting themselves to a crawling position if rolled onto their backs and of circling to the right and/or left in search of mom and littermates. They cannot defecate or urinate without mom's stimulating lick, and they are unable to regulate their own body temperatures so they must stay snuggled against mom and each other. About 90 percent of their time is spent sleeping while their bodies absorb nourishment and their nervous systems rapidly develop. During this stage, small amounts of gentle handling by careful humans appear to strengthen the puppies' physiological development and have a beneficial behavioral effect. Does the breeder of your prospective Dal puppy know this, and has he provided appropriately?

The Transitional Period

The transitional period occurs from the second to the third week of the puppies' lives (14–21 days). This period is packed with important developmental milestones. Their eyes open and their vision sharpens from blurred images to the recognition of distinct features. They start cutting teeth, walking on four legs, defecating on their own, and even leaving the nesting area to urinate/defecate and then returning to the brood. Although their senses are on "overload" during this period, it is extremely important to continue with gentle handling by the humans in their environment to stimulate motor development and prepare them for socialization. Normal household noises become a part of their lives as well.

period encompasses so many activities that it can almost be broken down into further sub-categories. From the 22nd day on, the puppies become aware of their surroundings, can hear and distinguish between different noises, begin to eat food in addition to nursing, bark, wag their tails, and begin to chew on their littermates. At 28 days, growling, teeth-baring, chasing, and prey-killing games begin. At 36 days, weaning onto solid food begins and the pups' curiosity about their environment increases.

"Who me? I didn't make that puddle!" Eight-week-old Paisley's Honey's Chocolate Chips (L) has the look of puppy innocence. Owned by Dan and Janice Maguire.

Was the litter from which you are considering purchasing a Dal puppy raised in the middle of household activities, or were the pups isolated in a dim, quiet room or, even worse, the garage or a shed in the back yard?

The Socialization Period

The fourth week, beginning on the 22nd day, inaugurates the socialization period, which lasts until 10–12 weeks of age. This

They have little fear and the pack order is established as they engage in group play and mock sexual activities. At 49 days, their vision and hearing development have reached adult capacity, their brains have reached the final stage of development, and they have the courage to explore beyond the whelping box, investigating anything. At 56 days, there is a short period of fear of sudden and loud sounds and unexpected movement, and the pups develop caution about new things in their environment.

During this period of rapid development, other things are happening as well. Mom, if she is a good brood bitch and has been allowed to remain with her puppies, has taught them how to be good canine citizens. She has disciplined them with growls, quick barks, or rapidly applied nips that won't harm them, but that will send them squealing. She has taught them by example how much biting is too much, when too much playing becomes annoying, and when to step back and respect their elders' rights to eat first or chew on the best bones. If puppies are removed from the litter too early, they miss this invaluable training and may have difficulties associating with other dogs when they reach adulthood. How young was your puppy when you took it home? Did he miss out on this important training from mom?

Human contact must be in steady supply during the socialization period in order to produce puppies that are not afraid or wary of interaction with humans. Proper exposure to a variety of humans results in

puppies' thinking of humans as part of their "family" and treating them with the same respect they accord adult dogs. This respect, or pack discipline, is what allows you to train and maintain control over your pet. How much human interaction did your puppy receive?

Human and canine interaction is not the only important ingredient that goes into the making of a good pet. From the neonatal period through the 49th day, the neurological system of a pup completes its growth and comes to full potential. Certain physical activities can be done with each pup during this period that will enhance this development and help produce superior pets. Research has determined that a small amount of stress to neonatal puppies during their rapid neurological growth stage will increase the capacity of their systems, resulting in improved cardiovascular performance with stronger heartbeats; more efficient adrenal, hormonal, and pituitary glands; and greater resistance to stress and disease. The US military actually developed a program in an effort to improve the perfor-

Tattersall Howie Looya, "Howie," at 12 weeks of age.

mance of dogs in the military. It is a series of five exercises that is performed with each pup, for three to five seconds per exercise, every day during the neonatal and transitional periods. Once the puppy enters the socialization period, the breeder begins to enrich the puppies' environment by supplying a variety of toys in different shapes and sizes. The pups are introduced to a variety of different surfaces such as wooden floors, carpeting, concrete, gravel, and grass, as well as obstacles such as stairs, boxes to crawl into, and tubes to crawl through. Normal household noises such as radios, TVs, vacuum cleaners, washing machines, doorbells, children's voices, etc., are part of the daily routine. Overcoming the mild stress provided by these stimuli gives the puppies self-confidence. Proper socialization produces a confident puppy with a frame of mind that is receptive to learning.

CHOOSING THE PET DAL PUPPY

You now know that Dalmatians have high energy levels, possess quick minds, and tend to dominate their surroundings. Within a litter, however, these characteristics will vary in the intensity of their expression. The trick is to determine which puppy in the litter will be best suited to your family situation.

Before puppy shopping begins, sit down together as a family and write a brief description of your personalities, your daily lives, your favorite activities, and your thoughts on how the new puppy will fit into your lifestyle. Do you tend to be assertive or a little shy and quiet? Are you an active family, always on the go? Or do you prefer the more sedentary life of relaxation on the couch after a hard day's work? Are there kids in the family and, if so, how do they expect to relate to the puppy? These thoughts will give the breeder a good idea of which puppy's temperament is best suited to you and your family.

Some breeders will have given each puppy a "puppy aptitude test" and others know their bloodlines well enough to discern the temperament varieties among the

Rockstar's Paisley Night Moves, "Seger," at seven-and-a-half weeks of age. Owned by Pam and Bob Fisher.

pups without testing. Most breeders, knowing each puppy's characteristics, will attempt to guide you in your selection. Their goal is to match each puppy closely to their new families so that they will remain in their new homes forever. And while any good breeder will take a puppy back if the placement does not work, it is obviously to everyone's benefit to place a puppy in the proper home from the start.

As an average pet-owning household, you are not looking for a challenge from your Dal puppy. The average family does not want a top performance dog, nor do they want to stretch patience to the limit. Knowing that the Dalmatian has the tendency to be independent, you should pick a puppy that shows more of an inclination to come to you and to follow you willingly as you walk away. Knowing that the Dalmatian has the tendency to be dominant, you should pick a puppy that does not nip at your face and hands when he comes to you, and that doesn't pounce on your feet, bite your pantlegs, and get underfoot when following. Knowing that the Dalmatian can hides under the chair and avoids contact with you.

If the breeder has not done any aptitude testing, you can still check for general characteristics by asking to see the puppies

A basket full of Dal babies as adorable as these can make anyone's choice difficult. Liver pups owned by Helene and Pauline Masaschi.

also show aggressive behavior, you would not want to choose a pup that growls, snaps, or refuses to be held down. Knowing that the Dalmatian can be an overly active dog, you should look for the puppy whose responses are a little slower, yet is still willing and happy. Knowing that early socialization with humans is a key ingredient to proper development you would not choose a puppy, no matter how appealing, that sits shyly in the corner or one at a time and gauging their responses. You can kneel down and call them to you, get up and walk away, gently turn them on their backs and hold them for a few seconds, sit them in front of you, and stroke them head to tail. Throw one of the dog toys and see if the pup goes to get it and brings it back. These simple tests will give you a general idea of each pup's personality as well as suitability for youngsters.

PUTTING THE PIECES TOGETHER

This very brief description of the critical stages in a puppy's development should give you an idea of how important it is to have each ingredient added to the "mix" at the proper time in the proper amount to produce a well-adjusted puppy. You now understand the importance of "mom's" role in training the pups to be good canines and the importance of the breeder's role in selecting the proper genetic mix and then supplying the appropriate stimulation for optimum development. It would certainly not be to your advantage to pick a pup that has been removed from mom at four weeks of age, crated and shipped to strangers, and placed in the sterile environment of a Plexiglas cage with no littermates, no toys, and little human interaction.

It is also important to understand that the socialization period continues until 10–12 weeks of age. When the new puppy has come home with you, he still needs stimulation in the appropriate amounts and of the proper type to mold him into the well-behaved, well-adjusted pet you were hoping for. The third period of the enrichment stage is *entirely* up to you, as it lasts for the remainder of the pup's life, builds on the foundation that was set during his first few critical weeks, and is provided by the daily activities you engage in with him.

BUYING A SHOW PUPPY

Conformation

So you've decided that you want to show a Dalmatian. Welcome to the world of Dals and dog shows. If you've done your homework, you know that just because a dog is AKC-registered and has a few champions in its pedigree does not mean that the dog is show quality. Even the best dogs when bred together generally produce only a small percentage of show-quality puppies. Dals are not an easy breed to get right, and there are many things that can keep a puppy from being considered show quality.

Assuming that you've studied the Dalmatian standard, you know that Dals must have proper construction, sound movement, correct markings, the right kind of bite, and a steady disposition to be successful in the show ring. Such dogs do not come from the pet shop nor do they come from the Dalmatian owner who did nothing more than breed together two dogs "with papers." The vast majority of AKC-registered pups are bred by dog owners who will raise only one or two litters and could more correctly be called "puppy raisers." Although the pups may be healthy and well socialized, they are rarely more than average in quality. Their parents were bred together only because they were both Dalmatians, not because anyone was looking for the perfect match or expected the pups to be any better than their parents.

A smaller percentage of puppies is bred by people who are actually small-scale commercial breeders but sell directly to the buyer rather than through brokers. They advertise in local papers and sometimes

Future Am-Can. Ch. Cheshire's Northern Lights (L), also known as "Kajsa," as a puppy. Owned by Cheryl Steinmetz.

even in dog magazines, may talk about champions in the pups' pedigrees, and perhaps even offer what they call "show puppies." Some of these people can be quite convincing, so it's best to be very careful when answering such an ad.

A registerable dog with no disqualifying faults is not the same as a puppy with actual show potential, and the average novice breeder or puppy raiser has absolutely no idea what constitutes show potential. A dog might be "showable" without having any show potential whatsoever. None of the above-mentioned sources will prove satisfactory, and the person who wants a quality dog with potential to win in the ring must look elsewhere. *Show potential puppies come from breeders who show and win with their own dogs*. But where do we find them?

There are many ways to find quality breeders and quality dogs. Check to see if there is a regional Dalmatian club in your area. Most responsible breeders will be members of a regional Dalmatian club, if there is one in your area, and/or members of the Dalmatian Club of America (DCA). The conscientious breeder will follow the ethical guidelines of the DCA. People with computer access will find an astonishing amount of dog-related information on the Internet. The American Kennel Club and many national and regional breed clubs have web sites and home pages, as do some individual breeders. The Dalmatian Club of America's breeder referral coordinator as well as its corresponding secretary will be listed there, along with a variety of useful information on Dalmatians. A great deal of useful information also can be obtained by contacting the American Kennel Club.

Many potential buyers find the right breeders by attending dog shows. Watch the Dalmatian judging and talk with the exhibitors, but remember that most of them have more time to chat after the judging. Some of the exhibitors may be breeders, while others will own one or two dogs but may be able to put you in touch with the person from whom they purchased their dog(s). Breeders who don't have any litters planned will often refer you to a breeder who does. Remember though, your immediate goal is learning, not buying, so ask lots of questions and don't buy the first puppy that's available.

Attend a few dog shows to watch the judging. Inquire about the possibility of a Dalmatian specialty show in your area. Study the pictures in this book and in other Dalmatian publications. Buy or borrow a Chicagoland Pedigree book and study the pictures and pedigrees. Read and reread the standard and learn to apply it to dogs. There are many fine books on structure and soundness available at bookstores. The more you read and study, the better prepared you will be to purchase the right puppy and enter the world of dog shows. Remember that top breeders are more inclined to sell good puppies to buyers who have done their homework first. The more you know about dogs, dog shows, and Dalmatians, the better your chance of obtaining a genuinely good puppy.

It's a good idea to decide whether you would prefer a male or a female, a black or a liver, or whether you are willing to take the best puppy you can find. Males are often more fun to show and are great for learning about the breed and about dog shows. If you may want to become a breeder some day, a female is probably a more practical choice, but many breeders are less willing to sell a promising female pup to a novice show home. It might be better to buy a good young male, learn the ropes, prove your interest and commitment by finishing his championship and perhaps an obedience title as well, and then purchase a good female pup. You will be a familiar face or recognizable name, can supply references if needed, and will have made some useful connections.

Many buyers will purchase only one dog, finish its championship, and enjoy it as a special pet, while others will get hooked on dogs and dog shows and become serious breeders and exhibitors.

As you watch and learn you may find that there is a certain look or style that catches your eye, or you may notice that the dogs that consistently appeal to you are from one specific line or sired by a particular stud dog. Contact the breeder whose dogs you admire or the owner of the male whose often have waiting lists for puppies. Relatively few Dalmatian breeders have more than two or three litters a year. It's definitely worthwhile to be on a waiting list to get the right pup, but it's also a good idea to continue looking as long as you don't end up settling for less. Although it is generally

Liver pups at six weeks of age, bred and owned by Jeffrey Gillespie. The pup in front grew up to be Ch. Anchor Creek Spectacular.

offspring appeal to you, and express your interest in a show potential puppy. Explain exactly what you are looking for, give some background information about yourself, and offer to supply references if needed. Ask if there will be any puppies available or if they can refer you to another breeder who might have something that would interest you.

Be prepared to wait, as good breeders best for the prospective exhibitor to purchase his first show pup from an experienced breeder, the opportunity may arise to obtain a well-bred pup from a newer breeder. If that person has quality dogs that are winning in the ring and has a successful mentor or advisor, this can work out to everyone's satisfaction. Just remember that it takes an experienced eye to evaluate a puppy correctly and that an absence of disqualifying faults does not necessarily mean that a puppy has show potential.

Some buyers prefer to purchase dogs locally and, if there are good dogs in your area, this can work quite well. Responsible breeders work closely with their puppy buyers, thus giving the buyers the advantage of having a mentor who is readily accessible. It is sometimes possible to get a better puppy this way than you could otherwise, because the breeder will be able to keep an eye on things and be sure that the puppy is correctly raised and shown.

Don't hesitate to purchase a puppy from across the country if that's where you have to go to get the pedigree or the puppy you want. Most breeders can supply good puppy pictures or videos of their litters, and many of them are pleased to place quality dogs outside of their immediate areas. If the breeder has good dogs and a good reputation, and has sold winning dogs to other novices outside his area, you'll be just fine. Puppies are shipped cross-country to show homes all the time.

You may be offered a specific puppy or given the option to pick between several pups. Unless you have a strong preference for a certain puppy, it's probably better to tell the breeder that you would prefer the best overall puppy. Some litters do not have an obvious "pick" so if the pups under consideration are very similar, take the one that you find most appealing.

Breeders are often hesitant to sell a good puppy outright, particularly to a novice show home. If offered a puppy on co-ownership, be certain that you understand all of the terms of the sale. You may be able to purchase a better puppy or to pay less money in exchange for the breeder keeping some "strings" on the puppy. These might include the right to take the bitch back for a litter or the right to take one or more puppies from future litters. If the puppy is a male, the breeder may want to retain one or more stud services. Whatever the terms, it's very important that everything is in writing, especially the specifics on which party is

responsible for which expenses. Co-ownerships normally have an end date as well, such as when the dog finishes a title, reaches a certain age, or the breeder receives one or more puppies.

The AKC discourages co-ownerships because of the potential for misunderstandings, and unsuccessful co-ownerships often end up in court. Co-ownerships are very common in Dalmatians, and many longtime friendships have their origins in such agreements. A great many successful breeders got off to the right start because they were able to purchase an outstanding dog that way. If everyone understands and honors the terms of the contract, co-ownerships can prove very satisfactory to all concerned.

Any puppy you decide to buy should come from a background that is successful in the show ring as well as genetically healthy. The parents should be BAER tested for hearing, and should have had their hips x-rayed and evaluated by the OFA or Penn-Hip™. Many breeders also do eye checks and bloodwork, but hearing and hip evaluations are absolutely essential.

Before making a commitment to buy, be absolutely certain that you understand the terms of the sales contract and that you know what kinds of guarantees will apply. All contracts should be in writing and signed by both the buyer and the seller. Some contracts are very straightforward and simple, while others are exceedingly complex and detailed. Beware the sales contract that has too many strings attached.

The average show contract will identify the buyer and seller and should contain all of the information appearing on the registration application. It will guarantee the puppy's health for some period of time and offer a refund or a replacement if he is checked out by a veterinarian and found to have health problems. In addition, a show contract generally guarantees that the puppy will not develop disqualifying faults within a certain time period (such as two years) and will offer a refund or a replacement if that should happen. Many contracts also guarantee that the dog will have OFA-

This sophisticated young lady is Can. Ch. Avalon n Paisley Pawprints. "Katy" is owned by Janet Kumka and Rick Miller.

certifiable hips at the age of two. The buyer may also have to agree to certain conditions such as taking the dog through obedience training, keeping it as a house dog, or following through on the anticipated show career. If you have any questions about the contract, ask before you sign!

Obedience

Most obedience exhibitors started with a dog that was purchased strictly as a family pet or companion. It may have come from a responsible breeder, a pet shop, the local humane society, or an ad in the Sunday paper. The dog was signed up for obedience classes to teach it "manners" and the owner got hooked on obedience. Now it's time to buy a dog strictly for obedience, and how shall we do it this time?

Some obedience exhibitors

also want a potential show dog, one that can be shown in the breed ring as well as in obedience ring. In that case, the potential buyer would probably want to follow the same steps as the person seeking a dog strictly for the breed ring with the added provision that the breeder is knowledgeable about obedience, is willing to test all likely puppies, or will allow the obedience exhibitor an opportunity to test the puppies. There are a number of successful breeders who do both conformation and obedience with their dogs, and the potential exhibitor might do well to contact such a breeder.

If the obedience exhibitor has no interest in breed ring competition, or only requires a Dal that is good looking, sound, with a pleasant disposition, almost any responsible breeder might have a suitable puppy available. Most breeders will be perfectly willing to allow a prospective buyer to test the pups if they have not already been tested, provided the pups are not stressed or exposed to potentially harmful situations.

In breeds such as the Golden Retriever there are lines that are known for their obedience potential and trainability. That's less common in Dalmatians, but it's prob-

Paisley Matrix Rolling Stone at nine weeks of age. Not only did "Jagger" grow up to be a conformation champion, he earned his CDX title as well. Owned by Pam and Bob Fisher.

ably easier to find the right prospect if the breeder is also an obedience person. While puppy aptitude testing may prove very helpful in selecting a puppy, the breeder's observations may be equally useful. A pedigree full of obedience-titled dogs, particularly dogs who finished those titles with good scores, certainly indicates that at least some of the pups will have a better than average chance to be successful in the obedience ring.

A dog destined for an obedience career must be sound and athletic to stand up to the rigors of the sport, particularly if the buyer plans to go for advanced titles or is looking for a competition dog. At the very least, the immediate ancestors must have OFA- or Penn-Hip™-certified hips. It would be most unfortunate to put months or years of training into a competition dog and have it develop a crippling or degenerative health problem that would require an early retirement.

Evaluating a Litter

Whether you are evaluating your own litter or buying from another breeder, it may be necessary to make decisions on the relative merits of several pups in a litter. While it would take a crystal ball to predict *exactly* how any pup will look as an adult, there are a number of things to consider that will help to increase the accuracy of the predictions.

Most successful breeders have their own theories about the correct age and best method for evaluating a litter. Although some belong to the "pick 'em when they're wet" school, most breeders prefer to wait somewhat longer before making any kind of selection, however tentative. Some breeders will tell you that their current star was selected when he was three minutes or three days or three weeks old, but most simply watch the pups as they develop and make their initial selections at six to seven weeks of age. By that age it is possible to eliminate the obvious pets, including any pups with patches, large amounts of missing trim, or poor markings. Pups with sig-

nificant structural problems such as crooked legs, cowhocks, roached backs, and very long bodies are also quite evident, even to the untrained eye.

A six-week-old pup has its basic spotting pattern, ideally has complete eye and nose trim, should have a normal scissors bite, should have two palpable testicles if male, is coming up on its feet, and is starting to display its basic personality. Most experienced breeders agree that the dog's proportions and outline are pretty much evident by six weeks of age, and that gait can be assessed with a good degree of success. By the age of eight to ten weeks, many puppies have started to look long, leggy, and awkward, so it is usually best to stick with the earlier decision and not do too much second guessing.

Stacked photos (on a table) from all angles should be taken at six weeks because it is often possible to pick out things in a picture that are easily overlooked when watching a litter of active puppies. The pictures will also provide a record of each pup for comparison with previous and subsequent litters and are an important part of the learning process. It's much easier to evaluate pups that are not excessively fat, and it is best to take the pictures when the pups have empty stomachs. A videotape of the litter is nice to have, but snapshots are more helpful for study and comparison.

Unless the evaluator can understand and appreciate correct structure on an adult Dalmatian, it is certainly not possible to effectively evaluate a litter with any degree of success. Nice spots, ears that work, complete trim, a correct bite, and no patches are not sufficient to make any pup a show prospect, yet such pups are often sold as "show quality." It would be far better to classify such pups as "showable," which merely means that it is a registerable dog that has no disqualifying faults. Things like crooked front boning, flat feet, saggy or roached toplines, long backs, ewe necks, bad croups, and cowhocks are no more correct on pups than they are on adult dogs, and it is essential that the evaluator be objective about what he is seeing. It's wise to have several experienced breeders look at the litter and explain what they see on individual pups, and it's important not to be offended or defensive when the pups are faulted. If you want to learn, you need honest input. The evaluators don't even have to be Dalmatian breeders, as basic construction and movement are quite similar in many breeds.

Six-week-old pups can improve in many areas, so don't necessarily discard a pup that comes up a little short in a few areas at this age. Frosty spotting may clear, small pieces of eye and nose trim may fill in, high tails often come down, eye color can change, and feet may improve when the pup slims down or gets more exercise. However, if one or both parents have frosty spots, missing trim, high tails, light eyes, or poor feet, the chances of those things improving are not very good! This is where objectivity, a knowledge of the standard, and information about the dogs in the pups' pedigree become important. If the evaluator is unable to recognize the faults on the dam or is not aware of the sire's shortcomings, he may not be able to adequately evaluate the pups.

Don't be too quick to plan the show career of a six-week-old pup, however promising, as many things can still go wrong. Breeding is not an exact science and many unpleasant surprises show up in even the most well-bred, carefully planned litter. Just because the sire and dam are moderate-sized dogs with good markings and correct tail carriage, don't assume that the pups will all be the same way. If the pedigree contains an oversized grandsire, a granddam with a high tail, and some other badly marked dogs, it's entirely possible that one or more of the pups will have inherited those traits. There is a great deal of variation within any breed, which is why it is so important to know as much as possible about the dogs in the pedigree when planning a litter.

Size varies a great deal in Dalmatians and most lines will produce an occasional oversized dog. It's very hard to predict a pup's eventual size, and the smallest pup in the litter may grow to be the tallest adult. Again, the size of the puppy's immediate ancestors will provide the best clue as to its eventual size.

Although the basic spotting pattern is

A tubful of lovely Dal pups owned by Gilda Aquilera. A number of them went on to star in the breed and obedience rings.

apparent at six weeks, some dogs have spots that continue to grow and a well-marked pup may be too heavily spotted as an adult. Lightly spotted dogs must have good sized markings to be attractive, and a pup whose spots don't grow much will look too white as an adult. Some lines produce "ticking," small spots that fill in between the larger markings. Ticking often does not show up until after six weeks of age and it can ruin the appearance of an otherwise acceptable spotting pattern. Ticking is not desirable and any spotting that shows up after six weeks will normally be ticking rather than full-size spotting.

Spots should be round, clear, and uniform in size, with crisp edges and sharp contrast. Pups with ragged spots and mixed spot sizes are the most likely to add ticking,

Four-month-old litter brothers J Dream Lazy Acres General Purpose and J Dream Lazy Acres Model A. Bred by Jackie Jens and Kristy Stogdill.

and spots that are frosty (a mixture of colored and white hairs in the spots) at six weeks are more likely to be frosty on adult dogs. Some pups are born with shaggy coats and an overlay of long white hairs which normally begin to shed out by six weeks. A frosty-looking pup that is obviously shedding the long fuzzy hairs will probably end up with clear spotting. Some pups who were vividly colored at six weeks will get fuzzy edges to their spots a few weeks later, a process referred to as "blooming." The spot edges usually clear out again in a few weeks, leaving the pup with large vivid markings.

In some lines, all the pups in a litter will carry their tails high by six weeks of age. If the puppies' background consists primarily of dogs with good tail carriage, it's safe to assume that most of the tails will come down, but it's hard to predict which ones won't! Eyes that look very dark on black-spotted pups can lighten with age, while the eyes on liver-spotted pups normally darken.

Nose and eye trim may fill in a great deal after six weeks, but in most lines it fills in very little after that age, especially on liver pups. It has often been said that the pups sold to pet homes may end up with complete trim, while the ones the breeder keeps to watch never change at all!

Although overshot bites are not common in Dalmatians, undershot bites are seen from time to time and can appear in many lines. A puppy that is undershot at six weeks should be placed in a pet home, as the chances of its correcting are slim to none. It is more common for a puppy's bite to look fine at six weeks and go off at three to four months when the adult teeth come in. A very tight-fitting scissors bite on a pup should be watched carefully as this type of bite is more likely to end up undershot than a bite that shows a bigger overlap between the top and bottom teeth. Level bites on pups are also likely to end up undershot, and dogs with exceedingly small teeth seem more likely to have and produce bite problems. Some pups look slightly overshot

This cutie is Paisley Premonition, "Martin," at about three months of age. Owned by Tom and Anne Marie Gunther.

at six weeks while others appear a bit overshot at about six months. In most cases, these dogs turn out to have excellent bites.

When stacking the pups on a table, note which ones are relaxed and comfortable with alert expressions and wagging tails. Confidence is very important in a pup selected for showing. Some pups are easy to stack, while others absolutely refuse to stand still. It usually works best if the pups are tired from playing hard, but not too frantic about eating. Again, it will help to have an experienced person demonstrate the best way to get the pups to stand still.

A table with a rubber mat for good traction, an auto-focus camera, fast film, and a flash attachment will make the job easier. Some pups photograph particularly well because of their superior construction.

A pup that looks good in most of the pictures is normally a better bet than one that just happens to put it together for one picture. A properly constructed pup does not need to "have his pieces put together" to photograph well.

A good pup will be able to stand square with his front feet turning neither in nor out. A front that toes out *slightly* will normally end up fine if the dog has strong pasterns and good feet, while a front that toes in will always get worse. Some breeders prefer to see pups toe out slightly at six weeks of age, while others like the look of pole-straight legs, which may end up toeing in slightly on adults.

This is the time to look for crooked boning, since even at this age Dalmatian pups should have relatively straight legs and strong pasterns. Looking down from

Taking a break from the hectic pace of puppyhood is future CD and CGC Trigger Hill's I'm So Happy. Owned by Kris and Debbie Jamsa.

above should reveal elbows that are neither sticking out nor tucked in under the chest. When the hindquarters are stacked, the hocks should not turn in, nor should the rear feet turn out. The hocks may appear to turn out slightly at this age, and most breeders expect that kind of rear to become particularly nice. Some rears will stand wider and look like an inverted "U," while others will look like an inverted "V." In either case, the hindquarters should already show some muscle definition and stand true without any twisting.

Viewed from the side, the pup should show a relatively level topline and appear square or just slightly longer than tall, with plenty of neck. Some lines add leg after this age, and a pup who is quite square at six weeks may end up too high on leg as an adult. A soft back rarely gets better, but pups with very solid level backs may hump up slightly when stacked, especially if they are somewhat tense. This should not be confused with a roach.

The puppy should be stacked with his hocks perpendicular to the ground. If stacked with his rear overstretched, it will level out what may be a faulty topline. A bad croup

and low set tail generally worsen with age. A pup that stands with high withers and a ski-slope topline does not show correct construction and normally has straight shoulders and a short neck as well. Pups at this age often carry their tails high, but tails that are set on high will probably stay high.

Rear angulation can be seen at this age and a pup with straight stifles will grow into an adult with straight stifles. Some pups may show an impressive amount of angulation, but unless the pup also stands well on his rear and has sufficient muscle in his hindquarters, he will merely end up an over-angulated and cowhocked adult. Balanced angulation of the front and rear is necessary for the dog to move correctly.

Shoulder layback and the proportionate lengths of the shoulder blade and upper arm can be observed, although this is better evaluated by watching the puppy move and seeing how he uses what he has. The puppy should stand with his front legs set a bit under his body rather than coming straight down from his neck.

Heads vary a great deal in the breed, and even more so on puppies. The puppy should show parallel planes for the skull and muzzle, but some puppies have rather domey skulls which makes assesing the head planes more difficult. Ears should be set properly—high-set or low-set ears do not usually improve, but the ears on puppies are normally larger in proportion to the head than they are on adults. The puppy should be capable of bringing both ears forward in an alert expression and the front edges of the ears should lie close to the head. The head should be neither too broad in skull nor too cheeky. However, a head that appears short and blocky may end up just fine while a snipey head without enough underjaw will never be any better on an adult.

Good feet are very important in the Dalmatian, but the feet are often not quite finished on young pups. Some pups show good feet by six or seven weeks, while in other cases it takes a little longer for the pups to come up on their feet. Winter pups who are raised indoors and pups who are excessively heavy may spread their toes rather than show tight compact feet, but they must have relatively short toes and thick pads. Thin splayed feet and long toes without knuckles do not turn into acceptable feet.

Other things that can be evaluated at this age are width in front, amount of bone, and overall body length. The Dalmatian should not be a wide dog and the pup who is overly broad in front, especially if he also has a wide body and barrel-shaped ribbing, may move out at the elbows and have an awkward gait. By the same token, the pup should not be too narrow with both legs appearing to "come out of the same hole." Such dogs normally have restricted gaits and incorrect footfall. A six-week-old pup should have some forechest, and the pup with a big hole between his front legs will not improve. Dal pups must have plenty of bone for their size, but the amount shown by pups will vary somewhat between lines. The pups under consideration should not have less bone than their littermates, and they should have sturdy-looking legs. Notice the proportionate length between the pup's rib cage and loin area, as the rib cage should always be significantly longer than the loin no matter what the dog's overall body length.

It is quite possible to evaluate movement in young pups, but it takes patience as well as experience and the observer must be able to evaluate movement in adult dogs first. A correctly constructed pup normally trots much of the time,

while a less well-put-together pup seems to bounce or run when moving and rarely settles into a trot. Sit on the floor and evaluate the pups one at a time. It helps to have someone who the pups will follow around the room. A video camera is very useful here as it is possible to slow down the action and study the movement. It is particularly helpful if the pups can be convinced to trot up and down the sidewalk.

The pups should be able to trot comfortably and show relatively level toplines. Even at this age, the dogs with the long strides and smooth gaits are quite obvious. Avoid the pup with the short mincy steps, excessively high leg action, and bouncy topline. Such a pup may be eye-catching, but his movement is not correct. What you are looking for is the pup that appears to take "long steps" even when walking. Try to watch each pup down and back. The pup should be able to move in a straight line. As he moves away from you, his movement should be wide and strong, his hocks should not turn in nor his rear feet turn out, and you should never be able to see elbow action. Don't worry if he does not appear to single track when moving

Future Ch. Paisley's Perfect Timing, UD. Owned by Pat Mullin.

231

away at this age. As he comes toward you, there should be no flying elbows or flipping feet and he should show a tendency to single track. Don't confuse single tracking with a narrow-fronted pup who is crossing over. Pups that move parallel in front normally continue to do so and will move awkwardly as adults.

A properly socialized pup with a good disposition will be friendly and outgoing. He should be attracted to strangers and comfortable about being handled, although he may be wiggly and prefer to play with his littermates. Beware the puppy that does not come willingly to strangers or that appears frightened during the evaluation. Temperaments are not always perfect in Dalmatians, even in the best lines, so make no excuses for a puppy who is frightened or unfriendly. Dogs can go through fear periods at various times during their puppyhood, but six- to eight-week-old pups should always be friendly and fearless. A puppy aptitude test can be useful in selecting a young show prospect, especially when it includes such tests as sound sensitivity.

Sometimes a pup just stands out from an early age. In addition to having the structure and spotting that are required in a show dog, this pup also has an attitude that just makes you notice him—a way of carrying himself that suggests that he knows he's something special. Attitude and presence go a long way in the show ring, and a dog with that "special something" will often win more than a better constructed dog without it. A dog with a "show-dog attitude" is great fun to show, whether he is the novice's first show dog or is destined for a Specials career.

A champion mother and a champion son prove that quality dogs are produced from good breeding. Ch. Folklore n Firesprite Wm Tell and his dam Ch. Firesprites Trixi Dixi are owned by Robert and Diana Skibinski and Norma Baley.

Raising & Training the Dalmatian

GENERAL CARE

One of the best ways to establish a good rapport with your Dal puppy is to set aside time every day for a quick once-over of the grooming "check points." He really doesn't care what you are doing just as long as you are paying attention to him. As an added plus, he will become accustomed to submitting to thorough inspections such as those given by the veterinarian. Start with his head and work your way down his body.

wax seems to build up often or if you notice a strong odor when you lift the ear flap, the dog probably has an ear infection and needs medical attention. Other indications of ear problems are constant scratching at the ears, shaking of the head, or holding the head tilted to one side. Incidentally, you should never let the dog hang his head out of the window of a moving car; you run the risk of blinding him for life.

Eyes, Nose, and Ears

Check for a discharge and/or staining around the eyes; this is one of the first signs of ill health in other parts of the body. Some "sleep" in the corners is acceptable but excessive amounts indicate a problem. Look at his nose and check for a discharge; note the temperature and feel the texture of the nose leather. The nose of a normal, healthy dog should be cool to the touch, damp, and pliable. Examine the inside of the ear for any accumulation of wax or dirt and carefully remove it with a damp washcloth or soft paper towel. Never probe into the ear canal with anything smaller than your fingertip. If

Teeth

If you wish to go to the trouble, you can get your Dal puppy used to having his teeth brushed. A wild animal keeps its teeth clean by the chewing action needed to consume

Liver-spotted Bailey goes through the ritual of having her teeth brushed. Owned by Maureen Bouska and Mike Deer.

food, but modern society has removed this natural action by feeding commercial foods. Items such as rawhide, Nylabones®, or large dog biscuits can simulate this chewing action and save you the hassle of trying to brush your dog's teeth daily, but they don't do a complete cleaning job. Having his teeth cleaned annually by the veterinarian is a good routine to establish. If you insist on giving your pup bones to chew on, give only the commercially available sterilized shank bones found in pet stores and pet-supply catalogs. Rib bones, chicken bones, and

Safe and durable chew toys such as the ones made by Nylabone® will help keep your Dal's teeth clean in between brushings.

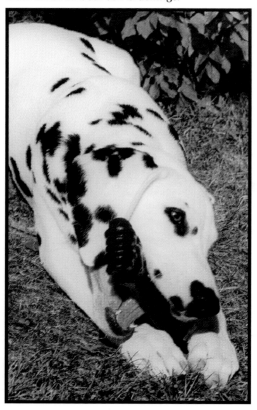

pork bones are *forbidden*, as they will splinter too easily, causing internal injuries.

Coat

Dalmatians *shed*. If the breeder you purchased your puppy from did not happen to mention this fact and you haven't caught on

to it from reading other chapters in this book, let us say it again. Dalmatians *shed*. Proper nutrition will keep his coat in prime condition but the Dalmatian typically replaces dead hair on a constant basis. Regular coat care can reduce the amount of hair left on furniture, rugs, and clothing. Brushing, even just a quick once-over, can help keep shedding to a minimum. Use a rubber brush or rubber grooming glove; bristle brushes do not remove dead hair effectively and wire brushes are too harsh. Follow each stroke of the brush with a stroke of your hand. This has two functions: it smoothes the coat into place and it allows you to check for small foreign objects or insects clinging to the skin.

Bathing the Dalmatian on a regular basis is not recommended; the Dal is typically a dry-skinned dog and the addition of soap and water will dry the coat even further. If he gets dirty, apply a damp wash cloth to the coat, rubbing in the direction that the hair grows. Most of the accumulated dirt will tend to stay on top of the coat and can be easily removed this way. A thorough brushing will remove the remainder of the dirt. If you feel that your Dal must be bathed, use tepid (body temperature) water and a very mild hypoallergenic dog shampoo designed for sensitive skin. Start with the head, using only water or a soapy wash cloth on the face and ears and being careful not to get water into the ears. Apply shampoo to the rest of the dog, working your way down the body and legs. *Rinse well.* Dry quickly with several thick towels, rubbing only in the direction in which the hair grows. Never brush a wet dog—this will remove too much hair. To hasten drying and to prevent him from catching cold, put your dog in a warm area and keep him active and on his feet.

Feet

Pick up each foot and examine the pads. You are looking for scabs, open cuts, small scratches, or punctures. Wash any wound thoroughly and treat with a non-poisonous disinfectant. Follow up with daily checks to be sure no infection develops. Note the texture of the pads—they should be thick and tough, yet resilient. Dry, scaly pads could indicate a nutrition problem.

Nails

Pet owners seem to be extremely intimidated by the thought of cutting their puppies' nails. Do not allow the puppy to convince you that nail trimming is traumatic—Dals are excellent actors. Failure to keep his nails trimmed can cause the puppy to change the distribution of weight on his feet. This change in distribution can put stress on joints that were not designed for such stress; they may develop abnormally, causing arthritis in later years. In addition, allowing the nails to grow overly long and then having the veterinarian remove them yearly will cost you an unnecessary expense and cause the dog unnecessary trauma. Allowing your Dal to set his own grooming rules is like letting a child tell you whether or not he intends to bathe or brush his teeth!

Weekly or bi-weekly nail care is ideal and will take so little time that the puppy will soon stop protesting. You want a minimum amount of nail to surround the "quick," or live portion. In a very small puppy it is easier to use a heavy-duty nail clipper designed for humans; as he grows you will need to switch to one of the many different types of clippers designed for dogs. There are guillotine-action clippers with replaceable blades and scissor-action clippers that must be periodically replaced. Try one type, and if it isn't comfortable to use then switch to another type. Taking small "nips" off the nail rather than one large chunk is an easy method for beginners.

Filing is another method of keeping the nails short. A fine-toothed wood rasp can be used to stroke the front, top, and both sides of the nail, keeping it trimmed to a proper length without the risk of cutting

"Do I have to?" Mandy is waiting patiently for her bath, but she doesn't look too excited about it.

"Mom needs more grooming before a show than I do!" Mandy waits for "mom" Karen Larson to get ready.

into the quick. However, filing is more time-consuming and your Dal may run out of patience before you run out of nails to file. People with many dogs to groom sometimes go to the expense of purchasing a small electric hand-grinder such as is found in hobby stores, plug-in or cordless, with a variety of interchangeable grinding heads. This does speed up the job once the puppy has become accustomed to the noise and vibration, but you must have patience when introducing this new method of nail grooming.

Should you happen to cut into the quick when clipping your Dal's nails there is no need to panic—breed history does not record any Dalmatians that have bled to death from such an accident! A wet tea bag applied to the end of the nail will help stop the flow of blood; a damp paper towel held tight to the tip of the nail will also

suffice, but takes longer. Purchase a styptic powder that you can dip the nail into, and a small bottle will last forever. In any case, your Dal will forget the incident and move on to new things much sooner than you will, so don't be intimidated by the experience.

NUTRITION

So much good information is available about canine nutrition that it is impossible to condense it into one chapter in this book, let alone a portion of a chapter, so we will give a general overview of nutrition basics. Relating these basics to the particular nutritional needs of the normal Dalmatian will be a little more difficult since no formal nutritional studies of the breed have been undertaken by professional laboratories or veterinary schools.

There is a big difference between a well-fed Dal and a Dal who is fed well. Keeping them "well-fed" is no problem—99.9% of the Dals in this world live to eat. On the other hand, a full stomach and a balanced diet are not always equal. The nutritionally ideal diet provides the proper amounts of proteins, fats, carbohydrates, vitamins, and minerals in the proper quantities to satisfy the dog. Failure to provide one of these elements can tip the scales enough to change the delicate balance existing between them and result in an inadequate diet for proper growth, health, and maintenance.

A puppy, a lactating bitch, a heavily campaigned show dog, a sedentary couch potato, and a geriatric Dal have different nutritional needs. The average dog food is nutritionally formulated to suit the average adult dog. Many owners use an inexpensive grocery-store brand dog food and think they can improve quality by customized supplementation. Beware! Under- and over-supplementation are equally dangerous, as this is one area where you can provide too much of a good thing. There has been such an improvement in manufactured dog food in the last decade that careful shopping can give you everything your Dal needs in one bag, with no supplements necessary.

Careful shopping starts with labels. Label language is regulated by the Food and Drug Administration (FDA), the Department of Agriculture (USDA), and the Federal Trade Commission (FTC). The label must contain the brand name, the product name, what animal it is intended for, a nutrition statement (i.e., formulated for puppies, older dogs, etc.), an ingredient list, and a guaranteed analysis. Ingredients must be listed in descending order by their weight. The guaranteed analysis must state the minimum amounts of crude protein and crude fat and the maximum amounts of crude fiber and moisture in the food as contained in the package before any additions are made by the consumer.

There are several important red flags here. Crude protein indicates the nitrogen content of the product as determined chemi-

cally, but does not guarantee the quality of the protein, its amino-acid balance, or how digestible it is. Protein, often the most expensive ingredient in dog food, can be of low quality—chicken beaks, claws, feathers, beef hooves, and horns can all be classified as protein but are not necessarily digestible or "available" to the system of the pet. Crude fiber is the amount of indigestible material contained in the food and is usually a derivative of plant products. Crude fat is that part of the food that is soluble in either; it contains 2.25 times the calories of the same amount of carbohydrates and protein. The term "crude" is technically a chemical analysis reference. It does not mean that dogs obtain 21% protein when the label reads "crude protein is 21%." The digestibility (availability) of the protein determines the actual percentage used by the pet and is

This Dal is trying to pick her own snack! Ch. Cyncar Miss Molly of Croatia is owned by Maureen Bouska and Mike Deer.

237

not always listed on the average label.

Generic brands—to feed or not to feed? The National Research Council (NRC) sets recommended levels of nutrients. In a study published in 1984, over 50% of the generic brands tested failed to meet their own labeled guaranteed analysis, 83% failed to meet the NRC levels for at least one nutrient, and up to 63% were insufficient in vitamin and/or mineral content or were not properly balanced, having either too little or too much of one or more minerals. Generics maintain their low prices by purchasing ingredients that are at a surplus on the market. Consequently, their ingredients change from month to month. Since protein is the most expensive ingredient, beaks, claws, and hooves are thrown into the recipe in order to maintain the "crude protein" percentage level, but it is not "available" protein.

A dog must have the correct proportion of proteins, fats, carbohydrates, vitamins, and minerals. Carbohydrates are the energy source and should comprise 70% of the dog's diet. They are found in cereals (wheat, rice, corn, oats) and sugars, and are high in calories. For maximum absorption, the cereals must be processed or cooked. If carbohydrates are lacking, the dog will use his body's proteins for energy. Proteins are necessary for growth and for the development and maintenance of body tissues. They should average at least 20% of the diet and are generally derived from meat, soybeans, fish, or other meat by-products. A small amount of fat is required to aid in the absorption of vitamins and minerals. Vitamin and mineral requirements vary with age and activity level, and foods formulated for these specific categories will generally have the proper levels.

Knowing the particular nutritional needs of your own Dal is the next step. The average growing puppy needs, per kilogram of body weight (a kilogram being equivalent to 2.2 pounds), 6.6 grams of protein and 130 calories. At six months, the level is 3.6 grams protein/100 calories, and, as an adult, 2.1 grams protein/65 calories. These figures produce an average growth rate in a dog with average activity levels. Underfeeding is preferable to overfeeding; studies have proven that overfeeding leads to abnormalities whereas underfeeding merely slows the growth rate. Underfeeding is not equated with malnutrition. It is defined as giving lesser quantities of a quality food whereas malnutrition is defined as the withholding of proper nutrients.

The nutritional needs of the pregnant bitch, the working dog, and the geriatric dog all vary widely from those of the average dog. The pregnant bitch should be switched to a formula for growth/lactation with no increase in the amount fed for the first four weeks, followed by an increase in the amount fed for the remainder of gestation and lactation. Caloric requirements increase sharply to 300 percent of normal during lactation.

The working dog's needs can vary so widely that it is impossible to gauge protein and caloric requirements. The diet should maintain proper weight, glossy coat, stamina, and general good health.

The nutritional needs of the geriatric dog could be an entire book in itself. Caloric intake is reduced to compensate for the reduced activity level and to avoid obesity; otherwise, the strain on the dog's limited organ reserve can shorten his lifespan. Reduced intake makes it imperative that a high-quality food is given. Fat supplements should not be added to the diet because they are difficult for the older dog to digest, can cause flatulence, and are high in calories. A quality food formulated for the geriatric dog will have the proper level of fat necessary to aid in the intestinal absorption of vitamins and provide for the manufacture of essential fatty acids. Geriatric dogs need more vitamins and minerals; reduced organ and intestinal tract function adds to the loss of these elements and they should be present in the daily food rations or supplemented as per your veterinarian's guidance.

A diet too rich in meat or one containing

It's dinnertime...and Ch. Hopi Kachina Mashanta just can't wait! "Chamita" and her more patient friends are owned by Ray and Cathy Nogar.

protein of poor quality creates an increased nitrogen load which must be handled by the liver and kidneys. Remember, protein is measured chemically by its nitrogen content. Excessive amounts of protein are waste products and indigestible proteins (nitrogens) from poor-quality sources also find their way to the kidneys. In addition, some food sources for protein are higher in "purines" than others (e.g., beef, organ meats, and certain vegetables). Excessive proteins, especially purines, are not needed by the Dalmatian and increase the risk of stones forming in the kidney or bladder. Look for a food that derives its protein from a source other than beef or organ meats. Energy needs are better met by giving carbohydrates that are cooked to break down starch granules than by increasing levels of the wrong type of protein.

The dog-food industry is pretty much self-regulated outside of certain items covered by the FDA. To determine which firms are reputable, find out if they do product testing and to what extent. Ask them for their sources of the protein, fat, and fiber content of their food. If grain-based, how do they process the grain? Cooked grains have complete nutritional availability; uncooked grains are more fiber than anything else. Monitor product labels over several months to see if percentages fluctuate and if ingredient lists vary.

Consider using a rice-based food for this breed, with easily digested lamb as its protein source. You can also use a rice-and-vegetable commercial product. Keep in mind the nutritional stage of your Dal. Assess the label for the nutritional value of the product and test the product over several months to give it a fair chance. Avoid excessive use of doggy treats—they add empty calories, have little nutritive value, and are usually made from beef and/or organ meat sources. Feed raw fruits and vegetables, except for the high-purine ones, as treats instead—they are nutritional and add to the dog's self-image as a small four-legged person/family member!

How Much to Feed

Presuming that the nutrition information has been understood and you are now feeding your Dalmatian a good-quality kibble designed for his particular needs, you may still have questions about what *quantity* to feed. Unfortunately there is no cut-and-dry rule that we can present you with because only you know the activity level of your Dal and how many calories he needs to consume to maintain proper weight. To start, check the label of the food you are using for the recommended amounts to feed based on the size of the dog being fed. Most experienced breeders will tell you that this is usually on the high side; you will probably find yourself decreasing that amount and still having a healthy Dal.

To gauge how much per meal to feed, take the recommended daily amount as found on the label and divide that by the number of meals you will be feeding per day. Feed this amount for one week and then analyze your dog's weight—has he gained, lost, or stayed the same? If he has gained/lost weight visibly in one week, decrease/increase the amount being fed per day by one-fourth to one-third. If his weight has not changed noticeably, continue feeding that amount for one more week and then assess his weight again. A weight gain/loss after *two* weeks calls for a *smaller* decrease/increase in the amount being fed. You want your Dalmatian to have a sleek, trim look without any ribs or spine showing. If his ribs are visible, he is too thin. If you can look down on his body from above and not see any indication of a "waist" behind his rib cage, he is too fat. If you are in doubt about proper weight, ask the breeder or your veterinarian for advice.

Frequency of Feedings

Most authorities recommend that dogs be fed in smaller amounts more often, so two feedings per day would be preferable to one large meal. This is much easier on the dog's digestive tract and helps minimize the possibility of bloat. A self-feeding schedule is not practical with this breed as the majority of Dalmatians would prefer to eat as much and as often as they could. Feeding the Dal his meals twice or three times daily allows you to gauge just how much food he is consuming, gives you the option of putting additives such as vitamins or other supplements in his food, and presents several opportunities for training as you make him sit and wait until the "OK" is given to eat. Most Dalmatian breeders advise that dry kibble be moistened before giving it to the dog, especially since the Dalmatian needs to consume as much water as possible to produce a more dilute urine. It is important to remember that *the Dalmatian needs access to water at all times* and should be encouraged to drink frequently.

The Dalmatian's particular characteristics of stone-forming are very important to be aware of; they are inherent in the breed, but not every Dalmatian will be a stone-former. You should be aware that it is possible to precipitate a stone crisis by feeding the Dalmatian improperly. Please read carefully on urinary-tract problems and their control.

TRAINING

So, you have a new puppy. How exciting! Puppies are such fun, so cute and cuddly, and oh so much work! But you're ready for all that. You thought about it for a long time before making the decision to add a puppy to your family and your already busy lifestyle. You did your homework and read everything you could find about buying a dog. You studied up on the breeds that interested you, went to a dog show and talked to owners of those breeds, visited several breeders, asked a million questions, and decided that the right breed for you was the Dalmatian. Or perhaps you've always wanted a Dalmatian and decided that now was the right time to get a pup. You've got the room, can make the time, and feel that you can afford the considerable expense that may be involved.

"Matilda" is caught being a "bad dog"—she isn't supposed to be up at the window. Ch. Korcula Waltzing Matilda is owned by Kay Arbuckle and Charles Garvin.

Hopefully you purchased your puppy from a breeder who explained both the negative and positive things about the breed. You were told that Dals are active, sometimes stubborn, and pushy by nature, and that they crave human companionship, require obedience training, shed year-round, and need to be raised with firmness and consistency. The breeder stressed how important it is to raise a puppy properly and how much time and effort that would require. You were told about contracts, crate training, housebreaking, vaccinations, obedience classes, chewing, digging, nipping, the right toys to buy, and all of the stages your puppy would go through.

Before you took your puppy home, you were given a "shopping list" of supplies and some recommended reading, a list that included informative books on how to raise and train a puppy. The breeder suggested that you buy or borrow several of the books and do some preliminary reading, and stressed that there was no one right way to raise a puppy. It was emphasized that the more you knew about dogs, dog behavior, and dog training, the better job you would do with your own puppy.

When you went to pick up your pup you were given a contract, the pup's health record, the registration information, a pedigree, and a booklet full of information, brochures, and useful articles. You were told to call day or night if you needed help or advice. The breeder asked you to please stay in touch and emphasized again that a responsible breeder cares about every puppy for its entire lifetime.

Or perhaps you did not buy quite so carefully. Perhaps you saw an ad on the bulletin board at work, checked out the pet column in the Sunday paper, or stopped (just to look!) when you saw a sign that read "Dalmatian Puppies For Sale." Perhaps your puppy came from a flea market or a boutique or you won him in a raffle. Maybe your pup came from the humane society because someone dumped the last few unsold pups from a litter that was more work and responsibility than he had anticipated. Perhaps your pup was an impulse purchase. It was so cute and really needed a home. So now you've got a puppy! What next?

Hopefully your pup is at least seven weeks old. Seven weeks is the age at which a dog's neurological development is complete. He's ready to face the world and become part of a human pack. Puppies need to remain with their dam and littermates for at least six weeks if they are to develop properly and grow up knowing that they are dogs. On the other hand, a puppy who lives with his littermates for longer

This litter of 12-week-old pups decided to help the Mastroianni family with after-dinner clean-up.

Above and below: "Hey, I know there was food here a few minutes ago...where'd it go?" Dal owned by Leslie Stanley.

the run of the whole backyard or use a dog pen? Who will be responsible for feeding, training, and walking him? Make these decisions now and stick with them. It's important to be consistent with puppies, and most Dalmatians do best in a structured environment. Don't keep changing the rules, or he'll learn to ignore all of them.

Buying and Using a Dog Crate

One of the most important purchases you can make is a dog crate. No, not a *cage*, the word is *crate*. Don't think in terms of "caging" your pup, think in terms of providing him with a safe little place to call his own—a den. You are providing him with a cozy place to sleep and a place to retreat to when things get too overwhelming or when he needs to rest. A crate makes housetraining much easier, helps to keep the puppy out of mischief when you can't supervise his activity, and gives you a place to put him when he is sick or when you have non-dog-loving company. If you will be taking the dog along when you travel, a crate will provide him with a safe place to ride and a familiar place to sleep, and he

It's a birthday party and Ch. All Around's Black Jack, CD is helping himself to a piece of cake! Owned by Jana Rodes.

than ten weeks must have individual handling by the breeder so that he is not too dependent on his littermates. It's important to remember that this is not a spotted child that you are adopting, but rather a dog. He will act, think, and respond like a dog, not like a person. Although he will bond with you and become part of your family, and may well be your best friend, he will always be your dog.

Decide on the Rules

It's important to make some decisions right away. Where will the pup sleep? Will he be allowed on the furniture? Will he eventually have the run of the house or will he be confined to a certain area? Will he be allowed to jump up on people? Will he have

can safely be left in his crate while you are sightseeing and when you go out to eat.

Crates come in many varieties, including the convenient metal fold-up crates and the inexpensive yet versatile plastic crates. Plastic crates are warmer in the winter, especially if your house is cool or drafty. If your house isn't air-conditioned, a wire crate will be more comfortable in the summer and you can throw a blanket over it to make it cozier. Perhaps you will want to buy several crates so that you can leave one in the car or the van. Buy a crate large enough for an adult dog and, if necessary, block off part of it while the puppy is small. Some pups will get into the habit of sleeping in one end of the crate and eliminating in the other end if the crate is too large.

Although some dogs are crated all day from an early age, this is not generally recommended for Dalmatians and is considered "crate abuse" by many. A dog will do his best not to soil his bed, but if he is crated for long periods of time before he has the necessary control to "hold it" all day, he will get into the nasty habit of crate soiling, which is something to be avoided at all costs. It is not healthy for a very young dog to try and control his bladder for that long of a time period. If someone is home all day, the pup can start using a crate right away. If the pup will be left for longer periods of time it is best to purchase a small wire pen (they are called "exercise pens" at pet-supply stores) and set it up in the kitchen or basement. Another possibility would be a pen in the garage with access to an outdoor kennel run or fenced yard.

If you choose to leave the pup with free run of the kitchen, a bathroom, or the laundry room, remember that bored or lonely dogs have been known to chew the corners of cabinets, pull up floor tiles, remove wallpaper, and eat through the wallboards!

Perhaps you can make arrangements with a neighbor to stop in once or twice a day and check on the pup, or perhaps a member of the family can get home for a few minutes at noon, at least while the pup is very young. A very young pup should never be left in a crate for more than a few hours at a time, except at night.

When using a pen in addition to the dog crate, leave the crate in the pen with the door open for a few days. If you are not using a pen, set the crate in a convenient spot, preferably in the kitchen. Put a blanket or towel and a few toys in the crate. Start feeding the pup in the crate, and put him in the crate when he is looking for a place to nap. Within a few days he'll feel right at home and you'll be ready to start crating him for a few hours at a time. When you start putting the pup in his crate at night, be sure you can hear him from your bedroom since most eight-week-old pups can not make it through the night without urinating. Take him outdoors to eliminate, then put him back into his crate.

Cover the floor of his area with a thick layer of papers. You are not paper training him as such, you are providing him with papers to use when no one is home during the day to take him outside. The papers will absorb any liquids and make cleanup easier for you. When you are home, you will be working on housetraining, not paper training.

In most homes, the best place for the crate is in the kitchen where the family spends lots of time, the floors can be easily cleaned, and a door to the outside is handy. You might prefer to have the crate in your bedroom at night, especially if you are gone for long periods of time during the day. The pup will benefit from the extra time with you. You might even choose to move the crate to the bedroom in the evening and then back to the kitchen in the daytime, or have a separate crate in the bedroom for nighttime use. Everyone's situation is different and there is no one right way to handle confinement.

It would be nice if all pups could go to homes where someone was at home all the time, but such situations are increasingly less common. People who are gone all day can do a perfectly satisfactory job of raising a puppy as long as they have sufficient time in the evenings and on weekends and they understand the puppy's need for companionship and training.

Housetraining

Using a dog crate makes housetraining a simple operation, but it still takes time and patience. Puppies need to eliminate often and should be taken out at regular intervals. They always urinate and defecate first thing in the morning and after each meal, and they urinate when they wake up from a nap. They tend to urinate at rather

more, remember that he will also urinate more often. (Once the puppy is housetrained, water should always be available).

If you are using a dog crate for housetraining, always take the pup outdoors as soon as he is taken out of the crate. When he cooperates, praise him enthusiastically, bring him back indoors, and let him run around and play for awhile. If he doesn't cooperate, put him back in his crate and try again in half an hour. When he is out of his crate, keep an eye on him and

All dogs, whether show dogs or companions, should be accustomed to a dog crate. Crossroads Checkers, CDX is relaxing comfortably.

short intervals, but this depends on the puppy and how much water he's been drinking. Some pups have marvelous control from an early age, while others take much longer to develop any kind of control at all. If you note when your puppy drinks, you'll have a better idea of when he will have to urinate, and if you take away the water bowl at 8:00 p.m., the pup will be more likely to make it through the night. When the weather is hot and the puppy drinks

dash him outside if he starts to circle, whine, pant, or look restless. Always stay outside with him and praise him when he performs.

Your initial goal is to teach the puppy that when he is taken outdoors, he is there for a reason and will be praised for cooperating. If he has an accident indoors, you should do nothing except clean up the mess. Puppies are not born knowing that it is wrong to eliminate in the house. It's your job to teach him that he should do it outdoors. If you catch him in the act, scoop him up quickly and take him outdoors, hoping that he'll have something left for you to praise him for! If you don't see him do it, just clean up the mess and say nothing. There is nothing to be gained from punishing a pup for doing something that he didn't know was wrong or was not able to control.

Don't make the mistake of giving him too much freedom right away. It's easier to housetrain a puppy that is confined to one room since it's easier to keep an eye on him. Don't let him get into the habit of wandering off and using the basement or one of the bedrooms as his toilet area. Use baby gates to confine him and let him earn house privileges as he becomes housetrained. If a housetrained pup starts to make mistakes he is either getting too much freedom, is not being watched carefully enough, or has a urinary-tract infection.

Once he understands the ropes, you can scold him mildly if you catch him eliminating indoors, but remember that pups have limited control and make mistakes. Perhaps he was busy playing and didn't realize he had to go until it was too late. Perhaps you missed his worried expression or his trip to the door. Don't expect too much too soon. Use common sense when housetraining, expect to backslide from time to time, and keep it all in perspective. Some dog owners report that their pups were trained in the first weekend and never had an accident inside—that means that the owners put a lot of time into those pups right from the beginning. Most dogs do not get housetrained that quickly.

When cleaning up after the pup, it is best to use a deodorizer made for that purpose or a mixture of white vinegar and water. Pups tend to go back to the same area each time, and if the odor remains, he's likely to use the spot again. Take advantage of that instinct by always taking him to the same area of the yard. He'll quickly catch on to what he is out there for, and you won't have spots of dead grass all over your lawn.

SOCIALIZING YOUR PUPPY

If your puppy was purchased from a responsible breeder, he has probably been well socialized so far. If not, you've got some work ahead of you to make up for lost time. It's very important that a puppy be exposed to a large variety of experiences during the socialization period (four to twelve weeks of age). A puppy that receives insufficient handling by people and is not exposed to a variety of situations and experiences during this time period will never be the confident and well-adjusted dog he could have been.

The puppy needs to meet and be handled by people of all ages, including men, women, adolescents, and the elderly. He especially needs to be exposed to gentle, well-behaved children; they act, smell, sound, and move differently from adults. A dog who has limited experience with children during the socialization period may grow up to be either fearful or aggressive around them.

The pup needs to go to a variety of places, both in the car and on leash. Ask to take him along to visit dog-owning friends. Take him to softball games where he can meet people and listen to the crack of the bat and the cheering of the crowd. Take him for walks in the park and past the school playground. The more things he does now, the more confident and adaptable he'll be as an adult. He should meet gentle dogs of other breeds during this period, but be sure that all of the dogs are up to date on their vaccinations. In areas where parvo is a problem, check with your vet before taking the pup to parks or other areas where he may be exposed.

If he tends to be shy in new situations, don't baby him as this will reinforce the shyness. Don't force him to do things that frighten him, but give him the opportunity to explore and praise him for going forward or holding his ground. Carry small biscuits in your pocket and encourage strangers to "give him a cookie," but don't inadvertently use treats to reward him for acting shy.

Expose the puppy to vacuum cleaners, lawn mowers, joggers, skaters, and bicycles.

Everyone likes dog crates! Ch. Bordal's Knight of Indalane, CDX, CGC and a friend. Owned by Richard and Evelyn Bordner.

Teach him to climb stairs, even if your house doesn't have them. Cut his nails, give him a bath, brush his coat, and get him used to a collar and leash. Expose him to all of the things he will be expected to accept as an adult.

At about eight weeks of age, a previously confident pup may go through a short "fear period" and display caution in situations that never bothered him before. This is not unusual and is no cause for concern. Continue the socialization process, but be careful that the pup does not undergo an exceptionally traumatic experience between eight and ten weeks of age. A very bad experience during this period will tend to stay with him.

It is vitally important to socialize a pup whether he was purchased for showing, obedience competition, coaching, hunting, or just to be a family pet. You can never make up for lost time if you do not work with your puppy during this time period. If you have difficulty finding time, consider hiring a responsible teenager to work with your puppy. Attending a puppy obedience class during this period is particularly useful for those with busy households.

EARLY OBEDIENCE TRAINING

All Dalmatians should receive some formal obedience training as puppies. Kindergarten Puppy Training is for dogs as young as eight or ten weeks of age. If the puppy does not attend KPT classes, try to start a regular beginners obedience class by the time he is five or six months of age. If your pup was purchased with the intention of showing him in the breed ring, an early obedience class is still an excellent idea—it is very good for confidence building.

Don't wait until you start obedience classes to start training your puppy. The basic exercises can be taught at home

Rosebrooks Red Alert (L) shows how to be a "good puppy" with his favorite toy. "Rescue" is owned by Nancy Welsch.

where there are fewer distractions. When you eventually attend obedience classes, your dog will have a head start and he will already have learned how to learn. Training at home is not a substitute for attending classes, as the dog should learn to behave properly in public and in the presence of other dogs.

Puppy training books emphasize teaching the basics to dogs as young as seven weeks of age. Young pups are ready and eager to learn and, although they have short attention spans, they usually catch on very quickly. Spend five or ten minutes several times a day working with your pup. Teach him to sit and to lie down. Teach him to stay. Tricks are fun, too, and everyone loves a dog that will shake hands. The more things he learns at an early age, the easier it will be to teach him additional things later.

The most important exercise to teach your dog is "come." "Come" is never used along with punishment, and you should never call the dog to you to correct him. If you have to correct him, go get him. "Come" should be a happy word with a positive meaning.

Carry small biscuits or pieces of dog food in your pocket and every now and then get down on your knees and call the puppy in a happy voice. When he comes running, give him a cookie and a hug. He should come happily and should always receive a reward at first. You're teaching him to associate the word "come" with a pleasant experience. As he catches on to this great game, you can practice from further away, hide in another room, or run in the opposite direction. When the pup hears you call him, he should eagerly seek you out and happily come to you.

PROPER TOYS

All Dalmatians should have toys of their own to play with. Popular choices include tennis balls, knotted rope toys, nylon bones, hard rubber balls or bones for chewing, and sterilized shank bones. Nylabone® offers safe Dal toys including the original Nylabone® and Nylafloss®. Never buy sponge rubber balls for a Dalmatian as the dog may bite off pieces and swallow them. Squeak toys are great fun but should be used with supervision as some Dals quickly "kill" the squeakers and tear the toys into small pieces. It's probably best to save the rawhide toys for special occasions, and they should always be used under careful supervision. Some Dals bite off large chunks, which can cause indigestion or even a blockage.

Never give the dog old shoes or slippers to play with, as the dog will logically assume that all such items are to be played with or chewed. Keep boots, shoes, and slippers shut in the closet when you have a new

puppy, and don't let him get started on what can be a very expensive habit.

Puppies chew while teething and many adult dogs chew for pleasure or when they are stressed. A good selection of toys and bones helps to ensure that the dog will choose one of his own toys rather than a table leg.

UNDERSTANDING PACK STRUCTURE

It's very important to understand the concept of pack structure. Dogs are social creatures and need to be part of a "pack," in this case, your family. They also need to understand their position within the pack. In your family "pack," the dog should always be the lowest ranking member. Dals tend to

A Nylabone® Frisbee® is a safe toy for your Dal to chew on, and it provides fun and exercise when you initiate a game of catch. *The trademark Frisbee® is used under license from Mattel, Inc., CA, USA.*

be a dominant breed and most of them are inherently "pushy." They would prefer to be near the top of the social structure, which can create all kinds of problems for their owners. The dominance issue is one of the most common reasons for dogs (of all breeds) to be given away or even euthanized. A dog owner must understand that the pushy dog whose behavior is not modified will eventually become a problem dog who is out of control.

There are a number of tests (such as the Puppy Aptitude Test) which can be used to assess a dog's degree of dominance or submission. The more dominant the dog, the more firmness that will be required to raise him. Although an excessively submissive dog is not desirable either, a slight degree of submission will help to ensure that the pup will be manageable within the family and amenable to training. Early training at home and a good KPT class will help reinforce proper behavior.

Most experts advise against wrestling and playing tugging games with a dog. Such games encourage the dog to growl, bite, and play roughly, and they send the wrong message, particularly to a dominant dog. Dad may be able to control the dog who gets too excited during these games, but that will not be the case when the dog tries to "play" in this manner with the four-year-old.

It's not necessary to be mean or to use excessive force to resolve the dominance issue, but it's important to be firm and consistent and to make sure that the dog understands that the house rules will always be enforced. Don't nag at the dog by giving him commands that you don't plan to enforce, and don't back down from things such as cutting nails if he protests—that sends the wrong message as well. It's easy to teach a young pup his place in the family pack, but it can be very difficult, if not impossible, to do the same with an adult

Daisy has found a substitute "pack member" to snuggle with—a stuffed toy is almost as good as a littermate! Owned by Barb Nordstrom and Sue MacMillan.

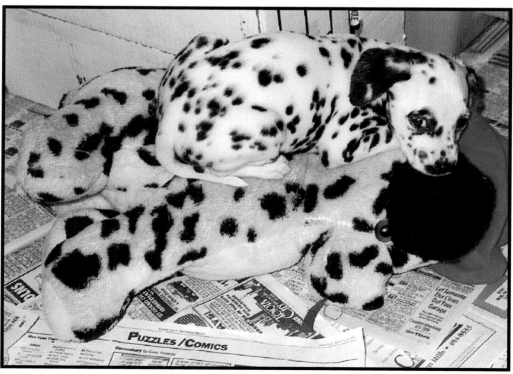

dog who is out of control. A dog who understands his place in the family is content, well adjusted, and more relaxed because he is not driven to keep testing his owners.

CORRECTIONS

There is a great deal of disagreement about the best way to correct a dog, although everyone seems to agree that a rolled-up newspaper doesn't work. Most Dals respond very well to a stern "no" or "stop" or to a loud "errr" (a growling noise). Some authorities suggest throwing a bean-bag or shaking a soda can filled with pennies to distract a pup from inappropriate behavior. Water pistols often work well to silence pups who are fussing in their crates. A scruff shake, where the owner grabs the pup by the scruff of his neck, lifts his front feet off the ground, and gives him a few shakes, works well in some situations but should be saved for the most serious infractions. A collar and leash are often used to correct jumping up or bolting out the door when it is opened. Very serious "crimes" may call for an alpha rollover (where the owner rolls the puppy over onto his back into a submissive position), while some authorities are totally against this method. Never resort to "spanking" your Dal. It is rarely an effective form of correction and may cause the dog to become fearful or "fight back." Proper puppy training reduces the need for corrections, and it's always wise to use the least amount of force needed to solve the problem. If professional help is required, don't put it off. Problems only get worse if they are allowed to continue uncorrected.

PUPPY PROBLEMS

Nipping

This is normal behavior for puppies, but that doesn't mean that it is acceptable behavior. If you watch a litter of puppies play together, you'll notice that they are

Morris and Newt on discuss "territorial rights"—in this case, who rightfully belongs on the bed. Morris is owned by Sue MacMillan and Newton is owned by Jeff and Julie Prentice.

constantly biting each other's faces, feet, tails, and ears. When a puppy bites too hard, his littermate lets out a squeal and a snarl to warn the aggressor that he is playing too rough. Mother dogs who are allowed to play with their puppies do the same. By playing these games, the puppies learn to control the pressure of their bites. When adult dogs play together, they often "mouth" one another without applying any pressure. Although it looks like biting, it's not, and it is normal dog behavior.

When puppies go to new homes, they treat humans like they treated their littermates and attempt to chomp on fingers, noses, earlobes, and ankles. That is also normal behavior, but it must be corrected. Nipping does not go away on its own and a nipping puppy often becomes a biting adult. A nip is just a small bite, but pups must learn that it is never acceptable to use their teeth on people.

Everyone has his own method for controlling nipping, and the new owner needs to find the one that works best for him and stick with it. Most puppies respond well to having their muzzles pinched while being told "no." Some trainers prefer snapping the index finger off of the thumb to flick the offender under the chin. Determined nippers may require a collar shake or a quick scruff shake, but don't use those methods unless the other methods don't work. If the pup is very excited and won't stop nipping, either put him in his crate to cool down or simply leave the room.

It will take several weeks to break a pup of nipping, and many pups occasionally forget, especially when playing hard or when having their nails cut. Games such as tug-o-war and wrestling, which encourage nipping and aggression, are not advisable. All dogs have the potential to bite and it is the owner's job to be sure that the dog understands that it is *never* acceptable to bite a person.

Stealing

Types of stealing, especially food stealing, are common problems for Dalmatian owners. Like many other problems, stealing is much easier to prevent than to cure. If the puppy is closely supervised and immediately corrected when he attempts to take food off the counter, tissues out of the trash, or laundry from the hamper, stealing will never become a problem. If he's crated or in his pen when no one can watch him, he won't have the opportunity to develop bad habits.

To reduce the temptation for the

"I can't believe I ate the whole thing!" Food stealing is a problem that many Dal owners encounter. Dal owned by Barrie Essner.

dog to get into the trash, it's probably best to use a covered container or to keep the wastebasket in a closet with the door shut. Most Dal owners quickly learn not to leave food on the counters. Once the dog gets into the habit of stealing, the only possible cures are mousetraps and "set ups."

A trap placed in an appropriate place may convince the dog to keep his nose off the counter or out of the trash. On the other hand, he may learn to spring the traps and carry them away to chew up! Pans balanced to fall when the dog puts his nose where it shouldn't be may work by startling him. It may work to leave something out where the dog will attempt to take it, wait right around the corner, and catch him in the act and correct him. If stacked pans are used at the same time, the pans will warn of an attempt, which can be followed up with a correction. Mousetraps and set ups will probably have to be repeated a number of times to be effective.

Chewing

Like stealing, chewing is a habit that is best prevented from the beginning. The puppy who eats the sofa should never have been left unsupervised long enough to do that. Dogs do not instinctively know that it's wrong to eat furniture or dig up floor tiles. If the puppy is properly supervised, he can be corrected the moment he attempts inappropriate behavior. A bitter-flavored spray can sometimes be used to reinforce corrections. This bad-tasting liquid can be sprayed on items the dog is determined to sample, and is also available in a formula that can be sprayed on the leaves of houseplants.

Be sure to have plenty of toys available for the puppy, and when he first begins to try his teeth on something inappropriate, merely take it away and give him one of his toys. The older pup who is determined to sample the piano leg may require a scruff shake to convince him that the leg is off limits.

Digging

Dogs enjoy digging. It's as simple as that. Although a few never dig, most Dalmatians are real trenchers when they are young and they dig just for the fun of it. When older Dals dig, it is usually a sign of boredom. However, a bitch in whelp will dig in an attempt to create a den for her upcoming puppies. There are many suggested cures for digging, some of which do work on individual dogs, but there is no definite cure. Filling the hole with water, cayenne pepper, or dog stools might work, or they might just cause the dog to dig in another spot. You can watch the dog carefully and correct him for digging, which might work if you catch him immediately. One canine behaviorist suggests giving the dog a special area of his own just for digging. If you want a perfect yard, probably the best way to handle a digger is to divide the yard into a "dog yard" and a "people yard" by cross-fencing the yard. Or you can build a pen for the dog and only allow him in the main yard when he can be supervised.

Some Dals love to dig...just look at the evidence! Hollywood's Achy Breaky Heart, owned by Dave and Lynn Rondot.

What has "Wally" gotten himself into this time? Ch. Paisley Willowood Trademark, TT (L) is owned by the MacMillans.

Barking

This is sometimes more of a problem for the neighbors than it is for the dog owner. No dog should be allowed to become a neighborhood nuisance, and prolonged barking can be very annoying. Don't teach your dog to "speak" on command, discourage him from excessive barking when he plays, and teach him that although it is fine to bark at the door, he should stop when told to do so. Again, it is much easier to correct a young dog for too much barking than it is to retrain an older dog.

Dogs who are left outdoors too long often become nuisance barkers. The Dalmatian's place is in the house, with his family. A dog who is left in a fenced yard without supervision will often start charging the fence and defending his territory, and that can lead to biting as well as barking.

If a dog was properly introduced to his crate, he will not normally bark when left there. If he is barking at noises outside, a radio left on will help mask the sounds from outdoors.

Separation Anxiety

This a very real problem for some dogs who become extremely agitated when left alone. They bark or howl continuously, tear up their houses, and relieve themselves indoors. The best prevention is proper use of a dog crate, which provides the dog with a feeling of security. A radio left playing will be soothing, and a few toys to chew on will help pass the time.

It is very important to make arrivals and departures low-key. If the owner spends 15 minutes apologizing to the dog for leaving, or returns home to greet the dog too enthusiastically and immediately take him out for a run, the dog may become agitated and overly excited. Just put the dog in his crate, give him a biscuit, and say goodbye. When you return, wait a few minutes before letting him out of his crate, send him outdoors to relieve himself, and then do a few household chores. Take him for his run a bit later when his initial excitement has worn off.

Pups should become accustomed to arrivals and departures at an early age and even if someone is home all day, the pup should be crated for a few hours. Then, if the schedule changes and he has to be left during the day, he can adapt quite easily.

Carsickness

This can be very frustrating, but most dogs do outgrow it. The puppy who drools or vomits when riding in the car should

Sounding the alarm are Am-Can. Ch. Five Alarm Truffle and her daughter Ch. Five Alarm Truffles' Trifle. Owned by Luane Williams.

travel in a crate or on the floor of the car. Don't feed him for a few hours before you expect to go in the car. Some people report good results from using motion-sickness medication or a gingersnap cookie to settle the puppy's stomach, while others are convinced that nothing helps. Getting the puppy accustomed to regular short trips in the car and giving the problem time are about the only sure cures. If you are attending obedience classes with a carsick pup, be sure to arrive early enough for him to recover before class starts. Don't err by leaving the carsick pup home. Carsickness does not go away without some effort and patience on the part of the owner.

Stool Eating

This disgusting habit causes owners a great deal of concern and is very difficult to cure. Apparently, the stools of animals still contain a lot of usable nutrition and some dogs find them palatable. While some dogs eat only their own stools, others eat only the stools of other animals. Many Dals are very bad about cleaning out cat boxes. An occasional dog will eat only frozen stools, or will bring them into the house to thaw on the carpeting. A change of diet might help and there are commercial products available that make the stools less palatable. Some dog owners sprinkle them with cayenne pepper, but it's just as quick to clean them up in the first place. A few Dal owners have noted that their dogs actually prefer the stools that have been "seasoned!" Cat boxes should be set out of the dog's reach or in an area to which the dog has no access. Although this habit is extremely disgusting, it is normal canine behavior.

Dalmatians in Conformation

Once you and your dog are in harmony as owner and pet, you might consider participating in one or more of the AKC-sponsored dog activities. There are conformation shows, obedience trials, and performance trials among others. In the conformation (or breed) ring, your dog can attain the champion title that people are so familiar with.

Conforming is complying with, adapting to, or being similar to an accepted standard. The breed ring is the proving ground for assessing your Dal's conforming to the breed standard. The American Kennel Club requires that all breeds accepted for registration have a "standard," a blueprint of what constitutes the perfect specimen for that breed. Conformation competition is a refinement of the process of selection—it is a useful tool in determining the suitability of an individual dog's place in a breeding program that is designed to pass on breed characteristics. It relies on the opinion of more than one person to judge the quality of these characteristics.

Ch. Spotlight's Spectacular (L) going BOB at DCA in 1993, breeder-owner-handled by Connie Wagner. The top-winning Dalmatian in breed history, she is now owned by Mrs. Alan Robson.

WHAT IS A CHAMPIONSHIP?

Conformation competition takes place at a show that has been pre-approved by the AKC and is sponsored by a club that is licensed by the AKC to hold such shows. It is a rating game wherein a judge, whose qualifications have been approved by the American Kennel Club, gives his opinion on how closely your dog conforms to the breed standard. His judgment is based on his understanding of the breed standard; he compares your dog to the picture in his mind of the ideal Dalmatian and to each of the other competing dogs. Each judge brings the sum of his personal experiences into the ring with him, and no two judges will evaluate a dog the same. The American Kennel Club, recognizing this, awards champion titles only after extensive competition in the breed ring. To become a champion, a dog must win 15 "points." Six or more of these points must be won at two different shows with ratings of three or more championship points ("major" points) each, and under two different judges. One or more of the remaining points must be won under a judge or judges different from those who awarded the "major" points. Points are awarded based on the number of eligible dogs competing in regular class competition for each sex, are awarded only to the Winners Dog and Winners Bitch, and range anywhere from zero to five points per show.

A schedule of points is approved each year by the American Kennel Club for the various regions of the country, taking into account the number of dogs in competition

Ch. Rockledge Rumble was BOB at DCA in 1967. He also went BIS under the famed Mrs. Flora Bonney at her last judging assignment. Owned and shown by Gloria Schwartz.

for each breed during the previous year. In California, for instance, it may require 20 Dalmatian bitches in competition to award a three-point major, while in Montana it may only require ten.

By now you are probably intimidated by the apparent complexities of obtaining the title of "champion" on your dog. Don't be! The process is actually quite simple, extremely enjoyable, and rather addictive. Like all things worth doing, it is worth doing

the particular faults and virtues your dog possesses. After studying the standard, you should attend a couple of licensed dog shows and sit at ringside to observe the various methods of presenting the Dalmatian. The show is also a good place to question exhibitors about handling classes in the area. Next, plan on observing several sessions of one or more of the recommended classes to decide which one offers the most. A good handling instructor com-

Ch. Lord Jim ("Jimmy") was the #1 Dalmatian for several years. He is a multiple-Group, BIS, and BOB winner and the sire of two of the breed's top producers: Ch. Tuckaway Traveler Indalane and Ch. Count Miguel of Tuckaway.

well, and so we advise starting with training classes.

TRAINING CLASSES

The dog show judge has a limited time to assess your dog's conformation to the breed standard. It is beneficial to have yourself and your dog trained and prepared to make the most of your time in the ring. To present yourself well, it is necessary to know and understand the breed standard, the traditional method of handling Dalmatians, and

municates his ideas well, demonstrates his methods clearly, can provide answers for any training situation, takes time to address individual problems, and praises the dogs extensively for their efforts.

TRAINING METHODS

The Dalmatian enjoys training sessions that have an atmosphere of fun and games. Positive reinforcement methods will produce a Dal with real ring presence; he approaches the show with an air of excitement and adventure. This attitude catches a judge's eye, holds his attention, and may influence his decision in awarding ribbons.

CONDITIONING

A Dalmatian, according to the breed standard, should be strong, muscular, and active, with smooth, yet well-defined, muscles. His coat should be sleek, glossy, and healthy in appearance. These things cannot be added the night before a show; they come from within the dog and reflect his good health and your good care. Proper nutrition is the foundation for building good bone and muscle, proper exercise tones up that muscle, and proper grooming on a

Dalmatian. If your normal routine is to walk the dog, use a flexible retracting lead that is approximately 25 feet in length; this will allow the dog to cover three to four times the ground area that *you* will cover during the outing. Joggers can also use the flexible lead, or can increase the distance of their daily runs if they are physically able. Biking is an option, provided you have trained your dog in basic obedience commands and are comfortable with the operation of a bike. There are many humorous stories told by Dal owners who thought that biking was a good way to exercise their dogs—until the neighbor's cat came along! There are several devices on the market that attach to the

Ch. Fireman's Freckled Friend ("Spotty") and his daughter Am-Can. Ch. Driftwood Chimney Cricket CD ("Cricket") are one of only three father-daughter combinations to go BOB and BOS at DCA.

regular basis puts on the finishing touches.

You know that your Dalmatian needs good nutrition and a considerable amount of exercise. Wisely, you and your Dal should already have a regular exercise and grooming routine. If good muscle tone is still not developing and the dog has grown out of the puppy stage, re-evaluate the quality of the food or the amount of exercise your Dal gets. This breed was designed to trot for hours and can cope with more activity than the average owner is normally inclined to provide.

There are several options open to you for conditioning the muscles of your mature

bike at one end and to your Dal's collar on the other, thus freeing both hands for controlling the bike. Golf carts have been used successfully by those with access to the carts and areas in which to drive them. Some owners even have driven their cars with their dogs on leashes alongside, but we do not recommend this method because of the hazards to dog, driver, and innocent bystander! For those lucky enough to own a horse with an area for riding, the reliably trained Dalmatian is the perfect companion and he will be getting into condition in a way that is natural for him. Of course, there is always the gym—a treadmill can be used if you have the equipment, the knowledge and the patience to accustom your dog to using it.

When and how much should the Dal be physically conditioned? Your puppy has been going on walks with you since you brought him home. As he grows, you can increase the length of your walks—if he doesn't take frequent rest stops, you can add more distance. As he matures, you will tire before the dog does. Under no circumstances should you submit your dog to the rigors of a steady trot for a prolonged period at too early an age, as you run the risk of building up muscles and stretching ligaments in areas that were not designed to handle such stress.

Conditioning also refers to the mental state with which your dog approaches new experiences. Your training classes have provided a firm foundation and you can build on that foundation by attending matches (practice shows) where the sights and sounds closely resemble the experiences you will both have at a licensed point show. Once show routines become familiar to both of you, you will relax and enjoy the showing experience. Mental conditioning benefits both dog and handler.

Condition, both physical and mental, is entirely dependent on your management as head of the team. A dog is in condition when he carries the right amount of weight for his size and has a healthy, properly groomed coat; firm muscle tone; clean ears and teeth; clear, sparkling eyes; and a happy outlook.

MATCHES

The informal practice show is called a match and is either a "fun" match (which are the least formal and frequently held by clubs not yet approved to hold AKC events) or a "sanctioned" match. Sanctioned matches are either "A-OA" or "B-OB," and are held for different purposes. "A-OA" matches are the most formal—clubs holding these matches are demonstrating to the AKC that they are capable of holding a point show or obedience trial and follow the

Am-Can. Ch. Shospots Standing Ovation, Am-Can. CD and Ch. Shospots Double Or Nothing, CD, winning the Brace class at DCA in 1977. Owned by Dan Mazlic and Linda Panter.

Int-Am-Can-PR-Ven-Dom-SA-Las Americas Ch. Keith's Mr. Major, Am-Can-PR-Dom. CD, Am. CDX, PR TT, CGC is one of the most titled Dals in breed history and is a recipient of the Dog World award.

same rules as actual dog shows except that no points are given. "B-OB," the most commonly held matches, are less formal in structure and are offered by clubs that are already licensed to give point shows. The flyer advertising the match will identify which type of match it is, what classes are available, and any restrictions that apply. No puppies under six months of age may enter obedience classes at any sanctioned match, and no bandaged or taped puppies or adults may enter the breed ring.

First place or group placements at a match do not guarantee that your Dal will be successful in the show ring; the win should be assessed in direct proportion to the quantity and quality of the competition.

Match regulations allow just about anyone to judge, and some people are more knowledgeable about your breed than others. Since the main purpose of a match is practice, it is wise to remember that you and the judge are both there to gain experience. Your match wins and losses will then fall into perspective.

As dress rehearsals for point shows, matches are usually closer to home, less expensive to enter, and less stressful for you and your Dal. They give you an opportunity to polish the skills you gained during training classes. Solicit comments from the judges as to your presentation of the dog, continue to observe other handling techniques, and above all—have fun!

Ch. Centennial Doctor Pepper (L) is a multiple-Group winner with over 100 BOB wins. He is also the sire of champions, both black and liver. Owned by Peter Capell.

THE AKC, SUPERINTENDENTS, AND SHOWS

We are presuming that by now you have registered your puppy with the American Kennel Club, received your registration certificate, and know what your puppy's registered name and number are. These will follow him throughout his career in AKC competitions of all types, so put them in a safe place. Enclosed with the registration certificate is more information about the AKC (including their general information address), the sport of dogs, and the various AKC publications and videos that are available. Write to the AKC to request copies of *Rules Applying to Registration and Dog Shows*, and perhaps the *Obedience Regulations*.

Subscribing to the *Purebred Dogs/American Kennel Gazette* magazine will also get you a monthly listing of upcoming shows and activities and the superintendents handling them, or you can write to the AKC to request the addresses of superintendents in your area. (Each licensed club usually hires a superintendent to oversee the mechanics of putting on their shows.) Write to a superintendent located in your area of the country and request to be put on his mailing list. Tell him how far you are willing to travel to attend shows. He will then begin sending you premium lists that describe the upcoming shows in detail and include entry blanks that have to be filled out and returned by a deadline should you wish to compete at a specific show.

The entry blanks are self-explanatory as to the information required and should be no problem until you come to (2) Dog Show Class and (3) Class Division. *Rules Applying to Registration and Dog Shows* (that you

Am-Can. Ch. Proctor's Dappled Duchess is the youngest Dal to win the DCA Futurity (6 months, 3 days). She finished her title as a puppy and was the #7 Dalmatian in 1990. Owned by Eva Berg and Lois Wilthew.

should have sent for) contains information on each of the classes and what is required for entry—become familiar with them. *Do not* enter more than one class in hopes of increasing your chances of winning the points. The right to compete for championship points is earned by winning first place in all classes in which you exhibit. So, if you take first place in one class but second place in another class, you are no longer eligible for points because you have been defeated by another dog and are therefore no longer a "winner."

Approximately one week prior to the show, you will receive a judging schedule in the mail detailing directions to the show, the time your breed will be judged, and in which ring. Your dog will be assigned a number (the judge will not know you or your dog's identity).

Arrive early on the day of the show, leaving plenty of time to locate the ring you will be competing in. You may wish to purchase a catalog for the day that lists details about all the competitors under the numbers they were assigned, and the en-

tries for each of the classes. The male class dogs will compete first, and the classes will be judged in this order: Puppy (6–9 months and 9–12 months), Novice, Bred by Exhibitor, American-bred, and Open. Females will follow, in the same order.

Each ring will have at least one ring steward who will check you in, hand you an arm band with your assigned number on it, and answer any questions you may have. By arriving early, you will have time to watch the judge's procedure; note where he asks you to stand your dog for the examination, what type of gaiting pattern he requests, whether he calls out his requests or simply indicates his wishes by gesture, and where the placement markers are so you know where to stand when you win! Some judges may request that the exhibitors enter the ring in "catalog (numerical) order," while others have no preference. If you are first in line, ask the steward before entering the ring exactly where the judge would like you to stop and stand your dog. Stack your dog (maneuver him into a flattering natural stance), keep one eye on the judge, and be prepared to gait your dog around the ring at a controlled trot on command. The judge will wish to see the class move around the ring as a unit and examine each dog individually as he makes mental comparisons to the breed standard. He has a limited time in which to do this, so you must make the best use of these few brief minutes to impress him with your dog's quality. He will then indicate his choices for the first place through fourth place ribbons among the entries in the class.

SHOW PROCEDURE

The competition at an AKC-licensed show is an elimination process, starting with the broad base of all dogs entered under their separate breed categories and narrowing down to one dog judged Best in Show over all of that day's competitors. The broad base consists of entries for each AKC-licensed breed in classes for non-champions, divided by sex. Each of the first place winners in the breed classes goes back into the ring for further competition, males to compete for Winners Dog, females to compete for Winners Bitch. Only the Winners Dog and Winners Bitch will earn points toward a championship. They are then eligible for further competition in a class called Best of Breed, which only champions of record may enter. The winner from this class is then, for instance, the best Dalmatian for the day and may now proceed to the next level of competition. The AKC has divided all of the breeds into groups based on the uses for which each breed was designed. The seven groups are: Sporting, Hound, Working, Terrier, Toy, Non-Sporting, and Herding. The Best of Breed winners from each of the breeds comprising these

Am-Can. Ch. Proctor's Dappled Hi-Flyer was in the Top Ten Dals from 1991–1994, #1 All Systems in 1992, and #1 in breed points from 1991–1993. He defeated more Dals in 1992 than any other Dal in breed history, and was in the Top Ten Non-Sporting dogs that same year. Owned by Ken and Eva Berg, Bob and Lois Wilthew, and James Anderson, pictured with handler Mike Stone.

Ch. Penwiper All The Right Moves. Breeder-owner-handled by Barbara DiMino, "Stash" went BOB at DCA in 1994 under Dr. Charles Garvin. He is a Group and specialty winner and a Top Ten Dalmatian.

groups will go into the ring with each other and the judge will decide which of them comes closest to their own breed standard. The first place winner in each of these groups will then go to the final level of competition where one of them will be chosen Best in Show.

USING A HANDLER

To successfully show a Dalmatian, you must objectively assess his conformation and be fully aware of his strong and weak points in relation to the breed standard. When exhibiting, you must develop the skills to show off your Dal's strong points and minimize his weak points. If handling classes, matches, and point shows have not given you the confidence needed to face competition in the breed ring or if you are continually walking out of the ring without a placement, perhaps the time has come to consider one of two alternatives: either the dog is not worthy of a champion title, or it is time to consider using the services of a professional handler.

How do you go about choosing a handler? You can get referrals from people you

know or you can simply observe handlers in the ring. But there are other considerations as well. Can you afford professional services? Will you be happy with the type of care your Dal will receive? How accommodating will the handler be to your wishes and your individual dog's needs? And what are the handler's ethics as regards winning, i.e., will the well-being of the dog be sacrificed for the points to be won?

Begin by observing the various handlers in the ring. Note whose dogs seem to be happy and willing workers and whose dogs have the bloom of good health and good care. Identify those who do not need to rely on shady handling tricks to put other exhibitors at a disadvantage. Follow the chosen handlers to their grooming areas and watch what type of attention the dogs are given outside of the ring. Are the crates and exercise pens clean, sturdy, and well secured? Check their methods of transportation and how the dogs are secured while traveling. Introduce yourself and explain your needs. The handler will no doubt request to see your dog and evaluate his chances for completing a championship.

Charles Garvin won the Leonard Brumby, Sr. Memorial Trophy as International Champion Junior Showman at Westminster in 1969 under Richard Cooper. He is the only person to win Junior Showmanship at Westminster with a Dal.

Be wary of someone who states that he thinks your dog is "finishable," but it may take a few more show entries to accomplish it. Perhaps you would be wiser to ask several reputable long-time breeders for their evaluations of the dog's quality before you go to the expense of hiring a handler.

If you decide to proceed, request a written schedule of fees and discuss transportation, grooming, and boarding charges. Will you be notified as to the number of shows entered? What happens if there is a conflict in ring times with other clients of the handler? You should fully understand the way in which expenses are determined before engaging the services of a handler, and you should request that information in writing.

Set up an appointment to visit the handler's facilities where your dog will be kept. Visit with the handler's assistants and ask them the same questions (except for fees and financing) that you asked the handler. Do you get a comfortable feeling from the people to whom you will be entrusting your dog? Handling can be tedious, hard, and tiring work and the majority of professional handlers are totally devoted to their dogs. Find one of these handlers and you will be happy with the service when your dog is losing (an inevitability) as well as when he is winning.

Before making your final decision, talk to some of the handler's clients. Ask them if they were satisfied with his services, with the care their dogs received, with the handler's attitude toward competition, and with his ring ethics. You will probably find that the majority of handlers receive high praise and are well thought of by their clients, other professional handlers, and your fellow exhibitors.

ADVERTISING

There are many facets to the sport of dogs, and once you have become involved in training and showing in conformation, your horizons will begin to expand. You may have initially set out to prove the quality of your Dal by obtaining his championship. Along the way you got hooked on the rush of adrenaline caused by show-ring competition, you began to enjoy the interaction of dog and handler as you became a team, and you've initiated a breeding program and had some success with it. You're proud of how far the two of you have come and would like to let people know it. Enter: the advertising game!

The majority of Dalmatian owner/handler/breeders join a regional Dalmatian club as their involvement in the sport increases. This may lead to membership in a local all-breed club and the national club, the Dalmatian Club of America. The local clubs have newsletters, many of which feature advertising as a means of raising funds and keeping members informed about each other's accomplishments. The national club has a quarterly magazine containing ads from breeders in all areas of the country. There are other magazines on the market, both all-breed and Dalmatian-only, to consider as well.

Be aware that many humorous articles have been written about the advertising game. Key phrases found in ads have been

At age 14, Diane Haywood (Bartholomew) going Best Junior Handler with Ch. Dalwood's Waggin' Master. She became the mentor for many Junior Handlers.

CONFORMATION

"translated into the vernacular," for example, everyone knows that "elegant" means lack of substance, "litter of eight show-quality puppies" means no disqualifying faults have shown up yet, "outgoing" means completely out of control, and "reserved" means just try and get your hands on the dog!

Before you compose your ad, sit down at the typewriter and in all capital letters type the word "HYPERBOLE"—then go look up the meaning. Type in the meaning, print it

is excellent, and his tail is set properly if the photographer caught him pulling back into a "roach" with his tail between his legs. You won't be able to explain to each of them how a stack of chairs crashed to the floor just at the wrong moment because none of them will be tying up the phone line to inquire about stud services. You will be paying hard-earned money for these ads, so make them count!

Jean Marie Lloyd at age 13 winning Best Junior at DCA in 1978. She was a top Junior Handler and went to Westminster three years, taking fourth in her class.

out, pin it to the wall above the typewriter, and study it intently. Notice how it can be shortened to "HYPE," which brings to mind Madison Avenue, which leads to thoughts of fact versus fiction. Do not get caught in the trap of over-enthusiasm or exaggerating the truth until it cannot be stretched any further. Keep it simple and keep it honest, and it will be much more impressive.

Choose a picture that flatters your Dal, emphasizes his good points, and leaves a favorable impression. Your ad will reach many people who may never have a chance to see your dog "in person." They won't know that his topline is strong, his angulation

JUNIOR SHOWMANSHIP

Dalmatians and children have a special affinity for one another, as we have already noted. This special relationship can be carried over to the conformation ring as the youngsters in your family participate in the Junior Showmanship competitions offered at most AKC shows. The classes are split into two age groups (Junior—ages 10 to under 14, and Senior—ages 14 to under 18) and two skill levels (Novice and Open). Unlike regular conformation competition, Junior Showmanship classes are judged on the ability of the handler, not on the dog's conformation. It is not a question of who has the best dog, but who does the best job handling his dog. For more detailed information on this aspect of the sport you may wish to consult the AKC's *Regulations for Junior Showmanship*, or purchase one or more of the excellent books devoted entirely to Juniors.

Junior Showmanship competition provides wonderful experience for young people techs, dog groomers, obedience trainers, dog psychologists, and professional dog handlers. Young entrepreneurs have started their own dog-sitting or yard-cleaning businesses. Some less obvious careers come to mind that also draw on the knowledge of dogs obtained from years of studying and working with them in the Junior Showmanship classes. These include drawing, painting, or photographing animals, and even

Julie Remmele (Rion) with Ch. Tuckaway Secondhand Rose, going Best Junior Handler at DCA in 1982.

who would like to continue showing dogs in the future, or, even if there is no intention to continue showing, it is a fun activity and confidence builder for those who like to work with dogs. Junior Showmanship can lay the foundation for an entire lifetime of involvement with dogs and open up many career opportunities. Many Juniors have gone on to the more obvious careers as veterinarians or veterinary technicians, lab careers writing about dogs and/or the sport. Many Juniors also continue in the sport by obtaining their licenses to judge the Junior classes once they are no longer eligible to compete in Junior Showmanship.

A list of all the young men and women who began their interest in purebred dogs by showing Dalmatians would be nearly endless, but suffice it to say that many of today's prominent breeders and breed judges started in the Junior ring showing the family Dalmatian.

A LIFETIME OF FRIENDSHIPS

One of the rewards derived from involvement in the sport of purebred dogs comes from the numerous friendships with other people throughout the country, and even in other countries. There is a distinct kinship felt between people who are daft over Dalmatians, and this love of the breed provides a common meeting ground on which friendships flourish. With computers and the Internet shrinking the spaces that separate us, these friendships are growing at an even faster rate.

Many Dalmatian families plan their vacations around the dates of the national specialty, where opportunities abound to meet with old friends and to make new ones while seeing the local sights. The modern family frequently relocates due to job trans-

Heather Haywood Johnston was the Best Junior at DCA in 1991, 1993, and 1994. She was in the Top Five Juniors with a Dal for three years and participated at Westminster three times. Pictured with Ch. Dalwood's Enchanted Knight.

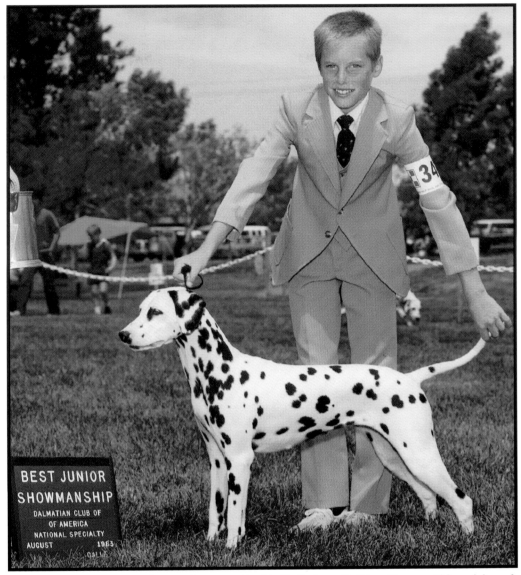

Ron Lloyd, winning Best Junior at DCA at age 13 with Ch. Dalwood's Disco Dancer. Although he only showed on a limited basis, he won several Best Junior titles.

fers, but previously established friendships with Dal families already settled near the new location make the transition that much easier. It's hard to feel like an outsider when you already have friends in that area. And no one accepts those little white hairs clinging to everything quite like another Dal owner!

That just about brings us full circle on this topic. There is one thought we would like to leave you with. You purchased a Dalmatian because you love the breed and you wanted to share your life with one. You enjoy your Dal and all the things you do together. If you wake up some day and realize that you are no longer having fun with all the extracurricular activities you and your Dal have gotten involved in, don't be afraid to beat a hasty retreat. The enjoyment of canine companionship is a prize not to be sacrificed.

Above: Ch. Fanfayre's Beau of Short Acre was BOW at DCA in 1982 and went on to become a multiple-BIS winner and one of the Top Dals in the US. Owned by Anne Nicholson. Below: Am-Can. Ch. Tuckaway Bottoms Up Gusto, CD (L) is a BIS and multiple Regional Specialty winner. He was strictly owner-handled throughout his show career and is the sire of numerous champions. Owned by Tom and Janey Baughn.

Above: Am-Can. Ch. Igdaliah M&M Candy Cain, CD, winning at DCA in 1987. He is also a Group winner and placer, Regional Specialty winner, and producer of champions. Owned by Bonnie Helt. Below: Am-Can. Ch. PGR Heiloh Samson, CD was a multiple-BIS and Regional Specialty winner, as well as a Top Ten Dal for several years and the sire of ten champions. Owned by Patricia Robinson.

Above: Ch. Green Starr's Major Houlihan was BOB and Group 3 at the AKC Centennial show in 1984, as well as BOB at DCA. She was ranked in the Top Ten Dals in 1985. Owned by Linda H. Lewin. Below: Am-Can. Ch. Godin's To Be or Not To Be, originally from Canada, finished her US championship and had a spectacular Specials career, exclusively owner-handled. She was the #1 Dalmatian in the US in 1991. Owned by Pauline and Helene Masaschi.

Above: Ch. St. Florian Pisces Jordache was the 1990 DCA Specialty winner under judge Mrs. Alfred Treen. Owned by Linda Fish and Dawn Mauel. Below: Am-Can. Ch. Korcula Midnight Star Bret D was the #1 Dal in the US (Pedigree System) in 1988, 1989, and 1990; and #1 All Systems in 1989 and 1990. Owned by Marie D. Zink and Dr. Charles Garvin, handled through most of his career by Tom Glassford.

Ch. Paradox Mad Max of Croatia was a multiple Group winner and ranked 20th in the US by 17 months of age. Owned by Narong Lohsomboon and Lynne Baum.

Ch. Tally Ho's Sir Charles was a multiple-Group and Regional Specialty winner. When he retired, he had 167 Bests of Breed. Owned by Mr. and Mrs. R. Thomas Ruark.

Am-Can. Ch. Belle Aire's Star E. Knight, CGC was a Top Ten Dalmatian for two years, with 21 Group Ones and multiple Regional Specialty wins. Owned by Tina Thomas Smith.

Ch. Daisydot Daphne of Dalwood was a Top Ten Dal with a Regional Specialty win, multiple Group wins, 79 BOBs, and a DCA Award of Merit. Owned by Tom and Carole Harris and Fran Redding.

Ch. Sunnyglen's Spencer For Hire was a multiple-Group and specialty winner and a Top Ten Dal. He was also an important sire. Owner-handled by Mary Widder.

Ch. Folklore n' Firesprite Wm Tell has been successful as a winner and producer. Owned by Robert and Diana Skibinski and Norma Baley.

CONFORMATION

Ch. Fiacre's Femme Fatale had a spectacular career as a class dog and as a Special. In 1994 she was BOS at DCA and at the Regional that followed. Owned by Carol Chase.

Ch. Centurion Coachman (L) is a multiple-Group winner and one of the first homebred liver champions for Centurion. Owned by Paul and Elaine Lindhorst.

Am-Can. Ch. Fireman's Becky Newsham is a multiple-BIS winner and was ranked in the Top Ten Dals for several consecutive years. Owned by Larry Stevesand and Robert Peth.

278

Am-Mex. Ch. Spottsboro Rebel Streak, CD is a multiple-specialty and Group winner, as well as one of the all-time top-winning BOB Dals. Owned by Donna McCluer.

Ch. Arora's Lacy Britches is one of the few Dal bitches to go BOB at Westminster. "Lacy" is a BIS winner and was the #6 Dal in 1989. Owned by Callie Norton.

Ch. Merry Polka of Tallara was the first show dog for Proctor. He was #9 in the US in 1969 and #7 in 1970. Owned by Ken and Eva Berg.

Am-Can. Ch. Deltalyn Decoupage was an All-Breed BIS, multiple-Group, and Regional Specialty winner, and was in the Top Ten from 1975–1977. Owned by Robert and Judy Rivard.

Am-Can. Ch. Coachman's Hot Coffee (L) was a multiple-Group winner who did much of her winning as a Veteran. Owned by Pauline and Helene Masaschi.

Ch. Deltalyn N Penwiper KisNCuzn, going BOS at DCA in 1991. She is also a BIS winner. Owner-handled by Barbara DiMino, co-owned with Robert Rivard.

Am-Can. Ch. Firesprite N Coachlight Gigilo (L) was a multiple-Group winner and Top Ten Dal, and the sire of 16 champions. Owned by Ray and Norma Baley.

Ch. Milky Ways Egyptian Goddess is one of the top-winning Dal bitches with 6 BIS, 3 specialty BOBs, and over 50 Group Ones. Owned by Dr. Richard Saxton and William Nilva.

Ch. Dakota's Victoria's Secret, winning her first BIS. Owned by Diane Ryan, Kris Benoit, and Anne Fleming, handled by John Benoit.

Am-Can. Ch. Legacy's Mt. Bryton Monogram, CDX, Can. CD, owned by Molly Martin.

Ch. Legacy's Pen Pal, owned by Molly Martin.

Ch. Madurhason's Top Marks of Fox, owned by Anne T. Fleming and Janeen Fox.

Am-Can. Ch. of the Americas Madurhason's Opening Night, owned by John and Kristine Benoit and Anne Fleming.

Am-Can. Ch. Esquire's Homespun Prophecy, CD, owned by Bob and Carol Altman.

Ch. Fireline's Double Dealer (L), owned by Karen Soule.

282

Am-Can. Ch. Robinwood Thief of Hearts, owned by Cynthia Klein.

Ch. Johnnie Walker of Watseka, owned by Beth Hallman.

Ch. Sugarfoot Dots Ring Dancer, owned by Anthony and Karen Mezyk.

Am-Can. Ch. Cheerio Willing and Able, CD, owned by Barry Gardner.

Ch. Centurion Center Stage, owned by Barry Gardner.

Ch. Snow Hill Sterling, owned by Suzanne Hughes, DVM.

Ch. Hideaway's Black Mariah, owned by Suzanne Hughes, DVM and Robert Georgiade.

Ch. Esquire's Sleight of Hand (L), owned by Barbara Greenspan.

Ch. Maricam's Saucy Suzy, CD, owned by Mariann Witherspoon.

Am-Can. Ch. North's Sir Wags Alot (L), owned by David and Sandra Slattum and Grant Peters.

Ch. Pacifica's Regal Adonis, owned by Duane Baier and Fred Klensch.

Ch. Hill-N-Dals M'Lady Mercedes, owned by Jan Hill.

Ch. Moonlight's Rising Son, owned by Tim and Cindy Gonzalez.

Am-Can. Ch. Clockgate's Candlelight, owned by Mary Lou Volz and Harold Howison.

Am-Can. Ch. Barker's Best Game of Magic, owned by Diane Blackstone and Elizabeth Barker.

Ch. Rowdy J. Rambler, CD, owned by Clark and Dawn Mauel.

Ch. St. Florian Sunspot Ad-Lib, CD, owned by Clark and Dawn Mauel.

Int-Am-Mex. Ch. Briarfield Princess Sonrisa, owned by Lou and Evelyn Cabral.

CONFORMATION

Ch. Avalon Taylormade By Paisley (L), owned by Rick and Ruth Miller.

Ch. Ivy Lea's Russet Herald (L), owned by Jeanne P. Brewer.

Ch. Hapi-Dal Knight Strider, owned by Susie Wilson-Carroll and Diana and Kristy Wilson.

Ch. Volanta Venturian of Snow Hill, owned by Kathryn Vandelogt.

Ch. DotzInk's Dippity Doo Dot, owned by Paula Hollingsworth and Lyra Partch.

Ch. Bottoms Up Tuti Fruity (L), owned by Tom and Janey Baughn.

Ch. Dromgoole's Nalova, owned by Armond and Marilyn Dromgoole.

Ch. Madurhason's Aberdeen (L), owned by Denise Powell and Ron Zimmerman.

Ch. Dalmino's Allegro, CD, owned by Lori Decker.

Ch. Angel's Nest Hollywood Star, owned by Lynn Rondot.

Am-Can. Ch. Remarkable Rambo of Croatia, owned by Cheryl Hayton.

Ch. Texas Ranger V. Tucwinn, CD (L), owned by Barry Martin.

287

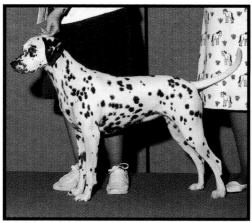

Ch. Misty's Echo of Denell (L), owned by Leonard and Paula Lisciotto.

Ch. Paisley's Natural Healer, CD (L), owned by Kimberly Cartright.

Ch. Alfredrich Mirliton of Culurien, CDX, owned by Stan and Sue Sommerfield.

Ch. Buccaneer Black-Eyed Bart, owned by Gerald and Frances Brennan.

Am-Bah. Ch. Ravenwood Yankee Clipper, Am CDX, Bah. CD, owned by Kathy and Lee McCoubrey.

Ch. Rambler's Lady Sarah Jane, owned by Stephanie and Cliff Seigneur.

Ch. Erin n' Acorn's Autumn Leaf, owned by Pauline Caton and Sharon Lyons.

Ch. Thidwick's Bungee Jumper, CD, owned by Lizabeth Hancock.

Am-Can. Ch. London's Cadbury Fudge (L), owned by Leonard and Sharron Podleski.

Ch. Firebuster's Oscar dla Renta, owned by Elaine Gewirtz and Julie Vick.

Ch. Rojon's Betcha By Golly, owned by Wayne Peterson.

Ch. Roadking's Raindrop, owned by Susan Brooksbank.

Ch. Bearded Oaks Astra's Lyra, CD, owned by Carolyn Bolt.

Ch. Snowood Superstition Bret D, owned by Meg and Mike Hennessey.

Ch. Snowood Ja Sam Jedan (L), owned by Meg and Mike Hennessey.

Am-Can. Ch. Snowood Black Cherry Optimist, owned by Meg Hennessey and Laura Keidaisch.

Am-Can. Ch. Cheshire's Northern Lights (L), owned by Cheryl Steinmetz.

Ch. Cheshire's Signature Silhouette (L), owned by Kirk and Tracy Seltz.

Ch. Cheshire N' Sunset Spellbound, owned by Cheryl Steinmetz.

Ch. Erin's Wildwood Luke McGyver, owned by Sharon Lyons and Ann Thornhill.

Ch. Erin's Wildwood Abby Road, owned by Sharon Lyons and Sue Mangina.

Ch. Erin's Irish Whiskey, owned by John and Sharon Lyons, Tony Costellano, and Michelle Sager.

Ch. Coachman's Paisley Candybar (L), owned by John and Sharon Lyons.

Ch. Harmony Real People, owned by Jan and Doug Nelson.

Ch. Harmony Wishful Thinking, owned by Jan and Doug Nelson.

Am-Can. Ch. Sunkist Singalong (L), owned by J. Richard Millaire and Al Kay.

Am-Can. Ch. Alfredrich Bay Colony Hytime (L), owned by Sue McCord and J. Richard Millaire.

Am-Can. Ch. Merry Go Round XKE, owned by Rod and Patti Strand and Terry and Karen Wissinger.

Ch. Merry Go Round Mardi Gras, owned by Rod and Patti Strand and Terry and Karen Wissinger.

Int-World-Am-Mex-Las Americas Ch. Splash O Ebony's Woodbury's Jaki, owned by Debbie Nierman.

Ch. Tongwood's Once In A Blue Moon, owned by Michael Swartwood and Susan Tong.

Ch. Indalane Winsome Wench, owned by Fran and Ed Stueber.

Ch. Merry Go Round Bentley, owned by Rod and Patti Strand.

Ch. Merry Go Round Rocket Man, owned by Rod and Patti Strand and Dr. Michael Manning.

Am-Can. Ch. Robbsdale's Puttin On The Ritz (L), owned by Tim Robbins.

Ch. Firewag'ns Krackerjack, owned by Peter Kingan, Tim Robbins, and Karen Haworth.

293

Ch. Morgan's Highlander Harper, owned by Peter Kingan and Rick Weyrich.

Ch. Esquire's Devilstar Mirage (L), owned by Karen Soule, Barbara Greenspan, and James Holbrooks.

Ch. Heiloh Ramsey Sundar, owned by Patricia Robinson.

Ch. Classic All That Jazz (L), owned by Sharon Rucksdashel.

Ch. S&P Starlet of Summerhill, CD, owned by Edith and Nelson Gladstone.

Ch. Esquire's Black Talisman, owned by Elaine Thomas.

Ch. Spottsboro Sungold Streaker, CD (L), owned by Donna McCluer.

Ch. MGR's Black Mystical Jewel, owned by Stephen and Lorraine Chmela.

Ch. Devlstr Snygln Rich n Spirit, owned by Sharon McCann and Mary Klein.

Ch. Roundhill Blacksmith, owned by Mary Klein and Sylvia Howison.

Ch. Cheshire Signature Scoundrel (L), owned by Kirk and Traci Seltz and Cheryl Steinmetz.

Ch. Heartland's Romeo of Croatia, owned by Carl and Ingeborg Hartung and Forrest Johnson.

Ch. Mr. Diamond Chips of Croatia, owned by Forrest and Audrey Johnson.

Ch. Reicrist Tsingi of Toleak, owned by R.P. Zemke.

Ch. Deltalyn Bold Lancer (L), owned by Robert and Judith Rivard.

Am-Can-Bda. Ch. Pacific's Boston Bandit (L), owned by Helene and Pauline Masaschi.

Ch. Paisley's Ebony of Coachlight, owned by Sheila Wymore.

Ch. Rambler Quintessence, CD, CGC, TT, owned by Jim and Joanne Nash.

Ch. Beauregard O'Hara of Proctor, owned by Eva Berg and Cindy Dix.

Ch. Paisleys Cause Celebre, owned by Ron Rajala and Sue MacMillan.

Am-Can. Ch. Paisleys Pointblank (L), owned by Sue MacMillan.

Ch. Whinemaker's One for the Road, owned by Sandra Turner.

Am-Can. Ch. November's Mister Frost Debut, owned by J. Richard Millaire.

Am-Can. Ch. Tateland's Top Gun, owned by Dr. Anita L. Tate.

Dalmatians in Obedience

OBEDIENCE TRAINING

Obedience training for the beginner usually starts as a formal program of lessons for the new owner and puppy, although dogs of all ages will benefit from obedience training. These lessons can be classes of a dozen or more handlers and their dogs with an instructor, or private lessons with one handler, one dog, and the instructor.

The goal of basic obedience training is to have a well-behaved dog who is a pleasant companion in the home. The Dalmatian normally enjoys obedience work and appreciates the extra attention, as well as having a job to do. This is an intelligent breed that can easily become bored, and a bored Dal can get into a lot of mischief! A well-trained Dalmatian is a happier dog and certainly more pleasant to live with than an untrained dog. This rule applies to all Dalmatians, no matter how good his temperament is or how willing to please he is. Obedience training benefits everyone (human and canine), and every Dalmatian should attend at least one series of classes.

For information on obedience schools and instructors, check with the dog's breeder, your veterinarian, a dog-owning friend, or someone who shows in obedience competition. Before signing up for lessons, try to visit the class and observe the training methods. If your dog has personality problems or if he is extremely stubborn or "hard headed," top-quality instruction is an absolute necessity. Ask the instructor about his experience with the breed, and if you are not comfortable with his response, it might be well to look elsewhere.

Obedience training is essential for Dals (and all breeds, for that matter!) and most of them enjoy training classes. Note the variety of breeds graduating from this Kindergarten Puppy class.

This obedience class produced 13 dogs who went on to earn their CD titles. The Dal is Tongwood's Spotted Storm, CD. Owned by Mr. and Mrs. Joseph Crone.

Most obedience classes basically train the handler and the dog with the intent that training continues at home. It is always wise to remember that the owner and his dog get only as much out of a class as they put into it. Obedience training requires time, effort, consistency, and commitment. It is essential to attend classes regularly and to work with the dog daily. Obedience training is not something that either "takes" or "doesn't take." Obedience is a pattern of behavior that is taught and then practiced throughout the dog's lifetime. It may be necessary to go back and take a "refresher" course, especially when dealing with an easily distracted puppy, high-spirited adolescent, or hard-headed adult.

Many new dog owners sign up for a series of eight or ten lessons for the purpose of learning how to teach the dog to come when called, sit, and lie down. They have no plans to exhibit in obedience trials. These owners just want good behavior at home. At some point during that first set of lessons, the owner may decide to continue with a second set of lessons. They may learn about the American Kennel Club's Companion Dog obedience title and start to work toward earning it. They begin a process of acquiring skills and coordination while keeping their dogs motivated to work. In spite of the ups and downs, many new owners will be bitten by the obedience bug. They shift from training only for home obedience to working toward obedience titles, tracking titles, agility titles, etc, etc.

KINDERGARTEN PUPPY TRAINING

Many Dal owners and breeders suggest Kindergarten Puppy Training (KPT) classes for Dalmatian puppies. These classes are for younger puppies and are normally followed by a regular beginner's class. Obedience schools, training clubs, and private trainers vary as to the ages of the puppies they accept and what is taught in their KPT classes. The classes are normally for pups ranging from ten weeks to four months of age, but some classes are open to pups as young as eight weeks and as old as six months. The traditional methods of dog training require a dog to be six months of age to attend an obedience class. However, by that age, Dalmatians are large and strong and may have already developed bad habits. Starting classes much earlier gives the puppy an opportunity to *learn how to learn* and teaches the owner how to control and communicate with his dog.

KPT classes are especially useful for first-time dog owners and for owners of particularly active and/or dominant pups. They are also exceptionally nice for winter pups in northern climates, where the pups might not otherwise get out enough to be properly

OBEDIENCE

socialized. Dal owners who exhibit in the breed ring also find KPT classes handy for socializing their young show prospects. Attending a KPT class ensures that puppies get out at least once a week, get used to riding in the car and entering strange buildings, become accustomed to new surroundings and a variety of noises, meet new people, and have the opportunity to socialize with other dogs. Timid pups will develop

dogs' behavior before it becomes a real problem.

Most classes get the pups started on basic obedience exercises and the pups learn to sit, lie down, walk nicely on leash, come when called, and perhaps retrieve a ball or toy. Many classes emphasize dominance and restraint, issues which are often significant when dealing with young Dalmatians. Some classes have obstacle courses

Sixteen obedience-titled Dals, nine of whom are also breed champions, pose for a group photo. All are Rambler owned, bred, or related.

confidence as they master their lessons and receive praise for good behavior.

KPT classes should always be fun! Dogs learn at different speeds and some are far more distractible than others. Going to class should be fun for both the owner and the Dal pup, and practice sessions at home should be short and positive, ending with a play session. If there is a graduation ceremony, the owner should not get upset if the pup seems to have forgotten everything. Puppies are like that!

It's best to attend a class run by an experienced dog person, someone who can answer questions and do some problem solving if needed. Small problems are usually easy to resolve if caught early, but may be exceedingly difficult to deal with later. An experienced trainer will notice minor problems and make suggestions as to how they can be handled. Dogs with dominance problems will be identified early on, and the owners will have a chance to modify their

(much like agility courses) and these are wonderful confidence builders for pups as well as great fun for their owners.

Class discussions may include such issues as dominance, aggression, reading a dog's body language, the proper use of dog crates, how to cut nails, puppy bathing, dogs and children, canine anatomy, health care, flea control, and other useful topics. Many schools have handouts and suggested reading lists.

It's important that pups stay current on their shots, are flea-free, and that the owners use common sense when exposing their pups to new situations and strange dogs who may be older and larger.

THE PURPOSE OF OBEDIENCE TRIALS

According to the American Kennel Club (AKC) in their *Obedience Regulations* pamphlet, "The purpose of obedience trials is to demonstrate the usefulness of the purebred

This young Dal is learning to walk through a tunnel at KPT class. This exercise is a great confidence builder.

dog as a companion to man, not merely the dog's ability to follow specified routines in the obedience ring." Furthermore, the goals of the trials are to produce "dogs that have been trained and conditioned always to behave in the home, in public places, and in the presence of other dogs, in a manner that will reflect credit on the sport of obedience."

WHAT DOGS MAY ENTER OBEDIENCE TRIALS?

A purebred dog of either sex that is eligible for registration with the AKC may compete in obedience trials. Spayed or neutered dogs are also eligible to compete in obedience although they are ineligible for the conformation ring. In addition, a dog with an ILP (Indefinite Listing Privilege) number may compete in AKC obedience. An ILP number refers to a dog of either sex that has been accepted by the AKC as looking enough like a specific breed to be allowed to compete in obedience trials. This is the perfect option for the adopted dog or rescue dog that is obviously a purebred Dalmatian but did not come with registration papers. Dogs must be spayed or neutered to receive an ILP number.

AKC OBEDIENCE TITLES

To earn the CD (Companion Dog), CDX (Companion Dog Excellent), or UD (Utility Dog) titles, a dog must score at least 170 out of a total of 200 points, including at least 50 percent of the points allotted to each exercise. Each time the dog qualifies in this manner, he earns a "leg" toward the title as well as a green "qualifying" ribbon. He must earn three legs under three different judges to qualify for each title.

Companion Dog (CD)

This is the basic AKC title, and the class is called Novice. During this competition, the

KPT offers a wonderful opportunity for socialization with strangers and other dog breeds. These youngsters practice sit-stays.

OBEDIENCE

dog "heels" (walks at his handler's left side) and sits when the handler stops. The exercise is performed both "on lead" and "off lead," at various speeds, and with left, right, and about turns, which are 180° turns. The dog must neither pull on the lead nor lag behind the handler. "On lead" heeling also requires the dog and handler to walk in a figure-8 around two people. "Off

Two-dozen-plus Dals prove that obedience training makes for a photo opportunity that will leave you "seeing spots."

lead" work requires the handler to leave the dog in a "stand for examination" and walk 6 feet away while the judge approaches and examines the dog, who must not move out of position. During the "recall" exercise, the dog must wait where he is left, come on the first command when the handler calls from across the ring, sit in front of the handler, and move to the "heel" position on command. The last exercises are the "long sit," where the dog must remain in the sit position for one minute, and the "long down," where the dog must remain in the down position for three minutes. The dogs perform these two exercises lined up in a row, with their handlers on the other side of the ring.

Tri-color Dal Rainbow was High in Trial at the DCA National Specialty in 1984 under judge Mrs. Alfred Treen. Owned by Sally Anne Walser.

The Novice class exercises are very practical for all dogs to know and most dogs can acquire CD titles without too much difficulty. Most dog and handler teams compete only for a CD, but some handlers get hooked on the sport and choose to go on to the more advanced classes.

"Brambles" demonstrates attention and proper heel position at DCA in 1993. She went on to win High in Trial for the second consecutive year. Alacameo Blackberry Bramble, UD is owned and trained by Prue Stuhr.

Companion Dog Excellent (CDX)

The exercises in this class, called the Open class, are even more challenging. In the Open class, all work is done off lead including the figure-8. During the "drop on recall" exercise, the handler tells the dog to come and then gives him a command to "drop," and the dog must lie down immediately. On the second command to "come," the dog returns to his handler and sits in front of him, then goes to the "heel" position on command. There are two retrieving exercises in this class, one "on the flat" and the other over a "high jump," whose height is proportionate to the dog's height at the shoulder. The "broad jump" is a set of

Ch. Melody My Rockaby Baby, CDX's flying ears give her "lift" over the high jump. Co-owned by Nancy Werhane and Beth White.

Dals love to jump and really enjoy the challenge of the Open class. A dog that receives his CDX may continue to compete in Open B.

Utility Dog (UD)

This title requires a great deal of patience, persistence, and practice, but is one of the most rewarding to achieve with any breed. The Utility class exercises include the "signal exercise," where the dog obeys a

Page's Editor in Chief, CDX demonstrates perfect form in retrieving over the high jump. Owned and trained by Judith Hackett.

Dynasty's Ultimate Rival, UD is the first Dal in breed history to have earned the CD, CDX, and UD titles in less than one year. Owned by Jacqueline McIlhenny.

boards raised just a few inches off the ground and spaced to cover a distance twice that of the high jump's height. In the Open class, the "long sit" is for three minutes and the "long down" is for five minutes. The dogs are again lined up in a row, but this time their handlers are out of sight.

Although Dalmatians are not always natural retrievers like many of the sporting breeds, they are usually reliable if properly trained, and many are outstanding retrievers. Most

series of hand signals from his handler without any verbal commands. In the "scent discrimination" exercise, the handler places his scent on a metal article and a leather article. The scented articles are individually placed with a number of unscented articles and the dog must identify and retrieve the scented articles. The "directed retrieve" requires the dog to retrieve one of three canvas gloves spread out across the end of the ring. The handler uses an arm signal and a voice command to direct the dog toward the correct glove, which the dog may not even be able to see from where he's sitting. The "moving stand and examination" requires the dog to heel, do a stand-stay while the handler keeps moving, accept an examination by the judge, and return to heel position when summoned. In "directed jumping," a high jump and a bar jump are placed along opposite sides of the ring. The dog is sent to the far end of the

Round Tower's Hickory Smoke, Am-Can. CD clears the high jump with ease. Owned by Cheryl Fales Steinmetz.

ring and is ordered to sit. He is then directed to jump over one of the obstacles and return to sit in front of his handler. The

Down-stay: In the Open class the dogs must remain down for five minutes with their owners out of sight. Dals are Sophie Leah Lehmer, UD and Am-Can. Ch. Paisley Peterbilt, Am-Can. CDX. "Sophie" is owned by Jan and John Wilson, "Jocko" is owned by Sue MacMillan.

exercise is repeated over the other obstacle.

Utility is the most challenging class for both dog and handler as it requires the dog to think and to pay close attention to the handler on each exercise. When the Dalmatian gives that kind of attention and response, he is truly a well-trained companion.

Utility Dog Excellent (UDX)

Upon earning the CD, CDX, and UD titles, a dog and handler can compete for the UDX. To achieve this award, the team has to qualify in both Open B and Utility (or Utility B) at ten shows. It is not necessary to win or place, but achieving this title calls for a great deal of consistency.

Obedience Trial Champion (OTCh)

This is the ultimate obedience title. It is the most difficult title to win, and the dog must have earned his UD before competing for an OTCh. The requirements are:

• Accumulate 100 points in competition.

• Win a first place in Utility with at least three dogs competing.
• Win a first place in Open B with at least six dogs competing.
• Win a third first place in either class under the same conditions.
• Win these three first places under three different judges.

The points required for an OTCh are awarded only to the dogs who place first and second in Open B and Utility (or Utility B) and are based on the number of dogs in competition. Since many Open B classes have entries of 40 or more dogs, some of which are already OTCh dogs that are continuing to compete, winning first place can be very difficult.

THE *DOG WORLD* AWARD

Many obedience exhibitors try to earn the coveted *Dog World* award while competing for their titles. This unofficial award is given to dogs that complete a title in their first three consecutive shows with scores of 195 or better. It is also given to dogs that complete all three titles within one year.

The directed retrieve requires the dog to retrieve one of three gloves. The correct glove is indicated by a hand signal from the handler.

Dynasty N Erins Justa Star, UD demonstrates scent discrimination. "Star" is the first Dal in breed history to earn the CD, CDX, and UD titles in less than six months. Owned by Jacqueline McIlhenny.

THE DALMATIAN'S PERSONALITY AND TRAINABILITY FOR OBEDIENCE

Can. OTCh. Beautysweet Cindi, UDT was the first UDT Dal. Owned and trained by Marilyn Suthergren.

The Dalmatian is a highly trainable breed that is alert and intelligent. However, Dalmatians are not, in obedience parlance, "push button" dogs. They do not rely on their owners to tell them every move to make. The Dalmatian forms a bond with his owner and is very willing to please even though he retains a certain amount of independence. Dalmatians also appear to get bored easily. It is the trainer's responsibility to make training fun, add new exercises, and not let the dog lose interest. Almost all top working obedience Dalmatians are trained with the use of toys, food, tennis balls, and a lot of praise. The only way a dog knows he is correct is if he is praised. Even if he has to be shown or physically placed where he is supposed to be, he still needs the praise, and the praise must be sincere. The smart Dal knows immediately if the handler does not mean what he says. A good handler uses a calm, firm, and authoritative, yet friendly, voice. A handler that loses his temper can cause the dog to lose respect and trust. It is best to put the dog away until the handler has regained his composure and a positive attitude. Since Dalmatians are very intelligent and sensitive, they pick up signals constantly from tone of voice and body language.

Short lessons with much praise and no more than ten minutes of training, followed with play such as retrieving a ball or toy, will keep the Dal bright, interested, and working. As training advances, take short play breaks and then get back to work. The intelligent Dal learns quickly that when he works well and pays attention, he will be rewarded. Food can be used effectively as a training tool and as a reward, and works very well with most Dals. At first, it should be used as a reinforcement every time an action is completed. Later, it can be used intermittently to encourage the correct response.

OTCh. Candi's Skagit Belle (L) finished her OTCh. title the weekend of the 1981 DCA National under judge Ken Nagler. She was the first Dal OTCh. Owned by Rex and Becky Auker.

There will come a time when your Dalmatian will test you to see if it is really necessary to do an exercise. At this point, when the dog knows the exercise and is plainly testing you, it is time to give a firm, quick correction. With many Dals, voice disapproval is quite enough, but sometimes it is necessary to give a leash correction. Learning from an experienced instructor how to give the correction followed by motivation is exceedingly important. The correction needs to fit the mistake and should be appropriate for that particular Dalmatian.

It's very important to keep your sense of humor when training your Dalmatian. This will be of great benefit, because Dals can certainly be real clowns at times!

Ch-OTCh. Crossroads's Wandering Star, UDX is the second Dal to earn an OTCh., the first breed champion to do so, and has earned her UDX. She is breeder-owner-handled by Jeannine Kerr.

TYPES OF OBEDIENCE TRAINING

Today there are many types and methods of dog training. Always keep in mind that the Dalmatian will retain a certain amount of independence, even though he would give his life for the owners he loves. With Dalmatians, it is best to avoid harsh training methods. The traditional or historical method, in which the handler popped the lead and praised the dog when the dog was in proper position at the knee, was a popular method for a long time. This method was effective as long as the handler learned how to use the lead with just enough force to control the dog. Sitting the dog physically and praising for the sit were also part of the traditional system.

Incentive training uses food, toys, and other motivators as a system of rewards for work well done. A combination of training methods is often used. Since Dalmatians

Wendell Sammet and Roadcoach Frou Frou, CDX as part of a Dalmatian obedience team in the early 1950s. Frou Frou was also a road trial winner.

are intelligent and easily become bored, repetition can be uninteresting unless there is an incentive for the Dal to continue to work.

An attention course is a specialized form of incentive training used to prepare dogs for serious obedience competition.

The judge has called for this team to halt—Jocko watches his handler carefully and is not distracted by ringside commotion.

Various methods are used throughout the country to teach basic attention. Using toys or food is very much a part of this motivational approach. However, attention training is not just a matter of randomly holding out a toy or food to encourage the Dal to look at the handler. Instead, the Dal is trained to look at the handler whenever the handler or trainer gives the cue, which can be a word like "ready" or "watch." On cue, the dog's head will tilt upward to look at the handler's face. The dog then receives a cue that the handler is walking faster or slower, turning left or right, or is ready to execute an about-turn. Through this approach, the Dalmatian becomes more successful in the obedience ring by finding it easier to maintain the correct heel position. Formalized attention training has been developed within the last 20 years, and is a major change in dog training. This approach has proven to be a good one for Dalmatians and their handlers.

Attention training is often an eight-week course. A handler can purchase booklets and videos and learn about attention training without actually attending a seminar, but the Dal owner could certainly benefit from attending a seminar and having an instructor present for reinforcement and correction. In order to locate seminars, videos, and instructors for specialized training, obedience handlers may wish to subscribe to the monthly newspaper for obedience puppy attention training courses. They demonstrate how to teach the puppy to watch the handler for heeling, recalls, sits, downs, stays, and finishes. Training for retrieving and scent articles can also be started. Puppy attention training can start at eight weeks of age and continue throughout puppyhood.

Obedience training can lead to a much happier life for Dalmatians and their owners. The Dal becomes a better canine citizen and gets regular quality time with

Attention! "Cody" demonstrates the willing attitude, proper heel position, and total focus that have made him a multiple-High in Trial winner. U-CDX Touchstones Ace In The Hole, CDX is owned and trained by Marie Jenkins.

handlers called *Front and Finish* (PO Box 333, Galesburg, IL 61402). Nationally recognized instructors advertise their seminars, which are often sponsored by local obedience clubs. Some local training schools also offer attention classes as one of their training options.

Some obedience instructors teach his owner. The handler enjoys great satisfaction and a feeling of nurturing and teamwork. As he becomes absorbed in working with the dog, it can become a very satisfying form of relaxation. A tight bond is created between handler and Dalmatian, and this bond enriches both of their lives.

Above: *Ch. Cal Dal Chocolate Chip, UDT was the third Dalmatian to become a champion UDT. He was also the #1 Dal in obedience in 1976. Owned by Jon Mett. Below: Ch. Forrest Jilia O'Brogan, UDTX, CGC, TT (L) is one of the three champion UDTX Dalmatians. Owned by P. Karen McDonnell.*

Above: *Dominique's Rusty Nail, UD (L) was a Dog World award winner, High in Trial winner, multiple-High Combined winner, and one of the Top Obedience Dals in the US in 1978 and 1979. Owned by Carol Simmons and Elaine Newman. Below: Driftwood Sunspot Rambler, CDX finished her CDX with two all-breed firsts and a specialty High in Trial. She was ranked sixth overall in 1984. Owned by Kathryn Blink.*

Above: *Ch. Gardorand's Lone Star Corie, UD with her array of obedience trophies. She was a Top Ten Obedience Dal for four years, including #1 in 1986. Owned by Dorothy Anderson.* Below: *A different type of brace: Bordal's Mystical Tai Magic, CDX, CGC and Bordal's Buckeye Battle Cry, CDX, CGC do obedience together. They won at DCA in 1992 and 1993. Owned by Jim and Karen Geissinger.*

Above: *A many-titled family! Front (L to R): Ch. Blacktowers Nevertheless, UD and Ch. Tear Drops Magic Roundabout, CD. Back (L to R): Tear Drops Mario Andretti, CDX; Tear Drops Tiger In The Tank, UD; and Ch. Tear Drops Lively Carousel, CD. Owned by Ronald and Catherine Cookson. Below: Am-Can. Ch. Paisley Peterbilt, Am-Can. CDX, TT earned a Dog World award in Canada and is a multiple-HIT winner in Canada and the US. Owned by Sue MacMillan.*

U-CDX Touchstone's Ace In The Hole, CDX is a multiple-Dog World award winner and a specialty HIT winner. Owned by Marie Jenkins.

Ch. Pompeii's Promise of Glory, CDX, Can. CD (L) was a multiple-all-breed High in Trial winner and a Dog World award winner. Owned by Sandra Ling.

Ch. Korcula Pickles of Sunnyglen, CD went High in Trial with a score of 197. Owned by Mary Widder.

Ch. Coachmaster's Pride Sparkler, UDTX became the third champion UDTX Dal at the age of nine-and-a-half. Owned by Paulena E.C. Verzeano.

M&M's Hobo of Bearded Oaks, UD was a multiple-all-breed and specialty HIT winner, and a Dog World award winner. Owned by Jon Mett and Susan Brooksbank.

Ch. Korcula Midnight Max of M&M, CDX is a High in Trial winner. Owned by Jon Mett, Charles Garvin, and Susan Brooksbank.

Dominoe's Winter Midnight, UDT was ranked in the Top Ten Obedience Dals from 1973—1980, and was the #1 Obedience Dal in 1978. Owned by Michael Pumilia.

Dottie, UD was one of the overall Top Obedience Dals every year she was shown. Owned by Leslie Stanley.

Dancourt Wedgewood Bon Jovi, CDX (L) was the #9 Obedience Dal overall in 1990—1991. Owned by Nola Jacqueline Krieger.

Lady Madonna Madiera, CD, CGC, TT completed her CD with two second places in classes of about 40. She was ranked #6 in Obedience. Owned by Camilla Gray-Nelson.

Bordal's Buckeye Battle Cry, Am-Can. CDX, CGC was ranked #3 Novice Dal in 1989 and was #10 in Open competition in 1992. Owned by Jim and Karen Geissinger.

Can. Ch. Paisley N Tuck's Derby, CD (L) went High in Trial with a 197.5 from the Novice class. Owned by Kathleen Charlton.

319

Left to right: Ch. The Enchanted Flame, CDX; Ch. Gardorand's Brazen Raisyn, CDX (L); Ch. Gardorand's Lone Star Corie, UD; and in front, Ch. Gardorand's Great Adventure, CDX. Owned by Dorothy Anderson.

Dalwood's Miss Valentine, CDX was a multiple-HIT winner and was in the Top Ten Overall and Novice in 1976. Owned by Georgiann Rudder and Herbert Lloyd.

Igdaliah's Miriam of Indalane, CDX went High in Trial at the Chicagoland Dalmatian Club Specialty in 1983. Owned by Bonnie Helt and Eleanore Hilen.

Ch. Karefree's Crackshot, CD was the #10 Obedience Dal in 1990 with a 194.83 average. Owned by Nancy Reiter.

Karefree's Cool Hand Luke, CD was the #10 Obedience Dalmatian in 1978 with a 193.67 average. Owned by Bruce and Nancy Reiter.

Can. Ch. Karefree's Question Mark, Am-Can. UD was the #7 Obedience Dal in 1979 with a 194.67 average. Owned by Bruce and Nancy Reiter.

Touchstone's Hello Holly, UD's first time in the obedience ring— she went High in Trial with a 198.5 from Novice B. Owned by Gilda Aquilera.

Hollytree's Good Time Alex, UD finished his CD and CDX in 1987, and ended the year as #5 overall. Owned by Gilda Aquilera.

Ch. Hollytree's Copper Chelsea, UD (L) finished her CDX in 1986 and tied with her dam for #8 overall. She was #6 in 1987, and she finished her UD in 1991. Owned by Gilda Aquilera.

Hollytree's Macho of Chelsea, CDX (L) was a High in Trial winner who ended up #8 overall before retiring. Owned by Gilda Aquilera, Mavis Barr, and Jeannie Jett.

OBEDIENCE
QUALIFYING SCORE
PRESTIGE SPEC. CLUBS
OF ATLANTA
OCTOBER 1987
PHOTO BY *Graham*

Happy Go Lucky, UD won tenth place at the Gaines Western Regional in 1976. She was a multiple-HiT winner and a Top Ten Obedience Dal. Owned by Linda Fish.

Pisces Rambler Sunspot Dawn, CDX won the Veterans class at DCA when she was nine years old. Owned by Linda Fish.

FIRST
VETERAN
DALMATIAN CLUB OF
AMERICA
NATIONAL SPECIALITY
MAY   1990

RFBCN Lidgate's Triever Franc, CDX was High in Trial at DCA in 1990. Owned by Jim and Linda Fulks.

Lidgate Charles of Seaspot, CDX was the #1 Open Dalmatian in 1989 (according to DCA statistics) and won a Dog World award for his Open scores. Owned by Jim and Linda Fulks.

Touchstone's Mountain Man, CD was shown only in Novice and was a multiple-HIT winner. Owned by Cathy Murphy.

Ch. Touchstone's Yosemite Sam, UD, TT was a multiple-specialty HIT winner and was in the Top Ten Overall from Open for two years. Owned by Cathy Murphy.

Ch. Touchstone's Wheeler Dealer, CDX, CGC, TT has been ranked in the Top Ten both for Overall and for Open. Owned by Cathy Murphy.

Colonial Coach Classy Chassi, CDX, amidst some of the 250 trophies that she won in obedience competition. Owned by Cathy Murphy.

Breeding Dalmatians

GENERAL INFORMATION

Let's face it—the world would survive nicely if no more litters of Dalmatian puppies were ever bred! They are not necessary to the ecology, nor are they a breed working for their keep. However, those of us who love their distinctive characteristics would find it hard to fill the void in our hearts should this breed die out. And that must be the one and only reason for producing a litter of Dalmatians—pure love for the breed based on a knowledge of the history that shaped their character and a desire to preserve and protect the best that this breed has to offer. Breeding, properly done, requires a depth of knowledge, a dedication of purpose, and a commitment of vast amounts of time.

If you purchased your Dalmatian strictly as a pet, then you should have already spayed or neutered the pup and, therefore, aren't concerned with the topic of breeding. Or did you purchase with the intent that possibly down the road...maybe just one litter...

Did you purchase a pet? Did you intend to show? Or breed? If so, did you purchase the best specimen from the best litter? What is your purpose for breeding—do you really think you will improve the breed or are you just going to "pupulate" the world? Do you know the genetic problems that this breed is disposed to? How about the genetic problems in the line your Dal is from?

"But," you say, "my Dalmatian is AKC-registered!" Well, that's a good start, but an AKC pedigree is not a guarantee of quality. The American Kennel Club guarantees that your Dalmatian pup is pure Dalmatian, with no other pure breed's or mixed breed's blood in his genes. The AKC's intent is to protect the purebred dog only. They are keepers of records and they can trace your Dalmatian's family back further than you can probably trace your own! The AKC encourages the responsible breeding and selling of purebred dogs, but their legislative and punitive authority does not extend beyond that pertaining to misrepresentation of pedigrees. The only exception is their ability to choose to withhold registration privileges from individuals charged and/or convicted of animal abuse.

Are you having a litter just to educate the children? Public television is doing a remarkable job of introducing the world to the miracles of reproduction. Perhaps you should visit the local humane society first and become educated about how many unwanted puppies there are in the world. Most responsible breeders would be willing to allow you and your children to watch the whelping of a litter, either in person or on videotape. Viewing the birth of just one puppy usually convinces the majority of children that it is more mess than miracle—they'd rather not have to attend the birth of an entire litter. Breeding and placing a litter take a great deal of time and effort if done properly. Done improperly, you may eventually be contributing to the population of the humane society you took the time to visit.

Spaying and Neutering—A Healthy Choice

The unspayed bitch runs a greater risk of developing mammary tumors, whether she has been bred or not. If a bitch is spayed prior to her first season, the risk of developing these tumors is significantly reduced. Spaying after the first heat cycle is still beneficial, but waiting until the bitch has matured has little or no effect on reducing her chances of developing tumors. Most families decide, after putting up with two or three annoying seasons, that it is time to spay their pets. They are tired of the bloody discharge produced for at least three weeks' time every six or seven months, tired of the unwanted male canine guests hanging around and marking everything they can. So, in the interests of her health and your peace of mind, why not just have your female Dal spayed before trouble starts and while you can still give her the maximum health benefits?

Neutering a male is a whole separate topic, isn't it? Must be a gender thing—the majority of men are a little reluctant to discuss the removal of their male pup's reproductive organs. Comedians have created entire routines based on the subject. But it really isn't so funny when it's *your* male that keeps straying from home to find the neighbor's bitch in heat and then proceeds to leave his calling card all over *their* property. Neutering keeps the neighborhood peaceful, and keeps Spot happily at home.

The health benefits of neutering a male, while they do exist, are not as much of an influencing factor as the effect that neutering will have on Spot's temperament and trainability. It is difficult to get and keep the attention of a male whose brain cells are suffused with testosterone, whose scent glands are assaulted with the fragrance of "eau de bitche." Once neutering removes those obstacles to learning, you will have a virtual four-legged genius on your hands. The temptation to "mark" territory in or out of the house will also diminish, as will the desire to fight with Spike next door over who has the breeding rights to the neighbor's bitch.

But won't he miss it? Do it early and he won't miss what he's never known. *But won't that stunt his growth?* Studies have proven that full growth potential will be reached and male body type retained. *But doesn't spaying and neutering cause obesity?* Taking in more calories than you burn off causes obesity. If spaying/neutering creates a less anxious pet who is more tractable and has less excess nervous energy, it means that fewer calories are burned and less food should be fed. Overfeeding causes obesity, not the lack of reproductive organs.

Chances are that if you did your homework before purchasing your Dal puppy, you are under a contractual obligation to spay/neuter when the time comes. Responsible breeders only allow the best representatives in their litters to reproduce and thereby improve the quality of the breed. Sure, you think your pup is the best—and he is, *for you.* Show you care; keep him or her happy and healthy. *Spay or neuter.*

A Popular Breed

The American Kennel Club maintains statistics on how many litters of a given breed are registered and how many indi-

*Disney's animated **101 Dalmatians** caused a rapid rise in the breed's popularity in the 1960s. "Tack" clowns around with animator Frank Thomas, who is pretending to be the film's "Mr. Dearly."*

BREEDING

vidual dogs are registered from those litters. Since the 1980s, the number of registered Dalmatians has steadily increased, causing the Dal to jump from 35th in popularity out of approximately 130 recognized breeds to (hopefully only briefly) one of the top ten most popular breeds.

What has caused such a rapid rise in popularity? Well, what attracts you to this breed with the startling markings, the striking good looks, and the adorable pudgy pups made famous by Disney? You see them in magazines, on billboards, in TV commercials, etc. They are photogenic and they draw your attention instantly. Once they were discovered by advertisers,

their race to the top of the popularity charts began. Those flashy ads with the well-trained Dals don't include glimpses of muddy paws from uprooting the rose bushes and paw prints all over your shirt when he kisses you in apology. No TV commercial shows you how rapidly a Dal's tail can clean off the coffee table or how hefty an adult Dal feels as he tries to climb onto your lap for some late-night attention. The furniture ads in the magazines don't show what a bed-hog your pet Dal will be or what the new couch will look like with little white hairs embedded in the material. With only the most favorable features portrayed in the advertisements, who wouldn't be duped into buying one of those gorgeous "designer Dals"?

"Tack" (Am-Can-Mex. Ch. Coachman's Classic, CD) poses for Disney artist Frank Thomas. Tack was the model for **101 Dalmatians'** *"Pongo." Owned by Maria Johnson.*

The commercials were only meant to catch your eye and sell you the product of the day; however, little did we realize that they were selling Americans on the Dalmatian itself. And having created a market, albeit unwittingly, the merchandising machine stepped in to supply that market.

Supply and Demand

One aspect of a capitalist society is that someone is always willing to turn circumstances into cash, and such is the case with the

Three eight-week-old Altamar puppies, Rollo, Asti, and Heidi, are sketched by Disney production supervisor Eric Larson.

market for Dalmatians. Enterprising individuals stepped up to produce Dal puppies to fill the demand, treating them only as a viable commodity, an agricultural product no different than corn, wheat, or cotton. Pedigreed brood bitches and stud dogs were purchased and bred with no concern for temperament, health, genealogy, or the suitability of the mated pair to each other. Brood bitches were fed well and vetted properly because, after all, you don't want to kill the goose that lays the golden egg. But no bitch is so healthy that she can produce a litter with every heat cycle and not suffer the consequences, or have her later litters of pups suffer with her. Most pups were removed from their mothers at four weeks of age and prepared for market so as not to compromise the bitches' health any further. When their ability to

produce good litters declined, these poor bitches were cast aside for fresh stock.

Puppy "farmers" are not always located several states away from you or in the middle of the agricultural belt—they may be as close as a neighbor's back yard. The term actually describes anyone who breeds large numbers of litters each year and places them for profit, frequently sells individual puppies or whole litters to pet stores, doesn't bother to interview prospective buyers any further than questioning their ability to pay, doesn't match the proper puppy to the proper home, never expects to see either the puppy or the buyer again, and places puppies "the sooner the better" because older babies need vaccinations, which cut down profits.

You are adopting another living creature

to become part of your family for the rest of his life—how would you prefer him to have spent his first few weeks of life? What happens to those babies who are not allowed to stay with "mom" to finish out the socialization period properly? Many of them appear in pet stores nationwide to

This is not to say that pet stores do not sell physically healthy pets. Obviously it is in their best interests to keep their products alive or they will have nothing to sell, hence no profits. But innumerable research projects have determined what factors are absolutely necessary to produce a puppy who is

Tack and "DeeDee" (Ch. Williamscrest Dainty Dancer) model for the parts of Pongo and Perdita at Disney Studios in Burbank, California.

feed the Dalmatian craze. Even an educated public is susceptible to the cute little puppy in the cage. Because they feel sorry for the poor creature, they buy him and bring him home...thereby creating an empty cage that must be filled with *another* Dal puppy. The only way to break this cycle is to educate the consumer, train him to be more discerning, and research the product carefully.

mentally healthy as well, and who is best suited to become a part of family life. The very nature of the agricultural process involved in mass-producing puppies for the commercial market precludes the incorporation of socialization, both human and canine, into rearing the puppies.

Having researched what ingredients go into producing a good pet, the intelligent purchaser will search out those breeders

ized, this spotted dynamo becomes such an aggravation that the ultimate solution is to give him away to another unsuspecting family or take him to the humane society.

To the Rescue

Excess baggage. Throwaways. Unwanted Dalmatians with no one to love or to love them. They're out there in humane societies and animal shelters scattered across America, put there by people who just couldn't cope any longer and had no one to call on for help. Almost as rapidly as they come in, many of them are being rescued by caring Dalmatian fanciers throughout the country. The members of the Dalmatian Club of America, regional Dalmatian clubs, and independent rescue groups and individuals are overwhelmed by the enormity of the job, but they still manage to bring the unwanted Dals home, clean them up, spay or neuter them, vaccinate them, train them, and place them in good homes. Many slip through the cracks, but many more are saved to be loved and to return that love.

With the scarcity of good homes, many people are choosing not to breed and instead recommend that inquirers look into adopting a rescued Dalmatian. Regional

Rob and Morris at Minnesota's annual Pet Fair. This is an opportunity for local breed clubs to distribute information and educate the public about their breeds.

who invest time, money, and love into raising their puppies. Concerned breeders with true love for the Dalmatian will be there to educate the potential buyer about the breed, smooth out the bumps, and help keep their puppies with the families who purchase them. No puppy "farmer," pet store, or pet store clerk is going to be there to help a new owner solve the myriad of problems that can arise while a Dal puppy is maturing. But until the cycle is broken and the puppy-buying public becomes educated, what is going to happen to the excess of puppies purchased by people who didn't realize what owning a Dalmatian entailed? Too many families become disillusioned when the cute little Dal baby rapidly grows into a rowdy, undisciplined bundle of energy. Left to his own devices in the back yard, untrained and unsocial-

Morris does some Dal PR at the Minnesota Purebred Dog Breeders education building. During the Minnesota State Fair, many breed clubs give presentations to the public.

clubs and rescue groups have taken a proactive approach to combating the over-population problem by running ads in local newspapers with headlines such as "Call for info before you buy," or "Don't buy a Dal." They offer free information packets about the pros and cons of owning this breed, and they provide resource materials about training and problem solving. To offset the enormous expenses of these efforts, fundraising events are necessary and the profits usually don't begin to cover the costs of the rescue. All of this tremendous effort is out of a love for each Dalmatian, no matter where they were conceived, how they were whelped, or how they came to need rescuing. It is the hope of rescue people everywhere that the Dal-owning public will become educated about the overpopulation of the breed and choose not to randomly reproduce Dalmatians. Rescue groups hope that this "negative" publicity about the Dalmatian will make people stop and think carefully, and then make responsible purchases.

To those of us who love these spotted clowns, there is no other breed worth having.

GENETICS

A dog has 78 chromosomes, which are arranged in 39 pairs. One chromosome in each pair is inherited from the sire, and the other is inherited from the dam. These chromosomes are made up of DNA, and genes are segments of that DNA. There are many factors that determine how genes will be expressed and, therefore, what traits and characteristics the dog will inherit. Chromosome pairs contain gene pairs, and the genes in each pair may or may not be identical. A *homozygous* gene pair has two identical genes for a specific trait, but a *heterozygous* gene pair has two different *alleles* (alternate forms of expression) of that gene. One of the alleles will be *dominant* and will be expressed as a visible trait; the other allele will be *recessive* and its effect will be hidden.

Other factors include *epistasis*, which is a reaction between gene pairs that occurs when certain genes at one site have the ability to mask the influence of other genes at another site. Other genes are not very influential individually, but in sufficient numbers can affect a main gene pair. These genes are known as modifying polygenes, or *modifiers*, and the extent of modification depends on the number and the nature of the polygenes involved.

While a trait such as color inheritance is usually quite straightforward, most physical characteristics are more complex and considerably less well understood. Things such as "good shoulders" are composed of a variety of characteristics, all of which may be affected by a number of genes. While the length of a specific bone may be inherited as a simple dominant or recessive gene, how that bone relates to and interacts with the rest of the shoulder assembly may be difficult to predict.

It has been suggested by some authorities that most correct features are dominant, while most genetic defects are recessive. If this is true, once a desired feature is lost to a breed, it can never again be found in the breed's own gene pool. An example of this might be normal uric acid metabolism, which apparently does not exist in purebred Dalmatians. Any faults that are dominant can be easily bred out because they are always expressed (visible) when present. However, when faults are recessive, they are very difficult to eliminate because they can go into hiding and only reappear when two dogs carrying the same recessive genes are bred together. This doesn't take into consideration the presence of modifiers, but breeding would be a good deal simpler if everything was simply dominant or recessive.

Unfortunately, this is not the case. Other possibilities include *incomplete dominance* and *incomplete penetrance*. Sometimes two different alleles on the same series will combine to produce a phenotype that is intermediate in appearance. An example would be leg length. If long legs are dominant and short legs are recessive, and if a breeding between a long-legged dog and a short-legged dog produces dogs of intermediate leg length, the allele for long legs is said to be *incompletely dominant*. Short legs would still be considered recessive if two long-legged dogs bred together produced a variety of leg lengths but two short-legged dogs bred together produced only short legs. Incomplete dominance appears to be very common, but it may be difficult to determine if one is dealing with *incomplete dominance* or with the presence of modifiers.

When the recessive gene must be present in duplicate for the trait to be seen, it is a simple recessive and an example of complete penetrance, which is the normal state of affairs. In some cases, the heterozygous trait may look like either of the homozygous phenotypes. They are not intermediate in type but look distinctly like *either* the dominant or the recessive phenotype. This is called *incomplete penetrance*.

It is important to remember that heredity affects more than just physical traits. In addition to such things as height, eye color, hearing, and tail carriage, we must also consider temperament and health. Although temperament can be modified by environment and training, the dog's basic disposition is inherited. All the training in the world will not prevent an aggressive dog from passing aggressive tendencies on to a percentage of his offspring. Although a shy dog can be desensitized to his surroundings, he will always have the potential to overreact to stress as well as the potential to pass this trait to his offspring.

Genetic health is equally important. Allergies, seizures, and hip dysplasia are only a few of the inheritable health problems that must be considered, and breeding stock should be tested whenever possible. Many breeders also feel that there is a hereditary basis for such things as the formation of urate stones and the tendency to be hypothyroid. Great care must be taken that existing health problems are not passed on to future generations.

All Dalmatians intended for breeding must have stable temperaments and must be readily trainable by using normal training methods. Dogs with significant health problems that might be hereditary must never be bred. All dogs should be BAER tested for hearing and have their hip x-rays evaluated by the OFA or Penn-Hip™. Many breeders also choose to do eye exams and blood work, though related problems are not (yet) common in Dalmatians. With the increased incidence of hypothyroidism in all breeds, a thyroid profile may also be advisable. It goes without saying that dogs who seizure should not be bred.

Although a dog will function just fine with a curly tail or light eyes, a dog that is highly allergic or bites small children is not a desirable companion. The breeder must remember that however gorgeous the dogs he breeds, they must also be healthy and able to function as companions to man in a normal environment.

The aspiring Dalmatian breeder is probably best served by learning to identify optimum soundness and the physical features that go into creating it. This, along with a feeling for acceptable breed type, the ability to identify and appreciate good health and correct temperament, and an understanding of the Dalmatian's original purpose will give the breeder a direction and a goal. The successful breeder must be able to recognize the faults in his own dogs, identify the opposing virtues in other dogs, and combine them in a fashion that won't cause him to lose existing virtues while attempting to correct faults.

Being a breeder is more than mating two show dogs and hoping for more show dogs. The breeder's goal is to create dogs that are better than their parents, so that each generation is an improvement on the previous one—not just in show wins, but in overall quality, health, and disposition. Each breeding should be thought of as a link in the chain, a step forward that brings the breeder ever closer to perfection. One fine dog can be the result of luck, but a prepotent line, i.e., a line that consistently passes on its virtues in high percentage to successive generations, that consistently produces top-quality dogs is the breeder's dream and ultimate goal.

SELECTING THE STUD DOG

Before selecting an appropriate stud dog, the breeder must understand the breed standard and be able to apply it to actual dogs. No dog is perfect and all dogs display some degree of faultiness. Learning to recognize faults is not particularly difficult. Learning to assess the degree of faultiness and its relative significance can be a great deal more difficult, and learning to recognize virtues (particularly in another's dogs)

is sometimes the greatest challenge of all.

Dogs used for breeding must have virtues, and the absence of faults does not automatically mean that the animal in question has any virtues to pass on to its offspring. Only the best dogs should be used for breeding, dogs that have something to pass on to succeeding generations. An attractive pedigree does not automatically classify a dog as breeding quality, and, in fact, most puppies from even the best breedings go to pet homes to be spayed or neutered.

The prospective breeder may wish to decide in advance whether to outcross, linebreed, or inbreed as this will reduce the number of stud dogs that need to be considered. Some breeders feel that the pedigrees are more important than the individual dogs. This is referred to as breeding "on paper." Others prefer to pick a specific dog that has the desired features and consider the pedigree of secondary interest. This is called breeding "dog to dog." Most breeders normally use a combination of both methods.

Am-Can. Ch. Deltalyn Decoupage ("Cooper"), winning the Stud Dog class at the Greater New York Specialty. His son and his daughter were Winners Dog and Winners Bitch.

A pedigree is actually of little use to an aspiring breeder unless he knows something about the dogs that it represents.

Outcrossing is the breeding of unrelated dogs, although all dogs within a breed are related to some degree. For practical purposes, we can consider a breeding with no common ancestors in the first four generations to be an outcross. Outcrosses are very useful for picking up characteristics that do not exist in a breeder's line or for correcting a feature which tends to be faulty in the bitch and in her pedigree. Outcrosses are generally more successful if both dogs are themselves linebred. *Quality dogs from unrelated lines often produce well when bred together, as the breeding is not likely to double up on undesirable recessives.*

However, though outcross produce may be very good in appearance, breeding them will rarely be as predictable as breeding from the original line.

Linebreeding is the breeding of related dogs, but a pedigree in which the same kennel prefix appears multiple times is not necessarily linebred. Linebreeding means several crosses to a particular dog whose name appears on both the sire and dam side of the pedigree, usually within the first few generations. It's important to remember that the dog being linebred upon must be a *good* dog! Unknowing breeders often linebreed on a familiar name without knowing anything about the dog itself. It's advisable to make some inquiries before deciding to linebreed on any dog. Linebreeding on a particularly good dog increases the chances of reproducing his good features, but his faults or the faults in his pedigree are also likely to show up! *A novice breeder with a linebred bitch from a winning line would probably do well to breed back into the line, unless the bitch is especially faulty in an area in which the line is not particularly strong.*

Inbreeding is the mating of closely related dogs such as father/daughter, mother/son, or brother/sister. Although inbreeding is blamed for a multitude of sins, it only concentrates the things that are already present in the genetic makeup of

Am-Can. Ch. Alfredrich Handsome Tall N' Dark won BOB and the Stud Dog class at DCA in 1992. Among his offspring is 1993's #1 Dalmatian. Owned by J. Richard Millaire and Al Kay.

the dogs. It also brings to the surface unknown recessives that may exist in the line. If continued over many generations, it has been shown to increase neonatal death and decrease the general viability of the produce. Inbreeding is best practiced by experienced breeders who know the dogs in the pedigree, are willing to take the risks that may be involved, and will cull if necessary. Inbreeding can be used as a tool for testing breeding stock to identify undesirable recessives that may be present. *An outstanding inbred dog has a greater than average chance of being able to pass on his good traits.*

An aspiring breeder would be well ad-

about her sire and dam as well as her littermates. Perhaps it would be worthwhile to pay the breeder a visit and see as many of the dogs as possible, especially if you have not done so before. *The more you know about your bitch's background, the better your chances of picking a suitable stud dog.*

List the features you would like to improve and then prioritize them. Don't expect to correct everything in one litter. Decide on what you most want to improve this time, but don't completely overlook the other features. Perhaps your bitch has poor feet, a long back, and light eyes. Poor feet are a major fault, a long back is a significant fault,

Left to right: Am-Can. Ch. Coachman's Chuck-A-Luck ("Brewster") with offspring Ch. Lord Jim ("Jimmy") and Ch. Coachman's Canicula ("Nicky"), and Ch. Miquel of Tuckaway, the son of Jimmy and the grandson of both Brewster and Nicky.

vised to seek help when choosing a stud dog. If the bitch in question is a champion or even a top winner, she will still have features that need to be corrected or improved. As many breeders soon realize, it is much easier to see faults in other people's dogs than in your own, and it's human nature to accept as correct the things you're used to seeing. Ask the opinions and advice of breeders whose opinions you respect and don't take offense at honest answers. If the bitch was purchased from a successful breeder, start there. Find out all you can

and light eyes are a relatively minor fault, so concentrate on the faults in that order. If you find a suitable stud dog with great feet and nice proportions, he should also have at least adequate eye color. Although you are not trying to correct eye color this time, doubling up on an existing fault may make it even harder to correct later on.

Some faults are easy to correct and can be corrected in one generation, while other faults are much more difficult. For example, poor rears are invariably easier to correct than bad fronts. A fault that is relatively common in the breed may be more difficult to correct because it is harder to find a stud dog who is strong in that particular feature.

Don't try to overcompensate for faults, as this rarely works. If your bitch has a soft topline and carries her tail too low, don't breed to a dog with a roachy back and a high tail. Breed instead to a dog that has an excellent topline and carries his tail properly. If he is a linebred dog from a line with consistently good toplines and correct tails, so much the better. That gives him a better chance of producing those features. *Remember that a dog's phenotype (appear-*

magazines, but keep an open mind. Don't be taken in by a perfect picture, since pictures can be touched up. Just because an ad claims that a dog is sound doesn't mean that he actually is. Ask for a video of the dog or make arrangements to see him yourself.

When you locate a dog that really interests you, write to the owner and ask if the dog is available. Send pictures of your bitch and a copy of her pedigree. Tell the stud owner what you are looking for in a stud dog and where your bitch needs improvement. Ask whether or not the stud

Ch. Sunnyglen's Spencer For Hire, winning the Stud Dog class in 1989, pictured with his son Ch. Long Last Perfect For Paisley (WD) and his daughter Ch. Rambler Winning Colors (AOM).

ance) and genotype (genetic makeup) are not necessarily the same.

When looking for a stud dog, attend as many Dalmatian specialty shows as possible. Look at the class dogs as well as the Specials, and be sure to watch the stud dog classes. When you see a dog that catches your eye, check to see if he has any offspring entered. If you notice a number of outstanding dogs with the same sire, check him out, particularly if his offspring are good in the areas where your bitch needs improvement.

Buy or borrow a copy of the *Chicagoland Pedigree Book*. Study the ads in the DCA *Spotter*, specialty catalogs, and other Dal

dog may be able to help in those areas. Be honest with the stud owner and expect an honest answer in return. You may not get one, but you have to start somewhere. An honest and experienced owner will tell you what the dog can be expected to correct and in which areas he may be weak. The owner will also have the percentages on deafs, patches, and blue eyes. Don't forget to ask about such things as temperament, health, tail carriage, bites, missing trim, and size. Many stud owners won't volunteer this information, but will provide it if you ask. If the dog is not too far away, make arrangements to see him. Even if the dog is not currently being shown, his owner may be willing to bring him along to a show you both will be attending.

When you've finally decided on the dog and if your bitch has been accepted, inform the stud owner approximately when you expect her to come in season. Be sure the bitch is up to date on her vaccinations and is free of parasites. As the time approaches, check her daily with a tissue and notify the stud owner the first day you see any blood. Make an appointment with your vet for a brucellosis test and, if she will be shipped, a health certificate.

STUD OWNER RESPONSIBILITY

A stud owner must be both honest and objective. No dog is perfect for all bitches, and certainly no dog should be offered at stud unless he is totally healthy and has an excellent disposition. A stud dog can have a significant impact on a breed, but not always in a positive fashion. One that is widely used can have a very negative impact if he consistently produces health or temperament problems. Dogs offered at stud must be BAER tested and have OFA- or Penn-Hip™ evaluated hips. It's also advisable for stud dogs to have their eyes checked, have bloodwork done including a thyroid profile and a vWB test, and have a urinalysis done several times a year. Although certain canine health problems are not particularly common in Dalmatians, all it takes is one popular but untested stud dog to change all that. Good record keeping can be very useful for the purpose of fielding questions from the owners of bitches. Percentages of the deaf, patched, and blue-eyed pups produced should always be kept, and it's useful to break down these statistics according to whether the dams were blue-eyed or had unilateral hearing. The stud owner should request complete numbers from each bitch owner and ask that he be kept informed of anything else of significance, including large amounts of missing trim, bad bites, oversize, particularly bad tails, poor tempera-

ments, or health problems of any type.

Responsible stud owners no longer accept pet bitches for breeding, nor do they accept bitches owned by people who are breeding for the wrong reasons. In this era of the Dal's excessive popularity, and the resulting surplus of puppies, the breed does not need any extra litters of Dalmatians, especially litters that have no potential to produce quality dogs.

Anyone offering a dog at stud must understand the mechanics of dog breeding and know how to handle a stud dog. There are a number of dog breeding books that address this topic, but the assistance of an experienced stud dog owner is even more helpful. It should be remembered that most veterinarians are not reproductive specialists and are of little help in such matters.

All visiting bitches must be tested for brucellosis before breeding and the stud dog should also be tested regularly. He should be kept healthy, parasite-free, and up-to-date on his vaccinations, and he should not be overused. If several bitches will need to be bred at the same time, the stud owner should notify the bitch owners in case they would prefer to wait and use the dog at a later date.

Visiting bitches need clean, comfortable, and secure quarters, regular exercise, and a proper diet. Breedings must be closely supervised to avoid injury to either dog. Accurate records must be kept and the bitch owner should be notified as to the exact days of breeding. Bitches should not be forcibly bred before they are ready to stand, even though it might be more "convenient" for the stud owner. If a vaginal smear is required, then it should be done, but the bitch owner should always be notified first if an artificial insemination (AI) needs to be done.

Shipping arrangements must be thoroughly understood by both parties to avoid misunderstandings of any kind. All agreements and fees should be discussed in advance, and a written stud contract should be signed by both parties.

At the 1987 DCA Specialty, Ch. Fireman's Freckled Friend won the Stud Dog class. He is pictured with daughters Ch. Driftwood Chimney Cricket and Ch. Fireman's Becky Newsham.

BREEDING THE BITCH

A bitch is usually taken to the stud dog, either driven or flown depending on the distance and the owner's inclination. Most Dalmatians stand for breeding after the tenth day, and it is not unusual for them to wait until the 15th day or even later. One of the most common reasons for a bitch to miss is that she was bred too early. An experienced stud dog knows when the bitch is ready, while a young dog may try far too early. Owners of young males often worry unnecessarily and are absolutely convinced that their dogs will never get it right. Most Dals are good studs and do just fine when the bitches are actually ready to be bred.

If it is important that the bitch stay on her regular diet while she's away, send some of her food along with her unless the stud owner offers to supply it. Inform the stud owner of any peculiarities too, such as the bitch's ability to get out of a 12-foot chain link covered run. Send along her regular blanket and a bone or a toy so she'll feel a bit more at home. If the bitch doesn't normally wear a collar, buy one for this occasion. Any dog that is shipped or that is staying with someone else should wear a snug-fitting buckle collar with an ID tag. If she doesn't spend much time in a crate, get her used to it before she comes in season so that she will be comfortable when shipped or transported and while visiting the stud dog.

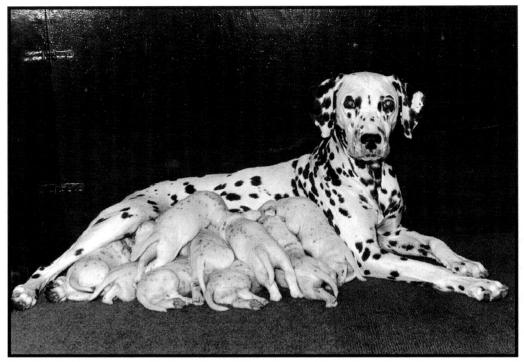

Ch. Melody Up and Away, CD (L) and her all-liver litter, which produced four champions. "Pooka" produced a total of 15 champions, 7 of which were also obedience-titled.

Dogs are normally shipped by air cargo in vinyl airline crates, although some airlines will take them "counter to counter" which means that they are loaded and unloaded with the luggage rather than with the freight. Most dogs need not be tranquilized before shipping as it may impair equilibrium, reduce the rate of respiration, and reduce the ability to regulate body temperature. Most Dals handle shipping very well, especially those who have been shown and are used to traveling. The crate should be in good condition, with all the screws in place and a bungee cord stretched over the door to make it more secure. A thick blanket or pad will make the crate more comfortable. Call the airline well in advance to make arrangements, and be absolutely certain that everyone involved understands the flight numbers, destination, and arrival time.

If you have not shipped a dog before, it's advisable to discuss the procedure with the stud owner or another experienced Dal owner. Check with other dog breeders in your area for information about your local airport as well as their preferred airline(s).

An alternative to shipping the bitch is to use chilled or frozen semen from the stud dog you have chosen. Chilled semen, which must be used fresh, is shipped counter to counter or by overnight express when the bitch is ready to breed. Frozen semen, properly stored, will keep for years. The insemination must be done correctly at precisely the right time in the bitch's cycle. Most veterinarians have no experience with this procedure so it may be necessary to consult with one who specializes in canine reproduction. Although this procedure is rarely less expensive than shipping a bitch, it may be easier for all parties concerned and it works well when the weather is too cold or too hot for shipping dogs.

PREGNANCY

When the bitch returns from breeding, it's important to remember that she may still be breedable for several days and should be kept away from all male dogs for at least a week. More than one Dalmatian has been shipped to a handsome stud and come home only to be bred by the mutt down the street!

The observant owner can often tell quite early if the bitch is pregnant since many of them show significant personality changes. Some become irritable and short-tempered, but most pregnant Dals are excessively affectionate and cloying. Many also display increased appetites from the very beginning, and when an otherwise well-behaved Dal starts stealing food off the counter, it's usually safe to assume that she's pregnant.

Physical changes include enlarged nipples and a vulva that does not shrink

These pups are from the first litter of AKC-registered Dals whelped from the use of frozen semen. Bred by Beverly Huer and Carol Schubert using the Seager Cryogenic System.

down to its pre-breeding size. Most pregnant bitches don't start to fill out until after the fifth week, causing many an owner to worry needlessly that there may be no puppies after all of that careful planning.

Breeders who absolutely can't wait will often take their bitches to be palpated between the 25th and 30th day. Some veterinarians and breeders are very good at this, but more than one breeder has been told that his bitch isn't pregnant, only to end up with a litter of 12! Ultrasound is also used to confirm pregnancies, but the equipment is very expensive and is not always available. Ultrasound uses sound waves to produce

Pregnant "Dia" could use a tummy rub. Ch. Ldy Daps Strsnstryps of DC's, CD is owned by Patrick and Linda Jones.

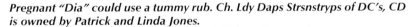

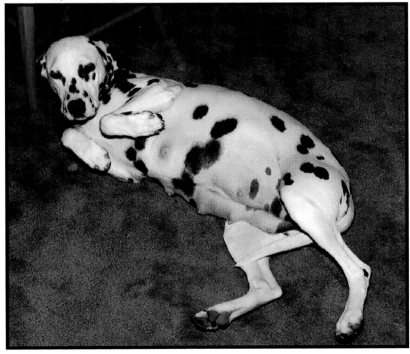

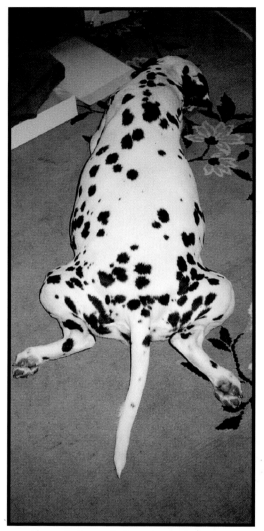

Just hours before whelping, "Lacy" can still do the "frog dog" position. Ch. Aurora's Lacy Britches is owned by Callie Norton.

Pregnant bitches should not be vaccinated, nor should they receive any medication that is not absolutely required. (Most authorities consider heartworm preventative safe for pregnant bitches.) A good brand of puppy food fed throughout the pregnancy and lactation will supply all of the additional calories, protein, fat, and calcium that she needs. If supplements are added, they should be limited to such things as hard-cooked eggs or cottage cheese. Extra calcium is not normally advised when puppy food is used. Some breeders are also convinced that raspberry leaves or raspberry leaf tea helps to ensure an easy whelping.

Bitches should not gain any weight during the first month of pregnancy (unless they are underweight to begin with) and should never be allowed to gain excess weight as that may lead to whelping difficulties. Bitches normally gain the equivalent of 15 to 25 percent of their pre-breeding weight during pregnancy, but that, of course, depends on litter size.

The bitch may be allowed to exercise as usual until the last few weeks of pregnancy, but care should be taken that she does not play too roughly. Jumping should be discouraged. If she is not normally active, a daily walk will help her maintain muscle tone and may make whelping easier. She should not be forced to exercise during the last week unless she wishes to do so.

The area designated as the whelping room should be ready at least a week before puppies are anticipated. Many bitches have strong nesting instincts and will spend the last few weeks trying to find the perfect place to raise a family. Unless you want puppies whelped in a hole in the backyard, in a window well, under the bed, or in the linen closet, it's best to select a cozy, quiet, and protected area for whelping. Although the puppies may eventually be moved to the kitchen or family room, it is better to start them off in an area where the bitch can have some privacy, such as an extra bedroom, home office, or the basement, if it is not dark and damp.

images much like the sonar used by submarines. It is normally used on about the 32nd day, but very sophisticated equipment can detect pregnancies even earlier. Ultrasound is not foolproof, as it may not detect all of the puppy skeletons. Even with both palpation and ultrasound, there is always the chance that the bitch will reabsorb the fetuses and the pups that could be felt or seen early in the pregnancy will no longer be present when the due date arrives.

There are many plans available for building a whelping box complete with adjustable sides and removable rails to keep the bitch from accidentally laying on a puppy. Whelping boxes can also be purchased commercially and are usually durable and easy to keep clean. Some breeders find that children's plastic swimming pools work well, while others use the bottoms of plastic crates with great success. A few swear by large cardboard boxes because they are durable, disposable, and free, and they can be reinforced with duct tape to make them stronger. Whatever type of whelping box is chosen, it should have sides that are at least a foot high and a solid bottom. It should be long enough for the bitch to stretch out full length, but not so large that the puppies can crawl too far away. If the floor tends to be cool, the box should be raised a few inches off the floor.

Setting the box inside a metal exercise pen will keep the bitch from moving the pups to a site that she prefers over the one you have chosen for her, and will keep the puppies from wandering too far from the box when they first begin to explore. If the room is carpeted, a sheet of heavy plastic can be placed under the pen and covered with a thick layer of newspapers. Local newspaper companies will often sell clean roll-ends of newspaper at reasonable prices.

Some breeders have had success using a large wooden whelping box with a nest area in one end and sawdust or wood shavings (not cedar) rather than newspapers in the other. Although sawdust and shavings are messy and

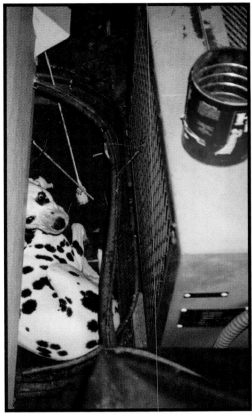

Some bitches prefer to choose their own whelping box. "Perdie" is quite comfortable in the window well. Ch. Paisley's Princess Perdita is owned by Kevin and Teresa Doran.

"Monkee" has lost her trim girlish figure! Proctors Queen of the Mt., two days before whelping a healthy litter of nine. Owned by Shirley Allegre.

The following series of pictures shows the birth of Monkee's pups. Each pup is born in its own sac.

tend to get tracked around the house, the pups will stay cleaner and there will be no bags of soggy paper to dispose of.

Some provision should be made for keeping the whelping area warm. Space heaters, heating pads, and heat lamps all work when it's not possible to keep the room warm without overheating the rest of the house. Great care must be taken with all types of auxiliary heat sources.

Monkee bites through the umbilical cord.

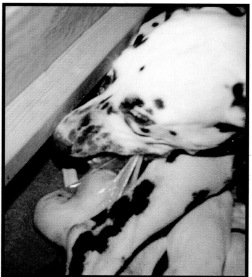

Space heaters should have tip-over switches and must not be accessible to the dogs. Heating pads must be used in a way that allows the pups to crawl to a cooler area if they become too warm, and the pads must never be hot enough to burn tender puppy skin. Heat lamps should not be attached to the box or pen where they can be knocked off and broken, but they work very well when suspended above the box. All cords should be inaccessible to puppies, and the puppies must always have the option of moving to a cooler surface. Temperature on the floor of the whelping box should be at least 85 degrees for the first two weeks.

Monkee bites the sac so the puppy can breathe.

WHELPING

Dalmatians are normally easy whelpers and good mothers, but all prospective breeders should own at least one good, up-to-date whelping book. There are several of them on the market and a good whelping

The puppy is out of the sac, but the cord is still attached.

Puppies are normally born on the 61st day after ovulation but unless testing was done to determine the exact day, the bitch can be expected to whelp anywhere between 58 and 63 days from the first breeding. It would be best to have all of the supplies ready by the 56th day and to have the bitch settled and comfortable in her whelping box. If she goes beyond 65 days, the veterinarian should be consulted. Be sure that your regular veterinarian will be available if needed, and get the name of a backup veterinarian if necessary. An experienced breeder who is willing to help out as a midwife can be a real blessing. Supplies that may be needed include:

book is almost as important as a good veterinarian. Although the majority of Dalmatian bitches need little or no assistance, a good book can be very useful, especially at 3:00 in the morning when things are getting worrisome and the veterinarian has not yet returned your call! Knowing what to do and when, and being able to recognize a true emergency, may enable the breeder to save one or more of the pups and maybe even the bitch herself. This text is intended merely to provide an overview of whelping and to discuss the specifics as they relate to Dalmatians.

Post-whelping—nine healthy pups, all clean and dry.

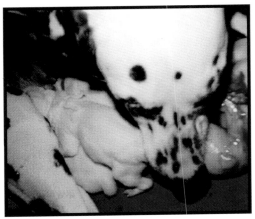

The whelping looks a little messy, but everything is proceeding normally.

- An up-to-date and complete whelping book
- A thermometer for taking the bitch's temperature
- Plenty of clean, dry newspapers for lining the whelping box
- A supply of clean towels for drying the puppies
- A plastic trash bag for dirty papers
- A clock for keeping track of the time between puppies
- A note pad and pencil for recording information on each puppy
- A means of identifying pups such as colored yarn, rickrack, a marking pen, or nail polish

- Sterilized scissors and perhaps a hemostat for cutting cords
- Heavy thread or dental floss for tying cords
- Sterile gloves in case it is necessary to check on the position of a puppy
- A puppy nursing bottle or tube feeding setup and some milk replacer

You might also want to include a radio, a good book or magazine, a thermos or coffee pot, and a comfortable chair for yourself.

The bitch's temperature should be taken twice a day during the last week of gestation. Her temperature will normally drop to about 99 degrees before whelping begins. A bitch whose temperature hasn't dropped will not normally whelp within 24 hours, but once her temperature goes down and

stays down, the bitch should not be left unattended. Most owners get up at least once a night during the last week to check on the bitch.

In normal whelpings, labor consists of three stages. In stage one, the bitch is typically restless. She may pace, shred papers, tear up her box, and appear to be uncomfortable. This stage may be as short as a few hours or it may last for several days. Stage two begins when the cervix is fully dilated. The bitch begins to have noticeable contractions and will pant in between contractions. If the contractions are strong, this stage may last for only a very short time. If the contractions are weak or intermittent, it can go on for several hours. Labor has actually begun once the bitch starts straining, and the first pup

The pups wear different-colored rickrack collars for identification.

should be born within an hour. During stage three, the pups and the placentas are delivered. The time between the pups varies but is not normally longer than three hours. Most pups are born 20 to 30 minutes apart, and occasionally one right after another. Large litters can be whelped in as little as a few hours or may take a day or even longer.

Although most bitches prefer to take care of things themselves, someone should be available at all times. A little assistance at the right time can make the difference between saving and losing a puppy. Some owners sleep in the same room as the bitch for the last few nights, just to make sure that they don't miss the birth of the first puppy. Although bitches have been known to come early and take care of everything with no assistance whatsoever, this is not advisable, particularly with the first litter.

Above: *Whelping is not for the squeamish! The blood, although messy, is from the cut umbilical cord and is a normal part of the process.* Below: *Ch. Woodwynd's Irish Pepper of Pal delivers her first litter. This puppy grew up to be Ch. Woodwynd's KC Masterpiece. Owned by Mary-Lynn Klevans.*

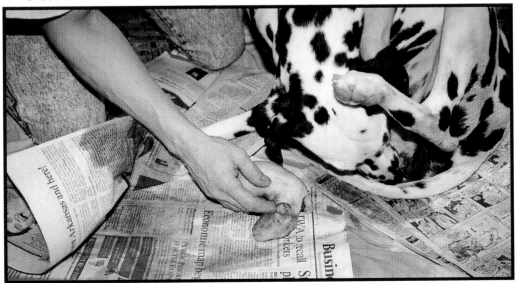

Each pup is contained in an individual fluid-filled sac. As the contractions move the first puppy down the birth canal, a dark "bubble" may be the first sign of an impending birth. It may take a number of contractions to push the first puppy out, so don't be impatient. The sac may rupture before the pup is born and the fluid will gush out, causing the bitch to lick frantically in an effort to clean things up. The pup should follow shortly.

The bitch's reaction to the birth of the first puppy varies a great deal. Many Dals are very businesslike about the whole thing and act as if they have done this all of their lives. Others deliver easily but seem astonished to see the wet and wiggly intruder in the box. However, after a few tentative licks they settle quickly into the routine. A few will panic at the birth of the first puppy, especially if the delivery is not easy and the puppy is large. Some scream when the pup makes his appearance and may try to leap out of the box. Taking the bitch by the collar, reassuring her in a calm voice, and encouraging her to lick the puppy will usually resolve the problem quickly.

Most pups are born in the sac with the cord and placenta still attached, though it is not unusual for the sac to break during delivery. Pups are also often born breech (feet first), and this does not seem to cause any problems. When a pup is born with the sac and placenta intact, the bitch will normally eat the placenta, strip the sac off the puppy, and cut the cord with her teeth. Some bitches are more concerned about cleaning up than they are about removing the sac, so you might want to assist by pulling the sac away from the puppy's head so he can breathe. If the bitch seems to resent this kind of interference, you should respect her wishes unless a puppy really needs assistance.

If the bitch does not attend to the newborn pup promptly, you will want to clean off the puppy and be sure that he is breathing. The umbilical cord need not be cut immediately, so give the bitch a chance to do it herself. She will chew through the cord and crush the blood vessels, which will keep the cord from bleeding. If she doesn't cut the cord, you can attempt to tear it or to cut it with scissors. Be careful not to pull on the cord, as you run the possible risk of causing a hernia. If a hemostat is attached about an inch from the puppy and the cord is cut on the side away from the puppy, it will reduce the chance of bleeding. If the cord does bleed, pinch it tightly between your fingers for a minute or tie it off with a piece of dental floss or heavy thread. If the bitch cuts the cord too short and it bleeds, the end should be tied. Don't forget to trim the floss or thread so that the ends don't tangle around the puppy, and also trim any ragged ends on the cord.

If a pup gets hung up with just his feet showing, it would be best to grasp his feet with a towel to keep him from slipping back up the birth canal. Don't pull on his feet, just hold on tight, and with the next few contractions he will probably slip right out. A slight downward pressure during each contraction may be needed if the puppy is large, but do not pull in between contractions.

Most breeders like to pick up each newborn pup to check sex and color and to dry it off a bit, but some bitches are concerned when their pups are pulled away. If the bitch does not immediately begin to lick the pup and roll him around, the breeder should take the pup and rub him dry with a warm towel.

If the pup is limp and not breathing, if he is gasping for air, or if he sounds "juicy" because of fluid in his lungs, he may need to be "swung," a maneuver that has been used to save many puppies. Place the pup in a towel and cup him between your hands, face up, supporting his head and neck with your index fingers. Lift your hands up over your head and swing them down between your legs in a smooth arc. This will normally cause the pup to gasp and start breathing. This motion may need to be repeated several times. Follow this up with brisk rubbing and encourage the bitch to lick the pup. Keep an eye on any pups that initially have trouble breathing for the first couple of hours and make sure that they continue to breathe normally.

Some breeders play a more active part in whelping and remove the sacs, cut the cords, and dry each puppy, but most Dals are perfectly able to take care of these chores themselves. Whelping books often suggest using a small box with a heating pad to keep the newborn puppies out of the way while the rest of the puppies are being born, but most bitches prefer to have their puppies with them and are normally very careful. You might help out here by moving the pups to one side so that they stay dry and relatively clean. Be sure that a placenta is passed for each puppy that is born. Retained placentas can cause serious problems, but this is a relatively uncommon problem in dogs. Some breeders prefer to keep the bitch from eating all of the placentas as they are often vomited and may cause diarrhea.

If the litter is large and the bitch gets tired, she may appreciate help, but some bitches become a bit nervy and are overly concerned about too much interference. Try to move some of the wet and dirty papers out of the box whenever possible, but don't make a big deal about it. During an interval between pups, you might want to take the bitch outdoors to relieve herself. Take along a towel just in case a puppy is born outdoors. While she is outside, the whelping box can be cleaned up a bit.

Most pups nurse within a few minutes of birth, and pups have been known to grab onto a nipple while still attached to the placenta. Bitches will normally allow the pups to nurse in between births, which is important if the whelping takes a long time. Smaller pups or those that are slower to catch on can be helped by squeezing a drop of milk from a nipple, opening the pup's mouth, and placing the mouth over the nipple. Most pups will hold on immediately, but some are slower to get started. A puppy that seems unable to nurse should be checked to see if he has a cleft palate, which would look like an opening in the roof of his mouth. A pup with a cleft palate should be euthanized.

When the bitch has finished whelping, she will usually relax and may even sleep, although it's not unusual for the last puppy to appear a few hours after the whelping seems to be over. The bitch should be taken outdoors while the box is cleaned up and can be offered a light meal and a drink. Many bitches insist on "eating in bed" for the first few days after whelping. She may have gotten rather messy during whelping, but a bath can wait until the next day.

Ch. Rambler's Lady Sarah Jane with her color-coded litter. A method of identification is needed because Dal pups are born all white (except for any patches). Owned by Cliff and Stephanie Seigneur.

Choco Chip Brandi Delight ("Brandi"), in the midst of cleaning her new litter. Patches are visible at birth—notice the two pups with dark ears in the foreground. Owned by Rosie Hadaway.

Some breeders recommend taking the new mother in for a check-up within 12 hours of whelping, while others prefer taking her along when the pups have their dewclaws removed. Unless the whelping

was particularly difficult or there is some question as to whether all of the placentas were passed, it's probably best to leave the bitch at home with her brood and just keep an eye on her.

When the pups are dry and breathing well, you may want to knot a piece of colored yarn or rickrack around their necks as a means of identification. Each pup should be recorded by time of birth, sex, weight, color, whether or not it is patched, and any other identifying marks. Other possible means of identification include a small diagram indicating the location of nose or ear color, or a dot of permanent marker or nail polish. If yarn or rickrack "collars" are used, they must be tight enough that the pups can't get their feet or legs caught, and the collars must be changed every few days as the puppies grow.

Patches are present at birth and are normally found on the head, although they occasionally appear at the base of the tail. They are very rarely found elsewhere on the body. The most common location of a patch is on the ear or around the eye. An ear patch may cover just a part of the ear or it may cover the whole ear and extend on to the head. An eye patch can be just a small circle or it can cover half of the head. Some pups have multiple patches, such as two ear patches or an ear patch and an eye patch. Don't forget to check the underside of the ear too, as under-ear patches are not at all unusual.

At one time, most responsible breeders chose to eutha-

Here are Brandi and her litter just a few weeks later. Notice how much they've changed in a short time.

contracts. It's an individual decision and there is no right or wrong. If the litter is very large and the bitch may not be able to raise so many pups, or if there are a limited number of homes waiting for pet-quality pups, the patched pups might well be culled.

Small areas of color along the front edges of the ears are not patches, but rather the color showing through in an area where the hair is extremely short. Although pups are born white (except for any patches), their skin is already spotted and it's possible to get an idea of the eventual spotting pattern by closely observing a puppy while he is still wet.

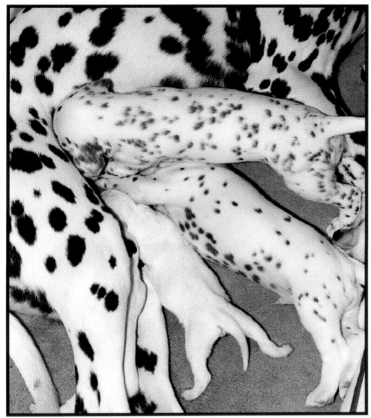

The white pup is about five days old, while the spotted pups are about three weeks old. The pups' markings become visible in the first few weeks. Mom Eloise is owned by Sue MacMillan and Ron Rajala.

nize patched puppies because it was suspected that there were health and temperament problems associated with patching. This was disproved some years ago and now breeders must decide for themselves. Some choose to euthanize newborn patches because they do not look sufficiently "Dalmatianly" and they can not be shown and should not be bred. Others choose to keep the patched pups and sell them on spay/neuter

A different type of patch—on top of the head.

351

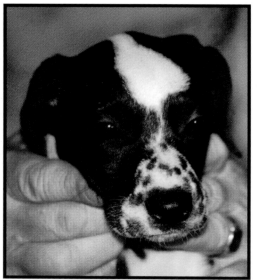

A very extreme patch. This pup is known as Boston Blackie, and he comes from a litter of five in which four pups were patched.

It's usually possible to tell whether the pups are black spotted or liver spotted when they are first born. It's easiest to tell with pups that have a lot of nose trim, although many litters are born with minimal amounts of trim. The noses on liver pups are either brown or a rather purplish color. Some liver noses are so dark that they appear almost black, while others are just a faint tan that will darken up during the first week. Liver pups are somewhat more likely to have pink noses at birth. If the pups have color along the fronts of their ears, this will also help separate the blacks from the livers. Liver patches are, of course, immediately recognizable. The skin spotting on newborn pups is usually less distinct in livers.

Some pups are born with very short thin coats, while others are quite shaggy. In some lines, new pups may show distinct waves in their coats, a sort of rippled effect which will disappear during the first week. The rippled look seems to be caused by a simple recessive gene, and two Dals who were wavy-coated at birth will produce entirely wavy litters. There is no difference in their adult coats.

Pups are sometimes born with kinks in their tails, and this is also something that is inherited, though the method of inheritance has not yet been identified. Tail kinks do tend to be more common in some lines than in others. Kinks are often not visible on newborns, but they usually can be felt in the last couple of vertebrae of the tail.

Cowlicks also occur in some lines and are normally visible at birth. They are most commonly seen on the shoulders but may also be present on the face or down the back of the neck.

RAISING THE LITTER

Although most Dalmatians are excellent mothers and need little help with their pups for the first two or three weeks, many breeders choose to stay home and be close to the new family for at least a few days, just to be sure that all is well. A bitch is often reluctant to leave her box at first, and a collar and leash may be required to take the new mother outdoors to relieve herself. Some bitches have trouble organizing the pups when they return and appreciate having the pups moved to one side so they can jump in without fear of stepping on them.

The puppies are best kept on clean papers until their umbilical cords dry up and drop off. Once that happens, washable

"What's going on over there?" Something has caught this liver-patched pup's attention.

throw rugs, squares of bathroom carpeting, or folded mattress pads make excellent bedding that can be washed regularly and changed as needed. Beware the bitch who digs in her bedding and buries her pups under the rug in her box. Her pups will probably be safer in shredded newspapers for the first week or two.

Be sure that the room is warm and free of drafts and that the whelping box is kept dry. Cold or damp puppies are at great risk of succumbing to the herpes virus infection. The temperature on the floor of the whelping box should be kept at about 85 degrees. Puppies can not regulate their body temperatures for the first few weeks, and a warm environment is essential. The dam should be able to move to a cooler place if she gets overheated, and water should always be available to her.

This is the time when new mothers need privacy. Don't let any other dogs into the room where the whelping box is located, and wait a while before inviting friends and neighbors to admire the new litter. Even the friendliest bitch may become protective at this time, so always use common sense when allowing people to see the puppies. Keep the box clean and the room quiet, and resist the temptation to over-handle the pups. If there are smaller pups in the litter, they can be helped by moving them to the best nipples. The rear nipples usually have the most milk, and the strongest pups get to those first.

Pups should be weighed daily and their weights recorded for the first week or two, just to be sure that all are gaining weight. Pups who are not gaining may be supplemented with a bottle or by tube feeding. Although bottle feeding can work just fine, tube feeding is much faster. Most good breeding books explain the tube feeding procedure. If bottle feeding is employed, allow the pup to suckle, being careful not to squeeze milk into the pup's mouth. You may inadvertently cause him to aspirate the milk and posibly develope pneumonia. Some breeders work very hard to save every puppy, while others feel that only the stron-

gest pups should survive and nature should be allowed to take its course.

Most breeders have the pups' dewclaws removed between the ages of one and five days. Dewclaws are the rudimentary thumbs that sometimes get torn on adult dogs, and they are easily removed on young puppies. This can be done at home, but most breeders prefer taking the litter to the veterinarian to be checked out and have their dewclaws

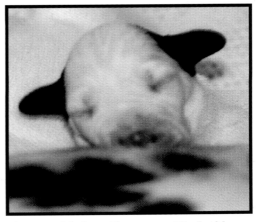

Above and below: Liver pup with double ear patch, pictured at two days old and seven weeks old.

removed at the same time. Pups that are appreciably smaller than their littermates, or any that are not strong and vigorous, should probably postpone this operation for a few days. To transport the litter, a sturdy box with a cover, lined with towels and containing a hot water bottle *wrapped in a towel*, will keep the puppies comfortable. The dam may be better left behind so she will not hear the pups cry. If she can be left with a patched pup or one of the smaller pups for company, so much the better; however, most bitches will manage quite well alone.

If the dam appears restless or frantic, is aggressive with the pups, or starts moving them around near the end of the first week, it might be wise to discuss her behavior with your veterinarian. These symptoms are sometimes caused by an excessively low level of calcium in the bloodstream. A calcium injection quickly resolves the problem, the bitch relaxes, and everything is soon back to normal.

The bitch's temperature should be taken at least once a day for the first couple of weeks and if it is above 103 degrees, a veterinarian should be consulted. Bitches normally show a brownish discharge for three or more weeks after whelping but, if the discharge is particularly copious or if it is bloody, yellow, dark greenish black, or has a strong odor, there may be a retained placenta. This can be serious and it must be checked out immediately. If the bitch appears listless, stops eating, won't tend to her puppies, or has breasts that are enlarged, hard and warm to the touch, she may be developing mastitis, a condition which also needs to be taken care of immediately.

Although some new mothers receive special diets that may include eggs, cottage cheese, meat, or canned food, most Dalmatian bitches do very well on the puppy formula of their regular dog food or whatever puppy food will be used for weaning the litter. The extra protein, fat, calcium, and calories provide a very suitable lactation diet. If supplements are added, they should not exceed 25 percent of the diet. Bitches with big litters may require large amounts of food to maintain their body weight during lactation, but there is no advantage in letting the bitch get excessively heavy.

Dalmatian pups are generally strong and vigorous. Normal-sized pups who are good nursers and who are kept warm and dry rarely have any problems. Possible health problems that could occur include staph infections and infected eyes. Staph infections will show up as small scabs or scaly areas, usually on the legs or the top of the head. This can be treated with an oral antibiotic or by bathing the affected area several times a day with an antibacterial shampoo. The puppy's eyes should be watched carefully, especially during the second week. If any of them appear to bulge out or look like "frog eyes," they will require warm compresses and must be gently opened and treated with an

Ivygate Magical Spotlight with her week-old pups. The pup in the dog dish is about to be weighed—many breeders regularly weigh their pups to check growth. Owned by Barry and Karen Moore.

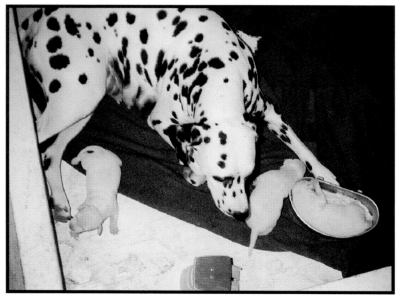

antibiotic ointment. Eyes that are not opened and allowed to drain will be damaged and the pup may be blinded in one eye.

Handling

Pups should be handled every day. Daily weighing is enough handling for the first few days, but as the pups become aware of their surroundings they require additional handling. Hold each pup in your arms, rock him back and forth, turn him upside down for a moment, and hold him on his back. Hold him up to your face and speak softly to him. Put him on your lap, rub his coat with and against the lay of the hair, and gently pinch his toes. Each pup should be handled at least once a day for a few minutes. This is a good time to cut the nails, too. Nails should be trimmed several times a week. Just snip off the pointed ends so that the pups don't scratch their dam or each other. Socializing young pups doesn't take much time, but it makes an enormous difference.

Hearing Testing

It is important to remember that deafness does occur in this breed and if you think that a puppy is deaf, he probably is. Wishful thinking will not make puppies hear, and the older the pups get, the harder it may be to identify the deafs with home testing. Deaf pups quickly learn to watch their hearing littermates and respond to their movements. Although it is very difficult to euthanize otherwise healthy puppies, responsible

breeders *never* place deaf puppies, and all puppies destined to become companions should be able to hear and respond to a human voice.

Puppies are born with their eyes and ears sealed. Their eyes begin to open at about 12 days of age, and they begin to hear on the 13th or 14th day. In most litters, the hearing puppies are obvious by 18 days of age and any puppies who do not respond by then may be deaf. Some breeders routinely test pups at a very early age and have identified any deaf pups by 15 or 16 days of age. Young puppies that are just starting to hear will normally respond to whistling, sharp hand claps, or a high-pitched voice. When testing small puppies, they should be asleep and lying spread out. If hearing puppies are laying next to deaf littermates, the movements of the hearing pups will cause the deaf pups to wake up, too. Pups that can hear will lift up their heads in response to the sounds. Some will get to their feet, while others may sit up and bark. Don't assume that the puppies who lay there and twitch their ears

Heiloh Moonlight Madness carries her day-old pup. Some Dals are not happy with their whelping boxes and move their pups to another spot, which is why breeders often put whelping boxes in an exercise pen or a room that can be closed or partitioned off.

355

can hear, as healthy pups are constantly jerking and twitching as they sleep.

A few breeders euthanize deaf pups as early as three weeks of age. Others wait a week or more before even begining to test the pups. When the pups are being weaned, they quickly learn to associate food with a high-pitched "puppy, puppy" call and leap to their feet when they hear the "food noise." Pups who sleep through dinner are invariably deaf.

Brainstem Auditory Evoked Response (BAER) testing is available in many parts of the country, and often breeders, prefer to test the whole litter and euthanize any deafs afterward. BAER testing is used to identify which pups hear bilaterally (in both ears) and which hear unilaterally (in one ear). Unilaterally-hearing pups make perfectly satisfactory pets, but most breeders and dog show exhibitors prefer to work with bilateral pups. Some breeders

feel very confident about identifying bilateral and unilateral hearing pups by home testing (unilateral hearing pups have no directional hearing), but most prefer to have their puppies BAER tested if at all possible. If you are unsure of the hearing status of a puppy, BAER testing will provide foolproof results.

Weaning

Dalmatian puppies are easy to wean. Forget all the stories about baby cereal, scraped beef, hard-boiled eggs, and teaching the pups to lap. Simply put mom in her crate for a couple of hours so the pups will be hungry. Take the puppy food you plan to wean them on, soak it in hot water until completely soft (if you grind it up first it will soften more quickly), and add enough warm water to make it soupy in consistency. The food should be approximately room temperature or a bit warmer. Pour the

Ch. Saratoga's Jesse's Girl with her first litter. Many Dal bitches allow their pups to continue nursing even after they have learned to eat from a bowl. Owned by Denver and Georgia Nichols.

It looks like some of these pups are hungry and some just want to play with mom! Ch. Firesprite's Trixi Dixi, CD and family are owned by Bob and Diana Skibinski.

mixture into a flat pan and introduce it to the pups. Some need to have their faces pushed down toward the food or have a little of the food placed in their mouths. Most will just climb right in and start eating. So much for weaning! Some breeders prefer to add cottage cheese, yogurt, eggs, canned meat, or milk to the puppy food, but puppies normally do very well on puppy food alone.

Most breeders begin weaning pups at about four weeks of age, but this depends on the size of the litter and how much milk the dam has. Hungry pups can start eating from a bowl as early as three weeks of age, but a small litter whose dam has plenty of milk may not start weaning until five weeks. Many Dalmatian mothers make it very clear when they are ready to begin weaning their pups by spending as little time as possible with them. Some will throw up their dinner for the pups, but may gobble it back down while growling at any pups who try to share. Once the puppies show an interest in food, it's best to feed mom

outside of the box so she can eat in peace.

Pups should receive one meal the first day, gradually increasing to four or five meals a day. Let them eat as much as they want for the first few weeks, though later on some of the gluttons may need to be pulled out of the bowl. Large round puppy bowls shaped like flying saucers (or hubcaps) make eating somewhat less messy, but the pups and their pen will probably need to be cleaned up after each meal. Mom is usually more than willing to take care of both chores.

From the time the pups get their first meal, water should be available in a low tip-proof bowl. The bowl must not be so deep that a pup could climb in and be unable to get out again. It's very important that Dalmatians drink enough water, especially during the weaning process. Food must be well soaked and should be decidedly soupy until the pups are drinking well.

As weaning progresses, mom will probably choose to spend more and more time away from the litter, but, if she is one of the more dedicated mothers, it may be necessary to keep her away from the pups for part of the day. By the time the pups are six weeks old, she will probably only be spending the night with them. This is a difficult time for some litters, while others don't even seem to notice their dam's absence. Pups should be completely weaned by seven weeks of age, the age at which they begin to leave for new homes.

Veterinary Care

Take a stool sample to the vet when the pups are about four weeks of age, or even earlier if worms may be a problem. If the sample is negative, many breeders still like to give a single dose of a mild wormer just as a precaution. It's possible that the pups have worms, but the worms may not be shedding eggs at the time of the fecal exam. Pups should be checked several more times over the next few weeks. Six-week-old pups with loose stools might have a infection such as coccidia or giardia. A fresh stool sample taken to the vet should answer that question, and treatment can be started immediately.

A pup that stops frequently to urinate in small amounts probably has a urinary tract infection. It's difficult to get sufficient urine for a urinalysis, and most veterinarians will treat the symptoms without actually testing. Fourteen days on an antibiotic usually does the trick, although infections occasionally flare up again and may need to be treated for a longer period of time.

All pups should be thoroughly checked out by the veterinarian before being sold. This can be done at six weeks when the first shots are given. It's a good time for the pups to take a car ride, but care must be taken that they are minimally exposed at the veterinary clinic. Keep the pups in the car until it is their turn to be seen by the veterinarian, and don't put them on the floor or let them associate with other dogs who might be sick.

There may occasionally be a pup that blocks up with urate crystals. No one quite knows why this happens, but it's essential

that pups drink enough water to prevent concentrated urine. A pup that is unable to urinate at all must be taken to the veterinarian immediately. This is not a urinary tract infection and the treatment is totally different. If the bladder feels full, the veterinarian will use a needle to withdraw urine directly from the pup's bladder. If the pH is acidic and the sample is full of urate crystals, the situation is serious. The blockage must be relieved and the pup must be placed on a special diet to reduce the formation of urate crystals.

Socialization

Socialization is one of the most important aspects of dog breeding and is particularly important when raising Dalmatians. Unless the prospective breeder has sufficient time to socialize the pups properly, raising a litter should never be considered. Pups must be raised in the house and handled every day. The way they are raised for their first seven weeks will have an enormous impact on their temperaments for the rest of their lives. Although pups may be genetically programmed to have sound temperaments, they must be correctly socialized in order to live up to that potential.

For the **first three weeks**, daily handling will be sufficient. It will accustom pups to the feel and smell of humans and provide the stimulation as well as the stress they need to develop properly. On or about the 21st day, the pups undergo a significant change. As if by magic, they cease being spotted blobs and turn into "little dogs" almost overnight. They are suddenly aware of their surroundings and they begin to recognize people, wag their tails, bark, and play with one another.

During the period from **three to four weeks**, pups need an enriched environment but they should not encounter any frightening experiences. If hearing testing hasn't already been done, loud noises should not be used for testing during this period. Don't be surprised if the pups duck out of the way when you reach for them too quickly. They are now beginning to notice things. Handle them gently, allow them to explore the area around their box, and give them some toys and bones to investigate.

This is the age when pups start keeping their nest clean, so allow them the opportunity to leave their box and eliminate on the papers around the box. Lower one side

Pups should be allowed to explore the area around their box, but be careful that they don't get lost and frightened at this age. Carry each pup around the house for a few minutes and show it the sights. Be sure that any adult dogs don't jump up and scare the pups.

Now would be a good time for the pups to meet a few gentle children. Have the

These five-week-old pups are eager eaters. The "flying saucer"-type bowl keeps the pups out of the food and ensures that each pup gets his share. Owned by Nancy Welsch.

of the whelping box or cut a doorway in whatever you used (cardboard box, plastic wading pool) as a whelping box. When visiting the pups, lift them out of the box and onto the papers, where they will urinate immediately. Cleanliness is a habit that should be encouraged from the very beginning. If using sawdust instead of papers, lift the pups into the sawdust when you visit.

children sit on the floor of the puppies' pen and allow the pups to climb on them and sniff them. Be sure that the children don't move around, scream, or try to carry the pups. Instead, encourage them to hold the pups gently on their laps.

Four-week-old pups are ready to start some serious exploring. Let them out of the pen several times a day and give them the opportunity to investigate their surroundings. You might want to move the puppy pen to the kitchen or to an area of the house where there is more activity. Provide the pups with balls, toys, and knotted socks, as well as boards and bricks to climb on and over. A box lying on its side makes a great hideout. An old stuffed toy is perfect for wrestling. As the pups become increasingly brave, take them in groups to explore other areas of the house. If the weather permits, they can spend time outdoors on the grass for a while each day. Have individual pups sit on your lap to watch TV in the evening. Now is the time for more visitors, but be sure that any visiting children are well supervised. They must never pick up the pups or step on them.

Five-week-old pups are ready to see more of the world. Weather permitting, let them spend more time outside tasting the grass, carrying leaves and small sticks, feeling the wind and sun. Take them to other parts of the house so they can hear the phone ring and the toilet flush. Let them hear the vacuum cleaner from the next room. Take them exploring in pairs, as some may not be ready to go it alone yet. The cautious ones will be more comfortable if you sit on the floor near them. Take them out of the pen one at a time to play. Roll a ball, show them a squeak toy, practice puppy sits, and start teaching them to stand on the grooming table if they are destined for show careers. Remember— the more toys the better! Barriers and tunnels are great fun, and a mini-obstacle course will help the pups build confidence and coordination. A raised platform will teach them to climb and prepare them for steps. If you have adult dogs who are gentle with pups, now would be a great time for the adults and pups to interact with each other. Visitors are welcome, but always supervise the way they handle your pups.

Six-week-old pups need to be individuals. Take each puppy away from his littermates for a few minutes each day. If the litter is out in the yard, the pups should take turns being in the kitchen with you. Teach them to chase a ball, practice stacking on a table, and work on restraint. Let the pups get used to a collar for a few minutes at a time, and perhaps let them drag a lightweight leash around. Teach them to climb stairs.

It's a good week for the pups to start riding in the car. This is the week to visit the veterinarian for a check up and a puppy shot. Perhaps a longer trip will be required for BAER testing. Let the pups ride together in one or two crates, and don't feed them right before the trip.

The pups can spend much of the day outdoors if the weather permits. They should meet as many new people as possible, especially children of all ages. Replace their box with a crate this week. The pups can be bathed now, weather permitting. Use a tearless shampoo and a mild spray, and dry them thoroughly. The more they do this week, the better prepared they will be for their new homes.

Seven-week-old pups are ready to take on the world. This is the perfect age for them to go to new homes. They are ready to leave their littermates behind and become members of a new family.

Puppies that stay with their littermates need to continue individual socialization, which becomes increasingly important at this age. They should go for short walks, first in pairs, then separately. Seven-week-old pups will follow well, even though they may fight the lead at first. They should continue to go for car rides and should receive some individual time and training each day. By ten weeks of age, each pup must be sleeping in his own crate at night and should be well started on housetraining. It's important that the pups not develop a pack mentality and become overly dependent on their littermates.

Any pup kept for more than ten weeks would benefit from "going to camp." He should stay with friends for at least a week to break the bonds with his littermates and dam and to learn to function on his own. This simple precaution will make the difference between a dog who is fearful and "kennel shy" and a dog who is self-confident and will be able to make the adjustment to a new home with ease at a later date.

Puppy Aptitude Testing

Many breeders use some type of puppy testing to help them evaluate the individual pups so that each pup may be placed in the most suitable home. One of the most popular tests is the Puppy Aptitude Test that was developed by Jack and Wendy Volhard. The test has been used for years and has proven to be very helpful when assessing a puppy's basic personality type. It measures the degrees of dominance, submission, independence, and social attraction, and the obedience and working potential of the puppy. The test results are not exact, and the pups' personalities may be modified through train-

Socialization is extremely important for puppies, and it's a "job" that most children love. An armful of spots is keeping this youngster's hands full!

BREEDING

ing, but the test gives breeders a better feel for the personality variations within the litter. The test can also be useful for identifying areas in which a puppy will require more work.

The test is normally given to pups who are 49 or 50 days old, since their neurological development is complete at that age. The tester is a person who the pups don't know, and the test is usually performed in a place that is unfamiliar to the pups.

PUPPY PLACEMENTS

Placing the puppies in their new homes must be done with great care. All potential buyers should be carefully screened and no pups should ever be sold to questionable homes. Buyers must be aware of both the good and bad characteristics of the breed and understand that adopting a puppy is not something to be taken lightly. The entire family should visit the breeder's home and meet any adult dogs in residence before viewing the puppies. The breeder can inquire about their experience with dogs and why they want a Dalmatian. He should ask about the buyer's current living situation, where the dog will spend the day, who will be responsible for the dog's training, and what their expectations are for the dog. Watching the way the buyers interact with the adult dogs can provide a lot of unspoken information. If there is any question whatsoever, no puppy should be sold. If anyone in the household does not want a dog, or if the children are unruly, this is not a good potential home.

If the breeder has pups that are old enough to be safely handled, the buyer and his family may be invited to help socialize the litter. This is a great chance to see the way they interact with puppies and whether or not a small puppy would be safe with them. Use great care when introducing unfamiliar children to small pups and never leave them unsupervised. Some breeders prefer not to place young pups in homes with small children.

Even if the potential buyer measures up and seems like he would provide a good

permanent home for a Dalmatian, no pup should ever be sold on the first visit. A verbal reservation can be taken and the buyer should be told to think about it overnight before making a final decision. Puppies should never be purchased on impulse—all potential buyers need a "cool down" period.

BREEDER RESPONSIBILITY

Breeders must understand that they have a permanent responsibility for every dog they produce. If prospective buyers are carefully interviewed and pups are properly placed, few dogs will become "unplaced." By staying in touch with the buyers, breeders can resolve small problems before they become big problems. The breeders can be sure that the pups are properly housetrained, learn to sleep in a crate, go through obedience training, and are spayed or neutered at the appropriate time. They can also provide support and encouragement when the pups go through the "terrible teens," the age at which many dogs are either given up or, unfortunately, abandoned.

Some dogs will be given up despite the best efforts of all parties involved. Divorce, illness, and allergies all contribute to a certain percentage of dogs needing second homes. A breeder must remind all buyers that it's important to him to know where his dogs end up and that dogs should never be taken to the humane society or a dog pound. If a dog needs a new home, the owners can make an attempt to find a suitable one. However, if things don't work out, the breeder must get involved and take the dog back if necessary. Occasionally a dog becomes unplaced and the breeder is not notified. For that reason, many breeders monitor the classified ads and check out any Dalmatians that show up at the local humane society.

If an adult dog needs a new home, it often works well to check with previous buyers and ask whether any of them might be interested in a second dog. Dals can be addictive, but many buyers prefer to skip the work of housetraining a second dog and would be delighted to adopt an adult Dal in need of a new home.

Deafness in Dalmatians

Probably the single most important question you can ask the breeder from which you select your new Dalmatian puppy is, "Have the litter, the sire, and the dam been BAER tested?" Statistics gathered from the tests of over 4500 Dalmatians to date have shown that approximately 8% of the Dalmatians born are totally deaf with another 22% being deaf in one ear—an amazing 30% of the breed with hearing defects! BAER refers to a clinical test that determines whether the Dalmatian hears with both ears, one ear only, or is totally deaf. Knowing that the puppy is physically capable of hearing verbal commands is a very reassuring thought to new owners. The unilaterally deaf (hearing in one ear) Dalmatian makes a very happy and satisfactory pet.

Training the deaf Dalmatian is an extremely difficult task that should never be undertaken by the inexperienced novice. It is seldom successful in the long term, even when accomplished by the most skilled trainer. Story after story has been told of the adult, trained, deaf Dal who was startled by the unheard approach of a child and reacted out of pure instinct for self-preservation—fight, then flight. Dalmatian teeth can do a great deal of physical damage in one quick bite, not to mention the almost certain psychological damage suffered by the child. Many an owner has seen his deaf Dal run out in front of a car and be killed because the dog could not hear the call to stop or come back. For these reasons, the Dalmatian Club of America has taken a position recommending that all litters of Dalmatian puppies be BAER tested if at all possible and that all bilaterally deaf Dal puppies be humanely euthanized.

THE HEARING EAR

Sound waves funnel through the ear flap and travel down the external auditory canal to the eardrum. In the middle ear, lying against the eardrum, are the ossicles—the hammer, anvil, and stirrup, with which we are all familiar. Acting like a system of levers, they convert the large but weak

One of the most important things you should ask before you take home a new Dalmatian puppy is whether or not the litter has hearing tested. Dals owned by Gilda Aquilera.

363

vibrations of the eardrum to smaller but stronger vibrations of the oval window of the snail-shaped cochlea. Within the fluid-filled cochlea are organ of Corti hair cells embedded in the tectorial membrane and nurtured by the endolymph produced by the stria vascularis. Movement of sound waves through the cochlea bends the hair cells and depolarizes them, activating nerve synapses. High-frequency sounds activate hair cells near the base of the cochlea while low frequencies best activate hair cells near the apex. Communication proceeds through the eighth cranial nerve to the central nervous system.[1] Congenital deafness in the Dalmatian is the result of loss of the stria vascularis, followed by collapse of the cochlear duct, degeneration of the hair cells of the organ of Corti, and collapse of the saccule.[2]

HISTORICAL RESEARCH

Hearing impairment in the Dalmatian was recorded as early as 1750 in the essays of M. de Buffon, the noted French naturalist, who wrote of the "inability to hear properly" as a characteristic of some members of the breed. A subsequent reference to deafness was made by Rawitz, an anatomist in Berlin, who reported degeneration of the inner ear organs of both ears and of the auditory regions of the brain in a "white dog with blue eyes" he had intensively studied in 1896. M.H. Lurie referenced the membranous labyrinth in a congenitally deaf Collie and Dalmatian in a work published in 1948. References became more numerous in the 1960s and 1970s, with more complete descriptions of the affliction in the Dalmatian, white Bulldog, and other white-coated animals such as minks, mice, and cats.

Data was being gathered on the nature of the affliction. The majority of cases featured the same inner ear pathology: the cochlear partition had collapsed, the organ of Corti had degenerated, the stria vascularis had atrophied, and the tectorial membrane had contracted. The auditory pathway from the outer ear to the brainstem was no longer functioning and the affected animal was unable to process sound waves and interpret them. This abnormality was observed to occur in one ear as well as in both ears. It appeared to be linked to the white coat color and possibly to the blue eyes.

HOME TESTING

Prior to the onset of clinical testing, Dalmatian breeders had been aware that bilateral deafness was a genetic problem in Dalmatians, but it was not until the early to mid-1970s that breeders throughout the United States gradually became aware of the existence of unilateral deafness in Dals. Through observation of behavioral characteristics in some of their Dals such as a lack of directional hearing (an inability to locate the sources of sounds), breeders realized that perhaps deafness was more of a problem than they had originally thought.

Out of necessity, breeders had developed a variety of home testing procedures to identify bilaterally deaf puppies. One of the easiest tests was to condition pups to respond to a specific sound, or "chow call" when "mom" arrived back in the litter box after a relief outside. The "chow call" could be a whistle, a tongue clicking, a chirping sound, or just calling out "puppy, puppy, puppy" in a sing-song voice. This "chow call" was also used when weaning began and solid food was presented to the pups by the breeder. Once the puppies associated the sound with food, each puppy was taken individually to a different room and allowed to explore the new environment. When his attention was fully diverted from the breeder, the familiar "chow call" noise was made. A hearing puppy would immediately throw up his head and come for the food he associated with the noise. Any puppy who continued his exploration without responding to the noise would be marked for further testing. A continued lack of response, especially by the age of six weeks, indicated deafness. If an ensuing veterinary exam confirmed open ear

A pile of sleepy four-week-old pups. Home hearing testing should begin with Dal pups as early as four weeks of age. Owned by Jackie Jens.

canals and no sign of ear infection, then deafness was confirmed and the affected pup was humanely euthanized.

A soft whistle is an excellent "conditioner," but care must be taken not to combine a whistle with the test of holding a pup up, facing away from you, and lightly whistling. The pup may detect the movement of air and wiggle his ear, thus giving a false impression of hearing response. (If a soft whistle is used, this can later be transferred to field or obedience work with a mechanical whistle—puppies conditioned to associate the whistle with food will continue to respond positively by coming to the owner.)

When doing home testing, care should be taken not to confuse a puppy's response to motion or vibration with a response to sound. Banging on a pan is not a reliable indicator of hearing response—affected puppies rapidly learn to compensate for

their defect by becoming more observant of motion, temperature change, and vibrations in their environment. Dropping a pan on the floor combines both motion and vibration. Whistling directed at an ear combines motion (of air) and temperature change.

Testing at home for *unilateral* deafness is extremely difficult and results are not 100% reliable. Keen observation, perfect timing, and developing a conditioned response in the puppy are crucial. The key to unilateral testing is to determine *directional* hearing, i.e., a sound will reach the closer ear a fraction of a second sooner than it reaches the farther ear. The brain computes the difference between the two and locates the source of the sound, or the *direction* from which it comes. Hesitancy in determining the direction of a sound source or inability to locate it at all can indicate unilateral deafness.

Testing should start as early as four weeks of age. One of the better tests requires four separate individuals and involves the "chow call" conditioning. The four testers sit at a table at all four points of the compass. For test description purposes, let's position tester #1, holding the puppy to be tested, on the west side while the breeder (or individual the puppy most relates the "chow call" to) sits directly opposite on the east side. Tester #2 is on the north side of the table, tester #3 on the south side. The breeder gives the "chow call" in a quiet tone and tester #1 releases the puppy when the puppy demonstrates a desire to go to the breeder. As the puppy heads toward the breeder, tester #2 (on the puppy's left) immediately gives the same "chow call," also in a quiet tone and *without any changes in facial expression or any physical motion*. The puppy should immediately turn his head toward tester #2, and possibly alter his course to go to that tester. This indicates the probable presence of hearing in the puppy's left ear. The procedure is repeated, but with tester #3 on the south side (on the puppy's right) quietly giving the "chow call" after the breeder's call. Again, the puppy should alter his course and turn toward tester #3, indicating probable hearing on the right side.

Another test for possible unilateral deafness is the use of floor mounted stereo speakers set at a distance from each other with the puppy in between. A noise that is interesting to the puppy, such as barking, whistling, or animal sounds, is played while the tester transfers the sound from the left to the right speaker and back again. The puppy's response to locate and go to the speaker from which the sound emanates should be *immediate and correct*; if not, unilateral deafness should be suspected.

Each breeder has developed his own method for testing throughout the years, but it should be emphasized that appropriate responses indicate *probable* hearing or non-hearing status. The only positive test is the properly administered BAER test with its accompanying certificate and/or a copy of the test results.

THE DEVELOPMENT OF CLINICAL (BAER) TESTING

Obviously, since home testing methods were not 100% reliable and were sometimes subjective in nature, there was a need to develop a positive clinical testing procedure for identifying the defect and determining the degree of penetrance in the breed. Concurrently, veterinary colleges throughout the country were beginning to use computerized electronic testing equipment to study neurological transmissions from the ear to the brain. The test, called **B**rainstem **A**uditory **E**voked **R**esponse (or BAER for short), was a simple, painless procedure which could determine whether sound waves were being picked up by the dog's ear and transferred neurologically to the brain for interpretation. A four-year in-depth study on the incidence of unilateral and bilateral deafness in the breed began in December 1984 at the University of California Davis campus with the cooperation of members of the Dalmatian Club of Northern California. During this period, 900 dogs of various ages were examined—749 of these were presented for testing by various owners/ breeders in a representative sample of the population at large; the remaining 151 were dogs that had been produced over a long period of time by the breeding program of a local veterinarian and member of the DCA and DCNC, Holly J. Nelson. Her breeding stock had been selected in favor of bilateral hearing. The test results showed that 72% were normal (or bilaterally hearing), 21% were unilaterally deaf, and 7% were bilaterally deaf.

Further statistics were gathered by Dr. George Strain from the School of Veterinary Medicine at Louisiana State University, who combined his test results with those of the Dalmatian Club of Greater Phoenix and Holly Nelson. This effort was supported by various regional Dalmatian clubs and the Dalmatian Club of America. More testing sites were established throughout the country as breeders became aware of this valuable diagnostic tool. The percent of affected Dalmatians remained relatively unchanged as the numbers of test results increased: 21.9% were unilaterally deaf while 8.0% were bilaterally deaf. It is therefore safe to conclude that 29+% of all Dalmatians born are genetically deaf. A unilateral (deaf in one ear) Dalmatian is expressing the gene(s) for deafness even though the other ear can hear.

While some phenotypic markers, such as blue eyes and lack of pigment on the retina, appear to be significant and related to the deafness defect, there is still no clear way to identify by physical characteristics which Dalmatians will hear bilaterally and produce bilaterally hearing pups. According to Dr. Strain's update on the research as published in Volume 24, No. 4 of the *Spotter*, the official DCA publication, there *is* a significant relationship between a Dal's hearing status and that of its parents. Bilaterally hearing Dals produce a larger number of bilaterally hearing offspring; conversely, unilaterally deaf Dals produce a larger number of unilaterally and bilaterally deaf offspring.

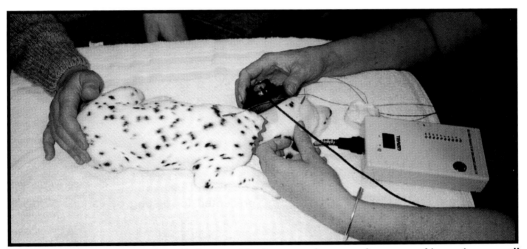

Above and below: *BAER testing a Dal puppy. The large earphone produces a masking noise; a small plug in the other ear produces the testing noise, which sound like "clicks." The electrodes are very small fine needles that are inserted under the dog's skin.*

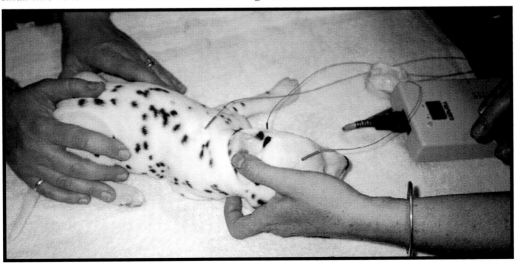

367

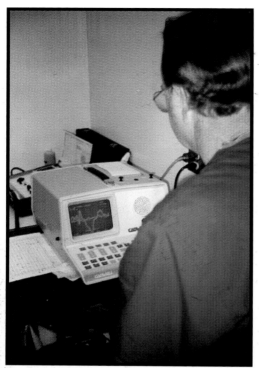

The monitor shows the characteristic peaks that indicate the transmission of sounds to the brain. This is a sight that all Dal breeders are relieved to see!

THE BAER TEST PROTOCOL

Tiny painless subdermal recording needle electrodes that are connected to a computer are inserted under the skin at strategic points of the puppy's skull. Measured clicks at 35 dB through 95 dB are administered by tiny earphones (sort of a "doggy Walkman") inserted into the ear canal of the test ear. Some testers also use a masking "white noise" of static administered to the non-test ear. As these clicks are perceived by the ear drum and transferred to the cochlea and beyond, the transmission to the brain through the brainstem can be monitored. Data is collected by the attached computer using an electrodiagnostic signal averaging system and a read-out (similar to the electrocardiogram most people are familiar with) is shown in wave form. The first wave, or peak, is generated by the cochlea; cochlear deafness is demonstrated by the absence of that peak and all subsequent peaks, i.e.,

a relatively flat line. As the sound is translated to nerve synapses in the cochlea, the cochlear nerve, and brainstem auditory pathways, additional waves (peaks) form. Every breeder of Dalmatians is exhilarated to see those waves forming as each puppy's test results appear on the monitor!

GENETIC INHERITANCE

Currently, no mode of inheritance of the deafness gene(s) has been clinically identified. The various theories include a dominant gene with incomplete penetrance, double dominant genes, and multifactorial recessive genes. Dr. Holly Nelson, an active member of both the Dalmatian Club of America and the Dalmatian Club of Northern California, was a practicing veterinarian trying to help Dal owners reach a better understanding of breed health problems. She wrote numerous articles for the DCA *Spotter* as well as a monthly "Ask Dr. Spot" column in the DCNC newsletter. Her observation of statistics gathered from numerous breedings led her to develop the theory that Dalmatian deafness is the result of the combined action of two dominant genes. This theory was published in the Fall 1985 issue of the *Spotter* (Volume 16, No. 1). However, experimental breedings done by Dr. Strain of a deaf dog to a deaf bitch produced bilaterally hearing puppies in numbers too large to agree with this proposal. Research is currently underway to identify genetic "markers." Conceivably, in the future a simple blood test will determine whether a Dalmatian is at higher risk to throw deaf puppies, allowing breeders to select away from this breed fault.

1. Strain, George M., Congenital Deafness in Dogs and Cats. *Compendium on Continuing Education for the Practicing Veterinarian*, Vol. 13, No. 2, February 1991.

2. Strain, George., et al, Brainstem Auditory Evoked Potential Assessment of Congenital Deafness in Dalmatians: Associations with Phenotypic Markers. *Journal of Veterinary Internal Medicine*, Vol. 6, No. 3, May/June 1992.

Your Dalmatian's Health

The Dalmatian is prone to some very unique breed-specific health problems, problems that every Dal owner and every potential Dal buyer need to know about. It is important to be able to provide routine preventive health care for your Dal as well as to understand the conditions that specifically affect the breed. The more informed you are, the better care you will be able to give your Dal for a lifetime of health and vitality.

Chestnut Venus of Rosebrook is the picture of health and vitality. "Venus" is owned by Nancy Welsch.

URINARY TRACT PROBLEMS AND CONTROL

Urinary Stone-Forming in Dalmatians and Other Dogs

Dalmatians, Bulldogs, and many other breeds of dog can form urinary stones. Innumerable stone-forming dogs, Dalmatians included, live out their lives happily and uneventfully without any signs that they are stone-formers, according to veterinary centers specializing in urinary stone problems. Other Dalmatians who never show any symptoms may not be stone-formers at all.

Most dogs who exhibit symptoms of stone-forming can be easily and successfully treated. Veterinary knowledge of canine urinary stones and their non-surgical treatment has expanded rapidly within recent years. Today, there are even two national veterinary centers that specialize in urinary stones: the Minnesota Urolith Center at the School of Veterinary Medicine of the University of Minnesota and the Urinary Stone Analysis Laboratory at the School of Veterinary Medicine of the University of California at Davis.

The best preventatives for stone-forming in Dalmatians are those of diet and sufficient water intake. Paralleling the splendid advances in veterinary knowledge, commercial availability of many special dog-food formulations for this problem has also evolved. Most of these are readily available at local pet stores and others are available by prescription. After being weaned from the mandatory puppy diet, maturing and adult Dalmatians (stone-formers or not) can now be fed from a variety of non-beef, non-meat dog foods (such as turkey-and-barley or vegetable-and-rice) and go their entire lives without the onset of urinary stones. In other Dalmatians, stones already formed can be non-surgically and successfully dissolved with certain medications and, from the veterinarian, prescription anti-stone-forming dog food. For the few Dals for whom bladder surgery is unavoidable, modern canine anesthetics such as Isofluorane make this procedure no more threatening nor complex than an appendectomy in a human.

Why Do Some Dalmatians Form Urinary Stones?

Dalmatians, humans, and some species of apes are unique for the way in which they metabolize those proteins known as "purine-yielding foods." Not every human will form urinary stones and neither will every Dalmatian.

It is not just the total amount of protein that causes the problem so much as the amount of purine-rich proteins. Certain foods such as liver and other organ meats are alarmingly high in purines while other foods like eggs and most vegetables and fruits are acceptably low in purine-yielding proteins.

When some humans ingest purine-rich foods, their diet may aggravate and bring on their gout or kidney stones. When some Dalmatians ingest those foods, they develop urinary stones most particularly those known as "purine" or "urate" stones. Dog foods containing high amounts of purine-yielding ingredients such as meat, beef, and "meat or beef by-products" should be avoided.

Feeding your Dalmatian meat or most other table scraps is unnecessary and ill-advised because these foods may increase the risk of urinary stones.

Of all stone-forming Dalmatians, the vast majority forms urate stones but a few may form other types. Treatment can be the exact opposite for each type of stone so your veterinarian will want to first obtain an accurate assay in order to prescribe the most effective treatment. Urate stones are composed of one or more of three types of purines: ammonium acid urate, uric acid, or sodium urate. Veterinary specialists report between 80 and 90 percent of stone-forming Dalmatians produces ammonium acid urate, a purine stone that is very responsive to simple non-surgical treatment with a program of anti-urate medication and anti-urate diet.

Urinary stones in dogs are either found in the upper system, such as in the kidneys, or in the lower system, such as in the bladder. Data collected from some 15 years of stone-forming Dalmatians showed that 97 percent of stones was either "passed" or found in their bladders where treatment and maintenance are much simpler than if the stones were found in the upper system such as in the kidneys.

The treatment of urate stones vs. "struvite" stones (the most common type in all other stone-forming dog breeds—they are so frequently seen and so identified with urinary infections that they are called "infection stones") is totally different and underscores the importance for an accurate assay by the veterinarian of the type of urinary stone being formed by the dog before treatment is started.

How is a Stone-Forming Dog Detected?

The most important detection by Dalmatian owners of urinary tract disease including stone-forming is by careful observation. Watch the way the Dalmatian urinates and examine the urine. Suspicious signs include any difficulty in urinating, any increase in the frequency of urinating (which may be less obvious in a male), any increased sense of urgency about urinating, or any urinating habits that change such as voiding in uncommon locations. Other signs include an increase in licking of the genitals (especially prominent in females), apparent soreness or tenderness in that region, or a change in general appearance such as arching of the back or a higher or lower carrying of the tail.

The urine of an affected dog may show cloudiness, gravel or sand, or even tiny blood stains, especially when the Dalmatian reaches the final emptying of the bladder. In the advanced stage of obstruction by a urinary stone, there may be very little or no urine at all so that the dog will visibly strain to urinate with little or no output. The dog will usually appear uncomfortable or in pain and may even cry out as it attempts to urinate.

Urinary obstruction by stones in male dogs will produce warning symptoms more obviously than females perhaps because of the marked differences in their normal urinary anatomy. As a large-enough stone travels down the urinary pathway, it can lodge within the male dog's penis at a dam-like narrowing of the cartilage, the "os penis." The same size stone would pass uneventfully through a female dog's urinary anatomy.

Some stone-forming dogs will suddenly succeed after several attempts to urinate with a copious outpouring of urine. In such an instance, it is probable that the stone creating the obstruction was "passed," thus restoring the normal flow of urine. Any obstructed dog, even those who quickly pass stones naturally, should be seen by the veterinarian for a workup and to embark on a program of prevention.

The signs and symptoms of urinary tract infection and urinary stone-forming are similar but either condition requires further investigation and treatment. Confirmed diagnosis is based primarily on a urinalysis performed by the veterinarian. This will show the presence in the urine specimen of abnormal crystals, red or white blood cells, and other diagnostic information. Most urate stones, the most common Dalmatian ones, do not show up under routine x-rays. They require certain special x-rays and contrast methods such as "indirect radiography" to be seen.

What to Do for Urinary Infections?

Because urinary infections and urinary stones frequently occur together, or either condition can produce the other, it is important than any urinary tract infection be diagnosed and treated whether or not stones are present. Treatment of urinary tract infection consists of eliminating any infection present with antibiotics, increasing the dog's water intake and, in the case of abnormal *urate* crystals or stones, greatly reducing the dog's intake of purine-rich food ingredi-

Water from the sprinkler is inviting to this Dal on a summer day, and it's important that Dals drink a sufficient amount of water to keep their urine properly diluted.

ents and the use of the anti-urate drug allopurinol. Special anti-urate food formulations are now commercially available including some by prescription only. Some owners of stone-forming dogs alternatively and successfully follow recipes for home-cooked anti-urate diets. The veterinarian may sometimes add a final adjustment of the urinary pH by a supplemental acidifier or alkalinizer, depending on what type of abnormal urinary crystals or stones have been assayed.

What to Do for Urinary Obstruction?

Blockage of normal urinary flow becomes progressively serious the more the urine backs up into the dog's system. The top priority, therefore, is to remove the obstructed urine from the bladder as soon as possible and as often as necessary while the obstruction remains unchanged and while treatment is being evaluated. The dog should be promptly taken to a veterinarian, who can usually accomplish this simply and effectively without surgery or anesthesia, and sometimes even without tranquilizers. One process is "cystocentesis," in which a needle is inserted through the dog's abdomen into the bladder and urine is tapped off. Most dogs tolerate this procedure well.

The veterinarian can also catheterize the dog in a special way by which the obstructing stone is "back flushed" into the bladder, thereby removing the cause of the obstruction and reopening the normal flow of urine. After a successful back flushing, some dogs do not ever obstruct again. Others may not obstruct again for years, although some dogs can obstruct within a matter of hours or days as a stone again moves down the system until it lodges without being passed. A second or even a third back flushing may be required to produce long-term relief.

Once normal urinary flow has been successfully restored, the dog can live out his years happily and uneventfully so long as his owner conscientiously adheres to a preventative program (mostly an anti-stone diet for Dalmatians). Most recently, many stone-forming Dalmatians have been given only distilled water (available from supermarkets' bottled water shelves), which has been of consistent benefit although no scientific documentation exists either for using it or for not using it.

General Preventative Guidelines for Stone-Forming Dalmatians

- Have your vet perform a routine, inexpensive urinalysis periodically. If centrifuging spins out sediment from the urine specimen, send it for assay only to one of the two urinary stone centers in the United States. (Minnesota Urolith Center does not charge.)

- Obtain "fresh" urine in a clean, chemically inert container (glass, plastic) for testing by the veterinarian. Do not obtain the sample after the Dal has recently urinated, as the bladder may have been flushed of crystals or small stones. Instead, obtain specimen either first thing in the morning, before feeding (after urine has sat unemptied in the bladder overnight), or after dog has not urinated for at least four to five hours. Deliver the urine to the veterinarian as soon as possible after collecting. Do not refrigerate.

- One major goal of prevention is to maintain a urinary pH of 7.0. Dipstick fresh urine frequently and keep a diary of pH readings. If the pH goes below 7.0 (into the acidic area of 6.0 or less) and stays there over the course of several dipstickings, consider reevaluating the Dal's diet/medications and consult with your veterinarian about additives to alkalinize the metabolizing of the dog's current food formulation.

- If the pH goes above 7.0 (into the alkaline area of 7.5 or higher) and stays there over the course of several dipstickings,

contact your veterinarian to rule out a possible urinary infection.

- Some stone-formers may benefit by drinking only distilled water for their entire lives. This type of water is available in any supermarket where bottled water is stocked and it is not expensive. Make sure that the label specifies "distilled water," not merely "drinking," "filtered," or "purified." (Filters on your water faucets or supply will not purify the water to the extent that distilled water is purified.)

- Formation of abnormal crystals and stones occurs in stagnant urine. Let the Dalmatian urinate as frequently as possible (at least every four to five hours) so that the bladder is flushed of crystals before they progress into stones.

Picadilly's Alexis of Dynasty jumps up to get a treat. It's important to watch what kinds of treats your Dal eats, as some foods increase the risk of stone-forming.

Dipsticking to Monitor Stone-Formers and Their Diets

Remember in high school chemistry when litmus paper revealed if a solution was either acidic or alkaline? Modern dipsticks from your veterinarian or from the drug store are "super litmus paper." They are simple for a Dalmatian owner to use and they show exact degrees of urinary pH. A quick dip into a dog's urine before feeding will indicate if the pH is acidic (how much below 7.0) or alkaline (how much above 7.0). With a program of regular dipsticking and keeping a diary of the results, any Dalmatian can be tracked to detect when and how long it is producing abnormal and unstable urine, often long before abnormal crystals progress into stone formation.

All Dalmatians are born with a tendency to acidic urine in which the occurrence and growth of abnormal *urate* crystals and stones thrive. The success of preventative anti-urate diets and drugs thus can be monitored by dipsticking and treatment regimens can be modified if the pH continues to be undesirably acidic.

Some dog-food formulations cause acidic urine to be produced, and dipsticking will help to reveal these foods that, therefore, should be avoided for stone-forming Dalmatians.

Emergency Procedures: What to Do if Your Dalmatian Cannot Pass Urine (Urinary Obstruction)

• Rush your dog to the veterinarian or emergency clinic! Obstruction of the urinary pathway quickly reaches life-threatening status within 24 to 72 hours as urine backs up into the body system instead of being expelled. It is not unknown for bladders to burst as urine continues to collect. Have the dammed-up urine easily but immediately removed from bladder either by cystocentesis or by catheterization. This may have to be done several times while diagnosis and treatment are being evaluated. Draining urine "buys time."

• Have the type of stone identified by urinalysis; abnormal urinary crystals are apparent and identifiable under an office microscope. Urates form in acidic urine (pH below 7.0). Struvites known as "infection" crystals/stones form in alkaline urine (pH above 7.0). Their treatment is different!

• Have the size of the stones confirmed by x-ray but remind the veterinarian that the most commonly-seen urate stones in Dalmatians do not visualize under normal x-ray procedures. Urates requires "indirect radiography" to be visualized in situ.

• Non-surgical clearing of the obstruction often can be accomplished by "hydropropulsion" whereby the stones are flushed back up into the bladder. This sometimes must be done two to three times before a free urinary stream is sustained. If stones quickly move down and constantly reobstruct after short periods of time, then bladder surgery may be unavoidable to restore normal urinary flow. Isofluorane is one of the modern anesthetics desirable if surgery is unavoidable.

• The last resort after all other anti-stone procedures have failed is a "urethrostomy," which is not bladder surgery. It is a surgical creation of a false urinary opening generally at the base of the scrotal sacs. It should be performed only by an appropriately trained and experienced surgeon, preferably one who is Board-Certified.

• Have your Dalmatian started on anti-biotics for an existing urinary infection or to prevent the onset of one. A bacterial culture that includes "antibiotic discing" may tell the vet the most effective antibiotic for the species of bacteria inducing the infection. Shift the stone-former to distilled water only.

• Rush the stones that were either passed, catheterized, or removed surgically—or the sediment centrifuging out during urinalysis—to one of the two urinary stone centers to confirm assay by electron micrography, chromatography, and other highly specialized testing procedures.

Remember:
- Normal urinary pH is probably 6.5 to 7.0.
- Acidic urine is below pH 7.0 (down to 5.0 or 6.0, for example).
- Alkaline urine is above pH 7.0 (up to 8.0 or 8.5, for example.

Purine-Yielding Foods

Foods Highest in Purines

Anchovies
Brains
Game meats (venison, etc.)
Gravies
Herring
Kidney, beef
Liver (calf or beef)
Mackerel
Meat extracts
Sardines
Scallops
Sweetbreads

Foods High in Purines

Asparagus
Breads and cereals, whole grain
Cauliflower
Eel
Fish (fresh and saltwater)
Legumes (beans, lentils, peas)
Meat (beef, lamb, pork, veal)
Meat soups and broths
Mushrooms
Oatmeal
Peas, green
Poultry (chicken, duck, turkey)
Shellfish (crab, lobster, oysters)
Spinach
Wheat germ and bran

Foods Lowest in Purines

Beverages (coffee, tea, sodas)
Bread and cereal (except whole grain)
Cheese
Eggs
Fats
Fish roe
Fruits and fruit juices
Gelatin
Sugars, syrups, sweets
Vegetables (except those above)
Vegetable and cream soups

OTHER POSSIBLE HEALTH PROBLEMS

Although stone formation is a major health problem for Dalmatian owners to be aware of, it is important to understand that Dals can be affected by one or more of the following problems as well. They are listed in alphabetical order rather than by the frequency of their occurrence in the breed and discussed here in an effort to make you a well-informed Dalmatian owner; an awareness of the signs may save your dog's life.

Bloat/Gastric Torsion

Gastric dilatation/volvulus syndrome (GDV) is the formal term for the more familiar bloat/gastric torsion problem in dogs. The canine's stomach is suspended internally somewhat like a hammock. A rapid accumulation of air in the stomach or a build-up of gas due to the natural digestive processes causes the organ to blow up like a balloon (bloat). Sudden movements on the dog's part or simply the natural effort of the stomach to search for more space can cause it to flip or twist around (torsion), closing off the esophagus and small intestine. As gas continues to build up with no outlet, pressure is put upon the surrounding organs—blood vessels collapse, blood flow to the heart decreases, and internal hemorrhage and subsequent tissue death occur. Shock becomes inevitable, and death will follow.

Large, deep-chested breeds seem predisposed to this condition, but there are a number of other potential causes that make all breeds susceptible. While the type of food eaten does not seem to be a factor, the speed with which it is consumed has a bearing. Other similarities among cases are overeating, unrestricted activity following meals, large amounts of water gulped quickly, stress, and surgical complications. Recent studies have indicated that perhaps aerophagia (air swallowing) is more causative than the gas as a digestive by-product. Physical factors coming into play include abnormal motility of the stomach, its shape and angle, and stretching of the ligaments holding it in place. Most bloat victims are physically mature, many are overweight, and a good majority are approaching middle age. Since body shape, length, depth, and breadth are influenced by heredity, bloat is considered to be an inherited weakness.

The typical Dalmatian is deep-chested with a zest for life, consuming food rapidly and maintaining a high activity level. In the Dalmatian, eight to ten years is the average age for onset of bloat problems. If there is a family history of bloat, then the dog should be monitored for signs and precautions should be taken. With a tape, measure the girth of the dog's stomach behind the rib cage, using his distinctive spots as markers so that you are always measuring the same area. If your Dal's stomach expands markedly after consuming a meal and gurgles a great deal, he may be a candidate for bloat. If the stomach has not yet twisted on itself an antacid can be administered; it may buy you time while you drive to the vet.

At the first signs of bloat, a veterinarian should be called as any delay in relieving the pressure and preventing the onset of shock could be potentially fatal. If torsion has already occurred the only option is surgery. Bloat is *not* a condition that can be treated at home with over-the-counter preparations alone. The survival rate has not been improved during the last ten years despite extensive studies that have been undertaken. The only option at this point is to become familiar with the signs, follow basic precautions, and know a good veterinarian.

These suggestions can decrease the possibility of death from bloat:

• Feed two or more smaller meals per day at times when you can be home to observe reactions; make dietary changes gradually; use an elevated bowl rack.

• Rest the dog for one hour before and after meals; do not feed before or after a period of vigorous activity.

• Limit water intake immediately following a meal.

• Be especially vigilant for signs of bloat during times of stress to the animal.

• Know the signs: abdominal swelling, unproductive retching, anxiety, whining, pacing, groaning, inability to find a comfortable position.

• Call the veterinarian immediately and be prepared to move fast—timing is critical.

Dalmatian Leukodystrophy

Similar to a rare disease identified first in Cairn Terriers and known as globoid-cell leukodystrophy (or Krabbe's disease in man), Dalmatian leukodystrophy was first studied in 1977 in Norway and is extremely rare. Cavities which impaired neural transmission were identified in the myelin of the cerebral hemispheres of the brain. In the seven litters studied, the onset occurred between three and six months of age and was characterized by failing vision and ataxia in the hind legs. The ataxia progressed to all four legs, with paralysis in the hind legs within four months of onset of the disease. Both males and females were affected. These litters all descended from one male, and had a ratio of 32 normal pups to 11 affected pups. The gene responsible is a simple autosomal recessive. Any bloodline contaminated with the defective gene will produce affected puppies when linebreeding on the source of the defect.

Hip Dysplasia

Hip dysplasia not only affects the larger breeds of dogs but also has been identified in breeds as small as Chihuahuas. It is characterized by a hip joint laxity and deformities wherein the femoral head (end of the upper leg bone) is displaced from its normal position within the acetabulum (socket of the hip bone). As the joint becomes more and more abnormal, an excessive movement of the femoral head occurs, the amount of synovial fluid increases, the attaching ligament enlarges (probably due to stretching beyond its intended capabilities), the protective cartilage is abraded, and the joint capsule thickens. This results in irreversible damage to the bones and pain on movement. In an effort to relieve pain associated with weight bearing, affected dogs shift their weight to the forelimbs. This results in disuse atrophy or weakening and loss of hind limb muscle mass. Decreased activity, a swaying and unsteady gait, hind legs drawn forward while standing, a "bunny hopping" type of running gait where both hind legs move forward together, and difficulty climbing stairs or rising from a sitting/laying position are visual evidence of the disease. However, *some dogs experience little discomfort despite abnormal changes*

All Dals should be screened for hip dysplasia and only those with normal hips should be bred. Active dogs like Dalmatians need healthy joints to be able to do what they love best.

in their joints. In other words, the genetic predisposition is present but is not identifiable by observing the actions of the dog!

Because the disease develops over the course of the young dog's bone development, it is currently not possible to know whether a dog is clear of hip dysplasia until it has reached maturity. Diagnosis is established by radiographic examination, preferably while the dog is sedated or anesthetized. The dog is placed on its back with its rear legs fully extended downward and its stifles rotated inward. In a normal hip joint, the head of the femur fits tightly into and conforms with the socket of the hip, more than 50% of the femoral head is shadowed by the acetabulum (hip socket), and there is no abnormal shape to either the femur head or the acetabulum. The finished x-ray is then sent to the OFA for evaluation and assignment of a registration number.

The Orthopedic Foundation for Animals (OFA) is a non-profit foundation established primarily to help breeders reduce the incidence of canine orthopedic diseases. One of their primary contributions is the maintenance of a registry of the hip status for dogs of all breeds in conjunction with a voluntary diagnostic service.

All x-rays submitted to the Orthopedic Foundation for Animals (OFA) are independently evaluated by three experienced radiologists; deviations from the perfect hip and the breed normal are interpreted and graded accordingly. Dogs who receive "excellent," "good," and "fair" ratings are considered normal and qualify for an OFA breed number; dogs with "borderline" hip joint conformation or "mild," "moderate," or "severe" hip dysplasia are ineligible for an OFA breed number. The results are kept on file for future reference by concerned breeders. Unfortunately, not all x-rays are turned in to the OFA for evaluation, especially if the examining veterinarians have identified them as dysplastic. The exact penetrance of hip dysplasia in the Dalmatian gene pool is unknown, but as of July 1991, with over 1036 x-rays examined by OFA, the "percent dysplastic" total was 6.3%. Considering that deafness is considered a major problem in this breed and that the incidence of bilateral deafness is currently 8.0%, it would appear that we are beginning to reach a "percent dysplastic" that can no longer be considered inconsequential.

Until recently there was no way to determine which puppies to select for show/breeding stock other than to choose from a litter with a large number of OFA-clear ancestors in the pedigree and then having the pup's hips x-rayed at two years of age. The University of Pennsylvania has developed a method, called PennHip™, of measuring joint laxity, the condition that allows movement of the femoral head within the hip socket. This procedure can be safely performed on puppies as young as 16 weeks of age.

Three radiographic views are submitted on each dog evaluated by the PennHip™ method. Veterinarians performing these exams must become certified to do so, insuring technical competency and reproducibility of results. Unlike OFA, which subjectively evaluates radiographs of hips positioned in their tightest configuration, PennHip™ scientifically determines the *laxity* of the hip joint. Remember, it is this laxity or looseness that causes the degenerative changes and pain defining canine hip dysplasia.

PennHip™ scores each hip on an absolute scale, called a distraction index, then compares the results to other dogs of the breed in question as well as all dogs tested. this tells the owner the percentile that her dog falls in. Although PennHip™ veterinarians make no official breeding recommendations, their studies show that breeders accomplished a tremendous reduction in the number of dysplastic dogs produced when using only parents who scored in the best 50% of the population.

Hip dysplasia can be crippling, but since some dogs never show any indications of a problem, radiography is currently the only way to evaluate breeding animals. The mode of inheritance is unknown at this point, but is suspected to be polygenic.

Sires and dams rated "clear" by OFA may produce progeny with hip dysplasia. This may be attributed to some inherent inaccuracy in OFA evaluations, as well as a multiplicity of genetic and environmental factors affecting hip joint conformation and function. Breeders must not only be cognizant of hip status of the parents, grandparents, great-grandparents, etc., but also of littermates and progeny. The incidence of hip dysplasia can be reduced significantly by selecting for breeding only those animals with disease-free hips as shown by scientifically accurate radiographic examination, with further selection based on family performance and progeny testing.

IgA Deficiency

Selective IgA deficiency is the most common primary immunodeficiency of humans with as many as one in 500 affected. The absence of IgA predisposes a person to various diseases such as infectious gastrointestinal diseases, upper respiratory and ear infections, seizures, chronic skin or urinary tract infections, and an increased incidence of allergies, autoantibodies, and autoimmune disease. The three most common autoimmune diseases associated with selective IgA deficiency are rheumatoid arthritis, lupus erythematosus, and autoimmune thyroiditis. IgA deficiency has been diagnosed in canines and research is being done to determine parameters for measuring the extent of the problem.

Although the clinical signs are well-documented, the mode of inheritance and the modus operandi of the defect are still unclear. All of the ingredients are present for normal secretion of IgA, but failure occurs. Some, but not all, individuals have suppressor T cells that selectively inhibit IgA production.

Holly J. Nelson, DVM, a DCA member whose valuable contributions to the breed were cut short by an untimely death, wrote a definitive article on the subject that explains it well:

The protein IgA is an immunoglobulin. It is a single part of the body's complex immune system. IgA protects epithelium, particularly that of the respiratory and digestive tract mucous membranes. In a sense, it "slimes" foreign particles. These can be viruses, bacteria, food proteins, etc. "Slimed" by the IgA, the substances are rendered harmless.

Without IgA's protection, the foreign particle can bind to the epithelial surface. It may then activate another immunoglobulin, IgE, which is associated with allergic reac-

One-week-old Dal babies nursing from their dam. Newborn pups receive the protein IgA through their mother's milk.

tions. Once established, viruses and bacteria can multiply and cause disease.

IgA in the newborn is obtained in the mother's milk. Puppies under three months of age do not have measurable amounts in their bloodstream. By six months of age, a significant quantity of IgA should be present. By a year of age, the serum level approaches normal, then continues to climb slowly over the next few years.

"Normal" for IgA varies slightly between laboratories, but all are similar. At UC Davis, normal ranges from 0.40 mg/ml up to 1.50 mg/ml. Measurements of 53 Dalmatians from 11 months to 12 years old ranged from 1.01 down. Only 4 were within the normal range. About half of the rest measured between 0.16 mg/ml and 0.38 mg/ml. The other half fell into the category "less than 0.15 mg/ml."

The normals (over 0.40) and half-normals (0.20 to 0.40) are generally very healthy dogs. Those between 0.15 and 0.20 vary a lot (in symptoms). Those less than 0.15 mg/ml nearly all show one or more symptoms, often quite severe.

Symptoms in the Dalmatian include recurrent otitis, foot-licking, staphylococcus folliculitis (bumps), itching due to inhalation and food allergies, epilepsy (seizures), colitis, and/or increased susceptibility to parvo and kennel cough.

There is no cure for IgA deficiency. Treatment is symptomatic, aimed at keeping the dog comfortable and acceptable as a pet.

IgA deficiency in Dalmatians is decidedly hereditary. With (a high percentage) of our show stock affected to some degree, we can't entirely eliminate deficient dogs from breeding at this point. We can, however, make it a factor in choosing mates. By recognizing that these skin problems are a hereditary entity that can potentially be eliminated, we can produce healthier Dalmatians.

PRA (Progressive Retinal Atrophy)

PRA is not one but a group of recessive inherited diseases affecting the dog's photoreceptors. Two forms of the disease exist and the speed with which it develops will vary from dog to dog. In early onset, the photoreceptors fail to develop properly and the disease is detectable during puppyhood and/or adolescence. In late onset, the photoreceptors have developed properly but begin to degenerate prior to the natural degeneration brought about by old age. Late onset may not become apparent before the dog reaches three to five years of age, sometimes even later than that. By that time the animal has probably already been used for breeding and the defect passed on to its offspring. Developing a genetic history in the pedigree by having ancestors and subsequent progeny tested for PRA will go a long way toward protecting your line from this genetic problem. A specialized test called an electroretinogram is recommended if you wish early detection of PRA. Otherwise, an exam using a slit-lamp biomicroscope and indirect ophthalmoscope can be done to detect the presence of the disease.

The most common form of PRA initially affects the rod photoreceptors, creating "night blindness." It progresses to difficulty seeing under dim lighting conditions and eventually affects the cones as well, rendering the dog completely blind. Another form of the disorder creates "day blindness" by destroying cone vision (which operates under bright lighting conditions) first and then progressing to complete blindness. Central PRA (CPRA) impairs central vision but leaves peripheral vision untouched.

The Canine Eye Registration Foundation (CERF) compiles and maintains statistics on all tested canines whose results have been submitted for recording. This non-profit organization will issue a certification number to each dog whose properly performed test indicates a normal eye. The test for PRA must be performed by a member of the American College of Veterinary Ophthalmologists to be valid. The disease can develop at any stage in a dog's life so it is necessary to re-test periodically. CERF does

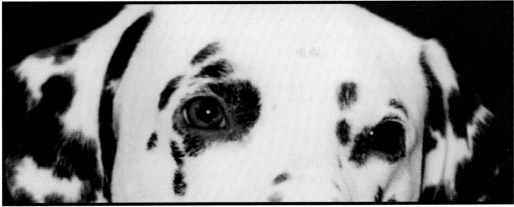

The Canine Eye Registration Foundation tests for PRA and certifies dogs with normal eyes, but periodic re-testing is necessary as the disease can develop at any time in the dog's life.

not have a significant database on the Dalmatian, perhaps because breeders—feeling that PRA is not a problem in the breed—do not test for it.

Seizures

A seizure is a convulsive episode with one or more causative factors, affecting one or both sides of the body and occurring singly or in recurrent stages or clusters. The normal neuron synapses in the brain are electrical currents that take place in the presence of certain chemicals. A seizure occurs when those neuron exchanges go awry, or "short out," and result in a complete lack of body control for the dog. Seizures that recur on a regular basis are termed epilepsy. If a cause can be found for the seizures, they are called symptomatic epilepsy; if no cause is found, they are called idiopathic epilepsy. Many times, symptomatic epilepsy will involve only area of the body whereas idiopathic epilepsy is usually generalized.

Normally, a symptomatic epileptic attack is brought about by metabolic disorders that can be diagnosed by blood, chemical, and urine analysis. These include, but are not limited to, hypoglycemia (low blood sugar), inflammation of the brain due to viral or bacterial infection, hydrocephalus (water on the brain), or brain tumors. Toxins and insecticide overexposure and trauma

may also cause seizures. Idiopathic epilepsy appears to be hereditary in that two epileptic dogs, when bred together, tend to produce offspring with a high tendency toward epilepsy.

During a seizure, a dog has no perception of its surroundings. Get him to the ground or the floor, clear the area of harmful objects, and leave him alone until the seizure passes. The episode may last from a few seconds to a few minutes, recovery may be instantaneous or may take a day or two, and each dog's reactions coming out of the seizure will differ. If the seizure lasts for more than ten minutes you have a medical emergency on your hands and need the assistance of a veterinarian.

Some dogs will give warning that a seizure is imminent by staring, trembling, salivating, or circling aimlessly, while others give no advance warning at all. During the seizure the dog may collapse, salivate, paddle, urinate, defecate, and show other signs of involuntary muscular contractions. After the seizure, the dog may be temporarily blind, disoriented, staggering, barking, hungry, or thirsty. Small seizures can also occur where none of the major muscular contractions takes place but the dog still shows the same symptoms of staring and being disoriented after the occurrence. The majority of seizures occur during the night when the dog is at rest.

It is important to have chemical tests run after a seizure in an attempt to identify the cause. Make note of any pertinent information about the dog's schedule prior to the incident: his diet, any toxins he may have come in contact with, etc. If the epilepsy is symptomatic in nature a cure may be effected by removing the triggering mechanism from the dog's environment. If no symptomatic causes can be found, investigate the dog's pedigree for possible occurrences in his predecessors; if there is a distinct pattern of epilepsy in the pedigree, seriously consider removing the animal from any breeding program.

Epilepsy can usually be controlled with the use of phenobarbital, but the course of treatment can be expensive and is not always reliable. Drugs rarely control seizures completely, but if the drugs are administered at appropriate levels for the dog, most seizures can be controlled for a period of years.

Thyroid Problems

There are two separate lobes in the thyroid gland of the dog, one on each side of the trachea. Their products are thyroxine (T4) and triiodothyronine (T3). Once released in the blood, more than 99% of both hormones becomes bound to various plasma proteins, leaving less than 1% of the hormone "free," or available, for diffusion into the tissues. This "free" T4 is converted in the tissues to T3, which is important for intracellular function.

Hypothyroidism (inadequate T3/T4 production) is one of the most common endocrine abnormalities in dogs. Hypothyroidism is either primary (due to a dysfunction of the thyroid gland itself) or secondary (due to injury or dysfunction of the pituitary with impaired secretion of its stimulating hormone, TSH).

The more common primary form occurs due to lymphocyte problems, atrophy, or destruction of the thyroid gland itself. (Lymphocytic thyroiditis is primarily an antibody-mediated process, although the cell-mediated immune system may play a role. The initiating factors are not well understood but are thought to be either genetic or due to previous damage to the thyroid gland.) Atrophy of the thyroid gland is normal in the aging process with onset at age nine. High risk, large, and giant breeds develop signs during middle age, perhaps around four to six years old. Onset of thyroid dysfunction at age two or younger is usually considered to be due to problems other than atrophy.

Clinical signs of hypothyroidism include lethargy, mental dullness, anestrus or decreased sex drive, decreased body temperature, thermophilia or heat-seeking, and a tendency to obesity even though the food intake is low. The hair coat is thin and the hairs are dry, lusterless, and easily shed. In advanced cases there is a tendency toward bilaterally symmetrical hair loss, particularly in the neck, lateral trunk, and spinal areas. The skin is dry, rough, scaly, and often overly pigmented. Hypothyroid dogs are often plagued with recurrent pyoderma and ear infections. Other less common, but equally indicative, signs of possible thyroid problems are cardiovascular signs such as heart arrhythmias, a weak apex beat, or cardiomyopathy; neuromuscular signs such as weakness, stiffness, reluctance to move, knuckling, dragging feet, or muscle wasting; gastrointestinal signs including diarrhea or constipation where other causes have been ruled out; and megaesophagus.

When outward physical signs resemble hypothyroidism, laboratory tests can be useful in confirming the diagnosis. A typical thyroid test will measure the total presence of the T4 hormone in the blood, the most reliable test being the RIA (radioimmunoassay). Veterinary endocrinologists currently recommend the inclusion of total T4, free T4, CTSH, and thyroglobulin autoantibodies in a complete thyroid profile. Normal levels may vary due to a number of outside factors such as length of fasting prior to testing, concurrent illness, presence of anti-thyroid hormone antibody, or administration of medications prior to testing.

The TSH response test measures thyroid

reserve by assessing the ability of the thyroid gland to release T4 hormone upon stimulation with an injection of TSH. Although the procedure is less convenient than a single measurement of serum T4/T3 or an RIA reading, it has a diagnostic accuracy of about 95% in cases of clinical hypothyroidism. However, in the early stages of progressive thyroid disease, the TSH response is usually normal (i.e., a false negative) because not enough of the thyroid gland has been destroyed and can still respond with the expected amounts of T4 release.

The serum cholesterol test is not specific for thyroid function but serves a useful purpose—few diseases cause the high cholesterol levels found in many hypothyroid dogs. In about one-third of hypothyroid dogs, however, the serum cholesterol level is normal, so the test is not diagnostic. When the cholesterol is elevated, it tends to return to normal with thyroid replacement therapy.

In some cases it is impossible to definitively diagnose hypothyroidism. A therapeutic trial of thyroid hormone replacement may be necessary.

Normal treatment of diagnosed hypothyroidism is sodium levothyroxine (T4 hormone), given in twice daily doses. Dosage recommendations vary, with some veterinarians determining dosage by body surface area rather than by weight. Initial dosage treatment is for the first four weeks; thereafter the level is reduced to the minimum amount needed to reverse the clinical manifestations. Any animal receiving thyroid supplementations should be examined every three to six months so the dose can be adjusted if necessary. With very few exceptions, thyroid hormone replacement therapy will be continued for the remainder of the animal's life.

Autoimmune Thyroiditis Theory— There is a growing movement among veterinary clinicians in support of an intermediate "thyroiditis" stage where dogs exhibit clinical signs of a dysfunctioning thyroid but test results are within the normal range. (They feel the diagnosis of "hypothyroid" should be reserved for the end stages when the animal's thyroid gland is no longer capable of producing sufficient hormone to sustain clinical health.) The theory is that the thyroiditis stage of the disease is an immune-mediated process that develops in genetically susceptible individuals and is characterized by the presence of antithyroid antibodies in the blood or tissue. Onset is around puberty, and the condition progresses to clinical hypothyroidism once the thyroid's glandular reserve has been depleted. Other systems may eventually show manifestations of immune-mediated disease.

Simplified, the body's immune system fails to recognize T4/T3 as a benefactor and forms antibodies to attack the suspected intruder. As the attack succeeds in lowering the T4/T3 levels in the system, the pituitary goes on the alert and signals the thyroid for higher production. The thyroid eventually wears itself out trying to cope with the higher than normal production requests. The thyroid antibody test may be useful in determining this early stage of hypothyroidism. While autoimmune thyroiditis is in the early stages of clinical study, knowledge of it may help diagnose otherwise unrelated signs in your dog.

Toxicosis

To indicate how common an occurrence poisoning is, there is a National Animal Poison Control Center, established in 1984, that provides a 24-hour hotline and that has currently logged over 250,000 reported cases in its computer system. The most offending substances by number of occurrences are rat poisons, caffeine (through chocolate or stimulant medications), and such common non-aspirin pain killers as ibuprofen and acetaminophen. The Dalmatian's natural curiosity, predisposition to a higher activity level, and propensity for eating anything in his path put him at risk for toxic encounters.

Toxic substances can be inhaled, absorbed through the skin and pads of feet, consumed completely, or absorbed through tissues in the mouth while chewing. Knowing the normal vital signs for a dog may make a life-or-death difference some day. The canine's normal rates are: 15 to 30 respirations per minute, 62 to 130 heartbeats per minute, and a temperature range of 100.9 to 102.5 degrees Fahrenheit. The

problems such as convulsions, paralysis, uncoordinated movement, and shivering. Watch the dog for unusual symptoms and actions such as pawing at the head, chasing the tail, biting himself, increased salivation, frequent swallowing, increased or unusual thirst, watery eyes or nose, dry mouth, numbness in tissues, pale gums, or dilated

A Dal posing in the springtime foliage makes a pretty picture, but be careful—some common plants and flowers can be hazardous to your dog's health.

variable range in respiration and heartbeat rates would be determined by "at rest" versus "active" check times. Check your Dal's rates, normal versus excited, and write them down and put them in a safe place for reference.

Signs of possible toxicity include breathing difficulties, digestive system upsets, temperature variations (high or low), heart problems, urinary problems, and nervous system

pupils. The veterinarian may need to take a blood test to analyze toxin levels.

Dog-proofing the environment is the ideal way to avoid problems, but you need to know what items are toxic in order to prevent access to them. A safe rule of thumb to follow is that if you don't want an infant to play with the item, you don't want a canine to play with it either. Gardening and lawn products, insecticides, cleaning compounds, automobile products, and, of course, the obvious rodent poisons are all to be kept out of reach. Flea and tick shampoos and dips are insecticides and their formulas vary; purchase these products from a veterinarian or ask his advice on the ingredients in the product you use.

Plants can also be hazardous to your dog's health. We have tried to list as many of the problem plants as possible, but this list is by no means complete. You may want to check with your county's agricultural extension service to identify regional toxic plants. Ideally, if you are not there to super-

COMMON PLANTS TOXIC TO DOGS

Amaryllis (bulb)
Andromeda
Apple Seeds (cyanide)
Arrowgrass
Avocado (pit)
Azalea
Bittersweet
Boxwood
Buttercup
Caladium
Castor Bean
Cherry Pits (cyanide)
Chokecherry
Climbing Lily
Crown of Thorns
Daffodil (bulb)
Daphne
Delphinium
Dieffenbachia
Dumb Cane
Elephant Ear
English Ivy
Elderberry
Foxglove
Hemlock
Holly
Hyacinth (bulb)
Hydrangea
Iris (bulb)
Japanese Yew
Jasmine (berry)

Jerusalem Cherry
Jimson Weed
Laburnum
Larkspur
Laurel
Locoweed
Marigold
Marijuana
Mistletoe (berry)
Monkshood
Mushrooms
Narcissus
Nightshade
Oleander
Onion (bulb)
Peach
Philodendron
Poinsettia (berry)
Poison Ivy
Privet
Rhododendron
Rhubarb
Snow on the Mountain
Stinging Nettle
Toadstool
Tobacco
Tulip (bulb)
Walnut
Wisteria
Yew

vise the dog, he should be crated or in a kennel run.

Von Willebrand's Disease

Von Willebrand's disease is a specific bleeding disorder in which the blood's ability to form clots is impaired. Carriers of the defect may show no signs or may be identified as "bleeders" when the flow of blood from an injury is difficult to slow or stop. It is a genetically transmitted disorder; the most common form of von Willebrand's (vWD) is "incompletely dominant with variable penetrance," which means that once you have it in your gene pool it is extremely difficult to breed out. Currently, 54 breeds of purebred dog have been identified as having vWD in their gene pools, with varying percentages of dogs affected. Dalmatian breeders nationwide who wish to protect their bloodlines are including a vWD test in their pre-breeding requirements.

To indicate the seriousness of the problem, let's illustrate two possible breedings. In the first, we have a normal dog bred to a carrier/heterozygote. This would result in 50% of the pups in the litter being normal and 50% being carrier/heterozygote. In the second scenario we have a carrier/heterozygote bred to a carrier. This breeding results in 25% normal puppies, 50% carrier/heterozygote, and 25% homozygote (dead or severely affected). A failure to identify vWD in breeding stock could mean that within several short generations, the defect could become so predominant that clear breeding stock is difficult to find and the problem nearly impossible to breed out. In 1979, 55% of the Doberman Pinschers tested were abnormal and 9% were bleeders. In 1987, (less than ten years later), 70% of the Dobermans tested were abnormal and 16% were bleeders. In 1989, after serious efforts on the parts of breeders to clear up the problem, the incidence had only been reduced 3%, with 67% testing abnormal.

The vWD, or von Willebrand factor, is produced almost exclusively from the cells lining the blood vessels. Any disease that

alters metabolism and protein synthesis can affect the vWD levels. Autoimmune diseases and thyroid disease can disrupt vWD factor production and function, which can lead to an acquired, rather than inherited, form of vWD. Finding low or low-normal levels of vWD through blood testing may be one of the early indications of a developing thyroid dysfunction. If the dog is already genetically predisposed to vWD and subsequently develops hypothyroidism, prognosis for long-term survival is not good. A simple blood test in which anticoagulated blood is drawn and a platelet count is taken may put your mind at ease about vWD.

FLEA AND TICK CONTROL

What Fleas Do to the Dog

Fleas can pose a serious health threat to dogs. Heavily parasitized dogs may become anemic from the amount of blood fleas ingest. More commonly, flea bites can cause itching in the dog whose subsequent scratching and chewing damages the protective barrier of the skin, allowing bacterial infections to ensue. These infections may take the form of "hot spots" (acute moist dermatitis lesions), generalized superficial infections, or full-blown flea allergy dermatitis.

At the very least, fleas are irritating pests that are responsible for transmitting other parasitic infections to their canine hosts. Fleas are intermediate hosts for the most common tapeworm in dogs. Flea larvae eat tapeworm eggs and, later, the adult flea is eaten by the dog and the larvae is released and grows to adulthood in the dog's intestine. Tapeworms are relatively benign, but may be responsible for an unthrifty appearance of some parasitized dogs. Therefore, dogs with fleas need to be treated periodically for tapeworms as well.

Life Cycle of the Flea

Adult fleas spend most of their lives on

the dog. In order to reproduce, the female flea must take fresh blood from her host for a couple of days. She then lays 20 to 25 eggs per day for 6 to 12 months. As the dog scratches, some of the eggs fall off and some of the eggs stay on. The eggs take about one to two days to hatch and form larvae, which feed from several days to several months. This pupal stage is the most resistant stage and lasts days to months depending on ambient temperature and humidity. Fleas produce best at temperatures of 65 to 80 degrees and humidity of 75 to 85 percent.

Flea Treatment

Effective flea control measures must ensure elimination of the flea population on the dog and in his environment (yard, home, kennel, and car). There are two approaches for treating and controlling fleas. One approach is with chemicals, and the other is with herbs and biopesticides.

The chemical approach traditionally has meant direct and frequent applications of adulticides, larvacides, and insect development inhibitors to the dog and all areas in which he spends time. Many of these products have potential side effects that make their use somewhat unpleasant at best. The introduction of several new topical and systemic products with very effective residual activity has revolutionized flea control for the average dog owner. According to Dr. Michael Dryden, noted flea authority from Kansas State University College of Veterinary Medicine, it is no longer always necessary to treat the dog's environment. Exceptions to this are heavy flea infestations in which cases rapid complete eradication is necessary.

Advocates of the herbs and biopesticides approach think that it is important to use these methods because the use of poisons or the simultaneous use of several chemical products can weaken the already compromised condition of the dog due to the flea infestation.

Treating the Dog

There are two methods of treating the dog for fleas. One way is to use a topical insecticide and the other is to use a systemic medication. Topical insecticides include sprays, dips, powders, flea collars, and liquid spot application. These products are applied to the animal's skin to kill the fleas as they crawl on the animal.

New topical products being used include imidacloprid and fipronyl, two agents that work as insect neurotransmitter inhibitors. They have one- to three-month residual flea-killing activity, respectively. Safety and efficacy studies as well as clinical trials show these products to be extremely safe for dogs and humans and extraordinarily effective at killing adult fleas before they bite the dog. This timeline is a great benefit to the flea-allergic dog, protecting it from exposure to allergens in flea saliva. By killing the flea prior to reproduction, these products eliminate the risk of further environmental infestation. These products are applied on the dog as "one spot" or spray treatments. Manufacturers of both imidacloprid and fipronyl claim that they remain effective on the dog after swimming or gentle bathing. Fipronyl is also labeled to kill ticks for up to one month.

Pyrethrins and permethrins are safe and relatively effective topical adulticides when applied frequently (every one to two days in active flea infestations). These topical insecticides are incorporated in sprays, dips, powders, and flea collars. These products may be used in conjunction with environmental insect development inhibitors. Herbs such as pyrethrins can be ground into a powder (using the flower heads) and mixed with other ingredients such as diatomaceous earth (food grade only) to produce a natural flea powder. You can order dried herbs or you can use concentrated essential oils. Diatomaceous earth is available for purchase either plain or already mixed with pyrethrins.

The systemic, or internal, products enter the animal's blood and kill the flea when it bites the animal, or cause the female to produce eggs incapable of hatching. The systemic lufernuron is another recently introduced product that can be effective without concurrent environmental treatment. Lufernuron is given orally to the dog on a monthly basis. It acts by preventing synthesis of chitin, the hard exoskeleton of fleas. Since mammals do not make chitin, it has virtually no effect on treated dogs and can even be used safely in pregnant and nursing bitches. Female fleas feeding on a lufernuron-treated dog produce eggs incapable of hatching. Larvae feeding on feces of treated fleas may also be suppressed from normal development. Lufernuron does not kill the adult fleas, so adulticides such as sprays and shampoos must be incorporated in a complete flea control program.

The older systemic products such as cythioate and fenthion require more frequent dosing, have reduced effectiveness compared to the newer products, and have a much narrower margin of safety. Both are cholinesterase inhibitors and should not be used with other drugs or insecticides that have this inhibiting activity.

Treating the House and Car

Thoroughly clean the car and home by vacuuming all of the carpets, particularly under the furniture, in the closets, and along the cracks and crevices of the walls. Immediately seal the vacuum bag so that any live fleas will not escape, and dispose of it. Concrete and tile floors should be mopped with a strong solution. Do not forget to clean the animal's bedding. It is best to provide new bedding if there is a heavy infestation of fleas.

Treat the area with an adulticide as well as with an environmental insect development inhibitor (IDI). IDIs work by mimicking the flea's juvenile hormones and preventing up to 85% of the population from maturing. Certain insect development inhibitors are stable in ultraviolet light (sunlight) and may need to be applied much less frequently than the adulticide. It is recommended that the adulticide be reapplied two and four

weeks after the initial treatment. There are spray formulations of pyrethrins and permethrins that are microencapsulated for longer lasting timed-release activity, have a low toxicity to humans and animals, will not stain upholstery, and are nearly odorless. Chlorpyrifos is potentially more effective as an adulticide, but also has a narrower margin of safety for dogs and humans.

Some exterminating companies have flea-control formulas that are guaranteed for one year. They use a patented powder process for the carpet and furniture that will not stain and is odorless. A similar formula is made up of five pounds of diatomaceous earth (food grade only), five pounds of borax, and one cup of table salt. Mix the ingredients together, sprinkle the mixture on the carpet, and rake it in. Allow the mixture to remain in the carpet for 48 hours and then vacuum the carpet.

Another method consists of sprinkling borax on the carpet and furniture after vacuuming. Do not vacuum after applying this powder—allow it to settle into the carpet. It is safe for humans and animals. The powder acts by desiccating (drying) the eggs, larvae, and some newly hatched adult fleas. It does not affect the pupal stage.

Treating the Yard and Outdoor Kennel Runs

If a chemical treatment is preferred, the yard should be sprayed regularly either by a professional exterminator or by using an insecticide in a hose sprayer. The best products will provide timed-release control on both adult and pre-adult fleas. Some are even effective after it rains. These products usually last for three to four weeks, and some are available in sprayer bottles that can attach to a garden hose for use by the home owner.

Another method is spreading pellets with active ingredients such as chlorpyrifos, malathion, or diazinon on the area. This has to be watered into the soil and animals should be kept off the area for several days. These compounds are organophosphates and may be associated with severe toxic reactions when ingested or absorbed through the skin of dogs or humans. It is not recommended for puppy areas as it can cause reactions in the nervous system. Reactions in animals can include profuse salivation, contracted pupils, muscle twitching, diarrhea, vomiting, hyperactivity, slowed

There are biopesticides on the market that use nematodes instead of chemicals to treat fleas in the yard. Nematodes are tiny worm-like organisms that eat grubs and the larvae of harmful insects. They kill flea larvae within 24 hours and continue to do so for up to four weeks. Once the nematode enters the flea's body, it releases

"I'm just resting my head." A group of Dal pups enjoys an afternoon nap in their outdoor run. All areas that dogs inhabit, indoors and out, must be included when treating for fleas.

heartbeat, and labored breathing, which can result in death.

Proponents of the herbal method of flea control suggest planting pennyroyal, a perennial, around the borders of the kennel. It has fragrant foliage and blossoms that smell like mint—fleas avoid it and it makes the kennel smell better, too. Other aromatic herbs that fleas avoid are sage, rosemary, and thyme. Trees such as eucalyptus and cedar also repel fleas.

a lethal bacteria. When the flea dies, the nematodes feed on the body, reproduce, and seek more larvae. After all of the harmful insects are gone, the nematodes die also.

Companies recently began selling nematodes under several brand names. They are applied with a hose sprayer or a tank sprayer. These products are safe for mammals, beneficial insects, and plants, so the treated area can be used immediately.

Nematodes can be purchased through a veterinarian.

Ticks

Most ticks affecting dogs are classified as Ixodids, or hard ticks, because of the shields on parts of their bodies. These ticks have three stages in their life cycles: larva, nymph, and adult. Between the cycles, the tick usually detaches from the host, crawls onto shrubs, trees, or walls, and drops onto a host again. Ticks can transmit serious diseases and some are reservoirs of a number of diseases such as babesiosis, Rocky Mountain spotted fever, tularemia and Lyme disease. The tick's saliva contains toxins that may cause paralysis.

Common Canine Ticks

American Dog tick (*Dermacentor variabilis*)—The adult female remains at-

Rocky and Ringo love exploring the woods with their owner, but wooded areas are a favorite hideout for ticks. All dogs should be checked carefully after spending any time outside.

tached to the host until fully engorged. The adult male feeds for short periods and moves around, breeding with the attached females. The fully engorged female drops to the ground and lays thousands of eggs. After hatching, the larvae attach to passing small animals where they feed on blood and then drop to the ground. During the nymph stage, they climb onto grass and then onto passing animals where they feed on blood and then drop to the ground. At this point, they molt into the adult stage and attach to a host. The entire life cycle ranges from three months to two years and the tick can hibernate during the winter. This tick is an important vector of Rocky Mountain spotted fever in the eastern USA and it also transmits tularemia and causes paralysis.

Brown Dog tick (*Rhipicephalus sanguineus*)—This is the most widely distributed tick in the world. It infests dwellings, likes warmth and moisture, and can hibernate. It is capable of feeding on the same host in all of its life stages. The females will usually lay eggs in cracks and crevices within three days of detachment from the host. The adult males are not parasitic. The life cycle ranges from two months to two years. This tick transmits *Babesia canis* and *Ehrlichiosis* as well as protozoal, viral, and Rickettsial infections.

Rocky Mountain Wood tick/Rocky Mountain Spotted Fever tick (*Dermacentor andersoni*)—This tick has an unusually long life cycle, frequently requiring two to three years to reach maturity. It is the most important parasite of the northwestern USA and is the vector of Rocky Mountain spotted fever, tularemia, and Colorado tick fever in humans. It also is the chief cause of tick paralysis.

Deer tick (*Ixodes: dammini, scapularis, pacificus*)—There are three stages in its life cycle. The adults are much smaller in size than other ticks; they are usually the size of poppy seeds. This tick is the most common known carrier of Lyme disease.

Lone Star tick (*Amblyomma americanum*)—This tick is prevalent from

Texas to Missouri and eastward to the Atlantic. It transmits Lyme disease, tularemia, Rocky Mountain spotted fever, and paralysis.

Pacific Coast tick (*Dermacentor occidentalis*)—This tick has no obvious site preference on the host. It is a vector of Colorado tick fever in humans and Lyme disease.

Diseases Caused by Ticks

Paralysis—Toxins secreted can cause paralysis. In most cases, once the tick is removed, the dog recovers rapidly. Signs of paralysis are incoordination of the hind legs followed by paralysis of the front legs and chest, and abnormal respiration. Death can occur within one to two days after the onset of respiratory failure.

Tularemia—This is caused by a non-spore forming gram-negative organism, is serologically related to *Brucella*. Symptoms include fever, stiffness, weakness, lassitude, increased respiration, coughing, and diarrhea. It can be treated with tetracycline.

Rocky Mountain spotted fever—This is a rickettsial disease characterized by a waking and waning fever, depression, hemorrhages of mucus membranes, and, especially in the chronic phase, lameness and joint pain. The organism multiplies in the cells lining the small peripheral blood vessels. Infections in dogs may be subclinical or acute. Treated dogs usually begin to respond within 24 to 48 hours of initiation of appropriate antibiotics.

Babesiosis (*Babesia canis*)—This is a microscopic parasite that lives inside red blood cells. Symptoms include lethargy, anorexia, and signs associated with anemia such as weakness, pale mucous membranes, and exercise intolerance. Diagnosis can be difficult as most laboratories are unfamiliar with the organism's appearance. Autoimmune hemolytic anemia (AIHA) causes almost identical symptoms. Dogs may require

Keeping your yard neat and well maintained will make it a less inviting spot for ticks and safer for your dogs. These pups found a patch of grass that was just right to curl up and nap in.

multiple treatments and should have blood tests regularly. If left untreated, babesiosis progresses quickly and causes death.

Lyme disease—Many types of ticks carry Lyme disease: Deer ticks, Western Black-legged ticks, Lone Star ticks, American Dog ticks, and Pacific Coast ticks. This is a bacterial disease affecting humans and animals. Symptoms include arthritis, sudden onset of severe pain and lameness, fever, lethargy, loss of appetite, and depression. There is a great deal of controversy regarding Lyme disease in dogs. While many veterinarians routinely vaccinate against this disease, some researchers believe that studies have not shown conclusively that dogs become clinically ill with Lyme disease. Others believe that the signs are self-limiting. Many researchers are concerned that the vaccine may actually cause immune-mediated arthritis in dogs. It is impossible to confirm a diagnosis of Lyme disease with a blood test since many completely healthy dogs show a positive titer. At this time it is inappropriate to recommend vaccination for Lyme disease in all dogs. This issue should be considered on a case-by-case basis.

Removing Ticks

In checking the dog for ticks, check between the toes, the pads of the feet, the dorsal area of the body, and around the head and ears (especially the inner folds and pockets). A tick crawls toward the head, neck, and shoulders of its host. To remove a tick, grasp the tick as close to the dog's skin as possible and pull it straight out. It is important to get the tick's head out as it can cause infection and swelling. Clean and treat the area on the dog in order to promote healing.

Tick Prevention

Fipronyl is a topical parasiticide that is also effective against ticks. It is applied to the dog's back and begins working within hours. It works on the skin's surface, killing ticks on contact. Ticks do not have to bite the dog to be killed by the chemical, which is important for dogs suffering from flea and tick allergies.

Treating the House, Kennel, and Yard

All crevices and cracks should be vacuumed thoroughly, and as much organic debris removed from the area as possible. Sprays such as 1% ronnel or 2% chlordane may be used repeatedly for several days. Ticks will crawl upward, so be sure to check the walls. Keep the lawn and fields mown to minimize the tick's environment.

SKIN AND COAT DISORDERS

Skin and coat problems are among the most commonly encountered problems in veterinary medicine and are often among the most difficult to treat. Unfortunately, as noted in most dermatology texts, the Dalmatian is among the breeds most commonly affected. Problems often encountered include allergies such as allergic inhalant dermatitis, allergic contact dermatitis, flea bite dermatitis, and food allergies; superficial and deep pyodermas; and the controversial Dalmatian Bronzing Syndrome. Less common problems include acral lick dermatitis and demodectic mange.

Allergies

Allergies are quite common in dogs, affecting a large percentage of the canine population to a varying degree. Dogs may be allergic to any number of things including airborne pollens, a variety of food ingredients, molds, house dust mites, flea saliva, shampoos, and household cleaning products. Most dogs with allergies are typically allergic to more than one thing.

An allergy is the body's abnormal response to a normally harmless environmental factor. The substances that trigger these responses are referred to as "allergens." The dog is said to be "sensitized" to these substances and he produces antibodies to resist the allergens, thus causing the allergic reaction and resultant discomfort.

"Keep scratching...you've found the right spot!" P-Nut is owned by Dennis and Kathy Syrkowski.

Although a dog might show signs of irritation upon his first exposure to a new substance, it takes repeated exposure to produce an actual allergic reaction. One flea bite will not cause a flea-bite allergy, but continual exposure to flea bites may do so. Dogs that develop food allergies have often been eating the same food for years. Allergies may show up as early as six months of age or may appear at any time during a dog's life. They often worsen with age, and a dog who once had allergies only during the pollen season may eventually have problems year-round.

Allergic inhalant dermatitis is the canine equivalent of hay fever, and like hay fever, it tends to run in families. It is more common in some breeds and may be more prevalent in certain lines within a breed. While hay fever causes respiratory symptoms in humans, it normally makes a dog itchy and is often the cause of foot licking in Dalmatians. Although many scratching dogs do indeed have fleas, identical symptoms can be caused by something as mundane as ragweed pollen. Since there is an inherited tendency toward this type of problem, it is something that a breeder must always take into consideration when planning a breeding.

Allergic Dalmatians may scratch frantically, chew at themselves, or rub their faces on the carpet. Many Dals also lick their feet in an attempt to relieve the itching, and the resultant saliva will stain the haircoat deep orange. The ears may be involved as well; dogs with allergy problems often have chronic ear infections. Possible complications include seborrhea (characterized by thickened skin and greasy or flaky dandruff), "hot spots," open sores caused by scratching, and, very often, superficial pyoderma.

Dogs with mild allergies may be helped by the avoidance of the offending allergens, the use of antihistamines and fatty acid coat supplements, and regular baths with soothing shampoos and cool water. Antihistamines are relatively harmless even when used for long periods of time and, as is the case with people, different antihistamines work better on some individuals than on others. It is best to experiment with several different brands in an attempt to find the one most helpful for each individual dog. Antihistamines must be given regularly at high enough dosages to be of any use, but they may cause drowsiness in some individuals. If antihistamines are found to be effective, they may need to be used several times a day throughout the allergy season, especially when pollen counts are high. "Sustained release" products may also be used.

The omega-3 and omega-6 fatty acid supplements are increasingly recommended for dogs with skin problems and seem to be particularly useful for those with inhalant allergies. These naturally occurring fatty acids have a mild anti-inflammatory action and no apparent side effects, and may reduce the incidence of lesions even when they do little to relieve itching. These supplements are available through veterinarians and large pet-supply dealers, and should not to be confused with the fatty-acid supplements that are sold in pet shops and merely intended to produce shiny coats.

Soothing shampoos may be used to remove surface debris and possibly allergens as well. It is best to use either hypoallergenic and moisturizing shampoos and rinses or those with "anti-itch" ingredients such as oatmeal. Dals with skin and coat problems, especially those who are very itchy, should always be bathed in cool water and blotted, rather than rubbed, dry. It might also be well to double-rinse any towels and make sure that they are not dried with fabric softener sheets, as laundry products may also cause allergic reactions in susceptible dogs.

Dogs with severe inhalant allergies should have intradermal skin tests to identify the offending substances. A series of shots to hyposensitize the dog to these substances then becomes a possible treatment option. These procedures are not inexpensive, but they are of some benefit in perhaps 60% to 75% of the cases and can provide some degree of long-term relief. Not all veterinary clinics are equipped to handle these procedures and it may be advisable to get a referral to a veterinary dermatologist.

Corticosteroids such as prednisolone are often used to treat allergic skin problems because they relieve the itching and quickly make the dog more comfortable. However, they only treat the symptoms rather than the cause, and the side effects from long-term therapy can be quite significant and lead to far more serious problems. If the allergy is only a seasonal one this might be justifiable, but corticosteroids should not be considered the treatment of choice for long-term use. The long-acting injectable corticosteroids are even more potent and less desirable unless all other treatments are unsuccessful.

It is sometimes possible to reduce the dog's exposure to the environmental factors that trigger his allergies. Dogs who are allergic to pollens may be kept indoors at certain times of the year. Those who are allergic to molds must be kept in clean dry areas and all humidifiers, dehumidifiers, and air conditioners must have proper filters and be kept clean and in good repair. The dog's bedding should be washed regularly and kept dry, and the dog should be kept out of damp basements and not be allowed to play in wet grass or fallen leaves. Cedar shavings should be avoided for an allergic dog's bedding. Just as is done for children with allergies, carpets and furniture should be vacuumed regularly and hard floors should be damp-mopped to help the dog who is allergic to house dust mites. Furnace filters and vacuum cleaner bags must be changed regularly. As house dust mites are most common in bedrooms, it is best to keep affected dogs out of those rooms.

It is important to understand the "threshold concept" of allergies. A dog may be allergic to multiple substances and still do quite well until the cumulative effect is too great, at which point he reaches his "allergic threshold" and starts to show signs of discomfort. By reducing his exposure to some of the offending substances, it may be possible to reduce the total level of exposure to a point at which he can still remain comfortable. However, it must always be remembered that allergies are never cured, they are only "managed."

Estimates of the prevalence of **food allergies** in dogs vary from 5% to 20% of the canine population. This problem should probably be referred to as adverse food reaction or food intolerance, as many cases are not actually allergic reactions. Typical signs include such diverse reactions as itchiness, hives, and skin lesions, as well as chronic ear infections, vomiting, diarrhea, and flatulence. Although less common than inhalant allergies, food allergies are much easier to treat once the problem foods are identified.

Commercial dog foods contain many individual ingredients and the affected dogs are allergic to some of those ingredients rather than to the product itself. The ingredients may include beef, pork, chicken, eggs, soy, wheat, corn, yeast, and milk products, as well as preservatives. The dog may have eaten the same food for years but, for some reason, has become sensitized to one or more of the ingredients in that food.

It may be possible to simply change the brand of food and solve the problem, but it must be remembered that most dog foods contain many of the same ingredients. Many breeders feel that Dalmatians have more problems with beef than other food ingredients, and have switched their dogs to lamb- or chicken-based food. However, these products are more than just lamb or chicken and may also contain other ingredients to which the dog is allergic.

Although lamb and rice foods are very popular today, there is nothing inherently "hypoallergenic" about a lamb-based food. These foods may work very well on dogs that have become sensitized to beef, but it is also possible that a dog could become allergic to lamb. As more dogs have been maintained on lamb-based foods for long periods of time, more dogs have become sensitized to lamb and need to be switched to other protein-source foods.

Intradermal testing is less satisfactory for food allergies than it is for inhalant or contact allergies, and a hypoallergenic diet trial is the best test for food allergies. This consists of maintaining the dog on food ingredients to which he has not previously become sensitized. The ingredients of choice used to be lamb and rice, before they became popular ingredients in commercial dog food. An appropriate elimination diet consists of one unique protein source and one carbohydrate source. Possible choices would be fish, rabbit, duck, or venison, combined with potatoes. The dog eats *only* the chosen foods for one to two months and if the signs disappear, it indicates that the dog is indeed allergic to one or more of the ingredients in his regular diet. The dog must eat no other foods at all during this period—no rawhides, dog treats, table food, or anything else. Other ingredients are introduced one at a time every five to seven days. The signs recur within a few days or even hours when one of the offending food ingredients is added. Hypoallergenic diet trials take a long time and should be done only under veterinary supervision, but, if done properly, are very successful in identifying the food ingredients that must be avoided. With the enormous variety of dog food on the market, most dogs with food allergies can still eat commercial diets.

Contact allergies are probably not a big problem in dogs, and are most obvious in areas where the dog has a thin haircoat, such as his chest, chin, stomach, and muzzle. However, if a dog has inhalant allergies, it might be advisable to avoid physical contact with the offending plants. Local irritations are probably more common than contact allergies. Dals seem to have rather sensitive skin and may show an adverse response to some coat products including medicated shampoos, coat whiteners, flea sprays and dips, flea collars, and even some ear-cleaning products, as well as household cleaning products, fertilizers, and insecticides. Bathing the dog in a hypoallergenic shampoo will remove the offending substance, and short-term use of corticosteroids may also be indicated. Care should be always be taken when selecting products to be used on a Dalmatian's coat and skin.

Flea bite dermatitis is a significant problem for Dals, especially in the southern part of the US where fleas are a year-round problem. Not all dogs with fleas will develop a flea bite allergy, but those who do often have concurrent allergies such as inhalant or food allergies, making the diagnosis and treatment particularly difficult. Dogs become sensitized to substances in the flea's saliva and even a single flea bite is enough to make the flea-allergic dog miserable for five to seven days. Flea bite allergy is usually characterized by frantic biting and chewing, particularly on the flanks and near the base of the tail, with sores, hair loss, and scaling obvious on those areas. Close inspection may reveal fleas or the tiny dark specks of "flea dirt," which are actually flea feces.

Flea bite sensitivity can be successfully diagnosed with a flea antigen test, but the use of flea antigen in allergy shots to hyposensitize an allergic dog is not usually very successful. Since flea-allergic dogs often have other allergies as well, it is not sufficient to find fleas on a scratching dog and assume that they are the cause of his problem. On the other hand, many owners do not even notice when a dog has fleas. It was previously assumed that fleas were present on the dog only when the fleas were feeding, and that they spent the rest of their time in the carpet, the dog's bed, or the yard. New data indicates that fleas actually spend their entire lives on a dog. When the eggs are laid (on the dog), they fall to the ground and eventually hatch. Once the flea finds an appropriate host, it normally spends its entire life on that host, eating and laying eggs. The only truly effective control for flea bite dermatitis is a good flea-control program. Fleas must be totally eliminated from the dog's environment if this is to be successful.

Pyoderma

A commonly encountered but often misunderstood problem in Dalmatians is pyoderma, which literally means "pus producing infection of the skin." Superficial pyoderma is usually found in conjunction with folliculitis, an inflammation of the hair follicles. Pyoderma is most commonly caused by *Staphylococcus intermedius*, a bacterium normally found on the skin of all dogs. Pyodermas are treated with antibiotic therapy and antibacterial shampoos, but it is often necessary to find the underlying cause to effect a cure.

Pyoderma is typically observed down the center of the back, and sometimes on the top of the head as well. It is usually characterized by small papules (lumps) or pustules (like pimples), which are particularly noticeable when standing behind the dog as they raise up the hairs on his back and give him a "crew cut" appearance. These dry up and the skin surface flakes off, with some attached hair, leaving small bare patches of skin that are brownish in color. The bases of the surrounding hairs are often discolored as well by the serum seeping from the inflamed hair follicles, and the dog has a distinctly "moth-eaten" and dirty appearance. Various stages of the process are often evident, so the affected dog may show small lumps, flaky skin, and discolored hair at the same time. Mild cases may show very few noticeable lumps, but close examination will reveal small discolored areas of skin accompanied by tiny areas of thinning hair, often with a tinge of brown at the base of the hair. Sometimes an outbreak will be preceded by an allergic reaction that includes hives, but it often seems to "just happen" without warning.

A variety of antibiotics have been used successfully by different veterinarians and in different parts of the country. An appropriate antibiotic must be given for a minimum of 21 days but if no response is noted within 10 days, an alternative antibiotic should probably be tried. It is extremely important that the full course of treatment be given.

Pyoderma in Dalmatians is probably triggered by allergies, stress, irritants that inflame the skin and leave it open to infection, or abnormalities in the immune system. Adolescent Dalmatians may have coat problems for a few months, especially in the summer or during periods of stress, and never display signs again. Like teenagers with acne, their fluctuating hormone levels and immune systems that are not yet fully functioning leave them vulnerable to temporary skin and coat problems and, like teenagers, they may simply outgrow these problems. It has been noted that dogs that are treated with corticosteroids during this period seem to be more likely to have problems with chronic or recurrent skin problems as adults.

If pyoderma is treated immediately, before the signs become severe, it will not normally become unsightly. If it is allowed to progress before treatment is begun, the coat will not look healthy again until the problem is resolved and the new haircoat has grown in. It is not possible to effectively whiten a haircoat discolored by pyoderma. A Dalmatian with allergic hives should be treated with antihistamines immediately and should be watched for signs of impending pyoderma. If the cause of the allergic reaction can be identified, it might be possible to prevent a recurrence, and it is possible that an observant owner can

An example of pyoderma, sometimes called "Dalmatian crud," on a Dal's neck and back.

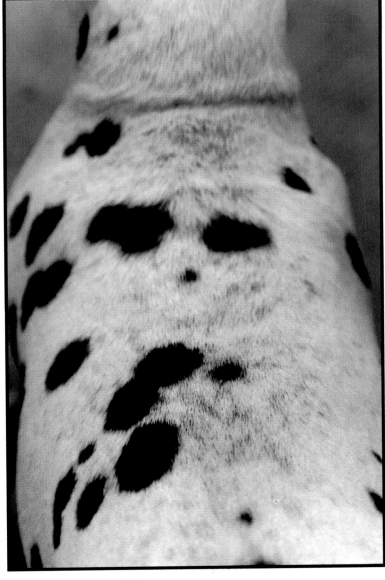

prevent a subsequent problem with pyoderma. The intelligent use of antihistamines may also work to prevent outbreaks of pyoderma.

If treated with an appropriate antibiotic (and perhaps an antibacterial shampoo as well) for a sufficient period of time, the pyoderma will normally appear to be resolved. However, if it continues to reappear when treatment is discontinued, it will be necessary to try and identify an underlying cause. Many medical and environmental factors are possible causes, but in some cases it seems impossible to identify the actual cause and the problem is referred to as *idiopathic chronic recurrent pyoderma*.

It should be noted that unless the pyoderma is associated with allergies, it is often not itchy and does not seem to bother the dog in any way; the problem is mainly one of appearance. However, it is possible that a superficial pyoderma could develop into a more serious problem, such as a deep pyoderma. Since an allergic dog will be more uncomfortable when pyoderma is present, and antihistamines seem to be less effective in such cases, a dog with an allergy problem must have the concurrent pyoderma resolved. This relatively uncommon but frustrating condition may require long-term antibiotic therapy. Some veterinarians suggest the additional use of an immune stimulant such as a staphylococcal vaccine that stimulates the immune system to fight off future staph infections.

Local irritation may be one of the contributing causes of pyoderma, as it injures and inflames the skin surface, leaving it vulnerable to attacks by the resident bacteria. Dogs who are shown extensively, bathed excessively (especially with harsh shampoos), or who experience periods of stress may develop pyoderma. Simple changes in lifestyle may be sufficient to control these cases. Show dogs who sometimes suffer chronic pyoderma may, upon retirement from the show ring, never exhibit signs of it again. It should be stressed again that dogs with allergies who are treated with corticosteroids, without addressing the underlying problems, are much more likely to develop chronic pyoderma. In cases of persistent and recurring pyoderma it may be necessary to consult with a veterinary dermatologist.

Dalmatian Bronzing Syndrome

The term "Bronzing Syndrome" appears in a wide assortment of veterinary literature, and was thought to be characterized by a variety of coexisting disorders including skin and coat problems, urinary abnormalities, protein or fat intolerance, and possibly even deafness. Various theories on the subject were proposed by an early researcher whose articles were widely read and distributed. It has become generally accepted that there is no particular relationship between these problems—no such "syndrome"—and that each problem must be addressed and resolved on an individual basis. The "bronzing" part was characterized by the discolored skin and hair and moth-eaten appearance, which are typically seen in cases of superficial pyoderma. "Bronzing" is the proper term for the discoloration of black spots when black hairs fade to brown on their ends. This is very occasionally seen along the back on young Dals and is normally a temporary condition. As described in the standard, this condition should not be mistaken for a tri-color.

Acral Lick Dermatitis

Lick granulomas, also called acral lick dermatitis, are occasionally seen in Dalmatians. They are characterized by the dog licking an area, usually on a leg, until the area becomes hairless, raw, and inflamed. A great deal of work is currently being done on this topic as granulomas can be very difficult to clear up.

Allergic Dals often lick or chew their legs and feet, so it is important to identify and correct the problem before it becomes a habit. There are many theories as to why dogs seem to lick for no apparent reason, including boredom, nervous disorders, and obsessive-compulsive behavior. Dals who are crated for long periods of time often lick excessively, particularly on the tops of their front feet, so the boredom connection may well apply to Dals.

There is no one treatment for granulomas and many different treatments may need to be tried before a cure is found. An Elizabethan collar is often used to keep the dog from bothering the area so that it has a chance to heal. Topical treatments, corticosteroids, and anti-inflammatory agents are used to assist in the healing process, and these may be sufficient to resolve the problem, at least temporarily. In other cases tranquilizers, antidepressants, and narcotics are used to modify the behavioral aspects of the problem. Treatments have also included the use of cobra antivenin injected into the site and radiation therapy.

Demodectic Mange

Demodectic mange is a noncontagious disease caused by the demodex mites that are normal skin inhabitants on both dogs and people. It is only when the host animal is unable to control the number of mites that the mites become a problem. Mites live in the hair follicles and are detected by applying pressure to an area of the skin to express the mites from their hiding places, scraping the surface of the skin with a scalpel, and examining this debris under a microscope. Diagnosis of demodicosis is based on finding a significant number of mites and eggs, as an occasional mite can be found on normal dogs.

Demodectic mange is most likely to appear on Dalmatians during the times they are teething, going through periods of rapid growth, or experiencing other periods of stress. There is a great deal of controversy surrounding the treatment of demodicosis, as its basic cause appears to be a poorly functioning immune system. If

Rudi has a lick granuloma, or "lick sore," on her back leg.

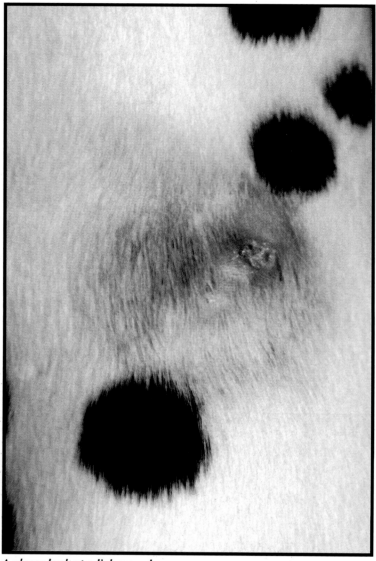

A closer look at a lick granuloma.

If the condition becomes more widespread, with extensive areas affected, it is said to be "generalized." This is a serious problem that can also result in secondary infections. The treatment of choice is a dip containing amitraz that is available only through veterinarians and must be used with care. The dog is dipped periodically and rechecked for mites until no mites are evident for some period of time. Many dogs require only a few dips, while others must be treated periodically throughout their lives.

Currently the only effective approved treatment for demodicosis is amitraz. Frequent dipping of dogs exhibiting only localized demodicosis increases the likelihood that resistant mites will develop. Therefore it is important that only those dogs with more severe cases be dipped. Since animals with defective immune systems should preferably not be used for breeding, it is important to differentiate between dogs with generalized and localized demodicosis. While some authorities feel that no dogs that require dipping to bring the demodicosis under control should be used for breeding, others feel that as long as any demodicosis was localized, such animals should not present a problem in a breeding program.

this problem is only temporary, as is often the case with young Dals, the dog will be able to overcome the mites on its own. Dogs with "localized" demodicosis will show only a few areas of thinning hair, usually on the face or legs or the back of the neck. This can be treated topically, or it can just be watched. In mild cases, demodectic mange will just disappear as the animal's immune system kicks in and brings the mite population under control.

You and Your Veterinarian

HOW TO CHOOSE A VETERINARIAN

If a dog is purchased from a local breeder, that breeder can recommend a veterinarian that is knowledgeable about caring for Dalmatians. If a dog is purchased from an out-of-town source, checking with a local kennel club, if one is available, for a suggested veterinarian could be helpful. Some veterinary offices are multi-veterinarian practices. The advantage of this is that more than one opinion can be readily obtained for major health problems and diagnoses. In recent years, there has been an increase in the

For several days following surgery for an infected cat bite, Jocko wore an Elizabethan collar to prevent him from bothering the stitches in his chest.

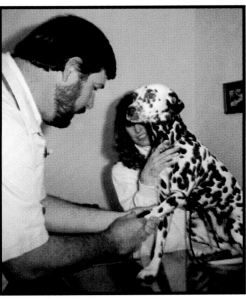

Monkee, owned by Shirley Allegre, is having blood drawn for a brucellosis test.

number of veterinarians who choose to specialize in a specific area of veterinary medicine. If the dog has a specific problem, it is reasonable to ask for a second opinion from a specialist.

Visiting various veterinarians' offices prior to purchasing a dog gives you the opportunity to check for displays of the veterinarians' state licenses as well as observe general office procedures and cleanliness. Observing the method used during the yearly exam helps to ascertain the veterinarian's competence. The veterinarian should check the dog's weight, heart, eyes, ears, skin, and sex glands for abnormalities in addition to checking the stool for worms, the blood for heartworms, and giving the yearly shots.

A veterinarian's office that is AAHA (American Animal Hospital Association) certified has met the highest standards. The office

Regular veterinary care is essential for any dog to stay in top condition. "Polly's" good health shines through in her appearance. Ch. Paisley Polyester is owned by Mike Rolling and Mary Oelrich.

has an on-site inspection every two to three years. The inspectors check the type of equipment used in the office and check to see if the laboratory is certified. If an in-house laboratory is used, the inspectors check to see if the quality controls have been documented. A special team reviews randomly selected cases, x-ray quality and readings, and patient records. Infractions of the standard usually have a period of one month to be corrected.

If a veterinarian loses his state license, it soon will be policy that the National Veterinarian Board will be notified, and, in turn, will notify all of the states.

AIDING THE VETERINARIAN IN DALMATIAN CARE

When making an appointment with the veterinarian, it is helpful to the office to briefly explain the reason for the visit (the sperm count on a stud dog, a complete physical, an eye exam, etc.). The correct amount of time then can be allotted for the veterinarian to accomplish these functions.

It is important for the dog owner to help educate the veterinarian about the particular abnormalities of the Dalmatian. As new information is disseminated through the

"Carlos" shows off the cast he wore for several weeks following an accident. Ch. North's M.T. Pockets (L) is owned by Dave and Sandy Slattum.

national and local Dalmatian clubs, a responsible owner will make the information known to the veterinarian.

There are general diagnostic procedures that a veterinarian will follow. For example, if there are indications of an infection, a culture is taken to ascertain the correct antibiotic to be used. If crystals are present in the urine, they will be identified so that the correct treatment can be initiated. (Since not all stones in Dalmatians are urate stones, they need to be assayed. Otherwise the treatment could hinder recuperation and even aggravate the problem.) For skin problems, a skin scraping and microscopic observation will be done to rule out the presence of mites and a culture may be taken to identify possible bacterial infections. If mites and bacteria are not present, then allergies should be considered. Possible causes and treatment options then should be discussed.

Crash got a little too close to a porcupine and ended up with 97 quills in his face and chest. Despite how painful this looks, he was just fine after having the quills removed.

The Senior Dalmatian

How old is your dog? Current trends equate a one-year-old dog to being approximately 13 years old in human years. A two-year-old dog is equal to 20 human years and a three-year-old dog is equal to 25 human years. From that point on, each dog year is equal to five more human years. An eight-year-old dog is 50 in human years and a 12-year-old dog is 70 in human years.

Generally, when the Dalmatian reaches the age of eight, he moves into the "senior" category and the owner needs to be aware of the dog's needs as a senior citizen. Common health problems in older dogs include obesity, kidney disease, heart disease, liver disease, diabetes, arthritis, disc disease, tooth and gum disease, impaired senses, tumors, and endocrine disease.

The senior citizen's diet needs to be taken into consideration. As organs such as the kidneys and heart age, they become less tolerant of the amount of phosphorus, protein, sodium, and calories typically found in commercial adult dog foods. Salt affects the heart; protein and phosphorus affect the kidneys; and, of course, calories contribute to obesity. The protein quality of the food is important because the older dog does not use as many of the amino acids and the excess is converted into waste materials that are excreted in the urine. Lower-protein diets help to maintain normal kidney function. If the dog has increased his intake of drinking water or there if is an unusually large or small amount of urine passed in a 24-hour period, consult a veterinarian.

Obesity is harmful to the older dog's joints, heart, and other organs. The correct weight for the dog can be determined by running your hands along the dog's sides. You should be able to feel the outline of the dog's ribs without pressing hard, and the dog's body should taper inward at the end of the ribs.

Exercise is important for an older dog. Regular walking once or twice a day is good exercise. If the dog is not affected by arthritis, chasing balls or sticks for a short time will get his circulation going.

Arthritis seems to be an affliction that many older dogs suffer from. Keeping the dog's nails short helps to ward off arthritis of the elbows. Acupuncture, the insertion of solid needles into specific points on the body called acupoints, and derivative techniques (electroacupunture, aquapuncture, and embedding) are known to relieve the pain and stiffness of arthritis. Gold bead implants are often used for relief from chronic arthritis.

Regularly examining the dog all over gives the owner the opportunity to check for lumps and skin abnormalities that might need to be checked by a veterinarian. Older females who have not been spayed are prone to mammary cancer, so these glands should be palpated regularly. Male dogs' prostate glands should be checked regularly for any irregularities.

Dental care is important. Plaque formation will result in gum disease, loss of teeth, and bad breath. There are various dog toothbrushes and toothpastes on the market that will help keep their teeth healthier. Also, the veterinarian should check the dog's teeth during his yearly check up. The spread of bacteria from an infectious tooth or gum into the bloodstream can be a serious risk to the older dog's health. If the dog has trouble eating hard foods or has bad breath, check his teeth and gums.

Eyes need to be periodically observed. A hazy bluish cast to the eye is normal with aging, but if a hazy whitish color exists, cataracts may be involved and the veterinarian should be consulted.

or become mentally or physically unable to care for the dog.

When the dog's health has deteriorated to the point that the dog is in constant pain or distress, or when the quality of the dog's life is in question, euthanasia is not at all inappropriate. In some situations, the whole family can be involved with

Senior-citizen siblings Jocko and Annie are taking it easy. Owned by Jerry and Mary-Lynn Wolfe.

Remember that the older dog needs to have his sleeping area clean, dry, and warm at all times.

SAYING GOODBYE

Providing for the care of a dog, physically and financially, in a will is becoming increasingly popular. This guarantees the owner that the dog will continue to be cared for in the manner the owner wishes if the owner should die

this decision. The term "put to sleep" can be misunderstood by younger children who may expect the dog to wake up or they may think that they, themselves, will not wake up like the dog. Explaining that euthanasia is a loving way to end the dog's life, because it is not going to get better, is sometimes helpful for children to understand. Two books that are written to help children understand a pet's death are *The Tenth Good Thing About Barney* by Judith Viorst and *When a Pet Dies* by Fred Rogers.

Making decisions and preparations for burial or cremation prior to euthanasia allows the time to choose the best course of action for everyone. Crying and grieving are important parts of the process as well as taking the time to say

Brochure, P.O. Box 150899, Denver, CO 80215.

ARRIVAL OF THE NEXT DALMATIAN

Getting a young puppy when the older dog is in reasonably good health can

Sharing a snooze with a friend is senior Dalmatian Windy. Both Windy and cat Kody are owned by Mr. and Mrs. Richard Heriot.

goodbye. Being present while the dog is euthanized can lower the dog's stress level. In some cases, a veterinarian will come to the house to eliminate the dog's stress of being transported to the veterinarian's office.

The University of California Veterinary School at Davis sponsors a pet loss hotline at (916) 752-4200 from 6:30 to 9:30 p.m. Pacific time, Monday through Friday. The American Animal Hospital Association has a free grief brochure that you can obtain by sending a self-addressed stamped envelope to Grief

sometimes give a boost to the old dog's attitude. In other cases, a young puppy can be too active and annoy the older dog. Both situations need to be monitored by the owner so that the best situation is established. Some proponents of bringing a young dog into the household say it softens the owner's sense of loss when it comes time to let the older dog die. A void is filled with new, young, vibrant life. Remember that the new dog has his own personality and should not be expected to be exactly like the old dog.

Living with Multiple Dalmatians or Dogs

Dalmatians are addictive. There's no doubt about it. That first adorable spotted puppy can change your life forever. Many owners start with one Dal and later decide that two would be even more fun. Sometimes the owner of a pet Dal gets interested in showing, adds a second dog, and eventually has a house full of them. Perhaps the Dal owner raises a litter and keeps one of the pups or takes a pup sired by his male as a stud fee. Perhaps a Dalmatian pup is added to a household that already has a dog, or perhaps a Dal-owning household takes in a rescue dog or adds a dog of another breed.

Above: *Taking each other for a walk are Tongwood's Spotted Storm and Tongwood's Bold Irish Starr. Owned by Mr. and Mrs. Joseph McCrone. Below: Three generations (left to right): grandson "James," Ch. Sunburst Chauffeur Driven; son "Kip," Ch. Centurion Cultured Kipper; and mom "Pearl," Ch. Centurion Cultured Pearl. James is owned by Martha Fritter; Kip and Pearl are owned by Elise Moloney.*

Will it work? How do Dals get along with other Dals? With other dogs?

Dalmatians vary a great deal in their ability to coexist with other dogs. Most do very well in multiple-dog households and many Dal owners have half a dozen or more dogs that live together peacefully. It's not unusual for adult unneutered males to have trouble getting along with each other, but in many cases even that works just fine. Some owners feel that their females have more trouble getting along than their males.

A male and a female, either altered or not, is the combination that is most likely to be successful; the combination of two unaltered males is the least likely to work. One dog dominant and the other submissive often makes it more likely that the combination will work. Two very dominant dogs, whatever the gender combination, can become a problem. An undisciplined single dog who thinks that he is in charge of the household is less likely to tolerate what he perceives to be competition for his position.

A group of dogs living together will normally develop its own pecking order and, unless there is serious fighting, it's best to let the dogs work things out on their own. However, a group of dogs can be difficult to control, and unless the owner can control the dogs as individuals, he can't possibly control the dogs as a group. If the

Crossroads Mountain Daisy, CDX, CGC and Crossroads Checkers, CDX pose with some spotted friends. Owned by Marilyn Gaffney.

Pile up! Robert is on the bottom, with daughter Sally Brown in the middle and daughter Erin on top.

Left to right: Sally Forth, Eloise, and Kitty are relaxing and enjoying a sunny day.

owner is not perceived as being alpha (the dominant leader of the pack), there is a much greater chance of the dogs fighting among themselves for the top spot.

It's not advisable to raise littermates together unless there is sufficient time to work with them separately as well as together. Never buy two dogs because "they will keep each other company." This results in two dogs who are excessively dependent on one another and have little interest in their owner. It's very difficult to teach them anything, and they won't bond properly with humans. Littermates, whether purchased or kept, need to be raised as individuals and separated as much as possible. They must

Ch. Rambler's Lady Sarah Jane as a puppy with housemate Picadilly's Sir Nigel. Owned by Cliff and Stephanie Seigneur.

Ch. Markmaker Never Say Never, CDX, CGC ("Pica") as a puppy with mom Markmaker Coriander, CD, CGC (L) ("Cory"). Owned by Carol Wells.

sleep in their own crates, eat from separate bowls, and attend training classes at different times. They should have individual walks as well as separate play times and training sessions. Both the dog who is taken out and the one who is left at home must be able to function without the other dog.

The same is true when adding a new dog to the household. He must be raised as an individual, not as "one of the pack." He is not a "pet" for one of the older dogs—he is *your* dog, and he must relate to *you*. It's much easier to let the older dogs teach him the routine, but it's not fair to the new dog. He has the right, as well as the need, to be an individual.

When littermates are raised together or a puppy is raised with his dam, each pup

Salem (left) and her brother Morris relax after a busy show weekend. Owned by Sue MacMillan, Salem co-owned with Lisen Overturf.

Dals owned by the Brennans enjoy a playful game of tug-o-war.

should go to stay with a friend for at least a week. This will break the bonds between the dogs and help them to function as individuals.

Many older dogs get jealous when a new dog is added to the family, although adding a puppy is usually easier than adding another adult. It's important that the older dog doesn't have his routine upset and that he doesn't lose privileges or get less attention

"Why don't you have spots?" Four-month-old Ringo (Dal) and Cogin (Golden Riever) enjoy each other's company. Owned by Luce Milhomme.

412

than he is used to. Dogs are social animals, and most of them quickly get used to another dog. Older dogs often learn to enjoy the company of a younger dog, and many of them seem to get a new lease on life.

When adding a puppy to a household with one or more older dogs, the puppy will normally be disciplined by the other dogs when he becomes too annoying. The older dog(s) will put up with puppyish behavior for a while and then warn the pup to back off. If the pup does not respond, he will be grabbed by the head and pinned to the floor or snapped at, and he may take off screaming. Unless the older dog is overly aggressive, the owner should not step in to "rescue" the puppy—he is frightened, not hurt. The older dog is just establishing his dominance and teaching the pup one of the pack rules. Younger dogs are expected to show submission to senior pack members and must learn the rules to fit into the group. A puppy who is not disciplined will grow up thinking that he can "take over" when he is

Dal pup Molly and her Whippet buddies Blaze (left) and Mad Dog (right). Molly is owned by Maureen Bouska and Mike Deer; Whippets are owned by D. Keller.

ready, which will eventually cause problems. In a household with multiple dogs, one or two of the dogs may take over disciplining the puppy while the others just stay out of the way.

If an adult dog is added, it's best to introduce the dogs to each other in a neutral setting, such as taking them both for a walk in the park. If an adult dog is brought directly into the house or yard, the resident dog may feel a need to defend his territory from a stranger. Great care must be taken for several weeks and the dogs should not be left alone with each other until it is absolutely certain that they are totally comfortable.

All dogs in the household should have their own crates. Normally, it's best to feed the dogs in their crates so that no dog can bully another over food and each dog can eat in peace. If there are dogs in the household who can't run together, they can alternate times being out of their crates. Each dog in the household should receive individual attention every day, even if it's just a walk to the corner or a ride in the car to get gas. Dals must absolutely have individual attention. If one of the dogs starts exhibiting behavior problems, a ten-minute daily training session with lots of praise will often solve the problem.

If the Dal owner has unspayed females and unneutered males, arrangements must be made for handling the situation when the females are in season. The easiest solution would be to board out one or more of the dogs, but this can be expensive. It might also work to swap dogs with a friend during the critical two weeks. The dogs can normally run together for the first week of the female's heat period, but as soon as the male(s) become interested, the dogs must be separated. Occasionally, bitches who usually get along just fine will start fighting with each other when one is in season, and males who normally get along may also have problems.

If the dogs are to remain at home, it is best if the female in season is moved to an area where she is not visible to the male(s). She should be exercised in an area to which the males have no access, since sniffing where she has urinated will cause the males to become agitated, especially when she is ready to breed. Chlorophyll tablets help to mask the odor, but experienced males are not fooled for long!

Although multiple dogs can be great fun, they are also a lot of work. Two dogs who are very obedient off leash when taken out separately may be very difficult to manage if taken out together. The challenge of seeing who can run faster and further tends to overshadow the owner's frantic calls. Two dogs can also think up a lot of mischief, and they may have a wonderful time playing tug-o-war with the sofa pillows or throw rugs. Before adding a second dog, be absolutely certain that the first dog is completely trained. Then put the same amount of effort into the second dog.

Pups Bear (top), Cali (middle), and Sony (bottom) think that there's no pillow more comfortable than their dad Paxten. Owned by James and Kathryn Ann Matheny.

Am-Can. Ch. Coachman's Carte Rouge (L) enjoys a spring day with four-week-old granddaughter Ch. Gallopade's V. Anne Gogh (L). Owned by Ellen Murray.

Above: *Ch. Bearded Oaks Astra's Lyra, CD loves to dive for toys in the pool. This photo won the AKC Gazette's 1994 photo contest. Owned and photographed by Carolyn Bolt. Below: "Should I or shouldn't I?"—testing the water with a spotted paw and contemplating a swim...*

WHERE TO GET HELP

Brochures and Pamphlets

Rules Applying to Registration and Dog Shows, AKC
Obedience Regulations, AKC
Tracking Regulations, AKC
Primer on Urinary Stones, Dalmatian Club of America

Videos

A Review of Color in the Dalmatian, DCA
The Dalmatian, AKC
Dalmatian Sensation, Bolt Action Video, 2610 Sunnyside St., Sarasota, FL 34239
Dogsteps, A Study in Canine Structure and Movement, Rachael Page Elliott, AKC
Eight Week Course on Attention, Demello, PO Box 458, Alexandria, IN 46001
Gait, Observing Dogs in Motion, AKC
Sirius Puppy Training, Ian Dunbar, Bluford/Toth Prod., Box 163, 496-A Hudson St., New York, NY 10014
Urinary Stone-Forming in Dalmatians and Other Dogs, Lecture by Joseph Bartges, DVM, Bolt Action Video, 2610 Sunnyside St., Sarasota, FL 34239

DCA Committees

Contact the DCA Secretary via the AKC for the current chairpersons and addresses of the following committees:
Dalmatian Rescue Coordinator
Breed Referral Service—location of breeders in specific areas
Research Sub-Committee on Deafness
Research Study Group on Urinary Stones
Membership
Regional Dalmatian Clubs—contact the DCA Secretary for locations

Testing and Evaluation Sites

BAER hearing testing sites—contact the DCA Secretary via the AKC
Hemopet (blood testing, immune deficiencies, and disorders)—Jean Dodds, DVM, 938 Stanford St., Santa Monica, CA 90403, (310) 828-4804
Orthopedic Foundation for Animals (hip and elbow x-ray)—2300 Nifong Blvd., Columbia, MO 65201, (314)442-0418
PennHIP™ (measures hip joint laxity)—International Canine Genetics, (800) 248-8099
Urolithic Assaying (crystals and kidney stones)—Minnesota Urolith Center, Dept. of Small Animal Practice, University of Minnesota School of Veterinary Medicine, C339 Veterinary Hospitals, St. Paul, MN 55108, (612) 625-4285
Urinary Stone Analysis Laboratory, Dept. of Medicine, School of Veterinary Medicine, University of California at Davis, Davis, CA 95616-8737, (916) 752-1363

Breeding

International Canine Genetics, Inc. (frozen and extended semen collection, ovulation timing tests) 271 Great Valley Parkway, Malvern, PA 19355
Seager Canine Semen Bank, Inc. (frozen and extended semen collection, storage and evaluation) Carol Schubert, 329 Sioux St., Park Forest, IL 60466

Service/Assistance Dog Training

Canine Companions for Independence, P.O. Box 446, Santa Rosa, CA 95402-0446, (707) 528-0830
The Phydeaux for Freedom, Inc., #1 Main Street, Laurel, MD 20708, (301) 498-6779

Veterinary Consultants

University Veterinary Teaching Hospitals
Morris Animal Foundation—information and research
Specialists—contact local veterinarians for specialists in the area.
Holistic Veterinarians—American Holistic Veterinary Medical Association, 2214 Old Emmerton Road, Bel Air, MD 21015
Veterinary Acupuncturists—International Veterinary Acupuncture Society, 2140 Conestoga Road, Chester Springs, PA 19425

Poison Control

National Animal Poison Control Center—(800) 548-2423 or (900) 680-0000

PUPPY APTITUDE TEST

puppy (color, sex) _____ litter _____ date _____

The following is a concise chart explaining each test and the scoring, a sample score sheet and an interpretation of the scores:

TEST	PURPOSE	SCORE	1
SOCIAL ATTRACTION: Place puppy in test area. From a few feet away the tester coaxes the pup to her/him by clapping hands gently and kneeling down. Tester must coax in a direction away from the point where it entered the testing area.	Degree of social attraction, confidence or dependence.	Came readily, tail up, jumped, bit at hands.	1
		Came readily, tail up, pawed, licked at hands.	2
		Came readily, tail up.	3
		Came readily, tail down.	4
		Came hesitantly, tail down.	5
		Didn't come at all.	6
FOLLOWING: Stand up and walk away from the pup in a normal manner. Make sure the pup sees you walk away.	Degree of following attraction. Not following indicates independence.	Followed readily, tail up, got underfoot, bit at feet.	1
		Followed readily, tail up, got underfoot.	2
		Followed readily, tail up.	3
		Followed readily, tail down.	4
		Followed hesitantly, tail down.	5
		No follow or went away.	6
RESTRAINT: Crouch down and gently roll the pup on his back and hold it with one hand for a full 30 seconds.	Degree of dominant or submissive tendency. How it accepts stress when socially/ physically dominated.	Struggled fiercely, flailed, bit.	1
		Struggled fiercely, flailed.	2
		Settled, struggled, settled with some eye contact.	3
		Struggled then settled.	4
		No struggle.	5
		No struggle, straining to avoid eye contact.	6
SOCIAL DOMINANCE: Let pup stand up and gently stroke him from the head to back while you crouch beside him. Continue stroking until a recognizable behavior is established.	Degree of acceptance of social dominance. Pup may try to dominate by jumping and nipping or is independent and walks away.	Jumped, pawed, bit, growled.	1
		Jumped, pawed.	2
		Cuddles up to testor and tries to lick face.	3
		Squirmed, licked at hands.	4
		Rolled over, licked at hands.	5
		Went away and stayed away.	6
ELEVATION DOMINANCE: Bend over and cradle the pup under its belly, fingers interlaced, palms up and elevate it just off the ground. Hold it there for 30 seconds.	Degree of accepting dominance while in position of no control.	Struggled fiercely, bit, growled.	1
		Struggled fiercely.	2
		No struggle, relaxed.	3
		Struggled, settled, licked.	4
		No struggle, licked at hands.	5
		No struggle, froze.	6

OBEDIENCE APTITUDE

TEST	PURPOSE	SCORE	1
RETRIEVING: Crouch beside pup and attract his attention with crumpled up paper ball. When the pup shows interest and is watching, toss the object 4–6 feet in front of pup.	Degree of willingness to work with a human. High correlation between ability to retrieve and successful guide dogs, obedience dogs, field trial dogs.	Chases object, picks up object and runs away. Chases object, stands over object, does not return. Chases object and returns with object to testor. Chases object and returns without object to testor. Starts to chase object, loses interest. Does not chase object.	1 2 3 4 5 6
TOUCH SENSITIVITY: Take puppy's webbing of one front foot and press between finger and thumb lightly then more firmly till you get a response, while you count slowly to 10. Stop as soon as puppy pulls away, or shows discomfort.	Degree of sensitivity to touch.	8–10 counts before response. 6–7 counts before response. 5–6 counts before response. 2–4 counts before response. 1–2 counts before response.	1 2 3 4 5
SOUND SENSITIVITY: Place pup in the center of area, testor or assistant makes a sharp noise a few feet from the puppy. A large metal spoon struck sharply on a metal pan twice works well.	Degree of sensitivity to sound. (Also can be a rudimentary test for deafness.)	Listens, locates sound, walks toward it barking. Listens, locates sound, barks. Listens, locates sound, shows curiosity and walks toward sound. Listens, locates the sound. Cringes, backs off, hides. Ignores sound, shows no curiosity.	1 2 3 4 5 6
SIGHT SENSITIVITY: Place pup in center of room. Tie a string around a large towel and jerk it across the floor a few feet away from puppy.	Degree of intelligent response to strange object.	Looks, attacks and bites. Looks, barks and tail-up. Looks curiously, attempts to investigate. Looks, barks, tail-tuck. Runs away, hides.	1 2 3 4 5
STRUCTURE: The puppy is gently set in a natural stance and evaluated for structure in the following categories: Straight front Front angulation Straight rear Croup angulation Shoulder Rear angulation layback *(see diagram below)*	Degree of structural soundness. Good structure is necessary.	The puppy is correct in structure. The puppy has a slight fault or deviation. The puppy has an extreme fault or deviation.	good fair poor

(Compiled by and first published in the *AKC Gazette*, March 1979.)

Straight front   Straight rear   Shoulder layback   Front angulation   Croup angulation   Rear angulation

INTERPRETATION OF SCORES FOR PUPPY APTITUDE

If the puppy scores:

Mostly 1's—This puppy will be dominant, aggressive, and inclined to bite if challenged. He is not suitable as a family dog and would do best with a very experienced handler. He could be a satisfactory guard dog or police dog if carefully trained.

Mostly 2's—This puppy is dominant and self-confident. He will accept leadership from an experienced trainer but is not suitable for most families, especially if there are small children. He might excel as a show dog, obedience dog, or working dog, but could become a problem dog and possibly a biter in a permissive home. *This type of personality is not unusual in Dalmatians but can be difficult for the average family to deal with*.

Mostly 3's—A puppy that scores mostly 3's will be a fine family dog if he receives sufficient training and exercise. He must be handled correctly and could be too much dog for a busy family or one with small children. These scores are ideal for a dog destined to become a show and/or obedience dog, but he will need training and structure to be an optimum family dog in most homes. *This type of personality is very typical in Dalmatians*.

Mostly 4's—This puppy will be perfect for the average family. He is not dominant, readily accepts restraint, and is usually mild mannered and gentle. He should be well socialized and must not be trained using harsh methods. He may be too "soft" for some situations, but if his score include a few 3's he will probably be suitable for all situations. *Most breeders would prefer their pet puppies to have this type of personality*.

Mostly 5's—This pup is submissive and lacks self-confidence. He must be carefully socialized but even then he may be somewhat shy. This is not a dog for a lively household—he would be more suitable for a single person with lots of time or an elderly couple. This type of dog does not make a good show dog and rarely makes a satisfactory obedience dog.

Mostly 6's—A pup who scores mostly 6's is normally very independent and has no need for people. Well-socialized pups of most breeds do not normally test this way and a pup who scores 6's should probably be retested a few days later. This type of personality is not common in Dalmatians, where personality faults are more likely to be aggression or shyness.

ETHICAL GUIDLINES

Introduction and Purpose

These guidelines are presented with the full realization that ethics cannot be legislated, and that most individuals desire and intend to do what is right. The purpose of these guidelines, therefore, is to set forth principles of practice that the Dalmatian Club of America would have all its members and those associated with Dalmatians adhere to as they strive to accomplish the club's goals and purposes so clearly stated in the by-laws. These guidelines present the minimum in ethical practices; how best to conform to these practices is better left to the educational efforts of individuals and regional clubs.

Practices

1. To ensure that all dogs in my care are provided adequate food, shelter, human companionship, and medical care.

2. To become educated in the fundamentals of owning, breeding, and exhibiting dogs.

3. To understand the basic laws of genetics, the standard of the breed, and the difference between the correct and the incorrect before attempting to breed.

4. To register all breeding stock with the American Kennel Club, and to keep complete, true, and accurate records of all matings, litters, and pedigrees. 5. To follow good business practices and ethics in sales and breeding contracts and to honor all agreements. Written agreements are encouraged.

6. To refrain from breeding unless there is strong assurance that a sufficient number of homes is available for the resulting puppies and to be willing to accept the return of unwanted dogs produced by my brood bitch or sired by my stud dog.

7. To ensure that no female will be bred before reaching 18 months of age nor before her second season and that no female will be bred after she has reached eight years of age. To ensure that no male will be bred before he has reached one year of age.

8. To be extremely discriminating when considering the acceptance of bitches for breeding to my stud dog, especially those whose owners have not pledged to adhere to these guidelines.

9. To ensure that the hearing status of all puppies and breeding candidates is known and taken into consideration in all breeding decisions. To ensure that all bilaterally deaf puppies produced by my brood bitch or sired by my stud dog are humanely euthanized as soon as the condition is detected and confirmed.

10. To transfer puppies only after they have reached at least seven weeks of age, to provide at least a three-generation pedigree, and to ensure that the buyer has the physical facilities to properly care for a Dalmatian.

11. To appropriately use AKC limited registration for puppies that are not of breeding quality. To avoid sales agreements which include "puppy back" clauses that may encourage unnecessary breeding.

12. To ensure that puppies and adults produced by my brood bitch or stud dog are never knowingly sold or consigned to pet stores, wholesalers, or commercial dealers. To not knowingly supply dogs for raffles, auctions, giveaways, prizes, or other such projects.

13. To recognize that careful follow-up of all genetic defects is the responsibility of the owners of both the sire and dam of every litter.

14. To ensure that all advertising is factual and not misleading. To never engage in malicious criticism and to separate fact from fiction before repeating comments heard from others.

15. To adhere to rules of the AKC while exhibiting; to practice the principles of good sportsmanship; and to consider competitors as a challenge, not a threat.

16. To ensure that while engaged in the art and science of judging that I will be influenced only by the quality of the animals to be judged.

17. To always ensure that my actions are directed toward the best interests of the Dalmatian breed, the Dalmatian Club of America and the American Kennel Club.

STUD SERVICE CONTRACT

The bitch named:

AKC #:

Owned by:

Address:

Phone:

Is bred to (dog's name):

AKC #:

Owned by:

Address:

Phone:

A stud fee of $_____will be paid at the time of the first breeding unless previous mutual arrangements have been made between the bitch and stud owners. These arrangements are (To be written in full):

_____

_____

_____

_____

CONDITIONS

1. This contract guarantees the actual mating of the listed dogs and does not guarantee pregnancy or puppies.

2. Veterinarian certification of health and breeding soundness of the bitch including free of worms, negative brucellosis and no vaginal infections.

3. The owner of the bitch is responsible for preventing accidental breeding to another dog. This, and/or the use of a pregnancy preventative shot, will unconditionally void this contract.

4. During pregnancy, the owner of the bitch has the sole responsibility for providing a safe and healthy environment for the bitch as well as a healthy and safe environment for whelping and raising the litter. The owner will also provide veterinary care for the bitch and pups as necessary. Failure to do so will void this contract.

5. Should the bitch fail to whelp _____living puppies, one additional service will be given free at the next season of the bitch provided ownership of the bitch and the stud has not transferred. No stud fee will be refunded, in whole or in part. If no pregnancy results from the return mating, this entire agreement is terminated.

6. In the event of a return breeding due to conditions listed in #5; if the stud dog dies or is not available for reasons of health, the stud dog owner will offer another stud dog he/she owns or a refund of half the original stud fee.

7. Papers for each patched puppy will be withheld by the bitch owner until the patched puppy has been neutered and proof thereof is submitted. Or, the patched puppies will be registered under limited registration with the AKC.

8. Deaf puppies will be euthanized by a veterinarian or shall be donated to the DCA deafness research laboratory.

STUD SERVICE CONTRACT (continued)

9. Owner of the bitch agrees **NOT TO KNOWINGLY SELL, CONSIGN FOR SALE, GIVE OR OTHERWISE TRANSFER OWNERSHIP OF ANY OR ALL OF SAID PUPPIES TO ANY PERSON ENGAGED IN THE RESALE OF DOGS TO THE GENERAL PUBLIC OR ANY RESEARCH LABORATORY** other than mentioned in #8. A fine of $_____ per puppy is payable to owner of the stud dog if there is an infraction of this clause.

10. Special variations (To be written in full. Verbal agreements which conflict with the terms of this contract will not be recognized.):

_____

_____

_____

_____

_____

11. It is specifically agreed hereby that the owner of the bitch will be liable for all attorneys' and/or legal fees incurred by the owner of the dog to gain performance of the above stated contractual obligations on the part of the owner of the bitch.

_____

Signature of stud owner (^)   Date

_____

Signature of bitch owner (^)   Date

DISCLAIMER

The Dalmatian Club of America is in no way responsible or liable, financially or otherwise, because of the use of this contract form by its members, or non-members who obtain and use it.

(FOR RECORD OF LITTER - NOT PART OF CONTRACT)

1st breeding date:			
2nd breeding date:			
Whelping date:			
Bitch whelped	male puppies and	female puppies on	, 19
Litter Registration #:			
Remarks:			

SALES AGREEMENT

The Dalmatian puppy described below is being sold as (encircle number applicable):

1. A potential conformation competition or breeding-quality animal.

2. A potential obedience competition animal.

3. A home companion.

Sex:	Color/Markings:
Date of Whelping:	AKC/Litter Reg.#:
Sire:	Dam:
Buyer:	Telephone:
Address:	
Seller:	Telephone:
Address:	
FOR THE TOTAL PRICE OF $	

This Dalmatian is guaranteed to be in good health at the time of sale and for 48 hours thereafter. The Buyer will be given a complete record of all innoculations and wormings done prior to sale. Buyer will also be provided with at least a four generation pedigree and properly completed and signed AKC registration papers. It is required that this Dalmatian be examined by the Buyer's veterinarian within 48 hours. Should any serious illness be found at that time, upon written certification from the veterinarian, this Dalmatian may be returned for a refund of the purchase price (the amount of cash actually paid by Buyer to Seller).

CONDITIONS OF SALE (encircle *only* those paragraph numbers which apply)

1. The Buyer agrees to provide this Dalmatian with a fenced yard and/or will not permit this Dalmatian to run loose outside its owner's yard. This Dalmatian is to be considered a companion and thus, a house dog which will not be left out in the weather. The Buyer shall never abandon this Dalmatian to an animal shelter or sell it to a research center.

2. It is understood that this Dalmatian is being purchased as a **potential show or breeding-quality animal.** Buyer agrees to act as insurer in this respect by following Seller's instructions on diet, training and grooming. Buyer shall offer this Dalmatian every opportunity of success in the show ring through proper conditioning and presentation including the possible services of a professional handler if deemed necessary.

3. This Dalmatian is guaranteed to be free of hereditary crippling and/or disabling defects visible by 24 months of age. Determination of what constitutes a hereditary defect is to be by the unanimous agreement of two (2) veterinarians agreeable to both parties. One of these veterinarians to be a tenured faculty member of an accredited university veterinary teaching hospital or Board-certified in the applicable specialty. Cost of the opinions are to be assumed by the Buyer. (Encircle one choice of following three (3) options, that choice to be initialed both by Buyer and Seller on lines to left of chosen option:)

_____ _____ a. Refund of _____ % provided the living Dalmatian and its registration papers are returned to Seller.

_____ _____ b. Replace with the next likely available prospect or mutually agreeable animal provided the living Dalmatian and its registration papers are returned to Seller.

_____ _____ c. Adjustment (to be filled in at time of sale): $_____.

4. Buyer agrees that this Dalmatian, if a bitch, shall not be serviced by a stud at least before she attains the age of 18 months and her second season. Special agreements concerning breedings are listed at the end of this contract and initialed by both parties. **NO PROGENY OF THIS DALMATIAN SHALL BE SOLD, GIVEN OR TRANSFERRED IN ANY MANNER TO PET SHOPS, IN LITTER LOTS, OR TO PERSONS CONTEMPLATING BREEDING FOR SALE TO COMMERCIAL DISTRIBUTORS OF DOGS OR GUARD DOG BUSINESSES.** Therefore, for each infraction a $_____ per puppy fine will be paid to the Seller.

5. If Buyer should ever decide that he can no longer keep this Dalmatian for whatever reason, Seller shall have the right of first refusal. Buyer shall offer said Dalmatian to Seller at a price equal to, or less, than that at which it will be sold to the general public. It is clearly stated and understood by the Buyer that returning the Dalmatian with its papers and acceptance by the Seller does not implicitly imply a refund or repurchase by the Seller. The Buyer agrees that any repurchase or refund by the Seller which might be agreed to, will be effected by costs of placing the Dalmatian in another home, retraining and any other costs incurred by the Seller subsequent to the return of the Dalmatian. Therefore, only written offers from the Seller to the Buyer will be honored. Expressly prohibited are any obligations on the Seller by the Buyer based on alleged verbal statements. The "re-purchase" of said Dalmatian and its papers by the Seller automatically voids any controls held by the Buyer.

SALES AGREEMENT (continued)

Said offer shall be made by certified mail, return receipt requested, and Buyer shall not sell the Dalmatian for 15 days after receipt of notice by Seller, and Seller shall have that 15 days in which to respond to Buyer's sales offer. If Seller does not respond or declines to purchase the Dalmatian, Buyer shall be free at the end of the 15 day waiting period to sell said Dalmatian to another person at not less than the price offered to Seller. Buyer and Seller shall keep each other advised of their current addresses. Buyer may not sell any Dalmatian from which Seller is entitled to puppies or stud service unless legal provisions are made to secure Seller's rights to the stud services or puppies due, or Seller has been paid compensation of $_____ per stud service and $_____ per puppy due.

6. Buyer swears he is not acting as an agent in the purchase of this Dalmatian and that he will not sell this Dalmatian to any agent, pet store, guard dog business or research facility. Buyer also agrees this animal will not be used as a guard dog for any business and will not be chained or attack-trained.

7. Special conditions: _____

_____

_____

_____

_____

_____

8. ENTIRE AGREEMENT - It is understood and agreed that Buyer by signing this form has read and understands the provisions of this contract. Furthermore, this written agreement constitutes all the conditions of the sale and no verbal statements either before or after the sale will be binding in any way.

9. A deposit of $_____ reserves said Dalmatian for Buyer until _____ at which time Buyer will pay the balance of the purchase price in cash and take delivery of the Dalmatian, or Buyer's deposit will be forfeited and Seller shall be free to sell the Dalmatian to another buyer. The undersigned have read this agreement, understand it, and agree to perform its terms on the day and date written below. This agreement shall not be in effect until both signatures are affixed and deposit has been accepted.

_____   _____

Signature of Buyer (^)   Date

_____   _____

Signature of Seller (^)   Date

ETHICAL GUIDELINES - THE DALMATIAN CLUB OF AMERICA

1. To become educated in the fundamentals of owning, breeding and exhibiting dogs.

2. To understand the basic laws of genetics, the standard of the breed and the difference between the correct and incorrect before attempting to breed.

3. To register all breeding stock with the American Kennel Club and to keep accurate records of all matings, litters and pedigrees.

4. To follow good business practices and ethics in breeding contracts and to honor all agreements. Written agreements are encouraged.

5. To transfer puppies only after they have reached at least six weeks of age, to provide at least a three-generation pedigree and to insure that the buyer has the physical facilities to care for a dog.

6. To insure that puppies or adults are never knowingly sold or consigned to pet stores, wholesalers or commercial dealers. To not knowingly supply dogs for raffles, giveaways, prizes or other such projects.

7. To insure that all advertising is factual and not misleading. Never to engage in malicious criticism and to separate fact from fiction before repeating comments heard from others.

8. To adhere to the rules of the AKC while exhibiting, to practice the principles of good sportsmanship and to consider competitors as a challenge, not a threat.

9. To insure that all dogs are provided adequate food, shelter and medical care.

10. To insure that while engaged in the art and science of judging, that the only influence will be the quality of the animals to be judged.

11. To always insure that actions be directed toward the best interests of the Dalmatian Breed, the Dalmatian Club of America and the American Kennel Club.

DISCLAIMER

The Dalmatian Club of America is in no way responsible or liable, financially or otherwise, because of the use of this contract form by its members or by non-members who obtain and use it.

THE BREED STANDARD

The First Dalmatian Standard—1921

Recommended by the Dalmatian Club

The Head should be of a fair length, the skull flat, rather broad between the ears and moderately well defined at the temples, i.e., exhibiting a moderate amount of stop and not in one straight line from the nose to the occiput bone, as required in a Bull Terrier. It should be entirely free from wrinkle.

The Muzzle should be long and powerful; the lips clean, fitting the jaws moderately close.

The Eyes should be set moderately well apart, and of medium size, round, bright and sparkling, with an intelligent expression, their color greatly depending on the markings of the dog. In the black-spotted variety the eyes should be dark (black or brown); in the liver-spotted variety they should be light (yellow or light brown). Wall eyes are permissible.

The rim around the Eyes in the black-spotted variety should be black; in the liver-spotted variety, brown—never flesh colored in either.

The Ears should be set on rather high, of moderate size, rather wide at the base and gradually tapering to a rounded point. They should be carried close to the head, be thin and fine in texture, and always spotted, the more profusely the better.

The Nose in the black-spotted variety should always be black; in the liver-spotted variety, always brown.

Neck and Shoulders.—The neck should be fairly long, nicely arched, light and tapering, and entirely free from throatiness.

The shoulders should be moderately oblique, clean and muscular, denoting speed.

Body, Back Chest and Loins.—The chest should not be too wide, but very deep and capacious, ribs moderately well sprung, never rounded like barrel hoops (which would indicate want of speed); back powerful; loin strong, muscular, and slightly arched.

Legs and Feet of great importance. The fore legs should be perfectly straight, strong and heavy in bone; elbows close to the body; feet compact, with well arched toes, and tough, elastic pads. In the hind legs the muscles should be clean, though well defined; the hocks well let down.

Nails in the black-spotted variety, black and white; in the liver-spotted variety, brown and white.

The Tail should not be too long, strong at the insertion, and gradually tapering towards the end, free from coarseness. It should not be inserted too low down, but carried with a slight curve upwards, and never curled. It should be spotted, the more profusely the better.

The Coat short, hard, dense and fine, sleek and glossy in appearance, but neither woolly nor silky.

Color and Markings—These are most important points. The ground color in both varieties should be pure white, very decided and not intermixed. The color of the spots in the black-spotted variety should be black, the deeper and richer the black the better; in the liver-spotted variety they should be brown. The spots should not intermingle, but be as round and well defined as possible, the more distinct the better; in size they should be from that of a dime to a half dollar. The spots on the face, head, ears, legs, tail and extremities to be smaller than those on the body.

Size—Height of dogs and bitches between 19 and 23 inches; weight, between 35 and 50 lbs.

General Appearance—The Dalmatian should represent a strong, muscular and active dog, symmetrical in outline and free from coarseness and lumber, capable of great endurance, combined with a fair amount of speed.

SCALE OF POINTS

Head and eyes	10
Ears	5
Neck and shoulders	10
Body, back, chest, and loins	10
	35
Legs and feet	15
Coat	5
Color and markings	30
Tail	5
Size, symmetry, etc.	10
	65
GRAND TOTAL	100

The 1950 Dalmatian Standard

The Head should be of a fair length, the skull flat, rather broad between the ears, and moderately well defined at the temple, i.e., exhibiting a moderate amount of stop, and not in one straight line from the nose to the occiput bone, as required in a Bull Terrier. It should be entirely free from wrinkle.

The Muzzle should be long and powerful; the lips clean, fitting the jaws moderately close.

The Eyes should be set moderately well apart, and of medium size, round, bright and sparkling with an intelligent expression, their color greatly depending on the markings of the dog. In the black-spotted variety the eyes should be dark (black or brown); in the liver-spotted variety they should be light (yellow or light brown). Wall eyes are permissible.

The rim around the Eyes in the black-spotted variety should be black; in the liver-spotted variety, brown—never flesh colored in either.

The Ears should be set rather high, of moderate size, rather wide at the base and gradually tapering to a rounded point.

They should be carried close to the head, be thin and fine in texture and always be spotted, the more profusely the better.

The Nose in the black-spotted variety should always be black; in the liver-spotted variety, always brown.

Neck and Shoulders—The neck should be fairly long, nicely arched, light and tapering, and entirely free from throatiness. The shoulders should be moderately oblique, clean and muscular, denoting speed.

Body, Back, Chest and Loins—The chest should not be too wide, but very deep and capacious, ribs moderately well sprung, never rounded like barrel hoops (which would indicate want of speed); back powerful; loin strong, muscular and slightly arched.

Legs and Feet of great importance. The fore legs should be perfectly straight, strong and heavy in bone; elbows close to the body; feet compact, well arched toes and tough, elastic pads. In the hind legs the muscles should be clean, though well defined; the hocks well let down.

Nails, in the black-spotted variety, black and white; in the liver-spotted variety, brown and white.

Gait: Length of stride should be in proportion to the size of the dog; steady in rhythm of 1,2,3,4 as in the cadence count in military drill. Front legs should not paddle, nor should there be a straddling appearance. Hind legs should neither cross nor weave; judges should be able to see each leg move with no interference of another leg. Drive and reach are most desirable.

The Tail should not be too long, strong at the insertion, and gradually tapering towards the end, free from coarseness. It should not be inserted too low down, but carried with a slight curve upwards and never curled. It should be spotted, the more profusely the better.

The Coat, short, hard, dense and fine, sleek and glossy in appearance, but neither woolly nor silky.

Color and Markings.—These are most important points. The ground color in both varieties should be pure white, very decided and not intermixed. The color of the spots in the black-spotted variety should be black, the deeper and richer the black the better; in the liver-spotted variety they should be brown. The spots should not intermingle, but be as round and well defined as possible, the more distinct the better; in size they should be from that of a dime to a half-dollar. The spots on the face, head, ears, legs, tail and extremities to be smaller than those on the body.

Size—Height of dogs and bitches between 19 and 23 inches; weight, between 35 and 50 pounds.

General Appearance—The Dalmatian should represent a strong, muscular and active dog, symmetrical in outline and free from coarseness and lumber, capable of great endurance, combined with a fair amount of speed.

SCALE OF POINTS

Head and Eyes	10
Ears	5
Neck and Shoulders	10
Body, Back, Chest and Loins	10
Gait	10
Legs and Feet	10
Coat	5
Color and Markings	25
Tail	5
Size, Symmetry, etc.	10
GRAND TOTAL	100

The 1962 Dalmatian Standard

The Dalmatian should represent a strong, muscular, and active dog; poised and alert; free of shyness; intelligent in expression; symmetrical in outline; and free from coarseness and lumber. He should be capable of great endurance, combined with a fair amount of speed.

Head—Should be a fair length, the skull flat, proportionately broad between the ears, and moderately well defined at the temples, and not in one straight line from the nose to the occiput bone as required in a Bull Terrier. It should be entirely free from wrinkle. *Muzzle*—Should be long and powerful—the lips clean. The mouth should have a scissors bite. Never undershot or overshot. It is permissible to trim whiskers. *Eyes*—Should be set moderately well apart, and of medium size, round, bright, and sparkling, with an intelligent expression; their color greatly depending on the markings of the dog. In the black-spotted variety the eyes should be dark (black or brown or blue). In the liver-spotted variety they should be lighter than in the black-spotted variety (golden or light brown or blue). The rim around the eyes in the black-spotted variety should be black; in the liver-spotted variety, brown. Never flesh-colored in either. Lack of pigment is a major fault.

Ears—Should be set rather high, of moderate size, rather wide at the base, and gradually tapering to a rounded point. They should be carried close to the head, be thin and fine in texture, and preferably spotted. *Nose*—In the black-spotted variety should always be black; in the liver-spotted variety, always brown. A butterfly or flesh-colored nose is a major fault.

Neck and Shoulders—The neck should be fairly long, nicely arched, light and tapering, and entirely free from throatiness. The shoulders should be oblique, clean and muscular, denoting speed.

Body, Back, Chest and Loins—The chest should not be too wide, but very deep and capacious, ribs well sprung but never rounded like barrel hoops (which would indicate want of speed). Back powerful; long strong, muscular and slightly arched.

Legs and Feet—Of great importance. The forelegs should be straight, strong, and heavy in bone; elbows close to the body; feet compact, well-arched toes, and tough, elastic pads. In the hind legs the muscles should be clean, though well

defined; the hocks well let down. Dewclaws may be removed from legs. *Nails*—In the black-spotted variety, black or white; or a nail may be both black and white. In the liver-spotted variety, brown or white; or a nail may be both brown and white.

Gait—Length of stride should be in proportion of the size of the dog, steady in rhythm of 1, 2, 3, 4 as in the cadence count in military drill. Front legs should not paddle, nor should there be a straddling appearance. Hind legs should neither cross nor weave; judges should be able to see each leg move with no interference of another leg. Drive and reach are most desirable. Cowhocks are a major fault.

Tail—Should ideally reach the hock joint, strong at the insertion, and tapering toward the end, free from coarseness. It should not be inserted too low down, but carried with a slight curve upwards, and never curled.

Coat—Should be short, hard, dense, and fine, sleek and glossy in appearance, but neither woolly nor silky.

Color and Markings—Are most important points. The ground color in both varieties should be pure white, very decided, and not intermixed. The color of the spots in the black-spotted variety should be dense black; in the liver-spotted variety they should be liver brown. The spots should not intermingle, but be as round and well defined as possible, the more distinct the better. In size they should be from that of a dime to a half-dollar. The spots on the face, head, ears, legs, and tail to be smaller than those on the body. Patches, tri-colors, and any color markings other than black or liver constitute a disqualification. A true patch is a solid, sharply defined mass of black or liver that is appreciably larger than any of the markings on the dog. Several spots that are so adjacent that they actually touch one another at their edges do not constitute a patch.

Size—The desirable height of dogs and bitches is between 19 and 23 inches at the withers, and any dog or bitch over 24 inches at the withers is to be disqualified.

Major Faults

Butterfly or flesh-colored nose. Cowhocks. Flat feet. Lack of pigment in eye rims. Shyness. Trichiasis (abnormal position or direction of the eyelashes).

Faults

Ring or low-set tail. Undersize or oversize.

```
SCALE OF POINTS
    Body, back, chest and loins ......................................... 10
    Coat .......................................................................... 5
    Color and markings .................................................. 25
    Ears ........................................................................... 5
    Gait .......................................................................... 10
    Head and eyes ......................................................... 10
    Legs and feet ........................................................... 10
    Neck and shoulders ................................................. 10
    Size, symmetry, etc. ............................................... 10
    Tail ............................................................................. 5
    Total ........................................................................ 100
```

The 1989 Dalmatian Standard

General Appearance—The Dalmatian is distinctively spotted dog; poised and alert; strong, muscular and active; free of shyness; intelligent in expression; symmetrical in outline; and without exaggeration or coarseness. The Dalmatian is capable of great endurance, combined with a fair amount of speed.

Deviations from the described ideal should be penalized in direct proportion to the degree of deviation.

Size, Proportion, Substance—Desirable height at the withers is between 19 and 23 inches. Undersize or oversize is a fault. Any dog or bitch over 24 inches at the withers is disqualified.

The overall length of the body from the forechest to the buttocks is approximately equal to the height at the withers.

The Dalmatian has good substance and is strong and sturdy in bone, but never coarse.

Head—The head is in balance with the overall dog. It is of fair length and is free of loose skin. The Dalmatian's *expression* is alert and intelligent, indicating a stable and outgoing temperament.

The *eyes* are set moderately well apart, are medium sized and somewhat rounded in appearance, and are set well into the skull. Eye color is brown or blue, or any combination thereof; the darker the better and usually darker in black-spotted than in liver-spotted dogs.

Abnormal position of the eyelids or eyelashes (ectropion, entropion, trichiasis) is a major fault.

The *ears* are of moderate size, proportionately wide at the base and gradually tapering to a rounded tip. They are set rather high, are carried close to the head, and are thin and fine in texture. When the Dalmatian is alert, the top of the ear is level with the top of the skull and the tip of the ear reaches to the bottom line of the cheeks.

The top of the skull is flat with a slight vertical furrow and is approximately as wide as it is long. The *stop* is moderately well defined. The cheeks blend smoothly into a powerful *muzzle*, the top of which is level and parallel to the top of the skull. The muzzle and the top of the skull are about equal in length.

The *nose* is completely pigmented on the leather, black in black-spotted dogs and brown in liver-spotted dogs. Incomplete nose pigmentation is a major fault.

The lips are clean and close fitting. The teeth meet in a scissors bite. Overshot or undershot bites are disqualifications.

Neck, Topline, Body—The *neck* is nicely arched, fairly long, free from throatiness, and blends smoothly into the shoulders.

The *topline* is smooth.

The *chest* is deep, capacious and of moderate width, having good spring of rib without being barrel shaped. The brisket reaches to the elbow. The underline of the rib cage curves gradually into a moderate tuck-up.

The *back* is level and strong. The loin is short, muscular and slightly arched. The flanks narrow through the loin. The *croup* is nearly level with the back.

The *tail* is a natural extension of the topline. It is not inserted too low down. It is strong at the insertion and tapers to the tip, which reaches to the hock. It is never docked. The tail is carried with a slight upward curve but should never curl over the back. Ring tails and low-set tails are faults.

Forequarters—The *shoulders* are smoothly muscled and well laid back. The *upper arm* is approximately equal in length to the shoulder blade and joins it at an angle sufficient to insure that the foot falls under the shoulder. The *elbows* are close to the body. The *legs* are straight, strong and sturdy in bone. There is a slight angle at the *pastern* denoting flexibility.

Hindquarters—The *hindquarters* are powerful, having smooth, yet well defined muscles. The *stifle* is well bent. The *hocks* are well let down. When the Dalmatian is standing, the hind legs, viewed from the rear, are parallel to each other from the point of the hock to the heel of the pad. Cowhocks are a major fault.

Feet—*Feet* are very important. Both front and rear feet are round and compact with thick, elastic pads and well arched toes. Flat feet are a major fault. Toenails are black and/or white in black-spotted dogs and brown and/or white in liver-spotted dogs. Dewclaws may be removed.

Coat—The *coat* is short, dense, fine and close fitting. It is neither woolly nor silky. It is sleek, glossy and healthy in appearance.

Color and Markings—*Color and markings* and their overall appearance are very important points to be evaluated.

The ground color is pure white. In black-spotted dogs the spots are dense black. In liver-spotted dogs the spots are liver brown. Any color markings other than black or liver are disqualified.

Spots are round and well defined, the more distinct the better. They vary from the size of a dime to the size of a half-dollar. They are pleasingly and evenly distributed. The less the spots intermingle the better. Spots are usually smaller on the head, legs and tail than on the body. Ears are preferably spotted.

Tri-color (which occurs rarely in this breed) is a disqualification. It consists of tan markings found on the head, neck, chest, leg or tail of a black-or liver-spotted dog. Bronzing of black spots and fading and/or darkening of liver spots due to environmental conditions or normal processes of coat change are not tri-coloration.

Patches are a disqualification. A patch is a solid mass of black or liver hair containing no white hair. It is appreciably larger than a normal sized spot. Patches are a dense, brilliant color with sharply defined smooth edges. Patches are present at birth. Large color masses formed by intermingled or overlapping spots are not patches. Such masses should indicate individual spots by uneven edges and/or white hairs scattered throughout the mass.

Gait—In keeping with the Dalmatian's historical use as a coach dog, gait and endurance are of great importance. Movement is steady and effortless. Balanced angulation fore and aft combined with powerful muscles and good condition produce smooth, efficient action. There is a powerful drive from the rear, coordinated with extended reach in the front. The topline remains level. Elbows, hocks and feet turn neither in nor out. As the speed of the trot increases, there is a tendency to single track.

Temperament—The temperament is stable and outgoing, yet dignified. Shyness is a major fault.

DISQUALIFICATIONS

Any dog or bitch over 24 inches at the withers.
Overshot or undershot bite.
Any color markings other than black or liver.
Tri-color.
Patches.
Approved July 11, 1989
Effective September 6, 1989

SCALE OF POINTS

General Appearance	5
Size, Proportion, Substance	10
Head	10
Neck, Topline, Body	10
Forequarters	5
Hindquarters	5
Feet	5
Coat	5
Color and Markings	25
Gait	10
Temperament	10
Total	100

DALMATIAN ROAD TRIAL REGULATIONS

Purpose

Road Trials are sport and all participants should be guided by the principles of good sportsmanship at all times. The purpose of a Road Trial is to demonstrate the use of pure-bred Dalmatians as a companion of man in the role that they have been bred to perform. The Dalmatian Standard states that the Dalmatian "should be capable of great endurance, combined with a fair amount of speed" qualities essential to his successful use as a horse/rider and horse/coach escort. A Dalmatian Road Trial is a performance event that provides a means of determining the degree to which these qualities are present.

All entrants are required to perform the same exercises over the same course so that the relative quality of the various performances may be compared and scored. Road Trials demonstrate Dalmatians' ability to behave in public places such as riding trails in the presence of other dogs in a manner that will reflect credit on the sport and on pure-bred dogs. The performance of dog and handler over the Road Trial course must be accurate and correct and must conform to the requirements of these regulations. However, it is also essential that the dog demonstrate willingness and enjoyment of his work throughout.

Chapter 1—General Regulations

SECTION 1. **Compliance with Regulations and Standards.** In accordance with the certification on the entry form, the handler of each dog and the person signing each entry form must be familiar with these Road Trial Regulations and by entering the Road Trial agrees to comply with said regulations.

SECTION 2. **Risk.** The owner or agent entering any dog and horse in a Road Trial does so at his own risk and agrees to abide by the rules of the American Kennel Club and the Road Trial regulations. The host club, group, or individual, its Road Trial Committee, and any and all of its members or officers shall not be responsible for or assume any liability in the event of any accident or misfortune, to either dogs, horses, exhibitors, or escorts participating in the Road Trial.

The host club, individual, or group shall reserve the right to determine an exhibitor's riding ability before allowing him to compete in their road trial. Should it be determined by the host that a rider might present a safety hazard to himself, his horse, or others, he may be excused from competition and his entry fee shall be refunded.

It shall be the exhibitor's responsibility to determine which medical inoculations are deemed necessary for his dogs and horse for the geographic area of a particular Road Trial. He may be required to show veterinary certificates of certain inoculations as specified in each Road Trial's premium list.

SECTION 3. **Equipment.** Exhibitors and escorts shall be required to wear safety riding helmets and riding boots or shoes with at least a 1/2 inch heel.

SECTION 4. **Use of Collar and Leash.** All dogs shall be kept on leash in the Start/Finish ring and exercise ring. Dogs should be brought to the course start on a leash. When each handler is ready to start on the course and when the judge is ready to start judging, the steward shall remove the leash and/or collar and place them behind the judge's table and shall return them to his handler as the course is completed. There shall be collars and leashes available at the Mid-Point Veterinarian check for exhibitors to use on each dog during his gaiting and veterinary examination.

No dogs shall be allowed to run on the course wearing a choke, prong, shock, or any other type of training collar, but a plain buckle collar may be worn at the handler's discretion. If wide, color-coded collars are used as the means of identifying each dog, the fabric should be lightweight, such as windsock material, and be fastened with Velcro or other such fastener that would yield should the dog become entangled on the course. It is advisable that each dog wear some means of identification such as a tattoo or tags.

Dogs should be kept on a leash when brought into the ring to receive awards.

SECTION 5. **Road Trial Hosts.** An all-breed dog show club may be granted permission to hold a Licensed or Member Road Trial in conjunction with its dog show; and a Dalmatian specialty club, any other group of Dalmatian fanciers, or individual may also be granted permission to hold a Licensed or Member Road Trial if, in the opinion of the Board of Directors of the Dalmatian Club of America, such club, group, or individual is qualified to do so.

A club may hold a Road Trial on the same day as its show or obedience trial, and the Road Trial may be announced in the premium list for the show or trial, and the Road Trial entries may be included in the show or obedience trial catalog. If the entries are not listed in the catalog for the show or obedience trial, the club must provide, at the Road Trial several copies of a typewritten sheet or sheets (the Road Trial Pamphlet) giving all the information that would be contained in the catalog for each dog.

If the Road Trial is to be held within seven days of the show or obedience trial, the entries may be sent to the same person designated to receive the show or obedience Trial entries, and the same closing date should apply. If the Road Trial is not to be held within seven days of the show or obedience trial, the club may name someone else in the premium list to receive the Road Trial entries, and may specify a different closing date for entries.

SECTION 6. **Road Trial Committee.** A Road Trial Committee must be appointed by the trial host and this committee shall exercise all the authority vested in dog show's bench show committee. If a dog show or obedience club holds its Road Trial in conjunction with a dog show, then the Road Trial Committee shall have sole jurisdiction only over those dogs entered in the Road Trial and their handlers and owners and only on the day of the Road Trial.

SECTION 7. **DCA Sanction.** Dalmatian Club of America sanction must be obtained by any club that holds a Road Trial in order for entrants in that trial to be eligible for existing challenge trophies and/or DCA Certificates of Participation.

SECTION 8. **Dog Show Rules.** All the American Kennel Club Dog Show Rules, where applicable, shall govern the conduct of Road Trials, and shall apply to all persons and dogs participating in them except as these Road Trial Regulations may provide otherwise.

SECTION 9. **Unentered Dogs.** Only dogs entered in the Road Trial shall be allowed within the show precincts, except dogs being used for the distraction exercise; dogs acting as official mascots, such as to escort the carriage or vehicle carrying judges and stewards to points along the course, or dogs confined to a specific crating area as designated by the road trial host.

There shall be no benching, offering for sale, breeding, or displaying of unentered dogs. If a club wishes to allow the presence of dogs in a particular area of the show precincts, these dogs shall be subject to all rules relating to health and conduct. The owners or agents shall be responsible for the care and safety of such dogs.

SECTION 10. **Unentered Riders.** An exhibitor is encouraged to choose for safety and enjoyment to have an unentered companion ride with him on the course. This escort may not at any time give commands or signals to any of the entered dogs and must ride and behave in such away as to not interfere with the exhibitor, his dog(s), horse(s), or carriage; the Mounted Judge or the Mounted Judge's line of vision; or the Course Judge or the Course Judge's line of vision during any portion of the Road Trial. This escort shall be subject to act in accordance with AKC Rules & Regulations governing dog shows.

SECTION 11. **Identification.** No badges, club jackets, coats with kennel names, or other identifying logos, markings, names, or ribbon prizes may be worn or displayed by an individual when exhibiting a dog in the ring or on the course. Dogs shall be identified on the course solely by either color-coded lightweight jackets or wide color-coded collars. Handlers shall be identified by a large number worn on their backs. Identification numbers worn by dogs and handlers shall be clearly visible to the judges and veterinarians. The catalog or Road Trial Pamphlet shall indicate both handler numbers and colors assigned to each of the dogs being handled. The numbers or colors assigned by the Road Trial Committee for each member of each team shall be printed in the show catalog or Road Trial Pamphlet. In the case of an exhibitor handling a single dog, the number displayed on the exhibitor may serve as sufficient identification for the dog.

SECTION 12. **Multiple Entries.** Each handler may enter up to six dogs on a single team in a Road Trial, and may enter up to two teams, but each team must be submitted as a separate entry and drawn by lot in accordance with Chapter 1, Sections 13 and 15.

SECTION 13. **Limitation of Entries.** The number of entries in a Road Trial shall be limited according to the starting time and the number of hours of light during the day of the trial, with teams leaving the starting line at approximate half-hour intervals, and with the last RD team leaving the starting line within three hours of expected time of dusk, or the last RDX team leaving the starting line within six hours of the expected time of dusk, dusk being defined as one hour after sunset.

After determining the maximum number of entries that can be judged at a particular Road Trial, which shall be designated in the premium list, and after the closing date for entries has passed, the Road Trial Committee shall conduct a drawing to determine which entries shall be eligible to compete and shall also select five alternates. Alternates shall be eligible to compete in the Road Trial should any entrant cancel or fail to appear by 7 A.M. on the day of the trial.

Those entrants selected to compete and the given alternates shall be notified by mail within five days of the closing date for entries and entry fees to all other entries shall be refunded. Entrants are encourage to notify the Road Trial Committee as soon as possible if they cannot compete so that an alternate can be notified as far in advance as possible. If an entrant should cancel after the closing date, no entry fees shall be refunded, except where an alternate has been selected and shall compete in his place, in which case one-half of the entry fee shall be refunded to the original entrant. Entry fees shall be returned to the alternates within five days of the trial should the alternates not have the opportunity to compete.

SECTION 14. **Change in Judges.** If for any reason an announced Road Trial judge is unable to complete his assignment, an alternate judge shall be named. Notification of this change shall be promptly made to the owner of each entry and the owner shall be permitted to withdraw such entry within seven days prior to the day of the show and the entry fee shall then be refunded. Should the change occur any time within seven days of the trial, withdrawn entries shall also be allowed and the entry fee(s) refunded.

SECTION 15. **Order of Running.** After the closing date for entries has passed and the entries have been selected with five alternates chosen, and prior to the printing of the show catalog or Road Trial Pamphlet, the Road Trial Committee shall draw by lot the order in which handlers shall begin the trial with their dog(s) and numbers and colors shall be assigned accordingly, as much as practical with the following considerations.

Each handler of two separate groups of dogs shall have submitted two separate entry forms indicating the grouping of dogs as he plans to run them, and the order of running shall allow him sufficient time to complete each course before being required to start with a subsequent group.

Carriage entrants competing on the 25-mile course shall be run first followed by horseback entrants competing on the 25-mile course, followed by carriage entrants on the 12.5-mile course, followed by horseback entrants on the 12.5-mile course.

Bitches in season, whether competing in the RDX or the RD class, shall be run last and in keeping with Chapter 1, Section 19 of these regulations.

SECTION 16. **Catalog Order.** Dogs should be judged in catalog or Road Trial Pamphlet order. It is the responsibility of each exhibitor to be ready with his dog(s) and horse at the Start/Finish Veterinarian ringside when required, without being called, and allowing time for the starting veterinary checks to be completed before his scheduled start time. The final veterinary check of dogs that have completed the course shall take precedence over dogs on teams that are just starting on the course. At the Start/Finish Veterinarian's discretion, he may request that an exhibitor whose dogs are ready and waiting at his ring be examined ahead of an exhibitor who is causing a delay. Once the starting veterinary check has been completed on each team, it is the responsibility of each handler to proceed immediately to the course starting line and await instructions by the Mounted Judge or the Start/Finish Steward. At the Mounted Judge's or the Start/Finish Steward's discretion, he may request that an exhibitor who is ready and waiting at the starting line be judged ahead of an exhibitor who has delayed proceeding to the starting line. At the Mounted Judge's or the Start/Finish Steward's discretion, and if agreeable to the Exhibitor, a team may start out on the course before the half-hour time interval from the departure of the preceding team has elapsed. Such early departure by one team shall not necessitate subsequent teams' being at the starting line before their scheduled start times.

SECTION 17. **Pure-bred Dalmatians Only.** As used in these regulations, the word "dog" refers to either sex but only to Dalmatians that are pure-bred and eligible for registration in the American Kennel Club stud book or a limited registration. An eligible unregistered dog for which an ILP number has been issued by the American Kennel Club may also be entered in such events provided the ILP number is shown on each entry form.

SECTION 18. **Dogs That May Not Compete.** No dog belonging wholly or in part to a judge, veterinarian, the Road Trial Secretary, Superintendent, or to any member of such a person's immediate family or household, shall be entered in any Road Trial, nor may any of these officials handle or act as agent for any dog entered in the Road Trial at which such person officiates or is scheduled to officiate.

No dogs shall be entered or shown under a judge at a Road Trial if the dog has been owned, sold, held under lease, handled in the ring, boarded or has been regularly trained or instructed, whether professionally or as amateurs, by the judge or by any member of his immediate family or household within six months prior to the date of the Road Trial, and no such dog shall be eligible to compete.

If the Road Trial is held within seven days of a dog show or obedience trial given by the same dog show or obedience club as gave the Road Trial, the Road Trial judges shall be eligible to compete in such dog show and/or obedience trial.

SECTION 19. **Disqualification and Ineligibility.** A dog that is blind or deaf or that has been changed in appearance by artificial means other than neutering may not compete in any Road Trial, and must be disqualified. Blind means without useful vision. Deaf means without useful hearing.

When a judge finds any of these conditions in any dog he is judging, he shall also obtain the opinion of one of the Road Trial veterinarians or when a veterinarian finds any of the conditions in any dog, he shall disqualify the dog, marking his book "Disqualified" and stating the reason. In the case of a disagreement, the opinion of the Road Trial veterinarian shall carry.

A judge or veterinarian must disqualify any dog that attempts to attack any person or horse on the grounds and the dog shall be immediately removed from the course. It is the handler's responsibility to immediately remove his excused dog from the course, and he must do so before continuing to compete with any other dog(s). A judge or veterinarian may excuse a dog that attacks another dog or that appears dangerous to other dogs on the course and require that this dog be immediately removed from the course. He shall mark the dog "Disqualified" or "Excused" and state the reason in his book and shall give the Superintendent or Show or Trial Secretary a brief report of the dog's actions, which shall be submitted to DCA with the report of the trial.

All awards made to any disqualified or excused dog at the Road Trial shall be canceled by the Dalmatian Club of America and the dog may not again compete unless and until, following application by the owner to the DCA Road Trial Committee, the owner has received official notification from the committee that the dog's eligibility has been reinstated.

Spayed bitches, castrated dogs, monorchid or cryptorchid males, and dogs that have faults which would disqualify them under the breed standard for Dalmatians may compete in Road Trials if otherwise eligible under these regulations.

A dog or a horse that is lame or otherwise unsound may not compete in a Road Trial. It shall be the Start/Finish Veterinarian's responsibility to determine whether a dog or a horse is lame or otherwise unsound before he starts out on the course and after he has completed the course. It shall be the Mid-Point Veterinarian's responsibility to determine whether a dog or horse is lame or otherwise unsound after he has completed approximately half of the course distance.

If in the Start/Finish Veterinarian's opinion or the Mid-Course Veterinarian's opinion a dog or horse is lame or otherwise unsound, the animal shall not be allowed to compete or to continue to compete and the official judge's book shall be marked "Excused-lame".

The Mounted Judge and the Course Judge may also at any point make a determination that a dog or horse is lame or otherwise unsound and shall immediately excuse the dog or horse from further competition.

Bitches in season shall be allowed to

compete if scheduling permits them to be run last, but they must be run last and at the owner's risk. It shall be the handler's responsibility to notify the Road Trial Committee by 7 A.M. on the day of the Road Trial if his bitch is in season. If in the opinion of either veterinarian or judge any bitch is in season whose handler has not notified the Show Committee by 7 A.M. on the day of the trial, the handler and bitch shall be barred from the competition and the official judge's book shall be marked, "Excused, in season, not reported."

No dog less that one year old may compete in an RD class and no dog less than one and one-half years old may compete in an RDX class at a Road Trial.

SECTION 20. **Disturbances.** Either of the judges or veterinarians of a Road Trial must remove from competition any dog or horse which its handler cannot control and may excuse from competition any dog or horse which he considers unfit to compete. The handler shall be immediately advised verbally that his dog or horse has been excused. If a dog or horse has been excused, the reason shall be stated on both the particular judge or veterinarian score sheet who excused the dog or horse and on the aggregate score sheet.

If a horse has been excused, the exhibitor shall be allowed to substitute another mount if such substitute mount is available within the time frame that would allow the exhibitor to complete the course within his originally allotted time.

Either judge or veterinarian may excuse from competition any handler who interferes willfully with another competitor or his dog or horse, any handler who abuses his dog or horse on the course, or any exhibitor who displays behavior contrary to the principles of good sportsmanship. Foul or abusive language by any exhibitor or exhibitor's escort in a Road Trial shall not be tolerated.

If a handler is expelled or excused by a judge or a Road Trial veterinarian, the reason shall be stated in the judge's book or in a separate report, and the exhibitor shall be prohibited from competing in future Road Trials until the matter has been resolved to the satisfaction of the DCA Road Trial Committee.

SECTION 21. **Misbehavior.** Any unusual display of fear or nervousness by the dog, or any uncontrolled behavior of the dog such as snapping; barking, except for a bark that warns of an impending danger; or running away, except that a dog starts after game encountered on the course but willingly returns on command; whether it occurs during a specific exercise or anywhere on the course, must be penalized according to the seriousness of the misbehavior, and the judge or veterinarian may excuse the dog from further competition. If such behavior occurs during an exercise, the penalty must first be applied to the score for that exercise. Should the penalty be greater than the value of the exercise during which it is incurred, the additional points shall be deducted from the total score under Misbehavior. If such behavior occurs before or after the judging or between exercises, the entire penalty shall be deducted from the total score.

SECTION 22. **Training on the Grounds.** There shall be no drilling nor intensive or abusive training of dogs on the grounds or premises at a Road Trial. Special training collars shall not be used on the grounds or premises at a Road Trial. The judges shall not permit any handler to train his dog by excessive verbal commands or by moving toward the dog to correct it in any way, nor to practice any exercise on the course before or after he is being judged, and shall excuse from further competition in the Road Trial any dog whose handler does either. These requirements shall not be interpreted as preventing a handler from moving normally about the grounds or premises with his dog at heel on leash, nor from giving such signals or commands in a normal tone of voice as are necessary and usual in everyday life, but physical or verbal disciplining of dogs shall not be permitted except to a reasonable extent in the case of an attack on a person or another dog. Likewise, physical abuse of a horse shall not be permitted. A dog whose handler disciplines it in the ring or on the course shall be excused from further competition and shall not receive a Qualifying Score. Any abuse of a dog or a horse in the ring or on the course must be immediately reported by the judge to the Road Trial Committee for action under Chapter 1, Section 26. The Superintendent, Road Trial Secretary, and the members of the Road Trial Committee shall be responsible for compliance with this section and shall investigate any reports of infractions.

SECTION 23. **Abuse of Dogs or Horses.** The Road Trial Committee shall investigate any reports of abuse of dogs or horses or severe disciplining of dogs or horses on the grounds or premises of a show. Any person who, at a Road Trial, conducts himself in such manner or in any other manner prejudicial to the best interests of the sport, or who fails to comply with the requirements of Chapter 1, Section 21, shall be dealt with promptly, during the trial if possible, after the offender has been notified of the specific charges against him, and has been given an opportunity to be heard in his own defense in accordance with Chapter 1, Section 26. Any abuse of a dog or horse in the ring or on the course must be immediately reported by the judge or veterinarian to the Road Trial Committee for action under Chapter 1, Section 26 and the exhibitor shall be excused from competition.

SECTION 24. **Decisions.** At the Road Trial the decisions of a judge or veterinarian shall be final in all matters affecting the scoring and the working of the dogs and their handlers. The Road Trial committee shall decide all other matters arising at the trial, including protests against dogs made under Chapter 19 of the AKC Dog Show Rules, subject, however, to the Rules and Regulations of the American Kennel Club.

SECTION 25. **Stewards.** The judges and veterinarians are in sole charge of their particular area of judging. Stewards shall be provided to assist each judge and veterinarian, but they may act only on the judge's or veterinarian's instructions. Stewards shall not give information or instructions to owners and handlers except as specifically instructed by the judge or veterinarian, and then only in such a manner that it is clear that the instructions are those of the judge or veterinarian.

SECTION 25A. **Start/Finish Steward.** The Start/Finish Steward will, acting on the Start/Finish Veterinarian's and the Mounted Judge's instructions, be responsible for maintaining an orderly flow of teams into the Start/Finish Veterinarian's ring and then onto the course. The Start/Finish Steward shall also record the time each team crosses the starting line and the finish line.

SECTION 26. **Discipline.** The Dalmatian Club of America shall have the right to suspend any person from the privileges of DCA for conduct prejudicial to the best interests of pure-bred dogs, Road Trials, or the Dalmatian Club of America, alleged to have occurred in connection with or during the progress of its Road Trial, after the alleged offender has been given an opportunity to be heard.

Notice in writing must be sent promptly by registered mail or hand delivered by the Road Trial Committee to the person in charge and a duplicate notice giving the name and address of the person charged and full details as to the reasons for the charges must be forwarded to the Dalmatian Club of America within seven days.

An appeal may be taken from a decision of the DCA Board of Directors. Notice in writing claiming such appeal together with a deposit of twenty-five dollars ($25.00) must be sent to DCA within thirty days after the date of suspension. The Board of Directors may itself hear said appeal or may refer it to a committee of the Board, or to a Trial Board to be heard. The deposit shall become the property of the DCA if the decision is confirmed, or shall be returned to the appellant if the decision is not confirmed.

Chapter 2—Overall Regulations for Performance

SECTION 1. **Time Limits.** Teams shall be required to complete the 12.5-mile course excluding the Mid-Point Veterinarian check within a time limit of three hours. Teams shall be required to complete the 25-mile course, excluding the Mid-Point Veterinarian check within a time limit of six hours. Faster times do not produce higher scores; a Road Trial is not a race.

SECTION 2. **Qualifying Score.** A Qualifying Score shall be comprised of Pass Ratings (50—100) on each of the exercises (Recall, Hock, Distraction, Long Sit or Down, Speed); *plus* a Pass Rating by the veterinarians at each of the course's beginning, mid-point, and end; *plus* the dog's having completed the course portion of the trial within the designated time limit.

SECTION 3. **Hands.** In all exercises on the course the handler's arms and hands shall be in a natural riding or driving position.

SECTION 4. **Commands.** Whenever a command is mentioned in these regulations, a single verbal command is preferable to be given by the handler and will be scored accordingly, but any extra commands are permissible if needed to keep the dog(s) under voice control. A handler may praise his dog(s) during an exercise, or use a voice correction, but this should not be excessive. Delay in following a judge's order to give a command must be penalized, unless the delay is directed by the judge because of some distraction or interference. Any unusual noise or motion may be considered to be a correction.

The dog's name may be used once immediately before any verbal command. In the case of a handler exhibiting more than one dog at the same time, each dog's name may be used once immediately before each dog is given any verbal command.

Excessively loud or gruff commands by handlers to their dogs create a poor impression and should be avoided. Commands which in the judge's opinion are excessively loud or gruff will be penalized.

SECTION 5. **Praise.** Verbal praise is allowed during, between, and after exercises. A handler may not carry or offer food on the course, but may offer his dog a snack and water provided by the trial-giving club at the mid-course check point.

SECTION 6. **Hock Position.** Hock Position as used in these Regulations for a horse/rider team means that the dog shall be straight in line with the direction in which the handler and horse are facing, within one horse's length of the horse at any point in a semi-circle behind the horse's head as close as practicable without crowding or obstructing the horse's motion.

Hock Position for a Carriage Team shall mean that the dog shall be straight in line with the direction in which the carriage and driver are facing, either directly behind the horse(s)' heels and under the carriage, as close as practicable without crowding or obstructing the horse(s)' or carriage's motion, or within one horse's length of the horse or carriage at any point in a semi-circle behind the horse's head. For either a horse/rider team or a carriage team, the dog(s) shall not go ahead of the horse's head during the Hock or Distraction exercises.

Dogs on a team with multiple entries shall not be penalized for allowing space for other dogs in Hock Position.

SECTION 7. **Orders and Minimum Penalties.** The orders for the exercises and the standards for judging are set forth in Chapter 8. The list of faults is not intended to be complete but the more common and serious

faults are specified. There is no maximum limit on penalties. A dog which makes none of the errors listed may still fail to Qualify or may be scored zero for other reasons that were not specifically stated in Chapter 8, but these faults shall be described on the judges' score sheets.

Chapter 3—Course Set-Up and Ring Conditions

SECTION 1. **Ring Conditions.** The gaiting portion of the Start/Finish Veterinarian soundness exams shall ideally be conducted in an outdoor ring at least 30' wide and 30' long, preferably no more than $1/2$ mile from the start of the course. The gaiting portion of the Mid-Course Veterinarian exam shall be conducted on as level and wide a surface as is available. The ground in both cases shall be as clean and level as practical, and the grass, if any, should be cut short.

SECTION 2. **Warm-Up.** After leaving the starting line and before beginning the Exercises, each team shall be allowed approximately a one-quarter mile warm-up stretch to allow the dogs and horses to settle. This warm-up distance shall be measured as part of the overall distance.

SECTION 3. **Overall Course Layout.** The course for a road trial shall cover a distance of 12.5 miles for the RD classes and 25 miles for the RDX classes and shall be marked with readily visible direction indicators. Course layout is at the host's discretion, and any portion of a course may be repeated in order for exhibitors to fulfill the required distances.

SECTION 4. **Course Layout, Mounted Judge Exercises.** A specific area shall be designated by the road trial host for the Mounted Judge to conduct the exercises under his jurisdiction. It is preferable but not required that the portion of the road trial under jurisdiction of the Mounted Judge be as close to the starting lines as possible to still allow for the required $1/4$ mile warm-up.

For the hock exercise, there shall be yellow-flagged course markers on either side of the trial indicating the measured distance is near, followed by green-flagged trail markers indicating the start of the 200 yard hock exercise distance, followed by red-flagged trail markers indicating the completion of the hock exercise distance. These markers shall serve as a general guide, and the Mounted Judge's orders shall in all cases take precedence over the location of the trail markers.

SECTION 5. **Course Layout, Course Judge Speed Exercise.** A specific area of the course shall be designated for the Course Judge to conduct the Speed exercise. It is preferable but not required that the portion of the road trial course designated for the speed exercise be as close to the section of the course that was used for completion of the Mounted Judge exercises as possible.

For the Speed exercise, there shall be green-flagged trail markers indicating the start and red-flagged trail markers indicating the finish of the 100-yard distance that the exhibitors are required to gallop. This 100-yard stretch shall not go downhill, but shall be flat or cover a gentle upward slope. The ground shall be as smooth as possible and free of holes or other hazards.

The Course Judge shall be situated in such a way as not to frighten the horse at a mid-way, preferably elevated point, and his stewards shall be instructed to remain quiet and still during this exercise.

SECTION 6. **Spectator Area.** The host must designate and mark an area for spectators that will allow the spectators to watch without enabling them to distract or interfere in any way with the performance of the exhibitors or their dogs or horses while they are being judged.

SECTION 7. **Course Check-Point(s).** There shall be at least one steward or sign-in sheet posted along the course at whatever point(s) deemed necessary by the trial host in order to verify each team's completion of the required distance.

SECTION 8. **Review of Course.** Whenever possible, the host shall conduct a review of the course with the exhibitors, judges, and, if possible, veterinarians on the day before the road trial, and shall notify the exhibitors of the time and date of this course review within two weeks of the date. It shall be the exhibitor's responsibility to arrive at the road trial site in time to attend this course review, and the host shall not be required to conduct subsequent review for exhibitors who fail to attend the scheduled review.

Chapter 4—Awards and Prizes

SECTION 1. **DCA Certificates of Participation.** The Dalmatian Club of America shall offer Certificates of Participation to each exhibitor who competes in a board-approved Dalmatian Road Trial.

SECTION 2. **Road Trial Trophies.** For Road Trials held in conjunction with the Dalmatian Club of America's National Specialty Show, the same trophies shall be awarded for class placements in the Road Trial as are offered for regular classes held at the national specialty show. For Road Trials held at locations and dates other than the annual DCA National Specialty, the host shall provide the trophies to be awarded.

SECTION 3. **Challenge Trophies.** For Road Trials held in conjunction with the Dalmatian Club of America's National Specialty Show, challenge trophies may be offered as approved by the DCA Road Trial Committee. These challenge trophies shall be displayed during DCA week on the trophy table and shall be held for safekeeping by the DCA Permanent Trophy Chairman during the period between Road Trials held in conjunction with DCA Specialty Shows.

Parties who offer challenge trophies are encouraged to provide the trophy's winner at each Road Trial with a momento of the award that shall be for the winner's permanent possession.

SECTION 4. **Road Trial Ribbons.** At Licensed or Member Road Trials the following colors may be used for prize ribbons or rosettes:

First Prize	Blue
Second Prize	Red
Third Prize	Yellow
Fourth Prize	White
Qualifying Prize	Dark Green
Highest Scoring Dog	Blue and Gold

Each ribbon or rosette shall be at least two inches wide and at least eight inches long, and shall bear on its face a facsimile of the seal of the Dalmatian Club of America, the words "Dalmatian Road Trial," the name of the prize and class, the name of the trial host, the date of the trial, and the name of the city or town where the trial is held.

SECTION 5. **Ribbons and Prizes.** All official ribbons, DCA trophies, and challenge trophies shall be awarded only to dogs that earn Qualifying Scores in the Road Trial. Awards for the four placings in each class shall be based solely on the number of points earned.

At the trial host's discretion, a certificate, ribbon of participation, or other form of recognition or prize may be awarded to dogs who competed in the Road Trial but who did not receive a qualifying score.

SECTION 6. **Highest Scoring Dog in Road Trial.** The dog receiving the highest Qualifying Score in any class at a Road Trial shall be awarded the ribbon and any awards and prizes offered for this placement, after announcement of final scores of the last class to be judged and any run-offs have been conducted.

Chapter 5—Regulations for Road Trial Veterinary Checks

SECTION 1. **Start/Finish Veterinarian and Mid-Course Veterinarian.** There shall be a Start/Finish Veterinarian and a Mid-Course Veterinarian at Dalmatian Road Trials.

SECTION 2. **Requirements for Veterinarians.** Any reputable person who is in good standing with the American Kennel Club and who has been duly qualified to practice his profession by law may act as a veterinarian for a Road Trial. It is preferable that the person have experience with Dalmatians, either in owning, breeding, showing (conformation or obedience), providing veterinary service, or having been a member of a Dalmatian Specialty Club for at least two years.

SECTION 3. **Overall Duties and Responsibilities of Road Trial Veterinarians.** At least one of the veterinarians shall be in attendance during the entire progress of the road trial.

The duties and responsibilities of Road Trial Veterinarians shall include: giving advisory opinions to the judges when requested, examining the health and well-being of dogs, and rendering medical attention to dogs in cases of sickness or injury occurring at the Road Trial.

The veterinarians shall not be called on to treat dogs or horses for physical conditions that existed before they were brought to the Road Trial.

Either veterinarians serving at a Road Trial will have complete authority to: (a) excuse any dog which he considers may endanger the health or welfare of other dogs; (b) excuse any dog from being shown in the Road Trial when he considers that the dog would impair the

dog's health; (c) excuse any dog who is blind or deaf or who has been changed in appearance by artificial means; (d) excuse any dog that attacks any person, horse, or other dog as described in Chapter 1, Section 19 of these rules; (e) excuse any bitch in season that has not been reported as described in Chapter 1, Section 19 of these rules; and (f) excuse any exhibitor or exhibitor's escort who abuses his dog(s) or horse or who uses foul or abusive language.

SECTION 4. **Duties and Responsibilities of Start/Finish Veterinarian.** In addition to the overall duties and responsibilities, it shall be the responsibility of the Start/Finish Veterinarian to check the condition and soundness of each dog and horse both before he starts on the course and after he finishes the course.

The first evaluation shall serve to (a) determine the animal's health and soundness before being allowed to complete and (b) establish a baseline for comparison to the final evaluation for each animal.

The Start/Finish Veterinarian shall observe and record temperature, pulse, respiration, capillary refill rate, hydration, respiratory character and quality, musculature, coordination, attitude and willingness, and any other tests as he may deem necessary and indicate these on the score sheet.

The Start/Finish Veterinarian shall record his observations for each dog and horse immediately and before starting to examine any other dog or horse.

The Start/Finish Veterinarian's observations shall be recorded on a separate sheet for each horse and team of dogs. The dog's condition at the start and at the finish shall be given an overall rating of either "pass" or "fail."

The Start/Finish Veterinarian's final evaluation shall include a score on a scale of 0—100, with 0—50 being a "fail" and 51—100 being a "pass" that indicates the relative condition of each dog. This score shall be included in the final compilation of scores to determine the overall ranking of the dogs.

The Start/Finish Veterinarian shall copy his pass/fail starting evaluation and the score of his final evaluation into the Official Judges' Book after he has judged all the teams.

SECTION 5. **Duties and Responsibilities of Mid-Course Veterinarian.** In addition to the overall duties and responsibilities, it shall be the responsibility of the Mid-Course Veterinarian to check the condition and soundness of each dog and horse at a designated check point and to observe each dog and horse during a rest period of a least five minutes, but not more than thirty minutes during which each animal is offered fresh drinking water.

This evaluation shall serve to determine each animal's health and soundness before being allowed to continue on the course.

The Mid-Course Veterinarian shall observe and record temperature, pulse, respiration, capillary refill rate, hydration, respiratory character and quality, musculature, coordination, attitude and willingness, and any other tests as he may deem necessary and indicate these on the score sheet.

The Mid-Course Veterinarian shall record his observations for each dog and horse on the mid-course score sheet immediately and before starting to examine any other dog or horse. The Mid-Course Veterinarians' observations shall be recorded on a separate sheet for each horse and team of dogs. The dog's condition shall be given an overall rating of either "pass" or "fail."

The Mid-Course Veterinarian shall copy his pass/fail rating for each dog into the Official Judges' Book after he has judged all the teams and returned to the starting area.

SECTION 6. **Time of Mid-Course Veterinary Check.** The Mid-Course Veterinarian shall record the check-in and check-out times for each team on each team's score sheet and this time shall be deducted from the exhibitor's total course time. He shall write the time required for each team's mid-course check into the Official Judges' Book after he has judged all the teams and returned to the starting area.

SECTION 7. **Standardized Veterinary Exams.** The same methods and standards must be used for rating dogs in the RD and RDX Classes. The veterinarians shall try as much as is practical to give standardized exams. One dog should not "fail" when another in very similar conditions has "passed," and vice versa.

A handler familiar with these regulations should be able to enter the check points knowing what checks the veterinarian shall conduct on his dog and horse.

In the case of a dog or horse that is in either veterinarian's opinion under stress or incapable of continuing, the animal must be removed from competition. Either veterinarian may conduct additional tests on the dog or horse other than what is specified in these regulations in order to determine the animal's health and soundness. The opinion of the veterinarian shall be final.

SECTION 8. **Qualifying Condition.** The veterinarians' certification in the Official Judge's Book of a Qualifying Score for any particular dog constitutes their mutual certification to the Dalmatian Club of America that the dog has performed all of the required tests at least in accordance with the minimum standards and that its performance would justify the awarding of a Road Dog or Road Dog Excellent title. A Qualifying Score must never be awarded to a dog who has not met the minimum requirements, nor to a dog that shows fear or resentment, nor to a dog that acts aggressively toward any other dog, person, or horse met along the course, nor to a dog whose handler disciplines it or abuses it in the veterinarian rings or on the course, or carries or offers food on the course, except at the mid-course check point.

In deciding whether a particular dog's condition warrants a "pass" score, the veterinarian shall consider whether the awarding of a road title would be justified if all dogs in the class appeared in similar condition at that particular point of the course. The veterinarian must not give a "pass" score if he decides that it would be contrary to the best interests of the sport if all dogs in the class were to be in the same condition.

SECTION 9. **Standard of Perfection.** The Start-Finish Veterinarian must carry a mental picture of the theoretically perfect performance and score each dog against this visualized standard which shall combine the utmost in condition as well as willingness and enjoyment on the part of the dog. Lack of willingness or enjoyment on the part of the dog must be penalized, as must any aggression by the dog, and/or roughness in handling or commands by the handler.

SECTION 10. **Official Judges' Book and Veterinarian Score Sheets.** The Official Judges' Book shall be kept by the Road Trial Chairman and shall contain an aggregate score sheet for each team entered in the Road Trial. The aggregate score sheet shall indicate each dog's score for each exercise, each dog's pass/fail status for the start and mid-point veterinary checks, each dog's score for the final veterinary check, the time each team crossed the starting line, the time each team crossed the finish line, and the time required for the mid-course veterinary checks, which shall be deducted from the total time for each team. This Official Judges' Book shall be made available for each veterinarian and judge to transfer their scores once they have completed their area of jurisdiction.

The Start/Finish Veterinarian and the Mid-Course Veterinarian must enter the scores of each dog on their respective score sheets immediately after each dog has been examined and before examining the next dog. These scores shall be transferred into the Official Judges' Book by the veterinarians after they have finished examining the last dog under their jurisdiction.

No person other than one of the judges or veterinarians may make any entry in the Official Judges' Book. All final scores must be entered in the Official Judges' Book by the judges and veterinarians, checked by the Start/Finish Steward, and verified by the judges before prizes are awarded.

SECTION 11. **Announcement of Veterinary Check Scores.** Each veterinarian shall notify each exhibitor of the pass/fail status of each dog as soon as the exam has been completed and the results entered on the score sheets, but he shall not disclose the points awarded each dog. If a dog or horse has failed any veterinary exam, he shall not be allowed to continue on the course.

Chapter 6—Regulations for Performance & Judging

SECTION 1. **Requirements for Judges.** Persons considered for assignment to judge a Road Trial should have the following minimum experience:

SECTION 1A. **Mounted Judge.** 1) Must be an experienced equestrian. 2) Must have earned an obedience title. 3) Must have a complete working knowledge of the Road Trial regulations. 4) Must have experience with Dalmatians, either in owning, breeding,

showing (conformation or obedience), or having been a member of a Dalmatian Specialty Club for at least two years.

SECTION 1B. **Course Judge.** 1) Must have earned an obedience title. 2) Must have a complete working knowledge of the Road Trial regulations. 3) Must have experience with Dalmatians, either in owning, breeding, showing (conformation or obedience), or having been a member of a Dalmatian Specialty Club for at least two years.

SECTION 2. **Standardized Judging.** Standardized judging is of paramount importance. Judges are not permitted to inject their own variations into the exercises, but must see that each handler and dog executes the various exercises exactly as described in these regulations. A handler familiar with these regulations should be able to enter the course under any judge without having to inquire how the particular judge wishes to have any exercise performed, and without being confronted with some unexpected requirement.

SECTION 3. **Standard of Perfection.** The Road Trial judges must carry a mental picture of the theoretically perfect performance in each exercise and score each dog/handler/horse team against this visualized standard which shall combine the utmost in willingness, enjoyment, and precision on the part of the dog, and naturalness, gentleness, and smoothness in handling. Lack of willingness or enjoyment on the part of the dog must be penalized, as must any lack of precision in the dog's performance, any aggression by the dog, and/or roughness in handling or commands by the handler.

SECTION 4. **Qualifying Performance.** The judges' certification in the Official Judges' Book of a Qualifying Score for any particular dog constitutes their mutual certification to the Dalmatian Club of America that the dog has performed all of the required exercises at least in accordance with the minimum standards and that its performance would justify the awarding of a Road Dog or Road Dog Excellent title. A Qualifying Score must never be awarded to a dog whose performance has not met the minimum requirements, nor to a dog that shows fear or resentment, nor to a dog that acts aggressively toward any other dog, person, or horse met along the course, nor to a dog whose handler disciplines it or abuses it on the course, or carries or offers food on the course, except at the mid-course check point.

In deciding whether a faulty performance of a particular exercise by a particular dog warrants a Qualifying Score, the judge shall consider whether the awarding of a road title would be justified if all dogs in the class performed the exercise in a similar manner. The judge must not give a Qualifying Score for the exercise if he decides that it would be contrary to the best interests of the sport if all dogs in the class were to perform in the same way.

SECTION 5. **Judges' Directions.** The judges' orders and signals should be given to the handlers in a clear and understandable manner, but in such a way that the work of the dog is not disturbed. The Mounted Judge shall take care that his horse does not come so close to any of the dogs so as to interfere with any exercise. Before starting the Recall, Hock, Long Sit or Down, and Distraction exercises, the judge shall state, "This will be the (particular) exercise," and ask, "Are you ready?"

For the Speed exercise, an official Course Steward shall, on signal from the Course Judge, state, "This will be the Speed exercise." and ask, "Are you ready?" At the end of each exercise the judge shall say, "Exercise finished," except that at the end of the Speed exercise there shall be a trial marker which indicates that the speed shall be reduced.

The judging of an exercise will begin when the judge or official Course Steward in the case of the Speed exercise gives the first order, not before.

SECTION 6. **No Added Requirements.** No judge shall require any dog or handler to do anything nor penalize a dog or handler for failing to do anything that is not required by these regulations.

SECTION 7. **Standardized Judging.** The same methods and standards must be used for judging and scoring dogs in the RD and the RDX classes.

SECTION 8. **Interference and Double Handling.** Any judge who is aware of any assistance, interference, or attempts to control a dog from outside the ring or along the course must act promptly to stop such double handling or interference, and shall penalize the dog substantially, or, if in the judge's opinion the circumstances warrant, shall give the dog a score of zero or a "fail" for the exercise during which the aid was received.

SECTION 9. **Rejudging.** If a dog has failed in a particular part of an exercise, it shall not ordinarily be rejudged nor given a second chance; but if in a judge's opinion the dog's performance was prejudiced by peculiar and unusual conditions, the judge may at his own discretion rejudge the dog on the entire exercise.

SECTION 10. **Ties.** In case a tie for any prize in the RD or RDX classes or for the Highest Scoring Dog in the trial, the dogs involved in the tie shall be tested by being required to individually perform the "Hock" exercise in a straight line for 100 yards. The Mounted Judge shall be the tie-breaking judge. The original scores shall not be changed.

SECTION 11. **Official Judges' Book and Judges' Score Sheets.** The Mounted Judge and the Course Judge must enter each dog's scores on their score sheets immediately after judging each team and before starting to judge the next team. The judges shall transfer these scores into the Official Judges' Book after they have finished judging all teams. The judges shall also copy the start and finish times from the Start/Finish Steward's sheets and deduct the mid-point veterinary check time from the total time on each team's aggregate score sheet.

The Start/Finish Steward shall note the start and finish times of each dog. The Mounted Judge shall mark the start and finish times on each team's score sheet and these times shall be transferred to the Official Judges' Book by the Mounted Judge.

No person other than one of the judges or veterinarians may make any entry in the Official Judges' Book. All final scores must be entered in the Official Judge's Book by the judges and veterinarians, checked by the Start/Finish Steward, and verified by the judges before prizes are awarded.

Judges may use separate score sheets or a tape recorder for their own purposes, but shall not give out or allow exhibitors to see such sheets or hear such recordings, nor give out any other written scores, nor permit anyone else to distribute score sheets or cards prepared by the judge. Carbon copies of the sheets in the Official Judge's Book shall be made available through the Road Trial Secretary for examination by owners, handlers, and spectators immediately after the prizes have been awarded in each class. If score cards are distributed by a club after the prizes are awarded, they must contain no more information than is shown in the judge's book and must be marked "Unofficial Score."

SECTION 12. **Announcement of Scores.** No judge shall be required to disclose any score or partial score to contestants or spectators until the public announcement of scores following the compilation of final scores in the Official Judge's Book and any run-offs, nor shall he permit anyone else to do so. He shall, in cases where a dog has been excused during the Road Trial as described in Chapter 1, Section 19 (Disqualification and Ineligibility) or Section 20 (Disturbances), immediately advise an exhibitor and his escort that the exhibitor, escort, dog(s) and/or horse has been excused and in these cases, the dog(s) and/or exhibitor and/or escort shall be immediately removed from the course.

The judges shall also advise an exhibitor if any dog has failed an exercise, and the exhibitor shall be given the option of continuing on the course. The judge is not required to explain his scoring and need not enter into any discussion with any exhibitor who appears to be dissatisfied.

After all the scores are given final verification, the Start/Finish Steward, after consulting with the Judges, shall announce the dogs involved in any run-off and after the run-off shall call for the dogs that have won Qualifying Scores to be brought into the ring. The Course Judge shall announce the scores, and all judges and veterinarians shall be in the ring during the announcement if at all possible. Before awarding the prizes, the Course Judge shall inform the spectators as to the maximum number of points for a perfect score, and shall then announce the score of each prize winner and announce to the handler the score of each dog that has won a Qualifying Score.

SECTION 13. **Explanation and Errors.** No judge or veterinarian is required to explain his scoring and need not enter into any discussion with any contestant who appears to be dissatisfied. At the judge's or veterinarian's discretion, he is encouraged to offer comment to interested handlers as to the performance of a dog. Any interested person who thinks that there may have been an arithmetical error or an error in identifying

a dog may report the facts to the Chief Ring Steward and to the Road Trial Secretary so that the matter may be checked and cleared up.

Chapter 7—Road Dog and Road Dog Excellent

SECTION 1. **Road Dog—A Class.** The Road Dog A Class shall be for dogs not less than one year old that have not won the title RD and that are being handled by an exhibitor who has not previously competed in a Road Trial.

SECTION 2. **Road Dog—B Class.** The Road Dog B Class shall be for dogs not less than one year old that either 1) have already earned the title RD or RDX or 2) are being handled by an exhibitor who has previously competed in a Road Trial. A dog who has already earned his RD or RDX title may continue to compete in this class, but only if the class has not been filled by dogs who have not yet earned an RD title.

SECTION 3. **Road Dog Excellent—A Class.** The Road Dog Excellent A Class shall be for dogs not less than one and one-half years old that have not won either the RD or the RDX title and that are being handled by an exhibitor who has not previously competed in a Road Trial.

SECTION 4. **Road Dog Excellent—B Class.** The Road Dog Excellent B Class shall be for dogs not less than one and one-half years old that either have won the RD or the RDX title or who are being handled by an exhibitor who has previously competed in a Road Trial. A dog may continue to compete in the class after it has earned the title RDX, but only if the class has not been filled by dogs who have not yet earned the RDX title.

SECTION 5. **Road Dog Class and Road Dog Excellent Class General Requirements.** The only difference between the Road Dog Class and the Road Dog Excellent Class shall be in the length of the course portion of the trial, the Road Dog being required to cover a distance of 12.5 miles, excluding the mid-point veterinary check within a period of three hours, and the Road Dog Excellent being required to cover a distance of 25 miles, excluding the mid-point veterinary check within a period of six hours.

Exhibitors must recognize that dogs must be properly conditioned to compete at these distances within these time frames.

Each dog in these classes may be handled by the owner or any other person. A handler may handle up to six dogs, run either all together, separately, or in two groups as pre-approved by the Road Trial Committee and designated in the catalog or Road Trial Pamphlet.

Each dog will be judged individually for each exercise, but dogs run in a group are required to perform the exercises held on the course in a group.

SECTION 6. **RD Title.** The Dalmatian Club of America will issue a Road Dog certificate to a dog and will permit the use of the letters "RD" after the name of each registered dog which has been certified by the Mounted Judge, the Course Judge, the Start/Finish Veterinarian and the Mid-Course Veterinarian to have passed a Licensed Road Trial in which the course portion measures 12.5 miles.

SECTION 7. **RDX Title.** The Dalmatian Club of America will issue a Road Dog Excellent certificate to a dog and will permit the use of the letters "RDX" after the name of each dog that has been certified by the Mounted Judge, the Course Judge, the Start/Finish Veterinarian, and the Mid-Course Veterinarian to have passed a Licensed Road Trial in which the course portion measures 25 miles.

Chapter 8—Exercises, Tests, and Scoring

SECTION 1. **Road Dog and Road Dog Excellent Exercises and Scores.** The exercises and tests for the Road Dog classes and the Road Dog Excellent classes are as follows:

SECTION 2. **Pre-Course Soundness. Mid-Course Soundness. After-Course Soundness.** The principal feature of these exercises is to determine that the dog is in sound condition before beginning the trial, at the mid-point of the course, and after completing the course.

These tests shall be conducted by the two Road Trial veterinarians, one who conducts the Pre-Course and the After-Course Soundness Tests, and the other who conducts the Mid-Course Soundness Test.

On request from the veterinarian, the handler shall place his dog on a table and hold his dog on a leash while the veterinarian shall conduct the tests described in Chapter 5 any other tests as he may deem necessary and indicate these on the score sheet. The handler shall then gait each dog on instruction from the veterinarian so that the veterinarian can check for any signs of lameness.

There shall be stewards at the Pre-Course/After-Course and Mid-Course checkpoints to hold the handler's horse(s) so that he may rest, and assist the veterinarian by holding his dog(s), and to old the escort's horse so that he may rest. Each team shall be allowed a rest of at least 5 minutes but not to exceed 30 minutes at this mid-course checkpoint, starting as soon as the veterinarian has finished his examination. Any dog that in the veterinarian's opinion requires more than a 30-minute rest period shall be excused from further competition in the Road Trial.

Orders are, "Place your dog on the table for a physical exam and hold him," "Move your dog at a trot in a counter-clockwise circle," "Move your dog down and back,"

1. Pre-Course Soundness Test	*Pass/Fail No Points*
2. Recall	*Pass(51—100)/Fail(0—50)*
3. Hock	*Pass(51—100)/Fail(0—50)*
4. Distraction	*Pass(51—100)/Fail(0—50)*
5. Long Sit or Down	*Pass(51—100)/Fail(0—50)*
6. Mid-Course Soundness Test	*Pass/Fail No Points*
7. Speed	*Pass(51—100)/Fail(0—50)*
8. After-Course Soundness Test	*Pass(51—100)/Fail(0—50)*
9. 12.5 or 25 mile Course	*Completion w/in time limit*
Maximum Total	*600 points + 8 Pass + Completion of Course within required time*

and "Exercise finished." These orders may be repeated at each veterinarian's discretion as often as he deems necessary.

The veterinarian shall also check each horse for any signs of stress or lameness and any horse that in the veterinarian's opinion requires more than a 30-minute rest period shall be excused from further competition in the Road Trial. Another mount may be substituted provided the exhibitor has made arrangements for this.

SECTION 6. **Pre-Course Soundness, Mid-Course Soundness, Scoring.** A dog must receive a "fail" and be excused from further competition in the Road Trial if he exhibits any lameness or excessive stress during these tests.

If the veterinarian is satisfied that a dog's condition is sound after conducting the tests, he shall give that dog a "pass" rating.

SECTION 7. **After-Course Soundness, Scoring.** A dog must receive a "fail" if he exhibits any lameness or excessive stress during these tests. The Start/Finish Veterinarian shall compare the baseline information recorded for each dog on the score sheet with the information recorded after the dog has completed the required distance in order to rate each dog's overall condition within a scale of 0—50 for "fail" and 51—100 for "pass."

SECTION 8. **Recall.** The principal feature of this exercise is that the dog respond promptly to the handler's command to "Come."

Orders are, "Call your dog" and "Exercise finished."

When the dog has run naturally to the front or has dropped back a good distance behind the exhibitor's horse, on order from the Mounted Judge the handler will give a command for each dog to Come while his horse is still moving forward at a walk. Each dog must come straight in at a brisk trot or gallop to the front of the horse or to the handler's left or right side On the judge's order, the handler will release his dog.

The Mounted Judge shall remain at least 20 feet away from the exhibitor's horse. An exhibitor's escort shall remain at least 20 feet away and take care not to interfere with any dog, the exhibitor, the Mounted Judge, or the horses or carriage.

SECTION 9. **Recall, Scoring.** A dog must be scored zero for failure to come when called.

Substantial deductions shall be made for a slow response to the come, varying with the extent of the slowness, and for a dog that comes partially in and then runs away once again before being released by his handler.

Minor to substantial deductions shall be made for dogs whose handlers repeat the command to come or who continue talking to the dog as he comes.

SECTION 10. **Hock.** The principal feature of this exercise is the ability of the dog to stay close to the horse and handler when required.

Orders for the exercise are "Call your dog to hock," "Trot your horse" and "Exercise finished." The judge shall standardize as much as is practical the place on the course that each dog is required to "hock." When the Mounted Judge announces, "This will be the Hock exercise. Are you ready?", the judge and handler shall be moving forward when the handler replies, "Ready" or "Yes." On the judge's order, the handler shall call each dog in and then give each dog a single command to fall into the hock position where they shall remain while continuing forward. Once in hock position, the team may begin a brisk trot with the horse, handler, and Mounted Judge. The handler may praise his dogs as the team continues forward and may give additional commands, if necessary, recognizing that the dog(s) will be scored accordingly. The dog(s) shall trot either close to the left or right side of the handler or horse, or driver or carriage; or up to one horse length from the horse's head or carriage without swinging wide, lagging, forging, or coming so close to the horse or carriage as to interfere with forward motion.

The Mounted Judge shall remain at least 20 feet away from any dog. An escort for a particular handler shall remain at least 20 feet away from any dog and make certain not to interfere with any dog, exhibitor, the Mounted Judge, or the Mounted Judge's line of vision during this exercise.

SECTION 11. **Hock, Scoring.** If a dog is unmanageable, or refuses to hock, the dog must be scored zero on this exercise.

Substantial deductions shall be made for excessively loud or gruff commands or signals to hock, or if a handler adapts his horse's pace to that of the dog.

Substantial or minor deductions shall be made for such things as lagging, forging, interfering with the horse or carriage's forward movement, going wide, or excessive barking.

Substantial deductions shall be made for a dog that goes ahead of the horse during this exercise, but who drops back into hock position on command.

Minor deductions may be made for repeated commands or praise during the hock exercise.

SECTION 12. **Distraction.** The principal feature of this exercise is to demonstrate a dog's ability to remain under the handler's voice control in the event of a distraction.

Orders are "Continue forward" and "Exercise finished." The Distraction exercise may be judged a trot, at the handler's discretion.

On signal from the judge, a hiker with a dog on a leash shall start walking toward the approaching handler, but while remaining on his right side of the trial at least 15 feet away while passing. The handler shall continue forward with his dogs in hock position from the previous exercise, and shall be allowed to command each dog to "Hock" or "Heel" when he has noticed the approaching distraction. When the handler and his dog(s) have gone past the hiker approximately 20 yards, the judge shall indicate that the exercise is finished and the handler may release his dog(s). The hiker and his dog shall remain on the down-course side of the handler and his dog(s) until after the Mounted Judge has completed judging the remaining exercise and has started back toward the Course Start.

SECTION 13. **Distraction, Scoring.** A dog must receive a score of zero if it attacks the on-coming hiker or dog, or if it disregards its handler's command to hock.

Substantial or minor deductions shall be made if a dog barks repeatedly at the distraction (a single warning bark shall not be penalized), if it starts to approach the distraction but comes back to hock on command, if it displays shyness, or if it moves out of hock position.

Minor deduction may be made for repeated commands or praise during the hock exercise.

SECTION 14. **Long Sit or Down.** The principal feature of this exercise shall be to demonstrate a Dalmatian's ability to wait under his handler's control until released.

Orders are, "Call your dog(s)," "Sit or down your dog(s)," "Command your dog(s) to stay," and "Exercise finished."

All the dogs being run together by a handler shall be judged at the same time for this exercise and a handler may give a separate command to each dog.

On order from the judge, the handler shall call his dog(s), command each dog to sit or down and command each dog to stay. It shall be the handler's choice whether to command each dog to sit or down, and different dogs on the same team may be given different commands. After placing his dogs in a sit or down, the handler shall remain mounted or in his carriage and shall assure that his horse does not come so close to the dogs as to threaten their safety while waiting for a period of one minute. The Mounted Judge and any exhibitor's escort must remain at least 20 feet away from the dog(s). Neither the exhibitor nor his escort shall move in any position that might interfere with the Mounted Judge's line of vision as he watches the dog(s).

After one minute from the time the handler has given the stay command, the judge shall say, "Exercise finished." The dog(s) must not move from the sit or down position until the handler has released them after the judge has said, "Exercise finished."

SECTION 15. **Long Sit or Down, Scoring.** During this exercise the judge's horse shall stand in such position that all the dogs are in his line of vision, and where he can see the handler without having to turn around.

Scoring of this exercise shall start as soon as the exhibitor responds "yes" or "ready" to the judge's question of "Are you ready?" Timing of the exercise shall start after the dog has responded to the handler's command to sit or down and as soon as the handler has given the "stay" command.

A handler whose dog assumes a position in such a manner that it could interfere with an adjacent dog or be too close to a horse for safety shall be required to reposition his dog.

A score of zero is required for the following: a dog's refusing to sit or down, moving at any time during the exercise a substantial distance away from the place where it was left, or going over to any other dog.

A substantial or minor deduction shall be

made for a dog that moves even a minor distance away from the place where it was left; for barking or whining during the exercise; for resisting its handler's command to sit or down; for not remaining in the position that was commanded (sits up from a down or lays down from a sit); or for overly loud or gruff commands to sit, down, and/or stay by the handler. A minor deduction may be made for commands or praise repeated during this exercise.

SECTION 16. **Speed.** The principal feature of this exercise shall be to demonstrate a Dalmatian's ability to exhibit a fair amount of speed, as specified in the standard for the breed, sufficient to keep pace with a galloping horse. One such demonstration shall be sufficient.

Orders are, "Call your dog(s)," "Extend your gait," and "Exercise finished" (which may be indicated by a trail marker).

On order from a steward acting on signal from the Course Judge, the handler shall call his dog(s) close to his horse or carriage. On further order from the steward, the handler shall gallop his horse (or do an extended trot with a carriage) for a distance of 100 yards, allowing his dog(s) to run in any position they choose. When the handler has passed the trial marker indicating the completion of this exercise, he shall reduce his speed. After completion of the Speed exercise, the exhibitor shall look back to obtain a go-ahead signal from the Course Judge. He may be rejudged if the Course Judge does not deem that the horse's speed was sufficient to determine the dog's/dogs' speed.

The Course Judge shall be situated in such a way as to not frighten the horse at a mid-way, preferably elevated point, and his stewards shall be instructed to remain quiet and still during this exercise.

SECTION 17. **Speed, Scoring.** A dog shall be scored zero for not attempting to keep up with the horse or carriage or whose handler does not exhibit any increase in speed.

Substantial or minor deductions shall be made for nipping at the horse or carriage; for falling increasingly behind the horse or carriage; for repeated barking; or for an exhibitor who adjusts his horse's pace to that of the dogs.

End

PLEASE NOTE: These rules were developed by the DCA Road Trial Committee (Charles Cyopik, Linda Fulks, Meg Ipsas Hennessey, Beth White, and Linda Myers, Chair) with help from many Dalmatian fanciers. They were updated in 1994 and approved by the DCA Board of Directors.

Copies may be obtained by writing to Linda Myers, 19809 N.E. 150th Place, Woodinville, WA 98072.

PLEASE, NO MORE "DALMATION"
by Carroll Weiss
Oh, woe is me! Oh, woe! Oh, woe!
Whenever will they stop the "O"?
"DALMATIAN"—the spelling is only with "A"s!
Like "aardvark," "acacia," and "alackadays."

There's Webster's Collegiate and Wagner and Funk,
Yet dog writers spell it as if they were drunk.
I learned, "I before E, except after C,"
But there's no spelling rule for a Dal pedigree.

Give me "coach dogs" or "fire dogs," I'll take either one,
But send misspelled "Dalmations" to oblivion.
You spellers with "O"s simply make me crazy,
Get rid of that letter and start being "A"zy!

Typographers tell me that the "A" is prettier,
It certainly makes this ditty dittier.
Compared to "O," the "A" is hotter:
An appropriate letter for the breed that's a spotter.

That Disney named Walt filmed Dalmatians to fame,
Folks buy the cartoon but still misspell the name.
Maybe spelling with "O" means you're old as gavottes,
If so, get thee hence from my world full of spots!

Why "A"s and not "O"s in "Dalmatian" you query?
'Cause they're needed for use elsewhere and here is why, dearie:
Take the misspelling "O" and what have you got
After filling it in? You guessed it! **A SPOT!**

Epilogue
"Dalmatian!" "Dalmatians!" Won't you now spell them right,
So I can calm down and lay back and at last sleep the nyght.

ALL-TIME TOP SHOW DALMATIANS THROUGH 1996

	BOB	BIS	G1	G2	G3	G4	Years
Ch. Spotlight's Spectacular (B) NM395664/01	362	62	272	36	18	4	1993—96
Ch. Green Starr's Colonel Joe (D) NS187661	336	35	138	76	51	17	1975—82
Ch. Korcula Midnight Hour (D) NM273670/06	298	7	92	75	23	8	1992—96
Ch. Midnight Star Bret D (D) NT88524	279	8	65	58	34	25	1986—95
Ch. Proctor's Dappled Hi Flyer (D) NT487885	275	5	57	58	32	31	1990—96
Ch. Fireman's Freckled Friend (D) NS753102	256	40	131	62	15	14	1983—89
Ch. PGR Heiloh Samson, CD (D) NS854415	245	2	21	47	45	27	1980—87
Ch. Spottsboro Rebel Streak (D) NS401414	219		8	9	17	21	1979—84
Ch. Fanfayre's Beau of Short Acre (D) NS612286	207	2	22	37	36	38	1982—86
Ch. Green Starr's Shamrock (B) NS888421	201	3	34	36	42	27	1985—88
Ch. Fire Star's Sonny Boy (D) NS394145	187	8	33	46	33	23	1979—83
Ch. Ye Dal Dark Brilliance (D) N350818	177	7	46	51	33	15	1958—65
Ch. Deltalyn N Penwiper Kisncuzn (B) NT604840	170	23	85	38	13	9	1990—94
Ch. Tally Ho's Sir Charles (D) NS129836	167		27	31	30	18	1975—81
Ch. Colonial Coach Son of York (D) NA573149	150		5	14	16	29	1967—73
Ch. Lord Jim (D) NA619679	149	13	50	35	20	13	1967—70
Ch. Rolenet's Ragtime Dandy (D) NS426849	144	8	36	34	23	21	1978—81
Ch. Panore of Watseka (D) NC1679	141	10	41	26	13	16	1971—77
Ch. St. Florian Pisces Jordache (D) NT45141	137	3	19	29	14	19	1986—90
Ch. Little Slam's Major Game (D) NB416211	136		19	26	23	20	1970—74
Ch. Godin's To Be Or Not To Be (B) NT281700	131	8	34	26	18	10	1987—92
Ch. Milky Ways Egyptian Goddess(B)NM405464/06	129	6	36	30	18	6	1993—96
Ch. Volanta Vici (D) NM264591/01	129	3	33	23	18	13	1991—94
Ch. Korcula Midnight Master (D) NT226750	127	1	31	39	18	11	1988—92
Ch. Roadcoach Roadster (D) N201878	127	17	75	33	7	3	1955—63
Ch. Deltalyn Decoupage (D) NS132793	126	1	12	14	20	15	1974—79
Ch. Farga de Montjuic (B) NT10344	125	5	44	23	12	11	1986—92
Ch. Pacifica Pride of Poseidon (D) NA39551	124	1	13	21	29	23	1965—70
Ch. Tuckaway Winged Foot (D) NM525524	124	5	42	28	15	8	1994—96
Ch. Coachman's Chuck-A-Luck (D) NA35983	121	3	31	37	15	11	1964—71
Ch. Volanta Venturian of Snowhill (D) NT620301	121	1	9	28	12	22	1991—93
Ch. Merry Go Round XKE (D) NT215546	119	3	17	23	9	12	1987—91
Ch. Valto's Chief Justice (D) NB104197	119		8	10	10	18	1970—74
Ch. Albelarm Starr of Summerhill (D) NS367514	114	1	29	19	14	13	1979—84
Ch. Blackpool Crinkle Forest (B) N706235	114	6	33	30	21	12	1962—66
Ch. Crestview Dan Patch (D) NS45762	112	4	29	26	18	7	1973—77
Ch. Swabbie of Oz Dal (B) N32668	112	8	62	32	7	4	1948—54
Ch. The Opera's Dappertutto (D) NM495713/05	110		12	21	5	8	1994—96
Ch. Paisley's Pointblank (D) NM398588/01	108	3	29	20	13	7	1993—96
Ch. Centennial Doctor Pepper (D) NT44817	105		2	5	9	7	1987—96
Ch. Fireman's Becky Newsham (B) NT163347	104	3	30	25	11	10	1988—93
Ch. Korcula's Salona, CD (B) NA407338	103		6	13	15	26	1966—72
Ch. Dalwood's Knight Traveler (D) NS733575	101		7	12	9	9	1983—88
Ch. Legacy's Pen Pal (B) NT595386	100		13	15	14	9	1991—96

APPENDIX

BEST IN SHOW DALMATIANS

Ch. Spotlight's Spectacular (B) NM395664/01	62
Ch. Fireman's Freckled Friend (D) NS753102	40
Ch. Green Starr's Colonel Joe (D) NS187661	35
Ch. Deltalyn N Penwiper Kisncuzn (B) NT604840	23
Ch. Four-In-Hand Mischief (D) A204760	18
Ch. Roadcoach Roadster (D) N201878	17
Ch. Lord Jim (D) NA619679	13
Ch. Panore of Watseka (D) NC1679	10
Ch. Fire Star's Sonny Boy (D) NS394145	8
Ch. Godin's To Be Or Not To Be (B) NT281700	8
Ch. Korcula's Midnight Star Bret D (D) NT88524	8
Ch. Rolenet's Ragtime Dandy (D) NS426849	8
Ch. Swabbie of Oz Dal (B) N32668	8
Ch. Ye Dal Dark Brilliance (D) N350818	7
Ch. Korcula Midnight Hour (D) NM273670/06	7
Ch. Blackpool Crinkle Forest (B) N706235	6
Ch. Milky Way's Egyptian Goddess (B) NM405464/06	6
Ch. Ard Aven Shamus (D) N265615	5
Ch. Farga de Montjuic (B) NT10344	5
Ch. Proctor's Dappled Hi Flyer (D) NT487885	5
Ch. Tuckaway Winged Foot (D) NM525524/02	5
Ch. Crestview Dan Patch (D) NS45762	4
Ch. Centurion Center Stage (B) NM255437/03	3
Ch. Coachman's Chuck-A-Luck (D) NA35983	3
Ch. Fireman's Becky Newsham (B) NT163347	3
Ch. Green Starr's Shamrock (B) NS888421	3
Ch. Merry Go Round XKE (D) NT215546	3
Ch. Mgr N Mika's Cause A Ruckus (B) NM300870/02	3
Ch. Paisley's Pointblank (D) NM398588/01	3
Ch. St. Florian Pisces Jordache (D) NT45141	3
Ch. Volanta Vici (D) NM264591/01	3
Ch. Devlstr Snygln Rich N Spirit (D) NT276436	2
Ch. Fanfayre's Beau of Short Acre (D) NS612286	2
Ch. Green Starr's Masterpiece (D) N190812	2
Ch. Greenwood's Rusty Nail (D) NM277921/02	2
Ch. Madurhason's Tanfastic (D) NS977669	2
Ch. Melody Dynamatic (D) NB753573	2
Ch. PGR Heiloh Samson, CD (D) NS485415	2
Ch. Rovingdale's Impudent Ingenue (B) N85612	2
Ch. Tuckaway's The Pill Peddler (D) NS364368	2

BEST IN SPECIALTY SHOW DALMATIANS

Ch. Korcula Midnight Star Bret D (D) NT88524	19
Ch. Alfredrich Handsome Tall N' Dark (D) NS991751	16
Ch. Korcula Midnight Hour (D) NM273670	10
Ch. Spotlight's Spectacular (B) NM395664/01	10
Ch. Deltalyn N Penwiper Kisncuzn (B) NT604840	9
Ch. Fireman's Freckled Friend (D) NS753102	8
Ch. Proctor's Dappled Hi Flyer (D) NT487885	8
Ch. Green Starr's Colonel Joe (D) NS187661	7
Ch. Pacifica Pride of Poseidon (D) NA39551	7
Ch. PGR Heiloh Samson, CD (D) NS485425	7
Ch. Panore of Watseka (D) NC1679	6
Ch. Tuckaway Winged Foot (D) NM525524/02	6
Ch. Crestview Dan Patch (D) NS45762	5
Ch. Deltalyn Decoupage (D) NS132793	5
Ch. Godin's To Be Or Not To Be (B) NT281700	5
Ch. Melody Fire On The Mountain (D) NT28303	5
Ch. Paisleys Pointblank (D) NM398588/01	5
Ch. Rolenet's Ragtime Dandy (D) NS426849	5
Ch. Acorn N' Erin's Doc Holliday (D) NM338597/02	4
Ch. Blackpool Crinkle Forest (B) N706235	4
Ch. Centurion Jaunty Jim (D) NT143824	4
Ch. Coachman's Hot Coffee (D) NS396998	4
Ch. Count Miguel of Tuckaway (D) NS173840	4
Ch. Countryroad Cool Classic (D) NS601600	4
Ch. Green Starr's Shamrock (B) NS888421	4
Ch. Indalane Bryan's Knockout (D) NS593413	4
Ch. Jameson of Shawnee (D) NS3260	4
Ch. Rockledge Rumble (D) NA211578	4
Ch. Sunnyglen's Spencer For Hire (D) NT50047	4
Ch. Tallyho's Sir Charles (D) NS129836	4
Ch. Zodiac's Snoopy (D) NB23085	4

ALL-TIME TOP SIRES THROUGH 1996

Ch. Fireman's Freckled Friend NS753102	94
Ch. Alfredrich Handsome Tall N' Dark NS991751	82
Ch. Buffrey Jobee NS895150	66
Ch. Long Last Perfect for Paisley NT392032	56
Ch. Karastella Cadillac for Mgr NS264806	54
Ch. Sunnyglen's Spencer For Hire NT50047	54
Ch. Tuckaway Traveler Indalane NS184707	54
Ch. Bob Dylan Thomas of Watseka, CD NS117730	53
Ch. Green Starr's Colonel Joe NS187661	52
Ch. Count Miguel of Tuckaway NS173840	49
Ch. Korcula Midnight Star Bret D NT88524	48
Ch. Panore of Watseka NC1679	47
Ch. Crown Jewels Black Diamond N716951	42
Ch. Tuckaway Augusta NT680694	39
Ch. Colonial Coach Carriage Way NS573084	38
Ch. Countryroad Cool Million NS328101	35
Ch. Roadcoach Roadster N201878	34
Ch. Pacifica Pride of Poseidon NA39551	30
Ch. Tamarack's Tennyson V. Watseka NA618272	28
Ch. Coachman's Chuck-A-Luck NA35983	27
Ch. Elmcroft Coacher 479155	27
Ch. Melody Dynamatic NB753573	27
Ch. Boot Black from Dalmatia N110039	26
Ch. Long Last Living Legend NS204698	26
Ch. Madurhason's Opening Night NT152238	26
Ch. Merry Go Round XKE NT21554	26
Ch. Tuckaway Bottoms Up Gusto NS670642	26
Ch. Erin's Wildwood Luke Macgyver NT108892	24
Ch. Melody Fire On The Mountain NT28303	24
Ch. Reigate Bold Venture A401493	24
Ch. Storm King of Quaker's Acre NA471805	24
Ch. Deltalyn Decoupage NS132793	23
Ch. Merry Go Round Cholo O Chelsea NS660736	23
Ch. Erin's Acer de Montjuic NS902123	22
Ch. Proctor's Dappled Hi Flyer NT487885	22
Ch. Coachman's Canicula NB611361	21
Ch. Dandy Dan of Coachmaster NS28836	21
Ch. Esquire's Razzamatazz NS658607	21
Ch. Igdaliah's M and M Candy Cain, CD NS815066	21
Ch. Robbsdale's Baron Von Cross NS323474	20

ALL-TIME TOP DAMS THROUGH 1996

Ch. Volanta de Montjuic NS764215	17
Ch. Korcula Midnight Mistress NS880002	16
Ch. Melody Sweet, CD NA445335	16
Ch. Melody Up Up and Away, CD NS11539	15
Ch. Tamara of Watseka N715069	13
Ch. Glen Oaks Contessa Leah NS856427	12
Crown Jewels Black Agate N965086	11
Ch. Indalane's Scarlett O'Hara NS378890	11
Ch. Sugarfrost Top Choice, CD NS232414	11
Ch. Coachman's Paisley Candybar NS246780	10
Ch. Miss Camielle of Croatia NS611974	10
Ch. Paisley's A Touch of Class NS132429	10
Ch. Indalane Nellie Bly NS411828	9
Ch. Korcula Midnight Serenade NS578724	9

ALL-TIME TOP DAMS THROUGH 1996 (Cont'd)

Ch. Labyrinth Hi Lili Heiloh NS845303	9
Ch. Labyrinth Sleigh Belle NB101339	9
Ch. Royal Oaks Liberty Belle NS171336	9
Aposta de Montjuic NS998085	8
Ch. Cheshire's Northern Lights NT27557	8
Ch. Cindarella's Coach Keeper NB214023	8
Daisy's Love Me Tender NS145812	8
Erin's Nutmeg Candy, CD NS484709	8
Ch. Firewagn's Lucinda of Croatia NS454356	8
Ch. Gladmore Gaylass 538830	8
Ch. Korcula Midnight Margie NS191329	8
Ch. Labyrinth Lalapaloosa NS621354	8
Ch. Limestone's Crescendo NS20138	8
Ch. Melody Crimson and Clover, CD NS11541	8
Ch. Paisley N Tucks Eureka NT531493	8
Ch. Pizazz of Watseka NS191303	8
Proctor Onyx Jewel of the Mt NS908369	8
Snowcap's Simonetta NS206427	8
Ch. Splash O'Ebony's Woodbury Jaki NS601259	8
Ch. Swood-Paisly-Cyncar Me Special NT675836	8

TOP OBEDIENCE AVERAGES

Year	Dog's Name	Class	Average
1971	Hapi Dal Doctor Peppi, UD	Novice	197.33
1972	Hapi Dal Casey, UD	Open	197.67
1973	Chardonnay Frosty Chablis, UD	Novice	197.67
1974	Beautysweet Cindi, UDTX	Open Competition	197.17
1975	Ch. Little Slam's Diamond Bid, CD	Novice	197.33
1976	Ch. Cal Dal Chocolate Chip, UDT	Open Competition	197.17
1977	Dallas, CDX	Open Competition	197.33
1978	Dominos Winter Midnight, UDT	Open Competition	198.17
	Dominique's Rusty Nail, UD	Open Competition	198.17
1979	Dominique's Rusty Nail, UD	Open Competition	197.67
1980	OTCh. Kandis Skagit Belle, UD	Open Competition	197.67
1981	OTCh. Kandis Skagit Belle, UD	Open Competition	198.83
1982	Touchstone's Hello Holly, UD	Open Competition	197.00
1983	Sneak Preview, UDTX	Open Competition	197.17
1984	Nickles Worth, CD	Novice	195.83
1985	Daphne, CD	Novice	198.17
1986	Ch. Gardorand's Lone Star Corie, UD	Open Competition	197.17
1987	Crystal's Rock Candy, UDT	Open Competition	197.17
1988	Dazdell Lady Dot of the Birch, CD	Novice	197.17
1989	Lidgate Charles of Seaspot, CDX	Open	196.33
1990	Alacameo Blackberry Bramble, UD	Novice	197.50
	Rowdy Ryleigh Ruckus, CDX	Open Competition	197.50
1991	Alacameo Blackberry Bramble, UD	Open	197.67
1992	Alacameo Blackberry Bramble, UD	Open Competition	198.17
1993	Alacameo Blackberry Bramble, UD	Open Competition	197.50
	Touchstone's Ace In The Hole, CD	Novice	197.50
1994	Alacameo Blackberry Bramble, UD	Open Competition	197.67
1995	Brewster's Beauty, UD	Open Competition	197.50
1996	Ch. OTCh. Crossroads Wandering Star, UDX	Open Competition	197.6

Index

Page numbers in boldface refer to illustrations. All titles have been omitted from dogs' names for the reader's convenience.

101 Dalmatians, 36-37, 80, 87, 95
Achilles, 9
Acorn Erin at Paisley, **409**
Acral lick dermatitis, 398-399
Acrobat, 105
Activities, 175
Advertising, 267-268
Age, 404
Agility, 91, 181
—titles, 182
Alacameo Blackberry Brambles, **303**
Albelarm, 48
Albelarm Starr of Summerhill, **48**
Albicans Dappled Peg, 121
Alfredrich Bay Colony Hytime, **292**
Alfredrich Handsome Tall N' Dark, **99**, **335**
Alfredrich Mirliton of Culurien, **288**
All Around's Black Jack, **243**
All Around's Playin the Banjo, **173**, **176**, **177**, **178**
Allegory of the Munster Peace Treaty, 104
Allergies, 392-396
—allergic inhalant dermatitis, 393-395
—contact, 395
—flea bite dermatitis, 396
—food, 395
Altamar, 36
Altamar's Acheson, **37**
Altamar's Annette, 66
Altamar's Aristos, **37**
American Kennel Club, 22, 28, 30, 86, 110, 222, 256
—breed ranking, 80, 86-87
—Centennial Show, 85
—championship, 257
—*Gazette*, 81, 87, 262
—*Obedience Regulations*, 262

—recognition of regional clubs, 84
—registration, 80
—*Regulations for Junior Showmanship*, 269
—*Rules Applying to Registration and Dog Shows*, 262
—standard, 81, 123, 426-430
—Stud Book, 22, 34, 81
Anchor Creek Spectacular, **223**
Angel's Nest Hollywood Star, **287**
Annie, **405**
Annle N Belrins Dylan Flyer, **117**
Anson, William, 33
Argentina, 116
Arnold, Mrs. Hastings, 88
Arro von Germannswald, **108**
Arthritis, 404
Assistance dogs, 193, 417
Asti, 329
Aurora's Lacy Britches, **279**, **342**
Australia, 91
—conformation, 93
—Dalmatian clubs, 93-94
—Dalmatian convention, 94
—"Moomba" festival, 94-95
—National Dalmatian Council, 94
—National Specialty, 94
Autoimmune thyroiditis theory, 383
Avalon n Paisley Pawprints, **225**
Avalon Taylormade By Paisley, **286**
Backcross project, 86
Backpacking, 195
BAER testing, 85, 363, 366, 368
—in Sweden, 122
Bailey, **233**
Banker, **134**
Barajas, Emilio, 110

Barker's Best Game of Magic, **285**
Barking, 254
Barnes, Miss, 102
Barney Oldfield In the Valley, 41
Barrett, Alfred, 45, 88
Barrett, Mary, 34, 45, **46**, 88
Bathing, 234
Battle of Mohaca, 9
Beachcomber's Mint Mark, **96**
Bear, **414**
Bearded Oaks Astra's Lyra, **14**, **290**
Bearded Oaks Astra's Ursa Major, **194**, 194
Bearded Oaks Jigsaw Puzzle, 187
Beau of Hollyroyde, 46
Beauregard O'Hara of Proctor, **297**
Beautysweet Cindi, **307**
Beekman, Ludwig, 104
Bell Ringer's Redrock Puccini, **35**, **175**, **184**
Bell Ringer's Sundance, 41
Bell, Mr. and Mrs., 112
Belle Aire's Star E. Knight, **276**
Beloved Scotch of the Walls, **30**, 56, **58**
Bengal, 10
Berolina, 105
Bespeckled, 49
Bespeckled Becky, 49, **49**
Bespeckled Charlemagne, **49**
Bespeckled Freckles, **49**
Bespeckled Jean, **49**
Bespeckled Kelly, **49**
Bessie (fire dog), 18-19, 22
Bessie (first registered Dal), 22
Best in Show dogs, 450
Best in Specialty Show dogs, 450
Beteta, Don Ramon, 109
Beteta, Mario Ramon, 109
Beteta, Mrs. Elizabeth, 109
Bewick, Thomas, 12

Biking, 204
Bingo, **178**
Biographical Sketches and Authentic Anecdotes of Dogs, 10
Birmingham Exhibition, 28
BJ, **178**
Blackpool, 38
Blackpool Crinkle Forest, **38**, 38, 60,
Blackpool Red Nora, **38**
Blacktowers Nevertheless, **315**
Blair, John and Mary Kay, 44
Blinko, Catherine, 96
Bloat, 376
Bobby's Bobbie of Tarzana, 57
Boel, Pieter, 11
Bohemia, 8
Bohom, Ms. Asa, 122
Bonney, Mrs. Flora, **37**, **46**, 46, **72**, **87**, 87-88
Book of the Dog, The, 28
Boomer, **201**
Boot Black from Dalmatia, **52**, 52, **73**
Bordal's Buckeye Battle Cry, **314**, **319**
Bordal's Knight of Indalane, **247**
Bordal's Mystical Tai Magic, **314**
Boston Blackie, **352**
Bottoms Up Tuti Fruity, **286**
Brandis, Mr. C. Willy, 104, 105
Braque de Bengale, **9**, 11
Braque de Bengale, **10**, 10, 12
Brazil, 116
Breed popularity, 327-328
Breed rescue, 331-332
Breed standard, 81, 123, 426-430
Breeders, 222, 223-224
—ethics, 421
—organizations, 417
—puppy placements, 362
—responsibility, 362
Bret D's Midnight Breeze, **174**
Briarfield Princess Sonrisa, 111, **285**
British Dalmatian Club, 84, 98, 102, 105

—*Handbook*, 102
—*Spots of News*, 102
British Kennel Club, 102, 103
Broadmoor of Birch, 57
Bromholm Dalmatian, **8**, 11
Bronzing syndrome, 398
Brooks, John and Monica, 8, 10
Brown, Captain Thomas, 10
Brutus, **178**
Brythennek Basil Fawlty, **102**
Buccaneer Black-Eyed Bart, **288**
Buch, Mr. Manuel, 110
Buffon, Count de, 8
Buffrey Jobee, **22**
Bulldog, 364, 370
Bullet, **178**
Cabaret Charivaris, 49
Caesar (fire dog), 20
Caesar (South Africa), 112
Calculator's Miss Sincerity, 66
Cali, **414**
Callea, Capt. Jim, 186
Cally, **20**
Cal Dal Chocolate Chip, **312**
Camacho, General Manuel Avila, 109
Canada, 95
—championship, 96
—Dalmatian "booster", 98
—Dalmatian Club of Canada, 96
—National Specialty, 98
—standard, 96
Canadian Kennel Club, 96, 98
Candi's Skagit Belle, **308**
Canine Eye Registration Foundation (CERF), 380
Canine Good Citizen, 196
Captain, 28, **28**
Captain Fiske, 30
Caravan Zagreb the Challenger, **115**
Carlo, 28
Carpay, Jacques, 96
Carsickness, 254-255
Cary, Mr. William, 22
Cassie, **200**
Castiglione, Francesco, 11
Castillo, Enrique, 110
Cee Kay Becky Thatcher, 183-184, **185**, **201**

Centennial Doctor Pepper, **262**
Centurion Center Stage, **283**
Centurion Cierra, **181**
Centurion Coachman, **278**
Centurion Cultured Kipper, **407**
Centurion Cultured Pearl, **16**, **407**
CERF, 380
Challenge Certificates, 93, 102-104, 108-109, 113, 114, 116
Championship, 257
Chance of a Lifetime, **174**
Chancellor, Dr. Philip, 110
Chapel of Santa Maria Novella, 11
Charley, **211**
Charlie's Pretty Penny, 45
Chasecourt Cheers, 92, 93
Cheerio Willing and Able, **283**
Chelsea, 187
Chereau, F., 12
Cherrymount Lucette, 93, **94**
Cheshire N' Sunset Spellbound, **291**
Cheshire Signature Scoundrel, **295**
Cheshire Signature Silhouette, **290**
Cheshire's Northern Lights, **221**, **290**
Chestnut Venus of Rosebrook, **369**
Chewing, 252
Chicagoland Dalmatian Club, 84
Chicagoland Pedigree book, 222
Chief, 186
Children, 208-213, 359
Chile, 116
China Doll of Dalmatia, **30**, **52**, 52, 54
Choco Chip Brandi Delight, **350**
Chousnick Castle, 8
Circa, 105
Classic All That Jazz, **294**
Clausentrum Red Dimples of Collaton, 112
Clockgate's Candlelight, **285**
Close, Glenn, 80

Club for Dalmatian Friends, 105

Club fur Dalmatiner Freunde, 106

Clydevale Mastermind, 92

Co-ownership, 224

Coach Dog of Reinagle, **11**, **12**, 12

Coaching, 12-16, 175
—position, 12-3, 177-178
—road trials, 33, 33-35, 90-91, 178

Coachkeeper Blizzard of Quaker's Acre, 49

Coachlane's Fireman's Blaze, **210**

Coachman, 49

Coachman's Callisto, 49

Coachman's Canicula, 72, **74**, **75**, **336**

Coachman's Carbon Copy, **50**

Coachman's Carte Blanche, **51**

Coachman's Chocolate E. Clair, **202**

Coachman's Chuck-A-Luck, 44, **44**, **336**

Coachman's Classic, **36**, 36, 49, **327**, **328**, **330**

Coachman's Cluster Bee, **191**

Coachman's Cup O' Tea, **50**

Coachman's Hot Coffee, **50**, **280**

Coachman's Lucky Cuss, **50**

Coachman's Paisley Candybar, **291**

Coachman's Red Carpet, **50**

Coachmaster's Pride Sparkler, **317**

Coat, 159, 234
—color, 159
—disorders, 392-400
—frosting, 168
—length, 172
—texture, 172
—ticking, 168

Cobbin-End Choirboy, **106**

Coeland Black Magic, **100**

Coeland Kado, **100**

Coeland Leader, **100**

Colonel Boots from Dalmatia, 52, **55**

Colonial Coach, 38

Colonial Coach Carriage Way, 76, **76**

Colonial Coach Cheshire, 39, 76

Colonial Coach Classy Chassi, **325**

Colonsay April Jest, **105**

Colonsay Blacksmith, 62

Colonsay Olaf the Red, 38

Colonsay Roll of the Dice, 92

Colonsay Tantivvey Claudia, 46

Color, 159
—genetics of, 160-168
—variations, 168

Come, 212, 248

Companion Dog (CD), 30

Complete Dalmatian, The, 16

Conditioning, 259-260

Conformation, 28, 221
—competition, 257
—disqualifications, 28
—early shows, 28-29
—entering a show, 262-264
—evaluating, 226-232
—first show, 28
—handlers, 265-267
—matches, 260-261
—selecting a puppy for, 221-225
—show procedure, 264-265
—training classes, 258

Consumer Reports, 208

Contracts, 224

Cooper, Abraham R.A., 12

Coprophagia, 255

Corrections, 251

Cottondale Woodland Lark, **181**

Count Miguel of Tuckaway, 60, **336**

Country Kate's Mandolin of MGR, 91, **175**, **182**, **188**, **202**, **215**, **235**, **236**

Countryroad Cool Million, **97**

Countryroad Polar Star, 112

Crane, Mr., 88

Crash, **403**

Crate, 213, 243-245, 360

Crestview, 39

Crestview Dan Patch, 39, 44

Crestview Diamond Jim, 39

Crestview Mr. Bently of Beaux, 64

Crib, 28

Croatia, 12

Cross-country skiing, 204

Crossroads Checkers, **19**, **206**, **245**, **408**

Crossroads Mountain Daisy, **201**, **408**

Crossroad's Wandering Star, **309**

Crown Jewels, 40

Crown Jewels Black Diamond, 40

Crown Jewels Oriental Pearl, **39**

Crufts, 98, 103

Culurien No Jacket Required, **193**, 194

Cyncar Miss Molly of Croatia, **237**

Dagwood, 94

Dahlstrom, Eric and Ardith, 70

Daisy, **184**, **250**

Daisy Dot Purrfect for Paisley, 186, **410**

Daisydot Daphne of Dalwood, **277**

Dakota Madurhason Andromeda, **409**

Dakota's Victoria's Secret, **281**

Dal Downs Dicie of Shadodal, **31**

Dal Downs Nordic, **32**

Dal Duchy's Georgeous George, 45

Dalhalla Thunderbolt, 41

Dallas Facsimilia, **119**

Dallas Inkspot, 118

Dallas Joyful Christmas, 118

Dallas Leading Lady, **122**

Dallas Super Star, **118**

Dallas Valonia Gardens, **119**

Dallmalli Hawk, **114**

Dallmalli Inthenews, **113**

Dallmalli Starsandstripes, **113**

Dalma Phantom, 112

Dalmatia (kennel), 52

Dalmatia (province), 8, 12, 60

Dalmatian Association of Queensland, 94

Dalmatian Association of Western Australia, 94

Dalmatian Club of ACT

(Australian Capitol Territory), 94

Dalmatian Club of America, 28, 34

Dalmatian Club of America, 87

Dalmatian Club of America, 222, 363, 366, 368

—Board of Governors, 81, 83, 84

—Breeder Referral Coordinator, 87

—educational programs, 80

—Endowment Committee, 86

—establishment of, 80

—ethical guidelines, 421

—first specialty show, 82, 88

—Judges' Education Committee, 84

—Membership Educational Committee

—National Specialties, 82-86, 89-91

—research committees, 80

—Research Sub-Committee on Deafness, 85

—*Rules and Standards Handbook*, 33

—special committees, 87, 417

—Standard Committee, 81

Dalmatian Club of America Foundation, 86

Dalmatian Club of Australia, 93

Dalmatian Club of Canada, 96

—*Transcanadals*, 96

Dalmatian Club of Greater Phoenix, 366

Dalmatian Club of Mexico, 110

Dalmatian Club of Northern California, 366, 368

Dalmatian Club of NSW,Inc., 93

Dalmatian Club of Queensland, 94

Dalmatian Club of South Australia, 93

Dalmatian Club of Victoria, 93, 94

Dalmatian Club (South Africa), 112

Dalmatian Club, The, 93

Dalmatian Handbook, The, 9, 11

Dalmatian, The (Frankling), 98

Dalmatian, The (Lauer), 16, 33, 178

Dalmatian, The (Willock), 10

Dalmatians, 10

Dalmatin, Jurij, 8, 9, 10

Dalmatiner Verein Deutschland, 106

Dalmatins, 8, 9

Dalmex Chicharrin, 111

Dalmino's Allegro, **287**

Dalquist Belle Charm, 66

Dalwood, 52

Dalwood's Disco Dancer, **271**

Dalwood's Dream Girl, 52, **55**

Dalwood's Enchanted Knight, **270**

Dalwood's Knight E Knight, 52

Dalwood's Knight Edition, 52, **55**

Dalwood's Knight Traveler, 52, **55**

Dalwood's Miss Valentine, **320**

Dalwood's Mr. Clown, **55**

Dalwood's Pat E. Kakes, **123**

Dalwood's Princess Candy Tuft, 52, **53**

Dalwood's Waggin' Master, **267**

Damm, Mr. Hugo, 105

Dams, 451

Dancourt Wedgewood Bon Jovi, **318**

Dandy Dan of Coachmaster, 57

"Danish Dog", 10

Dazdell Kingfisher Zeke, **189**

DCA Commemorative Keepsake 1980, 84, **85**

De Buffon, M., 364

De Hooch, Pieter, 11

Delta Society, 189

Deltalyn Bold Lancer, **296**

Deltalyn Decoupage, **280**, **334**

Deltalyn N Penwiper KisnCuzn, 72, **73**, **287**

Demodectic mange, 399-400

Denee, Mrs. C.F., 88

Denlinger, Milo, 16

Dalmatinerpost, 108

Deutscher Dalmatiner Club von 1920 e.V. (DDC), 105, 106

Deutsches Kartell fur Hundewesen, 105

Development, 215, 221, 242

—neonatal period, 216

—socialization period, 217-219, 221

—stages of, 216

—transitional period, 216-217

Devlstar Snygln Rich n Spirit, **295**

Diana and Her Nymphs, 11

Digging, 252

DiMino, Barbara, 72

Dipsticking, 374

Disney's Conscience Guides, 90

Disqualifications, 28

Dizzy, **162**, **167**

Doane, David, **30**, 56, **58**

Doane, J., **30**

Doane, Lt. Stephen, **56**

Doane, Mrs. David G., 56, **58**

Dodge, Mrs. Geraldine, 29

Dog, The (1847), 10

Dog, The (1872), 10

Dog World award, 306

Dogs of the British Isles, 28

Dogtowne's Firechief Rocky, 60

Dollar Tree of Warlike Eden, 116

Dolly, 187

Dominique's Rusty Nail, **313**

Dominoe's Winter Midnight, **318**

Don Benjamin de La Mancha, **111**, 111

Don Juan Tenorio de La Mancha, **110**, 111

Donahue, Lorraine, 62

Doriben's Mojave of Dallmalli, 113, 114

Dorini, Nilda, 96

Dottidale, 41

Dottidale Buster Brown, **42**

Dottidale Captain Nemo, **43**

Dottidale JoJo, 41, **42**

Dottidale Marco Polo, **43**

Dottie, **318**
DotzInk's Dippity Doo Dot, **286**
Driftwood Chimney Cricket, **152**, **259**, **339**
Driftwood Sunspot Rambler, **313**
Droesse, Mr. H., 105
Dromgoole's Nalova, **287**
Drury, Percy, 88
Duchess of Dal Downs, **30**
Dumbledeer Glenn, 94
Dumbledeer Jake, 94
Dyker, Christine, 60
Dylan of Watseka, 76
Dynasty N Erins Justa Star, **307**
Dynasty's Ultimate Rival, **304**
Eastern Dog Club, 30
Edgecomb D'Artagnan, 28
Educated Dogs of Today, 18
Educational programs, 80
El Archiduque de La Mancha, **11**
Elmcroft Coacher, **26**, 46, 76
Elvy, **109**
Ember, 186
Emergency procedures, 374
Emma, **209**
Emperor Frederick Barbarossa Before Pope Alexander, The, 11
Enchanted Flame, The, **320**
England, 98
—breeders, 98-99, 102
—conformation shows, 102-104
—Dalmatian clubs, 98, 102
—kennels, 98-99
English Pointer, 159
Epilepsy, 381-382
Epirote, 9
Epirus, 9
Eriksen, Melissa, 194
Erin n Acorn's Autumn Leaf, **289**
Erin's Irish Whiskey, **291**
Erin's Nutmeg Candy, 90, **90**
Erin's Wildwood Abby Road, **291**
Erin's Wildwood Luke McGyver, **291**
Erle v Nordenstadt, **107**
ES 82 Arko von Muhlenbache, **107**

Esquire's Black Talisman, **294**
Esquire's Devilstar Mirage, **294**
Esquire's Homespun Prophecy, **282**
Esquire's Sleight of Hand, **284**
Ethical Guidelines, 86,421
Euthanasia, 405
Exercise, 404
—senior dog, 404, 405
Fanfayre's Beau of Short Acre, **272**
Fanhill Faune, 102
Fanhill Festivity of Traveare, 112
Farga de Montjuic, **24**
Fawdry, Mr. J., 28
Federation Cynologique Internationale, 106
Feeding, 236
—amount, 240
—frequency, 240-241
—nutrition, 236-240
—purines, 370, 375
—senior dog, 404
Fenced-in yards, 214
Fessard, Claude, 11
Fetner, Bill and Jean, 49
Fiacre's Femme Fatale, **278**
Final Act de Nutwoot, 116
Findejs, Jan, 8, 9
Fire Brand, **67**
Fire dogs, 18, 183
Firebuster's Oscar dla Renta, **289**
Firechaser Phoenix, 20, 95, **95**
Fireline's Double Dealer, **282**
Fireman's Becky Newsham, **278**, **339**
Fireman's Freckled Friend, 93, **259**, **339**
Firesprite Firebird O'Land, **7**
Firesprite N Coachlight Gigilo, **281**
Firesprite Stingre O'Saratoga, **7**
Firesprites Trixi Dixi, **232**, **357**
Firewagn's Krackerjack, **293**
Firuski, Elviria, **89**
Fisher, Mr. Martin S., 11
Fiske, Loiuse Geddes, 30

Fitzsimmons, Ray, 110, **111**, 112
Five Alarm Truffle, **255**
Five Alarm Truffles' Trifle, **255**
Flea bite dermatitis, 396
Fleas, 386-390
Fleetwood Nu-Boot of Dalmatia, 118
Fleger, Ron and Natalie, 39
Flock, C.E., Jr., 56, 66
Flock, Ed, **59**
Florenza, 92
Floria Tosca de La Mancha, **111**
Flyball, 187
—titles, 189
Fobette's Fanfare, 44, 49
Fobette's Frishka, 49, **50**
Folklore n Firesprite Wm Tell, **232**, **277**
Forrest Jilia O'Brogan, **180**, **312**
Four-in-Hand, 41
Four-in-Hand Blackberry, 41, 46
Four-in-Hand Mischief, **26**, 39, 41, 49, 52
Foxhound, 10
Frankling, Eleanor, 98, 159
Freckles, 20
Frisbee®, 204
Frolish, Judy, 186
Front and Finish, 311
Frosting, 168
Frozen semen, 80, 85, 92-93, 417
Fulks, Jim and Linda, 200
Futurity, 84, 90
Fyt, Jan, 11
Gait, 152
—illustrations of, 152-158
Gallagher, Phil, 90
Gallopades Special Selection, **190**
Gardorand's Brazen Raisyn, **320**
Gardorand's Great Adventure, **320**
Gardorand's Lone Star Corie, **314**, **320**
Garland Pride, 72
Garrett's Ice Cream Checkmate, 118
Garvin, Chad, **211**

INDEX

Garvin, Dr. Charles, 60, **61**, **266**
Garvin, Dr. John and Betty, 60
Garvin, Jr, John, **208**
Garvin, Lynn, 60
Gastric dilatation, 376
Gemini of Tallara, **70**
General care, 233-236
—coat, 234
—ears, 233
—eyes, 233
—feet, 234-235
—nails, 235-236
—nose, 233
—teeth, 233-234
Genetics, 160-168, 332-334
—coat color, 160-168
—deafness, 368
Germany, 104
—breeders, 106
—certification for breeding, 108
—conformation, 108-109
—Dalmatian clubs, 105-106-early shows, 105
Geschichte und Beschreibung der Rassen des Hundes, 104
Gill, Dwight and Marianne, 194
Gladmore Gaylass, 89
Glover, Harry, 9
Godin's To Be Or Not To Be, 72, **135**, **274**
Golden Dawn of Coeland, **100**
Golden Dusk at Coeland, **100**
Goldfields Kennel Club, 112
Gonzalez, Alejandro, 110, 112
Good Times, 22
Gore, Catherine, 10
Great Dane, 10, 11
Green Starr, 56
Green Starr's Bit of the Walls, **56**
Green Starr's Colonel Joe, **48**, 49, 56, **57**, 72, **124**
Green Starr's Darling Dotter, 56
Green Starr's Dazzler, **59**
Green Starr's Dynamite, **56**
Green Starr's Follow Me

Mark, **58**
Green Starr's Jenny's Mark, **58**
Green Starr's King Pin, **59**
Green Starr's Major Houlihan, **274**
Green Starr's Masterpiece, **59**
Green Starr's Shamrock, 49
Green Starr's Undergraduate, **44**
Gren, 45
Gren's Coal Tar, 45
Gush, Mr. Geoffrey, 98
Gypsy Rose VII, 116
Hagen, Dr. George, 9
Hammarlund, Ann-Marie, 118, 122
Handlers, 265-267
Hans, 112
Hapi Dal Easy to Spot, **15**
Hapi-Dal Knight Strider, **286**
Happy Go Lucky, **323**
Hare, Lloyd and Briziade, 70
Harmony, 105
Harmony of Cheshire T. Redrock, **35**, **175**, **184**, 186
Harmony Real People, **291**
Harmony Wishful Thinking, **292**
Harpischord Adagio of Kilshane, 112
Harris, Tom, 91
Harrison, Mr. J, 28
Harrison, Tom and Barbara, 64
Harvey, Mrs. N.L., 22
Hawking Party, The, 11
Haywood (Bartholomew), Diane, 52, **267**
Hearing dogs, 194
Hearing testing, 355, 417
—historical research, 364
—home testing, 364-366
Heartland's Romeo of Croatia, **295**
Heidi (Altamar pup), **329**
Heidi (fire dog), 186
Heiloh Ramsey Sundar, **294**
Heiloh Midnight Madness, **355**
Her Majesty of Williamsdale, 46
Herding, 202
Hibbler, William, 76

Hideaway's Black Mariah, **284**
Higgins, Arthur and Muriel, 44
Hiking, 195
Hill-N-Dals M'Lady Mercedes, **284**
Hip dysplasia, 377-379
Hogan, John, 110
Holden, Dr. and Mrs. Eugene, 66
Hollytree's Copper Chelsea, **322**
Hollytree's Good Time Alex, **322**
Hollytree's Macho of Chelsea, **323**
Hollywood's Achy Breaky Heart, **253**
Holmes, Miss Rachael, 88
Homiller, Dr. John P., 88
Homiller, Mrs., 88
Hopi Kachina, 56
Hopi Kachina Indian Summer, **13**, 56
Hopi Kachina Kawaika, **59**
Hopi Kachina Mashanta, **239**
Hopi Kachina Melody Mocha, 56, **59**
Hopi Noki Kachina, 56
Housetraining, 245-246
Howison, Sylvia, 45
Hubbard, Clifford L.B., 9, 10, 11
Hull, Mr. Fred, 22
Hunting, 199
Hunting Party, The, 11
Hurst, Mr. and Mrs., 92
Hypothyroidism, 382
"Idstone", 10
IgA deficiency, 379-380
Igdaliah M&M Candy Cain, **273**
Igdaliah's Miriam of Indalane, **320**
Igor of Kye of Williamsdale, 46
Illyricum Pandora, **105**
Iman de Montjuic, **23**
Imports, 23
In the Valley, 41
Inbreeding, 335
Indalane Winsome Wench, **293**

Indi, **201**
Irishman's Lady Trixie, **195**
Istria, 10
Istrian Pointer, 10, 11
Ivygate Magical Spotlight, **354**
Ivy Lea's Russet Herald, **286**
J Dream Lazy Acres General Purpose, **228**
J Dream Lazy Acres Model A, **228**
Jack Daniels of Watseka, 76
Jackson, Christina, 64
Jagello, King Louis, 9
Jancsi of Korchula, 92
Jarrett, Dr. Henry, 88
Jaurequi, Mr. J.A., 110
Jaybar, 57
Jaybar's Black Label, 57, **59**
Jogging, 204
Johnnie Walker of Watseka, **283**
Johnson, Maria, 36
Johnston, Heather Haywood, 52, **270**
Johnstown's High Life, 114
Jordan, Carrie, 91
Journal of Heredity, 177
Junior Showmanship, 268-270
K-9 Corps, 195
Karefree's Cool Hand Luke, **321**
Karefree's Crackshot, **321**
Karefree's Question Mark, **321**
Kaylor's Hurricane Indy, **187**, **188**
Keeler, Clyde E., 177
Keith's Mr. Major, **261**
Kemp, Mr., 98
Kemp, Mrs. Fred, 14
Kennel Union of South Africa, 113
Kennel Union of Southern Africa, 112
Kennels
—Albelarm, 48
—Altamar, 36
—before 1965, 48
—Bespeckled, 49
—Blackpool, 38
—Coachman, 49

—Colonial Coach, 38
—Crestview, 39
—Crown Jewels, 40
—Dalmatia, 52
—Dalwood, 52
—Dottidale, 41
—Four-in-Hand, 41
—Green Starr, 56
—Hopi Kachina, 56
—In the Valley, 41
—Jaybar, 57
—Korcula, 60
—Labyrinth, 60
—Long Last, 62
—Majestic K'ls, 64
—major inactive, 36
—Melody, 66
—Oseau, 44
—Pennydale, 44
—Pill Peddler's, 66
—Pryor Creek, 44
—Quaker's Acre, 45
—Reigate, 45
—Roadcoach, 45
—Royal Oaks, 70
—Stablemate, 45
—Tally Ho, 46
—Tioga-Coach, 72
—Tomalyn Hill, 46
—Tuckaway, 72
—Watseka, 76
—Williamsdale, 46, 76
Kent, Bill, 194
Kief, 118
Kindergarten Puppy Training, 247, 250, 299-300
King, 56
Kingcrest Jack Tar, 49
Knightstone Huntsman, **27**
Knowles, William and Laura, 38
Konavlje Miss Gorgeous, **105**
Korcula, 60
Korcula John L. Lewis, **208**
Korcula King of Harts, **4**, **126**
Korcula Midnight Amanda, **18**
Korcula Midnight Margie, **61**
Korcula Midnight Max of M&M, **317**
Korcula Midnight Mistress,

60
Korcula Midnight Serenade, **60**, 60
Korcula Midnight Star Bret D, 60, **61**, **275**
Korcula Pickles of Sunnyglen, **316**
Korcula Salona, 60, **60**, 61
Korcula Waltzing Matilda, **241**
Krause, Carolyn, 183
La Mancha's Impossible Dream, 111
Labyrinth, 60
Labyrinth Big Spender, 62, **63**, **113**
Labyrinth Big Spender of Dallmalli, 112
Labyrinth Liveryman of Dallmalli, 112
Labyrinth Oscar Madison, **65**
Labyrinth Sleighbelle, 60, 72, **62**, **74**
Labyrinth Star Dot Star, 112
Labyrinth Tuckaway Julep, **65**, **74**
Lady Culpepper of Reigate, 45
Lady Madonna Madiera, **319**
Lane, George and Mary Leigh, 45
Larson, Eric, **329**
Larson, Karen and Stan, 91
Lathrop, Kurt, 186
Lauer, H. Fred, 16, 33, 88, 178
Ldy Daps Strsnstryps of DC's, **341**
Leash, 214
—retractable, 214
Led Astray, 94
Ledger B, 22
Legacy's Mt. Bryton Monogram, **282**
Legacy's Pen Pal, **282**
Leukodystrophy, 377
Lick granuloma, 398-399
Lidgate Charles of Seaspot, **32**
Lightning Sparks, 49
Limestone Zara Padraic, 116

Linebreeding, 335
Lipschutz, Amy and Elli, 41
Little Slam's Jack of Hearts, 111
Liver, 169
—brown, 170
—chocolate, 169
—red, 170
Lizzy, **214**
Lloyd, Jean Marie, 52, **55**, **268**
Lloyd, Ron, 52, **271**
Lola of Watseka, 76, **76**
Lomnice, Alena Meziricska, 8, 9
London's Cadbury Fudge, **289**
Long Last, 62
Long Last Black Chrome, 64, **65**
Long Last Link to Paisley, **65**
Long Last Living Legend, 64, **64**
Long Last No Frills, 64, **65**
Long Last Perfect for Paisley, **65**, **331**, **337**, **409**
Long Last Ripcord, 66
Long Last Solar Flare, 64
Lorbyrndale We Hail, 48
Lord Jim, 44, 49, 72, **258**, **336**
Louisiana State University, 85, 366
Lure coursing, 200
Lurie, M.H., 364
Machines Aren't Toys, 95
Mackie, Mrs., 98
Maclay, Alfred, 88
Madame Moose, 22
Madurhason's Aberdeen, **287**
Madurhason's Opening Night, **282**
Madurhason's Top Marks of Fox, **282**
Mahlib Jifft, 102
Majestic Cleopatra, 64
Majestic K'ls, 64
Majestic K'ls Bold Fella, 64
Majestic K'l's Ebon Mischief, 64
Majestic K'ls Ebon of Pearl, 64

Malone, Cyrill, **89**
Mange, 399-400
Maricam's Saucy Suzy, **284**
Mariscat Marigold of Dallmalli, 112
Markmaker Coriander, **411**
Markmaker Never Say Never, **203**, **411**
Mars-Dalmatia, 105
Martin, Miss M.W., 28
Mastiff, 9
Matchless Image of Folklore, **192**
Maurino, Mr. Luis G., 110
Maximilian, Emperor, 11
McCarthy, Chief John, 186
McManus, Jim, 39
McManus, Violet, 39
Meeker, Leo, 39, 41, 46, 70
Meeker's Barbara Worth, 30
Meerlus Angus, 114
Meistrell, Harland and Lois, 30, 34, 90
Meistrell, Lois, 177
Melbourne Royal, 93
Melody, 66
Melody Dynamatic, 56, 66
Melody My Rockaby Baby, **304**
Melody Ring of Fire, 66, **66**, 110-111,
Melody Rocky Top Cheerio, **67**
Melody Sweet, 66, **66**
Melody Up and Away, **340**
Merry Go Round Bentley, **293**
Merry Go Round Mardi Gras, **292**
Merry Go Round Rocket Man, **293**
Merry Go Round XKE, **292**
Merry Polka of Tallara, **279**
Mesabi of Watseka, 112
Mexican Dalmatian Club, 110
Mexican Kennel Club, 111
Mexico, 109
—kennels, 110
—National Specialties, 110-111
Meyers, Charlie, **41**
MGR's Black Mystical Jewel, **295**
Michigan State University,

86
Micklos, 9
Milet, Martin, 46
Milky Ways Egyptian Goddess, **281**
Minka, 112
Minnesota Urolith Center, 370
Misty's Echo of Denell, **288**
M&M's Hobo of Bearded Oaks, **317**
Molly, **413**
Molossian hounds, 9
Molossus, 9
Moonlight's Rising Son, **285**
Morgan's Highlander Harper, **294**
Morris and Essex show, 29
Morris Animal Foundation, 29, 86
Mossgiel Candlelight, **112**
Mr. Diamond Chips of Croatia, **296**
Mrs. Roseveare, 112
Multiple-dog households, 407-414
Musical Party, A, 11
Myers, Linda, 34
Nagler, Ken and Nan, 49
Nail trimming, 235-236
National Animal Poison Control Center, 383
National Dalmatian Council, 94
Natural History, 8
Nelson, Dr. Holly J., 366, 368, 379
Neonatal period, 216
Nero, 105
Neutering, 326
New Dalmatian, Coach Dog—Firehouse Dog, The, 8, 9, 10, 22
Newton, **251**
Nichols, Mr. W.J., 98
Niemeyer, Barbara, 57
Nigel of Welfield, 48
Nipping, 251
Noble, Edward, 14
Nogar, Ray and Cathy, 56
Northern California Dalmatian Club, 84
Northpleck Crackerjack, 92
North's M.T. Pockets, **403**
North's Sir Wags Alot, **284**

Nouveau Livre d'Animaux,
   12
November's Mister Frost
   Debut, **297**
Nursing, 349
Nutrition, 236-240
—senior dog, 404
Nylabone®, 249
Nylabone® Frisbee™, **24**
Nylafloss®, 249
Oak Tree Of Gypsy Rose VII,
   116
Obedience, 30, 83, 90, 225-
   226
—*Dog World* award, 306
—early competition, 30
—selecting a puppy for, 225-
   226
—titles, 30—33, 301-306
—top dogs, 452
—trainability, 307
—training, 247-248, 298-
   299, 309
—trials, 300-301
Obesity, 404
O'Dal, 39
Odyssey's Star-Lite Dazzler,
   203
Old Coach Trilj, **49**
Older dogs, 404
Orthopedic Foundation for
   Animals (OFA), 86, 224,
   226, 378
Oseau, 44
Oseau, Lloyd and Reba, 44
Outcrossing, 335
Owner responsibility, 206-
   208
P-Nut, **393**
Pacific's Boston Bandit, **296**
Pacifica's Regal Adonis, **284**
Page's Editor in Chief, **304**
Pack structure, 249-251,
   408-410, 413-414
Paisley Matrix Rolling Stone,
   225
Paisley n Snowood Sally
   Forth, **410**
Paisley N Tuck's Derby, **319**
Paisley N Tucks Eureka, **170**,
   351, **410**
Paisley Peterbilt, **305**, **310**,
   315, **401**, **405**
Paisley Polyester, **402**
Paisley Poppycock, **179**,

   179, 186
Paisley Premonition, **229**
Paisley Torch of Kirkland,
   116, **117**
Paisley Willowood
   Trademark, **254**
Paisleys Cause Celebre, **297**
Paisley's Ebony of
   Coachlight, **296**
Paisley's Honey's Chocolate
   Chips, **217**
Paisley's Natural Healer, **288**
Paisleys Peachy Keen, **171**
Paisley's Perfect Timing, **231**
Paisleys Pointblank, **171**,
   251, **297**, **331**, **411**
Paisley's Princess Perdita,
   343
Palmer, Chad, **209**
Pamela of Dal Downs, **30**
Panore of Watseka, 76, **77**
Pan's Crystal de Albo Atrum,
   116
Pappas, P.D., 112
Paradox Mad Max of
   Croatia, **276**
Paradox Prodigal Dotter,
   207
Patches, 28, 350-351
Patches (fire dog), 187
Pateshull Pucelle, 49Paul's
   Mischievous Bandit, 52,
   53
Paxten, **414**
Peabody, Miss Amelia, 34
Peacock, Mr., 112
Pearce, Rev. Thomas, 10
Pedigree Dogs, 14
Penn-Hip™, 226, 378, 417
Penny Parade of
   Williamsdale, 46
Pennydale, 44
Pennydale Deacon's
   Daughter, 111
Penwiper All The Right
   Moves, **265**
Perdita, 37
Peron, Juan, 116
Personality, 173, 307
Pet puppy, 219
Peters, Harry T., Jr., **46**, 88
Peters, Nick and Barbara, 38
PGR Heiloh Samson, **273**
Phaeland Patron, **105**
Phaeland Phorgetmenot,

   105
Picadilly's Alexis at Dynasty,
   202, **373**
Picadilly's Sir Nigel, **202**,
   410
Pickled Walnut from
   Pampard, **103**
Pill Peddler's, 66
Pill Peddler's Christmas
   Holly, **23**
Pill Peddler's the Nurses
   Aide, **69**
Pioneer Square Fire Festival,
   17, **21**
Pisces Rambler Sunspot
   Dawn, **323**
Poage, Lt. Larry, 20
Poca Dot Salute to Reveille,
   60, **63**
Pointer, 10, 12, 159, 165,
   199
Poison control, 417
Poisonous plants, 385
Pompadally Persephone, **10**
Pompeii's Promise of Glory,
   316
Pongo, 36, 95
Ponto, 33
Pottiger, Mr. George, 33
Pottiger's Bell, 33
Powell, John, 96
Powers, Helen, **89**
Pregnancy, 340-342
Price, J. Sergeant, Jr., 28,
   88, **88**
Price, Mr. Lloyd, 28
Price, Vern and Norma, 40
Princess Lillian, 49
Princess Lois of Loki, 49
Proctor's Dappled Duchess,
   263
Proctor's Dappled Hi-Flyer,
   122, **264**
Proctors Queen of the Mt.,
   343, **344**, **345**, **346**,
   347, **401**
Progressive retinal atrophy,
   380
Pryor Creek, 44
Psi Spolencenskych, 8
Psychic Power at Pampard,
   92
Puget Sound Dalmatian
   Club, 84
Puppy Aptitude Test, 250,

361, 418-420
Puppy placements, 362
Purines, 370, 375
Putty-Dalmatia, 105
Pyoderma, 396-398
Quaker's Acre, 45
Quintus of Caefel, 92
Rabbit Run Thunder Storm, **68**
Radcliff, Nelson, 76
Rainbow, **302**
Raindrop of Gypsy Rose VII, 116
Rambler Quintessence, **296**
Rambler Rose Tattoo, **191**
Rambler Winning Colors, **337**
Rambler's Lady Sarah Jane, **288**, 349, **410**
Ratner, Mrs. George, 41
Ravenwood Yankee Clipper, **20**
Rawitz, 364
Reeves, Lloyd and Stella, 34
Reeves, Stella, 66
Regional clubs, 84
Registration, 22, 262
Reichsgruppe Deutsches Hundewesen, 105
Reichsverband Deutscher Kleintierzuchter, 105
Reicrist Tsingi of Toleak, **296**
Reigate, 45
Reigate Bold Venture, 45, **45**, 56, 76,
Reigate Native Dancer, **45**
Reinagle, 12
Remarkable Rambo of Croatia, **287**
Remmele (Rion), Julie, **269**
Remmele, DVM, Sidney, 72
Remmele, Frances, 91
Rescue Me, **210**
Research committees, 80
Review of Color in the Dalmatian, A, 85
RFBCN Lidgate's Triever Franc, **324**
RFBCN Lidgate's Triever Watson, **199**
Riker, **212**
Ringo, **390**, **412**
Rivard, Robert and Judith, 72
Rivera Torres family, 110
Road Trial Committee, 34, 35

Road trials, 33, 84, 90-91, 178
—regulations, 33-35, 431-447
—titles, 35, 178, 443
Roadcoach, 45
Roadcoach Frou Frou, **33**, 34, **52**, 52, **310**
Roadcoach Racing Colors, 52
Roadcoach Roadster, 41,**41**, 45, **46**
Roadcoach Spice, **46**
Roadcoach Tioga, 72
Roadcoach Tioga Too, 72, **72**, 73
Roadking's Raindrop, **289**
Roadking's Rome, 44
Robbsdale's Puttin On The Ritz, **293**
Roberts, Henry, 11
Robinwood Thief of Hearts, **283**
Robson, Isabel, 48
Rockin Rudi Blues, 16, **399**
Rockledge Rumble, **257**
Rockstar's Paisley Night Moves, **219**
Rocky, **390**
Rodes, Jana, **176**, **177**, **178**
Rogers, Fred, 406
Rojon's Betcha By Golly, **289**
Rollo, **329**
Romany gypsies, 12
Rosebrooks Red Alert, **248**
Roundhill Blacksmith, **295**
Round Tower's Hickory Smoke, **305**
Rowdy J. Rambler, **285**
Royal Oaks, 70
Royal Oaks Liberty Belle, 70, **71**
Royal Oaks Ragtime Rambler, 70, **70**
Royal, Mr., 105
Rudder, Georgiann (Peggy), 52, **53**
Ruger, Mrs. E.W., 112
Rules and Standards Handbook, 33
Ruth H., 22
Sabre de Montjuic, **24**
Saddle and Bridle, **51**
Saint Rocco's Polka Dot, 44
Saldana, Rodolfo, 110
Salem, **411**

Sales agreement, 424-425
Sammet, Wendell, 34, **52**, 52, **54**, **73**, 118, **310**
Sanborn, Kate, 18
Saratoga's Jesse's Girl, **356**
Saunders, Mr. James, 98
Scent hurdle, 187
Schubert, Carol, **77**
Schubert, Don and Carol, 76
Schutzhund, 204
Scooter, **188**
Scott, 12
Scruff shake, 251
Seeing Eye dogs, 192
Seizures, 381-382
Separation anxiety, 254
Service dogs, 193, 417
Shadow, 20
Shadrach of Whitlee, **30**
Shad's Dotter of Whitlee, 56
Shaw, Vero, 28
Shimer, Geoffrey, **210**
Shospots Double Or Nothing, **260**
Shospots Standing Ovation, **260**
Show dogs, 449
Show puppy, 221
—co-ownership, 224
—selecting, 221-232
Sires, 451
Sit, 212
Skartoftas Clothilde, **120**, 122
Skating, 204
Skin problems, 392-400
—acral lick dermatitis, 398-399
—allergies, 392-396-bronzing syndrome, 398
—lick granuloma, 398-399
—pyoderma, 396-398
Skipper of Rabbit Run, 66, **68**
Sled dogs, 202
Sleeping, 213-214
Sleeping area, 405
Slovenia, 10
Smith (Noyes), Hope, 72, **72**, **73**
Smith, Dodie, 95
Smith, Mary Munro, 45, 90
Snitchal, 45
Snow Hill Sterling, **283**
Snowood Black Cherry

Optimist, **290**

Snowood Ja Sam Jedan, **290**

Snowood Superstition Bret D, **290**

Socialization, 212, 246-247, 358-361

Socialization period, 217-219, 221

Sony, **414**

Sophie Leah Lehmer, **305**

South Africa, 112

—breeders, 114

—championship shows, 113

—Dalmatian Club, 112

South America, 114

—championship, 114

Southern California Dalmatian Club, 84

Southern Dalmatian Club, 98

Southern New England Dalmatian Club, 84

S&P Starlet of Summerhill, **294**

Sparky, 20, 187

Spaying, 326

Splash O Ebony's Woodbury's Jaki, **292**

Sporting and Dramatic News, The, 11

Sporting Magazine, The, 12

Sportsman's Cabinet, The, 12

Spotter, 8, **82**, 82, 367, 368

Spotlight's Spectacular, **48**, 49, **256**

Spottsboro Rebel Streak, **279**

Spottsboro Sungold Streaker, **295**

Spring Classic By Apaloosa, **102**

Spur of Victory, 62

St. Florian Pisces Jordache, **153, 275**

St. Florian Sunspot Ad-Lib, **285**

Stablemate, 45

Standard, 81,123, 426-430

—1921, 426

—1950, 427

—1962, 428

—1989, 429

Stealing, 252

Steffens, Chief Jim, 187

Stephens, Miss Millie, **100**

Sterne, Vivian, 96

Stone, Mike, **264**

"Stonehenge", 13, 28

Stool eating, 255

Strain, Dr. George, 366, 367, 368

Strupp, Peggy Ann, **35, 175**, 186

Stud dog, 334

—contract, 422-423

—owner responsibility, 338

—selection, 334

Sugarfoot Dots Ring Dancer, **283**

Sullivan, Bob and Marge, 90

Sunburst Chauffeur Driven, **407**

Sunkist Singalong, **292**

Sunnyglen's Spencer For Hire, **277, 377**

Superintendents, 262

Sutphen, **162**

Swabbie of Oz-Dal, 72

Sweden, 116

—BAER testing, 122

—championship, 116

—shows, 120

Swedish Dalmatian Society, 120

—*Dalmatiner Kuriren*, 122

Sweepstakes, 84, 90

T-Cart Rasima, **120**

Tailgate of the Walls, **30**

Talbot, 10

Talk to Animals, 20, 95

Tally Ho, 46

Tally Ho Fore Thought, 89

Tally Ho Kathleen, 89

Tally Ho Last of Sunstar, 46, 89

Tally Ho Make Merry, 46

Tally Ho Sirius, **47**

Tally Ho's Sir Charles, **276**

Tamara of Watseka, 76, **76**

Tantivvey Georgina, 49

Taplin, 12

Tateland's Top Gun, **297**

Tattersall Howie Looya, **218**

Tattersall Tasmanian Devil, **213**

Taylor, Rod, 95

Tear Drops Lively Carousel, **315**

Tear Drops Magic Roundabout, **315**

Tear Drops Mario Andretti, **315**

Tear Drops Tiger In The Tank, **315**

Teeth, 233-234

—senior dog, 404

Temperament, 173

Tennyson of Watseka, 76

Tenth Good Thing About Barney, The, 405-406

Terboch, Gerald, 104

Texas Ranger V. Tucwinn, **287**

Theissen, C., **30**

Therapy dogs, 189

Thidwick's Bungee Jumper, **289**

Thomas, Elaine, 64

Thomas, Frank, **327, 328**

Thomas, Joseph B., Jr., 88

Thomas, Mr. J.B., Jr., 22

Thonssen, Ms. Decilia, 122

Thornhill, Ann, 90

Thyroid, 382-383

Ticking, 168

Ticks, 390-392

Tiger, 112

Tin Lizzy In the Valley, 41

Tioga Georgio of Dalmatia, **55**

Tioga-Coach, 72

Tomalyn Hill, 46

Tomalyn's Air Cadette, 46

Tomalyn's Rascality, 46

Tongwood's Bold Irish Starr, **407**

Tongwood's Once In A Blue Moon, **293, 407**

Tongwood's Spotted Storm, **299**

Top 20 competition, 91

Touchstone Topaz, **19**

Touchstones Ace In The Hole, **311, 316**

Touchstone's Firestarter, **204**

Touchstone's Hello Holly, **127, 322**

Touchstone's Mountain Man, **324**

Touchstone's Topaz, **193**, 194

Touchstone's Wheeler Dealer, **325**

Touchstone's Yosemite Sam, **325**

Toxicosis, 383-385

—poison plants, 385

Toys, 211, 248-249

Tracking, 84, 90, 178
—titles, 180
Training, 210, 241
—classes, 258
—crate, 243-245
—housetraining, 245
—methods, 258
—obedience, 247, 298-299, 309
Tramac Cinder Bandit, **18**, 186
Tramac's Sail Away With Me, 186
Transcanadals, 98
Transitional period, 216-217
Traviser, 28
Treen, Alfred and Esmeralda, 8, 9, 10, 22, 30, 44
Tri-colors, 28
Trigger Hill's I'm So Happy, **230**
Trimble, Harry C., 177
Tuckaway, 72Tuckaway Augusta, 72, **75**
Tuckaway Bold and Brave, **74**
Tuckaway Bottoms Up Gusto, **19**, 72, **272**
Tuckaway Dinah, **74**
Tuckaway Gallant Man, **74**
Tuckaway Jason James, **74**
Tuckaway Secondhand Rose, **269**
Tuckaway the Pill Peddler, 66
Tuckaway Traveler Indalane, 60
Tuckaway Winged Foot, 72, 91, **91**
"Turkish Dogs", 8-9
Twingates Blue Bonnet, **23**, **69**
Type, 146
—illustrations of, 147-151
Uhlan, 28
United States Agility Dog Association, 181
University of California Davis, 366, 370, 406
University of Michigan, 86
University of Minnesota, 370
University of Pennsylvania, 378
Uric acid, 85-86
Urinary tract, 370
—dipsticking, 374
—infections, 371-372

—obstruction, 372-373, 374
—stone forming, 86, 370-371, 417
—stone forming preventatives, 370, 373
Van der Veer, Marjorie, **89**
Verband fur das Deutsche Hundewesen, 106
Veterinarian, 358, 401-403
—consultants, 417
Vicor of the Ebony Spots, 116
Victor, Bill and Carol, 49
Victory, 12
Videos, 417
Viorst, Judith, 406
Volanta de Montjuic, **24**
Volanta Venturian of Snow Hill, **286**
Volhard, Jack and Wendy, 361
Volunteer Fireman's Discovery, **215**
Volunteer's of Touch of Soot, **215**
Volvulus, 376
Von Achen Ali of Almeida, 116
Von Willebrand's disease, 386
Wagner, Stephen and Connie, 49
Walker, George S., 30
Walsh, Mr. J.H., 13, 28
War Eagle Taps, 60
Wardell, Mr. Fred, 98
Washakie Belleamie, **27**
Washakie Dancing Brave, **103**
Washakie Indian Summer, **104**
Washington, George, 22
Watseka, 76
Weaning, 356-358
Weekes, John C., 46, 88
Weight pulling, 202
West, Mrs. C.G., 88
Westminster Kennel Club, 18, 29, 89
Whelping, 344-350
—care of newborn pups, 348, 352-358
—stages of labor, 346-347
—supplies, 345-346
Whelping box, 343
When a Pet Dies, 406
Whinemaker's One for the

Road, **297**
White, Beth, 66
White, DVM, Jack, 66
White, Evelyn Nelson, 46, 88, **89**
Whitney, Arthur, 88
Whitney, J., **30**
Widdington Kandy, 44
Wigglesworth, Mrs., 102
Willets, Howard, 88
Williams, Charles, 46
Williamscrest Dainty Dancer, **36**, 37, **330**
Williamsdale, 46
Williamsdale Rocky, 46
Williamsview, 76
Williamsview Carbon Copy, **78**
Williamsview Gaiety, **78**
Williamsview Gambler's Luck, **79**
Williamsview Jody, **79**
Williamsview Patrician, 76
Williamsview Riptide, 76
Williamsview Shane, 72, **72**
Willock, Franklin J., 10, 88
Willowmount Baron Brown, 45, **47**
Windgap's Honey Bee, **40**, 41
Windy, **406**
Windholme's Kip, 46
Wise, Lieutenant, 18
Wiseman, Mrs. Virginia, 45
Woodwynd's Irish Pepper of Pal, **347**
Woodwynd's KC Masterpiece, **347**
Woodyatt, Miss, 102
World Congress of Dalmatians, 84, 85
World Encyclopedia of Dogs, The, 11
Youatt, William, 10
Yugoslavia, 10
Yumani Ceasar, 114
Zagreb Enforcer, **115**, 116
Zagreb Hallmark, 116
Zagreb Hollywood, **115**
Zagreb Private Blend, 116
Zagreb the Challenger, 116
Zink, Debbie, 60
Zuccari, Federigo, 11
Zuma, **190**